I0138275

Holy Toledo

HOLY TOLEDO

Religion and Politics in the Life of "GOLDEN RULE" JONES

Marnie Jones

THE UNIVERSITY PRESS OF KENTUCKY

Publication of this volume was made possible in part by a grant from the National Endowment for the Humanities.

Scholarly publisher for the Commonwealth,
serving Bellarmine College, Berea College, Centre
College of Kentucky, Eastern Kentucky University,
The Filson Club Historical Society, Georgetown College,
Kentucky Historical Society, Kentucky State University,
Morehead State University, Murray State University,
Northern Kentucky University, Transylvania University,
University of Kentucky, University of Louisville,
and Western Kentucky University.

Editorial and Sales Offices: The University Press of Kentucky
663 South Limestone Street, Lexington, Kentucky 40508-4008

98 99 00 01 02 5 4 3 2 1

Frontispiece: Mayor Samuel M. Jones.
Courtesy of Toledo–Lucas County Public Library

Library of Congress Cataloging-in-Publication Data
Jones, Marnie.
Holy Toledo : the life and times of "Golden Rule" Jones / Marnie Jones.
p. cm.
Includes bibliographical references (p.) and index.
ISBN 0-8131-2062-4 (cloth : acid-free recycled paper)
1. Jones, Samuel Milton, 1846-1904. 2. Mayors—Ohio—Toledo—Biography. 3. Social reformers—Ohio—Toledo—Biography. 4. Toledo (Ohio)—Politics and government. 5. Socialism, Christian—Ohio—Toledo—History—19th century. I. Title.
F499.T6J66 1998
977.1'13'04092—dc21
[B] 97-52175

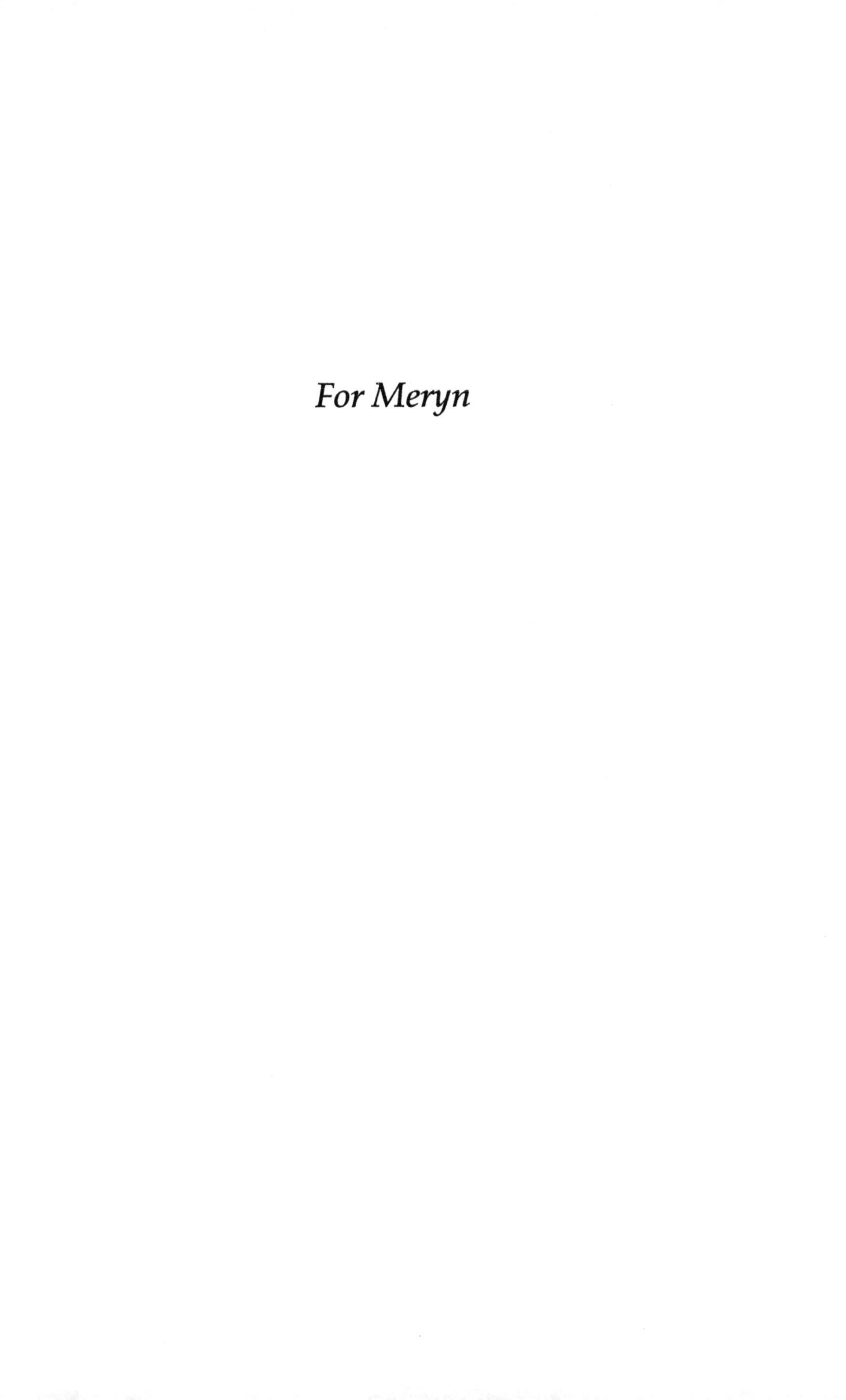
For Meryn

Let us hereafter, in speaking of the hot place in a man's consciousness, the group of ideas to which he devotes himself, and from which he works, call it *the habitual centre of his personal energy.* It makes a great difference to a man whether one set of his ideas, or another, be the centre of his energy; and it makes a great difference, as regards any set of ideas which he may possess, whether they become central or remain peripheral in him. To say that a man is "converted" means, in these terms, that religious ideas, previously peripheral in his consciousness, now take a central place, and that religious aims form the habitual centre of his energy.

—William James, *The Varieties of Religious Experience*

After nearly three years of a test, I am pleased to say the golden rule works. It is perfectly safe and worthy of a trial. It is nearly 1,900 years since Jesus gave it to the world, and I think the least his professed followers can do is to try it.

—Samuel M. Jones, *The American Fabian*

[Owain Glyndwr] is the Welshness in all Welshmen, whether they consciously acknowledge it or not. He is the spirit of their origins. That he achieved nothing material in the end is only apposite, for if there is one constant to the Welsh feel of things it is a sense of what might have been, tinged sometimes with despair. . . . His brief years of achievement have come to represent some crystallization of Welshness. His vision of the country was a vision of the place as a human entity, not just a country but a nation, not just a state but a fellowship, and a culture, and a heritage, and a sense of home, and a reconciliation of time, in which the affairs of the remotest past might overlap the present and engage the future.

—Jan Morris, *The Matter of Wales: Epic Visions of a Small Country*

Contents

Acknowledgments xi

A Word about Sources xv

Introduction: If You Knew My Inner Life, You Would Understand 1

Part 1: Personal Transformation

1. Stirred With Ambition To Better His Hard Lot 19
2. The Only Problem Worth a Man's Attention 38
3. The First Radical Move 65

Part 2: Factory and Municipal Reforms

4. Produce Great Persons, The Rest Follows 91
5. I Will Not Be the Mayor of Any Ring or Faction 105
6. The Time to Think About Someone besides Self 120
7. Like Christianity, Democracy Has Never Been Tried 139

Part 3: Political Defeats and Personal Victories

8. That I May Rid Myself of Guilt and Complicity 159
9. I'm a Man Without a Party and I'm Lonely 181
10. I Fail Utterly When It Comes to Depending upon Love 199
11. The Greatest Victory of My Life 218

Notes 239

Bibliography 270

Index 279

Illustrations follow page 104.

Acknowledgments

One cannot spend ten years researching and writing the life of a "Golden Rule" reformer without becoming self-conscious about the reciprocal nature of relationships. I end the process of writing this biography with a deep sense of indebtedness to many people whose help has improved the book. Early in the process of writing, Dick Bizot, Ron Burke, Jim Crooks, Betty Furdell, Alyson Meeks, Patricia Hamman and Bill Slaughter proved to be helpful readers. Ed Linenthal played a crucial role in helping the manuscript find a home.

My longest-term debts are to my first and best teachers, Nils Blatz and Lou Hamman, who read parts of the manuscript. Sam Kimball, David Courtwright, and Peter Frederick read the entire manuscript at critical junctures, and each helped me see my subject with new clarity of vision. My debts to them are incalculable.

Writing this book at the same time I directed the University of North Florida Honors Program was a great challenge. We try to do something like Sam Jones did on Segur Avenue: build community. I am beholden to the Honors Program faculty and staff, Marcia Ladendorff, Glenn Parker, Bill Slaughter, Lori Grandstaff, Michael Hurt, Alisa Hope, Benay Sinaikin, Melissa Morgan, Tina Carper, Matt Hankins, and Jennifer Cobia. Each of them, with gracious goodwill, shouldered extra responsibilities so that I could complete the manuscript. Thanks also to the Honors Program student directors, Danielle Liso, Heather Burk, Michael Hurt and Jason Spencer, who have taught me much about community.

Biographers are always indebted to their subjects in complicated ways, but I have a special connection to acknowledge. Samuel M. Jones was my great-grandfather. I began this project as a literary scholar with training in biography on the track of a good story. The familial connection was distant: Jones had died in 1904; I had not known his son, my grandfather, Percy; nor had I much contact with Golden Rule Jones's grandson and namesake, my father, Sam Jones. The connection, though, was established for me on my first day's research in Toledo. I began working with the Jones Papers at the end of his life, looking through the Memorial Scrapbook that was compiled at his death. As I turned the scrapbook pages, the genetic connection became real. I was struck by three photos and a caption: "The last photographs of Mayor Jones, holding his grandson and namesake Samuel M. Jones, II."

My research was supported at two critical junctures by the National Endowment for the Humanities, which provided a year's fellowship to write the first draft and a Summer Seminar in 1992 with Claude Welch, "The Church and Society in 19th Century Religious Thought," at the Graduate Theological Union at Berkeley. The University of North Florida supported my research travel twice through TSI grants and once through support from Afesa Adams, then dean of the College of Arts and Sciences.

I have followed Sam Jones's trail from Beddgelert, Wales, to Toledo, Ohio. There has been much joy in these detective forays. I followed Jones's footsteps so as to see the world that he saw. Research for this book took me to the north of Wales, where Elin Owen's Welsh and her intrepid handling of one-lane hairpin mountain roads led us to Sam's childhood home, Ty Mawr. There, Ruth Llywelyn Davies and Paul Orkney-Work, the owners, graciously showed me my great-grandfather's birth home. In Collinsville, New York, a local historian, Mary Teal, helped us explore the Black River region, where my daughter, Meryn, then six, was drawn like a magnet to the tombstone of her great-great-great grandmother, Margaret Jones, who was buried in the Turin cemetery in 1879. At Pithole and other ghost towns of the Pennsylvania oil fields, Alice Morrison helped me explore long-lost oil boom towns. In Toledo, I found family in my second cousin once removed, Mason B. Jones Jr. Others in Golden Rule Jones's extended family have enhanced my work in ways they cannot imagine: Ted Jones, like Mason, grandson to Sam through Jones's youngest son; Aled Davies, whose maternal grandfather was brother to Sam's father, Hugh; Helen Allen, who was Sam's brother John's youngest daughter.

Libraries, museums, historians and scholars have aided me as I sought to follow Sam Jones's footsteps. At the Toledo–Lucas County Public Library, which houses the Jones Papers, Jim Marshall and the staff at the Local History–Genealogy Department were unfailingly helpful and supportive during my frequent trips to Toledo. Permission to quote from the Jones Papers was granted by the Toledo-Lucas County Public Library. I benefited greatly from the important work in the 1970s of Morgan Barclay and Jean Strong, who collected the Jones Papers. The staffs at the Drake Well Museum, Titusville, and at the Lewis County Historical Society were most helpful in providing documentation for Jones's early life. Professor William Edgerton tracked down Ernest Crosby's letters to Tolstoy about Jones in the Tolstoy Museum in Moscow.

Finally, my biggest debt and greatest thanks go to my family: my husband, Buzz Thunen, and daughter, Meryn. For all of her life Meryn has had to share my attention, not with a sibling, but with her great-great-grandfather. My husband's love and support in this project were manifested in many ways; this book would not have been written or finished without his help. The words of thanks and appreciation to all those named here—but especially to Buzz—seem entirely inadequate.

A Word about Sources

I faced two different problems investigating the life of Samuel M. Jones. In 1953 Harvey Ford described a difficulty that has not been mine. In his Ph.D. dissertation, "The Life and Times of Golden Rule Jones," he observed, "The principal difficulty confronting a biographer of Jones is the lack of a collection of his papers" (1:iii). Seven years later, in 1960, workmen in the attic of the S.M. Jones Company on Segur Avenue in Toledo found trunks containing 15,000 documents and 145 volumes from Sam Jones's personal library. Mason Jones, Sr., Jones's last remaining son, donated the contents of those trunks to the Toledo–Lucas County Public Library. The books supplemented the 89 books from Jones's library which previously had been donated to the library by his widow, many were heavily annotated by Jones. Thus, though Harvey Ford had no primary sources that could give him access to Jones's mind, I have been inundated.

The Jones Papers contain both sides of his correspondence, letters to and from close friends and reformers of national importance as well as the hundreds of ordinary people who wrote to Mayor Jones. The collection provides a rich record of his developing thought and the mutual influence of his contemporaries. My problem, therefore, was to select from among the many treasures those best suited to reveal the man, for there are far too many to use.

The Jones Papers, housed at the Toledo–Lucas County Public Library, are available in the Local History–Genealogy Department. The librarians at the Toledo–Lucas County Public Library, in the 1970s, primarily Morgan J. Barclay and Jean W. Strong, did an exhaustive search of materials relevant to Jones's life. In 1976 a grant from the National Historical Publications and Records Commission made it possible to reproduce those documents to supplement the material found in the factory with copies of related material from twenty collections, including the Whitlock and Darrow Papers, both at the Library of Congress, the Dunbar and Gladden collections at the Ohio Historical Society, and the Lloyd Papers at the State Historical Society of Wisconsin. The Jones Papers, which now contain this added material, are available on microfilm from the Ohio Historical Society. A new scrapbook, kept by Jones, surfaced in 1990 and has been added to the collection. It is the only material, aside from Jones's heavily annotated personal library, not on microfilm.

I had only to look before the year 1897, however, to appreciate the rich documentary record that threatened to overwhelm me, for my second problem is the more vexing of the two. While Sam Jones's political career during the years 1897 to 1904 is amply documented by both his correspondence and the coverage he received in Toledo's two major newspapers, the direct original sources for his first fifty years are a complete blank. For most of his life Sam Jones was an ordinary person who left no record behind him. His first published book, *The New Right,* does contain an autobiographical chapter. With that as a lead, I have located secondary source material to help make sense of Jones's prereform life.

For the biographer who asks why Sam Jones changed from capitalist to socialist, the Jones Papers present a problem. The correspondence documents only his years as mayor, 1897-1904. A handful of letters from December 1896 survive. No personal documents from the crucial period of the founding of the Acme Sucker Rod Company survive. Consequently, in recreating the years 1843-96, the biographical detective work presented a different challenge. I turn, of course, to his own memory of his past found in his letters and autobiographical memoir. But that vision of the past was clearly colored by the reformer's present, the world of 1899. So the evidence itself is in some important ways suspect. The reader can share the biographer's quest to catch the "first" Sam Jones through the eyes of the "second" Jones. To cover the gap and document Sam Jones's world from some other vantage point than his retrospective view, I turned, wherever possible, to the recorded accounts of contemporaries: other Welsh immigrants dreaming the American Dream or eager young men at the end of the Civil War with "oil on the brain."

Introduction

If You Knew My Inner Life, You Would Understand

In 1897, in the most extraordinary election in American municipal politics, the Toledo Republican machine offered a socialist as mayoral nominee. Samuel M. Jones was well-known throughout the city as a manufacturer who literally ran his factory by the Golden Rule. The machine thought it could control this newcomer; it could not have been more wrong. Jones served as Toledo's mayor until his death in 1904; he had won three subsequent elections as a political independent. He continued to haunt the Republicans for two decades after his death: the party was unable to stop Toledo's independent movement until the early 1920s. But Jones's fame did not lie in his ability to limit the effectiveness of the Republican Party. During his lifetime he caught the nation's attention by offering a vision of a radically different America. His life presents a dramatic and poignant story for anyone today interested in poverty, community, and social justice.

Sam Jones lived the Golden Rule, but it gave him no peace. Many of his contemporaries thought his commitment extraordinary. The *New Orleans Sunday States* put it this way: "When a practical man can, through the application of common sense, make the golden rule a habit of daily life, he becomes not only a benefactor but a genius." Henry Demarest Lloyd, George Herron, Vida Scudder, and Walter Rauschenbusch each looked to Sam Jones as the one man in America who did the most to put the Golden Rule into action. Yet at his death, the *Denver Post* observed that Golden Rule Jones had broken his heart trying to change things a mayor could not change. Sam Jones lived his love for others, yet despite a decade of remarkable fidelity to the Golden Rule, he felt he failed. Just two weeks before he died, the Golden Rule mayor told a woman imprisoned for keeping a house of prostitution, "I am not as 'good' as many people think I am. . . . If you knew my inner life, you would understand . . . that it is not one of unalloyed happiness." His is the story of a deeply divided self: a successful businessman turned Progressive reformer painfully troubled by the inadequacies of his soul. This book examines how Sam Jones, a Welsh immigrant lad intent on making himself rich, became the Christian socialist Golden Rule Jones. It explores the religious and psychological factors that first drove him to make a fortune, and then, just as relentlessly, to give that fortune away.[1]

Jones applied the Golden Rule with a relentless selflessness. Late in life, in an attempt to escape from chronic asthma, Jones became a vegetarian, a devotee of exercise who ran the mile from his home to the mayor's office, and a firm believer in the meditative advantage of standing on his head. The newspaper reported that when he began speaking from that position, half a dozen fellows competed to get their heels over their heads. The paper dryly noted that the mayor's sanity was questioned. On another occasion, when he stood on his head in a downtown building, a crowd gathered to jeer him. A man on the outskirts of the crowd was heard to say in his defense, "Well, by heaven, none of anybody else's money fell out of his pockets." That comment had more truth to it than the crowd could realize. Jones used his mayoral salary to help the unemployed and homeless; sometimes it lasted only three days a month and he then turned to his private fortune. That happened so frequently that, although he was worth close to $1 million in 1897 when he became mayor and had a yearly income of $10,000 in addition to his salary, at his death eight years later his fortune had fallen to $333,000. The *Toledo Blade*'s headline read: "Sensational Developments: Cost Mayor Jones $100,000 a Year to Run Mayoral Office: Another Five Years Would Have Seen Him Depleted of Wealth."[2]

His first radical idea was to use the Golden Rule as a practical prescription for life. In 1894, at a time when employees in factories around the country were faced with long lists of rules to abide by or lose their jobs, he placed a tin sign on his new factory wall: "The Rule That Governs This Factory. 'Therefore Whatsoever Ye Would That Men Should Do Unto You, Do Ye Even So Unto Them.'" His factory had no other rules, no time clocks, and 50 percent higher wages than others. He went on to institute an eight-hour day in his oil fields to put more men to work; where previously six men had worked a drill for two twelve-hour shifts, now nine men did three eight-hour shifts. Soon he established a profit-sharing plan, paid vacations, a company cafeteria, and day care facilities. As mayor, he made Toledo the first U.S. city to place municipal employees on eight-hour days, worked for municipal ownership of utilities, and sought to overturn the work of the police courts, which he felt "perpetuate[d] more crime than they prevent." He stood virtually alone among middle-class reformers in arguing that crime, prostitution, and drunkenness were caused by the social system rather than by "vice." He argued against political parties so effectively that in 1899, when he made a nonpartisan bid for governor, he threatened the dominance of the president's Republican Party in William McKinley's home state.

The insights of the early twentieth-century press do much toward summing up the man and the meaning of his life. The *Milwaukee News* observed: "It is not of importance to the world at large that the mayor of Toledo is dead. The mayor of Toledo is of small consequence to the American people. But Samuel M. Jones was of interest to them—not simply because he was mayor of Toledo, but simply because he was a man who tried to help his fellows. He was not only of interest to them—Mr. Rockefeller and Mr. Carnegie are interesting personalities—but he commanded their sympathy." The *Cleveland Plain Dealer* noted: "It can hardly be maintained that his economic principles were the source of his strength with the people. . . . They may have cared much or little for his social and economic doctrines, but they believed firmly in Mayor Jones. They considered him brave, honest, sympathetic, kindly and as nearly right as the next. That alone would account for most of his political success." The *Detroit Journal* stated that "the moral which his spectacular career teaches does not lie in his theories or principles, but in the spectacle which his life presented of a generous, open-hearted, charitable man, tremendously energetic in the pursuit of his convictions."[3]

Sam Jones's ideas attracted the attention of his contemporaries because he was one of the most engaging of the early Progressive reformers. During his lifetime, he attracted so much notoriety that the national press regularly followed both his professional career and his personal life. The *Chicago Tribune* archly noted in 1902, while reporting his serious illness: "Ameri-cans would regret the untimely death of Mayor Jones. He is picturesque and unconventional. He preaches the golden rule and sometimes practices it. . . . It is to be hoped that Mayor Jones will not leave Toledo for another and better world—a world so much better that there will be nothing there for him to improve. He is not needed there as he is in the Ohio city which he rules."[4]

Golden Rule Jones's biography reveals that reformers were more complex and more various than historians, searching for patterns, have at times acknowledged. Jones's life should clarify our understanding of the reform impulse in America. For Sam Jones does not fit the pattern historians have traced. He came from an evangelical background, but he differed from many other reformers in his attitude toward middle-class morality. Paul Boyer persuasively demonstrates that reformers implicitly or explicitly assumed that the city should replicate the moral order of the village: "The story of municipal political reform in these years is a familiar and much analyzed one," he observes. Like most other historians, he then lists Jones with the other reform mayors of the period in a single sentence, failing to distinguish among them: "the battalions of 'reform' mayors, including Hazen Pingree in Detroit, William Strong and Seth Low in New York,

Charles Schieren in Brooklyn, Josiah Quincy in Boston, James Phelen in San Francisco, Samuel 'Golden Rule' Jones and Brand Whitlock in Toledo, and Tom Johnson in Cleveland. . . . What bears emphasizing here is how thoroughly all these movements were steeped in moral-uplift preoccupations. For municipal political reformers of the late nineteenth century, the worst thing about a corrupt and thieving municipal government, or one linked to vice interests, was that it poisoned the moral atmosphere of the entire city." Golden Rule Jones did not think that vice corrupted the city. "The popular conception of 'good government,'" he wrote Henry Demarest Lloyd, "seems to be confined to the thought of restraining saloons, gambling houses and brothels, but I think I have a larger conception, and in fact a better one, that will explain what I understand by 'good government.' It is expressed in the word Brotherhood. Any government that recognizes the idea and brings about a condition of brotherhood is good government."[5]

A brief story captures the essence of Jones's unique position among American reformers. In the last years of the nineteenth century, Toledo, Ohio, was often characterized, with some justification, as a "loose" city. The blue laws had not been enforced for years; the saloons in town, between six and eight hundred, quenched the thirst of a city of only 135,000 residents. The saloons were a known enemy. But in the past few years Toledo had seen the rise of a new threat, "wine rooms," which caused respectable men to blanch. For a wine room did not differ from a saloon in the nature of the beverage served but in the nature of the business transacted. These establishments provided lavishly decorated stalls, each complete with a couch, where prostitutes and their clients had some semblance of privacy. Toledo's most respectable men and women responded to this outrage by forming a committee that made its way downtown to the Valentine building, which housed the mayor's office, confident that their mayor would *do* something.

In early February 1898, Samuel M. "Golden Rule" Jones, a big, hearty, Welsh oil producer and manufacturer, had been mayor of Toledo for less than a year. The city's religious reformers had embraced him on election day, the previous April. After a narrow victory, he had ecstatically wired Washington Gladden, the Social Gospel minister, invoking the presence of a demon who would feature largely in his later political scuffles, that he had won "in spite of 600 saloons, traction company, and the devil."[6] Despite the original fears of the saloon keepers, the new mayor had left them alone—so far. As the committee members traveled the mile from their homes in the fashionable West End neighborhood to the Valentine, they knew that they spoke for those who had cast their ballots for Jones the previous spring. Although the nationwide prohibition movement temporarily was losing much of the strength it had gained in the past quarter-century, those en route to the mayor's office knew it was a still a highly charged issue in Toledo, despite the current lack of national consensus. The Ohio Anti-Saloon League had been founded in Oberlin in 1893 and exerted great influence throughout the state. As early as 1887, twenty temperance organizations in Toledo had tried to enforce the blue laws. Despite a decade of work with little to show for it, they were confident of victory now. After all, their new mayor, Golden Rule Jones, must be a moral, Christian man. He was, in fact, a neighbor; they knew him to be a lifelong teetotaler and an employer who at one time would dismiss an employee for merely standing *outside* a saloon.

Exasperated that their Golden Rule mayor had not done something about the scandalous goings-on of the wine rooms, the fashionable contingent met with their mayor. They were greeted by the good-looking, blue-eyed Welshman and taken in to his private office. As they looked about them, they saw a three-foot-long board upon which the mayor himself had carved: "JUDGE NOT LEST YE BE JUDGED." To the left a plaque proclaimed: "We are all children of God." These were sentiments they heartily approved of; they saw no warning that they would fail in their mission. They presented the facts and requested that the mayor close down the wine rooms and get rid of the women—preferably with police escort. Sam Jones listened carefully. His response startled them. "'But where shall I have the police drive them? Over to Detroit or to Cleveland, or merely out into the country? They have to go somewhere you know.'" Brand Whitlock, the novelist who later served as Toledo's mayor from 1905 to 1913, present at the meeting, observed that this "detail had escaped them." Then the mayor did more than startle, he shocked: "'I'll make you a proposition. You go and select two of the worst of these women you can find, and I'll agree to take them into my home and provide for them until they can find some other home and some other way of making a living. And then you, each one of you, take one girl into your home, under the same conditions, and together we'll try to find homes for the rest.'" There was silence. "'They looked at him, and then looked at each other, and seeing how utterly hopeless this strange man was, they went away.'"[7]

Sam Jones was a remarkable figure in the turn-of-the century reform community because he refused to repress new immigrant communities. Theodore Roosevelt, as New York's police commissioner from 1895 to 1897, had "waged a 'relentless war' against the 'bestial' rulers of 'commercialized vice.'" His friend Jacob Riis summed up the attitude of reformers hostile to the poor: "It is a dreary old truth that those who would fight *for* the poor must *fight* the poor to do it." Thus the "new abolitionists" of the 1890s sought to abolish prostitution and reform the sexual morality of American culture.[8] Sam Jones was virtually free of the general tendency among middle-class reformers to seek institutional means to repress the "vice" so prevalent in the urban ethnic wards. He saw both prostitution and alcohol in economic terms: the prostitute and the saloon keeper needed to make a living. With such a high incidence of immigrant women in prostitution, the concern among the middle class—like those who wanted to close down the wine rooms in Toledo—had as much to do with class-based fears as with concerns over morality. As mayor of Toledo, Sam Jones sought to use his power to make the municipality create a more humane environment. No better proof exists of his disinclination to impose morality than his regular habit of dismissing all cases that came before him when he sat in for the police judge.

Samuel Jones stands virtually alone among late nineteenth-century reformers in his refusal to use municipal powers to repress vice. Jones's position is especially striking because the impulse to evoke moral control through the institutions of the state spanned the entire political spectrum. The work of liberal, conservative, religious, and scientific reformers had the effect of increasing institutional moral control. It is hardly surprising, then, that concerned Toledo citizens would find his stand totally incomprehensible.[9]

Jones argued that the trappings of upper-middle-class life, not immigrant "vices," were what poisoned the atmosphere of the city. "I have more respect for many saloon keepers to-day than I have for a great many so-called 'good citizens' in the church and out of it, who are devoting their energies from infancy to old age, to the mere matter of getting money." Their only skill, he thought, was the ability to exploit others: "The brothel is not more hideous than the finely dressed lady, glittering with diamonds and jewels, purchased with profit made from the destruction of the lives of her sisters who toil for $2.50 and $3.00 per week."[10]

One of the clearest indications that the reform community linked vice to foreign immigrants comes from Josiah Strong. Observing that foreigners were bringing to America a "continental idea" of the Sabbath, thereby turning the Holy Day into a holiday, he wrote: "By far the most effective instrumentality for debauching popular morals is the liquor traffic, and this is chiefly carried on by foreigners."[11]

Sam Jones, unlike most turn-of-the-century reformers, saw the problems of poverty and the sins of "vice" as the inevitable results of the rapidly industrializing economy. Like Detroit's Hazen Pingree, he saw the conflicts of his city over municipal ownership and public transit in terms of private versus public interests. Because of his conviction that the environment has a great impact on people, he sought to build a city that could respond to the needs created by industrialization by building a commonwealth. Unlike his friend William Jennings Bryan, for whom he campaigned in 1900, Jones embraced the power of new technologies and sought to create humane urban communities. He was one of the very few reformers to reach immigrant, working-class voters. He was successful with them because he did not seek to transform them, to impose upon them middle-class notions of respectability: witness his response to prostitution. Sam Jones is remarkable precisely because he did not share the central concern of most reformers—to impose the values of old stock Americans so as to eradicate the "vices" of the lower class.[12]

Sam Jones's political career and his personal quest seem increasingly relevant as modern America struggles with issues of economic inequities and social justice. Jones's story provides us with an important vision of American political ideals. Functioning for three terms as an Independent who put "principle before party," Mayor Jones had the opportunity to educate his constituents to make them see the need for sweeping political and social change. Citizens of Toledo knew where he stood; he simply asked them to follow him. Sam Jones never hesitated, never changed his position, when the political winds blew cold. He serves as a strong reminder that at times politicians have been *leaders* whose convictions, rather than the latest poll, determined their votes. Despite declining support in his last four years in office, he never doubted the validity of his position.

The drama of his life resides in the conflict between Sam Jones's ideals and the political, economic, and social realities that he hoped to change. His agenda threatened others: the clergy; the upper middle class; his own family; business leaders; Republican party regulars; perhaps even President McKinley. Of course, Jones's vision of a postcapitalist world without competition, political parties, or prisons never materialized. Nor have solutions to the problems of poverty been found. The vibrant nineteenth-century Toledo is gone, but the homeless are not. They stand outside the doors of the Toledo Public Library, which houses the Samuel Milton Jones Papers, in need of food and shelter. Clearly, this is not just a story about who we once were, it is a story about who we are. Many of the issues of Sam Jones's day have not been resolved. His story may remind us that it is time they were.

The most poignant aspect of the drama comes in the inner conflicts with which Sam Jones struggled. He had a vision for this country, but his own psychic conflicts limited his effectiveness as a politician. Sam Jones has long been recognized as an important political figure. Other reformers, principally Gladden and Lloyd, took him seriously when he first ran for mayor in 1897; then the national press, including William Randolph Hearst and Lincoln Steffens, interested in the oxymoron of a Golden Rule politician, began following his career. Since his death, historians have identified Jones as the principal Progressive reformer who made the Golden Rule a habit not simply of personal life but of municipal life. Ernest S. Griffith, who finds corruption the conspicuous failure of municipal government, notes with some surprise that Sam Jones actually practiced the Golden Rule. Golden Rule Jones had a unique opportunity that Progressive reformers of the professional class did not: to change a city, to transform a political process. Nevertheless, an important aspect of this story is his failure as a politician. Toledo's city council and Ohio's governor frustrated many of Jones's reform initiatives. Understanding his psychological dilemmas is essential; his reform career is incomprehensible without understanding his inner life.[13]

Despite his failures, Sam Jones did have a lasting influence. The idea of nonpartisan politics has been more completely tested in Toledo than in any other American city. In the fifteen years that followed his death, other politicians were able to implement many of Jones's ideas. As a result of a legal battle initiated in 1902, by Jones, the Ohio Constitutional Convention drafted an amendment for municipal home rule for all Ohio cities ten years later; on January 1, 1916, Toledo's new city charter required that all municipal franchises be submitted to the voters. The most remarkable effect of the Jones legacy was that the charter mandated nonpartisan elections. And, in fact, national, state, and local organizations had little influence: neither political party sponsored a candidate until the Democrats nominated Edward J. Lynch in 1919. He finished third, losing to independent incumbent Cornell Schreiber and Socialist Solon T. Klotz.[14] Nevertheless, Sam Jones would have accomplished more had he become a skillful politician. His psychic battles made that impossible.

A few words are needed about my approach. Sam Jones's remarkable personal transformation, his factory and municipal reforms, and his political failures are all unintelligible without an examination of his inner life. This book depends on three perspectives to interpret Golden Rule Jones's life: phenomenological, psychological, and political-historical. These approaches provide different but essentially convergent perspectives, permitting us to understand how Jones saw himself but also to make connections that Jones was unable, or unwilling, to recognize fully.

On one level, I strive to retell Sam Jones's story from his own perspective. Sam Jones the reformer was, as I will show, remarkably articulate and deeply committed to understanding his world and his place in it. Thus this book is a phenomenological study of Jones's worldview: how he perceived himself and his world, how he articulated those perceptions within the

New Testament's moral imperative, and how he evaluated what he took to be his failure to live by the Golden Rule. Because Sam Jones was extraordinarily self-conscious about the direction and meaning of his life and because he recorded those introspections in two books, in scores of speeches and articles, in thousands of letters, and in the marginalia of his personal books, this approach seems particularly appropriate. Thus I trace Sam Jones's intentions but also stress the ways he represented those intentions to himself.

On the second level, I use psychological contexts to see beyond Jones's self-reckoning. One essential aim is to dramatize Jones's struggle to implement the Golden Rule, to analyze the difficulties it held for him, and to understand the consequences—to his inner self and his political career—of translating moral principle into political and economic programs. Psychological contexts permit us to see clearly beyond the limits of Jones's vision, but I want to emphasize that Jones attempted to make sense of himself in just this way. William James's *Varieties of Religious Experience* explored the psychology of religious conversion in 1902; Jones's annotated copy reveals that he read the book with great interest and care. James provides sound insight into the conversion process; this text can help begin to make sense of Sam Jones's ethical conversion and his spiritual and political journeys.

This biography also depends in essential ways on psychological contexts unavailable to Jones at the century's end. The perspective of developmental psychology, Philip Greven's *The Protestant Temperament,* and revisionist psychoanalytic theories of identity formation help to make sense of Golden Rule Jones's life and career, providing counterpoint to Jones's own sense of self. This is an interdisciplinary study that combines biography, history, psychology, theology, and literature.

We cannot see the world or the self as Jones saw them: our view of human nature itself has changed. At the end of the nineteenth century—at least within some elements of the Christian perspective—it was possible to see both the self and the world as coherent in a way that is no longer possible. Sam Jones believed in the possibility of crafting a coherent life that would, in turn, help to shape a more coherent world. Jones would have been unfamiliar with the psychoanalytic concepts that inform our understanding of the self today, however much we might quarrel with Sigmund Freud's particular theories. Current interdisciplinary work in sociobiology is further distancing our understanding of the self from that of the Progressive period. We are aware—in ways that Sam Jones could not have imagined—that forces beyond our intentions shape our lives. Our poststructuralist world is as confident about the utter absence of coherence as the Progressives were about finding order and meaning in the world. But biography, even in a poststructuralist world, is an art form that demands coherence. In choosing these three perspectives, I have shaped the story I tell. The perspectives of history and politics, theology and psychology, placed on a phenomenological analysis of Golden Rule Jones, make sense of the inconsistencies that mystified Jones and his contemporaries. It is not the only way to tell this story; I found it to be the story that demanded to be told.

It is essential to explore the compensatory nature of Sam Jones' vision and the shame and guilt he felt so intensely. His letters at the century's end contain a constant refrain of feeling responsible for the weight of the world's problems; his compensatory remarks seem to signal a deeply felt need for atonement. His wealth now seemed a defilement. The remainder of his life was, on one level, a series of compensatory acts. Beginning with the fair wage he paid his men, his willingness to lose money in the name of reform and donating his mayoral salary to the poor were gestures to compensate for having organized his first life around money. The Golden Rule establishes an ideal reciprocity. The simultaneous command to consider the self and to suppress it is inherent in Jesus' instructions to do unto others as you would have them do unto you. One must constantly monitor one's treatment of others in terms of the self: how would *I* feel treated in this manner? The focus continually reverts to the self. But then one must deny the self by putting the needs of the other before one's own. Sam Jones was extraordinarily willing to treat others as he would be treated. In fact, he treated others better than he treated himself precisely because of his discomfort with the self. Yet self continually intruded. The clearest example of the political problems that ensued was Jones's unwillingness to declare himself a candidate for office. He needed to make it seem as though he was serving the will of others, not answering the dictates of his own heart. Sam Jones's principal political "platform"—the Golden Rule—seeks to value the community over the individual. He was heir to the communitarian tradition, with its roots in the antebellum abolitionists such as Theodore Weld and Wendell Phillips, and to America's Puritan roots.[15]

We must understand how Jones saw himself and become familiar with the categories and vocabulary of self-reckoning that he adopted. Understanding Jones's psychology requires exploring the role of writing in his life. In his last years Jones identified himself through texts. Not only did he attempt to come to terms with the ultimate meaning of his own life by writing about his life, he refashioned himself into the Golden Rule reformer by internalizing a series of theological texts. The Golden Rule itself is a text—the one that came to define his life. His need for texts was an expression of his longing to free himself from his shame and guilt. Whatever money signified to him in his early manhood, it ultimately became an utterly inadequate sign for his desires. Like an alchemist, he seems to have longed to transform the base motives signified by money into a Golden Rule. It was, he thought, the difference between Mark Hanna, popularly thought to be the power behind the president, and himself: the Rule of Gold vs. the Golden Rule. The act of writing dominated his mayoralty because the written word became a means of entering into a contract of the heart, a contract of absolute reciprocity, of absolute fairness, with the world and with himself. His nickname declares this effort.

Sam Jones's intention to live a spiritual life was not a pathological impulse, but it is clear that his religious training had unfortunate psychological and political consequences. Jones's religiously induced sense of shame and inadequacy undermined his political successes. But it is also true that the religious world vision he absorbed as a child was the essential catalyst for his heroic attempt to live the imperatives of the New Testament. His conviction about the practicality of living by the Golden Rule and his nationwide reform fame rest on his remarkable ability to identify with others. This ability speaks to his extraordinary empathy and his great imaginative powers, but also to his very great needs. Psychoanalytic concepts help to make sense of the problem of identity, especially in relation to his internal disharmony, his need to "rid himself of guilt" and his belief—or was it dread?—that "love will accept no compromise."[16]

The book's third framework is political and historical. In his own lifetime, Jones's political and, hence, historical importance was recognized and either courted or feared by national figures as different as William McKinley and William Jennings Bryan, Mark Hanna and Eugene Debs. His thinking was infused with the ideals of George Herron, John Ruskin, and Leo Tolstoy. His Toledo reforms came out of conversations with Jane Addams and Henry Demarest Lloyd. Throughout the book readers will find Golden Rule Jones's national reform prominence and his local experiments in brotherhood and political failures connected to the reformers of his day. Other municipal reformers were far more successful in implementing Progressive policies than was Golden Rule Jones—Detroit's Hazen Pingree and Cleveland's Tom Johnson, and in Toledo, his own disciple, Brand Whitlock, come to mind. Comparison to Pingree, Johnson, and Whitlock, in the pages that follow, provides a way to measure Jones's limited political success.

The story of municipal reformers can tell us a great deal about the texture of the Progressive period. The four Great Lakes reform mayors, Hazen Pingree in Detroit, Samuel Jones and Brand Whitlock in Toledo, and Tom L. Johnson in Cleveland, made important contributions to American political culture. This is the first published biography of Jones, the most striking of these reform mayors. Jones's extraordinary willingness to apply Christian principles to municipal problems, his profound honesty in examining his inner life, and the presence of an unusually rich trove of manuscript material make Sam Jones's life of special significance. In many ways Sam Jones was an exception to the prevailing reform ethos. I will explore Jones within the context of the political and Social Gospel cultures. Readers should not, however, turn to this biography for a treatise on urban Progressive reform; that story has often been told. Jones, as I will demonstrate, was different. He had what he called a "larger conception" of political and personal change. I have tried to remain faithful to that larger conception by connecting Sam Jones to the centuries-old American religious sense of self and view of the world. Golden Rule Jones's Toledo—at least in his own mind—was a "city on a hill"; thus he was reenacting one of the great legends of American life. Jones displayed the quintessential American confidence that individuals and municipalities could start over again, reinvent themselves.[17]

Sam Jones sought to transform his adopted home. His vision, although he never explicitly cast it this way, was of a "Holy Toledo"—in the richest sense of the word holy. Its etymology reminds us of its essence: something whole, sound, happy. Sam Jones made his ideal of a nourishing, sound community real in one working class neighborhood. His values and his structural reforms helped the people create a place where everyone was respected, valued, and well treated. He struggled to seed the same transformation city-wide. As a reformer Jones embraced a holy cause by attempting to institutionalize selflessness in business and municipal government. Mayor Jones thought of the city as a family where respect was the order of the day, differences were honored and there was pleasure and fun to be had. Jones's Holy Toledo was to be life-affirming in every dimension. Open spaces and playgrounds characterized Jones's city on a hill, not Church steeples.

Jones's respectable neighbors outraged by immigrant sin and vice latched on to the narrowest conception of the word and would be outraged by the title of this book. Mayor Jones repeatedly asserted that the saloon offered more sustenance to the soul than did the Church. No wonder the professional clergy were his most vehement critics. I intend the title to shine a light on the richest sense of the word "holy," but also to emphasize that all but the very rarest of us confront the radical expectations of Christianity. Jones became deeply critical of the Church; he saw its essential hypocrisy in not ordering the world as Jesus instructed. The clergy and their congregations did not *live* the question "What would Jesus do?" on a daily basis. Mayor Jones painfully struggled to live that question and knew how far he fell short. The tenth chapter of Matthew haunted him. The young man who followed all the commandments asked Jesus what else he should do: give all your possessions away, he was told. Hearing this, he went away sorrowful. Sam Jones saw himself as that young man. He frequently bridled at his nickname, complaining that other businessmen kept eight out of every ten dollars their men earned for them but since he only kept seven they called him Golden Rule Jones.

Sam Jones had a rich sense of humor; he would approve of the title of his biography—aware of the several layers of meaning available. The origin of the phrase appears to go back to Toledo Spain's medieval skyline dominated by mosques and steeples. But its usage is quintessential mid-American awe; "Holy Toledo! I can't believe he caught that ball!" It is an expression of amazement and appreciation tinged with disbelief. "Holy Toledo! I can't believe the mayor gave all that money away!" "Holy Toledo! Sam Jones tried to run a city on the Sermon on the Mount!" His contract of the heart, an acknowlegement of his profoundly reciprocal relationship with others, was the device Jones used to make Toledo Holy.

At the end of the nineteenth century a politician with a religious agenda was, in some sense, the logical culmination of a peculiarly American process of Christian democratization. So intertwined was politics with religion that one cannot understand the politics of nineteenth-century America without understanding its evangelical religious culture. Nineteenth-century American Protestant religious culture was both democratic and populist in that it sought to associate virtue with ordinary people. Evangelical revivals throughout the century had yoked the Christian message to American democracy.[18] Sam Jones's ardent democratic strain had been inculcated by the message he absorbed at the Welsh Calvinistic Methodist Church, confirmed by his own experience in the oil fields, and reinforced by the reading of his favorite poet, Walt Whitman.

Even before the country's inception, politics and religion had been inextricably intertwined. Like the Puritans who settled New England, Sam Jones believed a community should take biblical injunctions as prescriptions for life in this world. He sought to transform industrial Toledo into a city on a hill. But Sam Jones's life story also confirms Sacvan Bercovitch's claim that the Puritan vision is central to America's ongoing self-description. Raised in a denomination with strong Calvinist leanings, Jones inherited the dilemma of Puritan identity. The essential paradox of the Puritan tradition was its call for self-examination and its simultaneous instruction to deny the self: thus the individual had to deny the self he was obsessively monitoring. The two cannot easily—ever?—be resolved. For selflessness indicates a preoccupation with the self that must be denied.

Consider Richard Baxter's words to measure the vehemence of the Puritan attack on the self: "Self-denial and the love of God are all [one]. . . . It is self that the Scripture principally speaks against. . . . The very names of Self and Own, should sound in the watchful Christian's ears as very terrible, wakening words, that are next to the names of sin and satan."[19] Sam Jones's political career and his identity were fundamentally shaped in ways he never saw by this conflict between self-examination and self-denial: he learned well the lesson of self-reflection, but he could never free himself from the Calvinist imperative to suppress the self. He would have been far more successful as a politician and a reformer if he had. He would have lived longer as well.

Sam Jones lived two distinctly different lives: first, that of a successful businessman who considered himself a good Christian, and later that of a man so tormented by images and recollections of poverty that he sought radical changes for society and within himself. This book traces Jones's transformation from a successful capitalist making the American Dream come true to a man who strove to live his life by the Golden Rule and the Sermon on the Mount. Shortly after Jones became mayor, he received a letter from a friend he had not seen in years. The friend wrote to inquire if the new mayor of Toledo really was the same Sam Jones he knew from Pennsylvania. Jones's response must have seemed enigmatic to his correspondent, but it is revealing to his biographer: "Yes, I am the same Jones you knew in Duke Centre, but am not the same man although I am the same Jones. The Jones you knew in Duke Centre has become quite another man."[20] How did he become that other man—the Golden Rule Jones of 1898 who baffled his well-to-do neighbors by embracing the prostitute and saloon keeper?

Jones's is a quintessentially American story. First, there are important continuities between Jones's ideas and the Puritan roots of our culture. Next, the American Dream plot so powerfully captured the American imagination because real people brought it to life. Sam Jones certainly did: he came to this country with his family as an immigrant lad from Wales searching for a better way of life and became immensely rich. Finally, it is the story of America's failures. Sam Jones, like many who have succeeded in realizing great wealth, found something missing, within both himself and his culture. Like the revolutionaries who founded this country, like his contemporaries protesting the social revolution brought about by industry, Golden Rule Jones envisioned a new American Dream. In 1894, in the midst of a severe economic depression, Jones began to question the system that had made him rich. What about his past and his sense of self led to those questions? What forces, both internal and external, combined to create and ultimately to limit this extraordinary American reformer? What happens to a man who attempted to turn his back upon everything he had been taught, everything he had hoped for, everything he had come to believe? Those are the questions addressed in this book.

PART 1

Personal Transformation

1

Stirred with Ambition to Try to Better His Hard Lot

In 1850, when Sam Jones was almost four, his family left their home high on Mount Snowdon in Wales in search of the American Dream. Hugh S. Jones had heard stories of prosperity and happiness that people had achieved from working in the New World. He "was stirred with ambition to try to better his hard lot," remembered his son. Although Sam Jones left Wales as a child, its culture had a deep effect on him. The democratic ideal of Wales as a nation seems to have shaped his reform self. But the Welsh Calvinistic Methodist Church was even more important to his identity. If there is a key to making sense of this man, which his well-to-do Toledo neighbors so concerned about the "vice element" did not understand, it is this Welsh church. Sam Jones was born into an evangelical family and culture and it shaped his entire life. If Calvinist notions of election dominated his first life, the Methodist doctrine of sanctification haunted him in his second. It is clear that Sam Jones never freed himself from the Methodist injunction to perfect the self.[1]

Welsh values do much to explain the trajectory of his professional careers, including his extraordinary commitment to reform late in life. The Welsh, wrote Jones in 1899, are a "highly spiritual people. It is to this feature of the Welsh character that I owe my enthusiasm for social justice."[2]

With its preponderance of consonants, the Welsh language sounds as rugged, as harsh, as beautiful, and above all as inexplicable as the land itself, where Sam Jones was born. *The Caernarvonshire Historical Society Transactions* sums up Sam Jones's biography in Welsh with these words: "*O Nantmor, Beddgelert; perchen gwaith olew mawr Toledo, Ohio, a wnaeth enw iddo ei hun fel dyngarwr; rhedai ei waith enfawr un ol y Rheol Euraidd. Cafodd angladd bron fel pe bai'n Arlywydd.*" In English it goes something like this: "From Nantmor, Beddgelert; the owner of a large oil works in Toledo, Ohio, who made a name for himself as a lover of mankind; he ran his large works according to the Golden Rule. He was given a funeral as if he were a lord." Nothing about his beginning would prefigure such an end. Hugh S. Jones,

Sam's father, and his father before him, "old Sam the draper," had nothing lordly about them. Hugh Jones, father to a man who would become a millionaire and a mayor, was a slate mason in a land so barren the best crop was stones. Their world was the forest of Beddgelert (pronounced Bethgelert) which covered the Pass of Aberglaslyn, a valley cut by the river Glaslyn from foothills of Mount Snowdon or "Yr Wyddfa," "the Eagles' Nesting Place." At 3,560 feet it is the highest mountain south of the Scottish border; it created a self-contained world then and guaranteed an insularity that continues to this day. For it is Sam Jones's part of Wales where the Welsh language is still spoken and the dream of separation from England lives on despite a union of more than five hundred years.[3]

Sam's Welsh identity was formed by the language he first used. Cymraeg, the Welsh language, is still spoken in the north, where they distinguish between *Yr Hen Taith,* "the old language of the country," and *Yr Taith Fain,* "the thin language of the English."[4] Once in New York, even in a Welsh community, Sam would have begun to learn that thin language. In Hugh Jones's day, the north was totally immersed in Cymraeg, which was linked to the land: *"Nid yw'r graig yn deall Saesneg,"* they said ("The rock doesn't understand English"). Cymraeg also linguistically stresses the concept of cooperation so essential to Jones's late-life philosophy. "The spirit of Welsh language was collectivist: '*cy*fraith, *cy*far, *cy*fnawdd, *cy*morthau, *cy*manfaoedd (custom, co-ploughing, co-protection, co-help, co-assembly,')" are the literal transcriptions. The language emphasizes cooperation with the cy- and the co-.[5]

Hugh and Margaret Jones lived with their family in a cottage imprecisely named Ty Mawr, "Big House," sheltered by a stone outcrop named Moel Hebog, "battle hill of the hawks." By the time Samuel was born on August 3, 1846, six people lived in that primitive cottage with a rough, flagstone-covered floor. When Sam returned triumphantly as a successful manufacturer in 1896, he was stunned that the flagstone floor was rougher than any he had ever seen used in a sidewalk. The cottage was twenty-three feet long and about ten feet wide: two rooms were downstairs, the kitchen with its huge chimney and a sitting room. The second story was only a loft, lighted by small skylights and difficult for adults to maneuver in because an oak truss crossed both rooms at shoulder height to support the roof (*NR,* 39). It is no wonder that Hugh and Margaret considered other options as their family grew to seven.[6]

Perhaps the pattern of names given the children indicates an increasing religiosity in the Jones family. The first three children, Alice, John Hugh, and Ellen, were named after family members; the last two born in Wales, Samuel and Mary, were given biblical names, as were two more sons born in the United States, Moses and Daniel. Perhaps the most striking choice is that of the first child born in New York. Moses Jones had not led them to the New World, a nineteenth-century Israel, but his naming suggests much about their vision of this country as a land of milk and honey and their covenantal relationship with God. In naming their last son born in Wales Samuel, Hugh and Margaret chose the name aptly, for Hannah had dedicated her son Samuel to the service of Jehovah, and Samuel, the prophet, "continued to grow both in stature and in favor with the Lord and with the people."[7]

When the Jones family worshiped God in the chapel in Beddgelert the area had a centuries-old religious heritage. Beddgelert existed as a town because ancient pilgrims took to resting there on their way down Snowdon to Holyhead and Ireland. A thirteenth-century church, dedicated to St. Kelert, was built on the site. For pilgrims heading east, back to England, it was the last rest before the most difficult part of the journey. The foundation of the church, which still stands, allows the town to make claim to being the second oldest Christian site in Great Britain.[8]

By the nineteenth century the Calvinistic Methodist Church had recreated Welsh morality in its own likeness. But it was not until the eighteenth century that the Methodist revival transformed Wales: it managed to do what Christian missionaries since St. Augustine had not been able to—deeply root Christianity in Welsh culture. The Christianization of Wales succeeded in large part because of the remarkable success of an eighteenth-century system of itinerant teachers. The Bible had come to define the way rural people saw life because of an extraordinarily successful educational system. For almost eighty years, the Welsh learned to read in an almost totally religious context. They came to define themselves in the language and concepts of the Bible.[9] Sam Jones the reformer would likewise express and define himself in biblical language and evangelical concepts.

The Calvinistic Methodist movement, which began in the 1730s, was characterized by a passionate interest in moral improvement. Chapel morality had become, by the Victorian period, Welsh morality—self-restrained, self-critical, and omnipresent. Nonconformist sects flourished in Wales, in part because the people viewed the established Anglican Church to be out of touch with all things Welsh: *yr hen fradwres,* they called it: "the old traitress."[10] Although Calvinistic Methodism had sprung from the Anglican Church, by Sam Jones's day it offered an intense emotional fervor the established church did not.[11]

Beddgelert was the site of the most intense nineteenth-century revival in religious feeling in Wales. The Second Great Welsh Revival, as it was known, began in the Beddgelert Calvinistic Methodist chapel in 1818, when

Hugh Jones was ten. One day the girls in the Sabbath Day class one by one burst into tears as they read the concluding chapters of the Gospel of John. The emotional intensity rose to the point that no one could continue reading. One of the brethren, Richard Roberts, of Caeygors, rose to address the entire school, when to the astonishment of everyone present he "became eloquent." He quoted a verse of a Welsh hymn which ends "The firmer hold's above." The word "above" possessed him: "It is from *above* that everything precious comes to us. The light comes from *above,* and the heat and the rain. The blessings of salvation came to the world from *above.* It is from *on high* that God pours his spirit. There is hope for the hardened sinners of Beddgelert *above.* If it is dark here, it is light *above.* If it is feeble here, it is mighty *above, above, above."* Those present reported feeling a great and mysterious presence. Many of the children seemed to be filled with dread. One boy ran to his father to say: "Oh my dear father! Here *is* the day of judgment! It *has* come." Within the week of the first experience, Welsh churchgoers erupted into continuous shouting at the opening of the first hymn. They "saw a gleam of hope that, lost sinners as they were, they should find [salvation] by the mercy of God in Christ Jesus and their pent up feelings burst over all bounds," observed a nineteenth-century historian. The shouting was so loud that no one speaking in a normal register could be heard. Word of the commotion reached the village and others who came to observe joined in, adding to the din. The uproar continued for hours, throughout the day and into the night. In Beddgelert, over the course of the next several weeks, other religious outbursts occurred; soon people from all over Wales were coming to Beddgelert to observe for themselves. The revival swept through the region. Since the sixteenth century religious enthusiasm had carried with it a pejorative connotation. The conventionally religious dismissed the enthusiasm of those who did not contain their passionate zeal. The Welsh were dismissed in some circles as "Jumpers" because their revivals were characterized by frenetic shouting and jumping.[12]

Both Hugh, in Beddgelert, and then Sam, in Collinsville, New York, were raised in a community of religious enthusiasts. Hugh Jones grew to young manhood in both the time and place of the most intensely felt religious revival Wales has ever experienced. Intense evangelical fervor swept his county; Hugh could not have remained untouched by the sense of a fire within kindling to a blaze or the glorious outpouring of the spirit. Certainly, his reformer son had an intensely emotional sensibility. And he was explicit that his parents truly lived their faith. His parents, he remembered, "were *really*—not merely professionally—religious." Their religion "was not a matter of 'belief' or 'creed.'" Consequently, in his last years he accepted the premise that "it is not a question of what I believe or what I think or what I say, but that religion is my life—what I do from Monday morning to Monday morning year in and year out."[13]

Hugh's decision to emigrate is surprising, given his age, the expense, and the grueling nature of the trip to the United States. It is clear that life in north Wales was immensely difficult: at century's end, Sam Jones thought the hardships his parents faced in Wales had helped shape what he saw as his "inborn love for a larger liberty." What is less clear is why Hugh chose to take his family to the United States rather than to the industrial south Wales. Hugh Jones left north Wales at a time when a major population shift was occurring, but his decision to emigrate was atypical. In 1841, counties in the west and north began a process of depopulation as the industrializing southeast lured people. When Hugh Jones and his family left Wales in 1850, they did so at the start of the last complete decade of significant Welsh emigration. By the 1860s, residents did continue to leave the flanks of Snowdon, but they moved in large numbers to the coal valleys of the industrial south.[14] But Hugh Jones ignored the lure of an industrial society in south Wales and settled in a rural community in New York with his roots and his emotional life still tied to the mountains of Snowdonia. His reformer son recalled that his father had heard "stories of prosperity and happiness that came as the result of toil in the new world, [and] was stirred with the ambition to try to better his hard lot" (*NR*, 39).

The families scattered around Yr Wyddfa's stony hillsides had been sending members for some years to Collinsville, now a successful Welsh settlement in upstate New York. The stories of their successes must have been encouraging and Hugh must have been a man of extraordinary ambition, for, at forty-one, he was uncharacteristically old to be making such a move.[15] Even with the ambition of a man almost half his age, Hugh faced another obstacle: the cost of the journey. Others seem to have had confidence in Hugh Jones's ambition for the family traveled as "assisted immigrants": he was able to pay their way thanks to a collection taken up by his friends (*NR*, 39).

Sam's childhood poverty determined the emphasis of his first life on business success and the radical reform agenda of his second life. The importance of poverty to his understanding of himself is clear. One of the first facts Jones presented about himself in his 1899 autobiographical memoir is that the family traveled as "assisted immigrants," who were not entitled to own land. The autobiographical memoir, in which he criticizes the system that penalized the poor in this way, provides a significant clue to how Jones made sense of his life. His presentation of himself as a child and both his concerted effort to amass wealth for thirty years and an almost desperate attempt to divest himself of that wealth in his last years indicate that Sam Jones always identified himself as poor. He organized his second life on the Golden Rule because on some deep internal level, everything he did for others in need was being done to himself. He did unto others as he would have been done unto. On a less healthy psychological level, the need to divest himself of his fortune and his possessions seems to have been his unconscious attempt to make his external self match his internal sense of himself. All his life long, it seems, Sam Jones was ashamed of his financial condition: first, his poverty, later, his wealth.

The dominant religious lesson of Sam Jones's life, as his reform years most dramatically suggest, was the importance of self-denial. Jones wrote in 1899 that the only real success in life comes from "the life of self-renunciation" (*NR,* 415). Using Philip Greven's paradigm of the "evangelical temperament" and the poignant clues in Jones's autobiography, it is clear that young Sam's religious culture taught him to deny the self and to conform absolutely to God's will. Such an upbringing, as recent theoretical models of the development of shame suggest, leads to a life with a propensity for shame and self-doubt.[16]

Shame shapes character. It differs from guilt in that one is ashamed for who one *is* while one feels guilty for what one *does*. One mode of responding to shame is to develop a perfectionist style to hide one's shame. The word's etymology reveals the characteristic response; the Indo-European root *skem* or *sham* means "to hide."[17] Sam Jones hid his sense of himself as shamefully poor behind his increasing wealth for most of his life, but there was no place to hide when he was a child. The shamed person seeks to break the link with the one who has seen one's weakness, but without question the Welsh community in New York knew of Hugh Jones's status: members of their own families still living in Wales would have helped to make the Jones family's passage possible.

Sam Jones retained no memory of his life in Wales. There is evidence to suggest that evangelicals, because of the rigor of their parents' attempts to suppress the child's emerging will, are less likely to retain memories of early childhood than other religious temperaments. Sam's lack of memory may suggest a great deal about his feelings over the loss of his home. The countryside around Ty Mawr may not have afforded adults much in the way of a living, but it would have been a delightful environment for a child. The hills, the hares, and the eagles' nests provided unlimited adventures in the summer of 1850 to a boy about to turn four. Then his life suddenly and unexpectedly altered. From the relative security of a mountain home and friends close enough to pay their passage, Sam was jolted to a life of change, discomfort, uncertainty, and the real threat of danger. He remembered none of it.

Everything about the transatlantic voyage was designed to make those traveling in steerage aware of their inferiority. The Jones family probably first made their way to the south of Wales and from there boarded a coastal vessel for Liverpool. The Welsh emigrants stayed at Welsh "teetotal" inns in Liverpool, a rough port city guaranteed to dismay the abstemious Welsh.[18]

Assisted emigrants traveled in steerage where food, light, water, and privacy were all in short supply. As the steerage passengers were floated out to the ship, moored half a mile from the Liverpool dock, they did well to pack a small bag with anything they would want for the next weeks or months. Once on board, they did not see their luggage again until they reached New York, and then they often found their boxes damaged, locks broken, and contents lost. The ships were magnificent—from a distance. Once on deck, one could barely walk because barrels, ropes, cooking equipment, and discarded masts and sails blocked the way. Everything was covered with smoke, tar, grease, and dirt. A fresh breeze or a beautiful view was blocked by handrails that were more than six feet high.[19]

Steerage passengers somehow crossed the masts, sails, and barrels to reach even more dismal quarters belowdeck. These sailing ships had not been designed to carry passengers. Yet as many as eight hundred passengers and fifteen hundred boxes were stowed with less consideration for the passengers than for the cargo. The passengers lived together for a month or more, sleeping, dressing, and cooking in a room sixty yards long, twelve wide, and five high. In bad weather they remained belowdeck in the dark. The only light came from lanterns that threatened to set fire to the ship as it rolled. Lack of ventilation stifled the voyagers once the hatches were battened down. The air was foul, sanitation was nonexistent, and water came from the last river in which the ship had been moored. Cholera was a constant threat. On some journeys the only way to observe the passage of time was by the rites of burial at sea. On three vessels alone in 1847, known in transatlantic shipping annals as the plague year, 313 passengers were buried at sea and an additional 322 were sick on arrival.[20] Three years later, Hugh Jones took his family on such a trip, with no assurance that they would fare well. Sam, huddled in steerage, alone among the children was old enough to understand that he had lost his home but not old enough to understand why.

The dream of prosperity and happiness led Hugh Jones and his family to settle in Lewis County, New York, linked to Wales both by its isolation and its inhabitants.[21] Collinsville promised the family a home away from home. So the seven Joneses made the arduous journey to this remarkably inaccessible spot to join those who had preceded them from north Wales. After a month at sea, the family reached New York. From there, they went up the Hudson River by canal boat to Waterford. They traveled the Erie Canal to Utica, then took a wagon for forty-five miles up and over the Oneida County hills and down into the Black River valley to the town of Collinsville (*NR*, 39).

In 1842, Welsh families, most from north Wales, had settled within six miles of Collinsville on the hills west of Turin in Lewis County. The Welsh Calvinistic Methodist Church of Collinsville had been formed in 1846 by twenty-four parishioners. When the Jones family joined their number in 1850, worship services still were held in homes, in shops, and in the stone schoolhouse. It was the one part of their week most like home; the service consisted of familiar songs, preaching, and prayers, all in their native tongue. By 1855, the Welsh Calvinistic Methodist Church numbered 170 members, and they constructed a building that became the center of their community. Over the following years, it became one of the largest Welsh churches in the country.[22]

Coming from the area of Wales most noted for its intensely religious fervor, the Jones family settled in its American equivalent, the region known as the "Burned-Over District." This region experienced a fervent revivalism not seen elsewhere. Western New York was inhabited by a "people extraordinarily given to unusual religious beliefs, peculiarly devoted to crusades aimed at the perfection of mankind and the attainment of millennial happiness."[23] The Welsh community was, in all likelihood, relatively isolated from the revivalism of native Protestants in this region. So it may be no more than a striking coincidence that Sam Jones, who later sought to implement changes to improve society and humankind, was raised in a region so intent on questions of millennial happiness.

Sam Jones was not alone in having his political ideals shaped in his church. In a period when people turned to the church, rather than the state, for everything, fundamental political assumptions were forged in church. By the time the Jones family moved to New York, the dominant culture was evangelical. Revivals had brought church membership to its highest point. At this period and especially in the Burned-Over District in New York, evangelism often led to progressive social reform. With Charles Finney as first professor of theology, Oberlin took a leading role in feminist and antislavery reforms: "Wherever he preached Christians turned their hands to reform."[24]

Sam Jones's view of the world was shaped by this evangelical Welsh community in ways he could not have foreseen and never acknowledged.

As a Christian socialist reformer, he seems to have inherited the anti-institutional bias of the first Welsh settlers of Lewis County. The eighteenth-century Welsh pioneers who settled upstate New York before him and the Puritans who settled New England before them all viewed the established church as an institution that could not change. This anti-institutionalism combined with the introspection of pietist and evangelical faith to form a powerful agenda for change. Jones's anti-institutional bias in late life, which seems incomprehensible in a politician, was the result of his lifelong introspective impulse and directly connects him to the dominant reform impulse in nineteenth-century America.[25]

As a young boy growing up in this Welsh community in upstate New York, Sam spent a good many hours listening to a people known for the art of their preaching. Their words and their expressive style took root in his soul and emerged in the last decade of his life when he found his voice. Again and again those new to Jones's political rallies at the turn of the century marveled at their religious qualities. "Wales is a land of preachers," says the classic Hastings edition of *The Encyclopaedia of Religion and Ethics*, "it is no wonder that the Welsh people have invented a name for the *je ne sais quoi* which makes preaching effective." The Welsh word *huil* sums up the "combination of nature, art, and grace. . . . It is the happiness of the preacher; it is the thing that grips the hearer" that makes preaching—inside the chapel or along the campaign trail—effective.[26]

As a reformer Sam Jones would have links to the communitarian tradition. Like the abolitionist Theodore Weld and later Progressives such as Jane Addams, John Dewey, and Frederic Howe, Jones's ideas about community were rooted in his experience in small-town American life. The small-town atmosphere seemed to intensify the Protestant emphasis on personal responsibility for the fortunes and morals of others in the community. The intimacy of small-town life created an environment in which people knew each other's needs and sought to meet them. The challenge for urban reformers at the century's end was to defeat the city's inevitable tendency to break down community.[27]

If the evangelical atmosphere of his home and his church formed his sense of self, specific religious doctrines left their imprint as well. His Calvinist training, with its doctrine of election, led him to his first life, where he was intent on creating great wealth and performing good works. The question is not, "What must I *do* to be saved? but How can I *know* I am saved?"[28] Both his increasing wealth and his life of good works assured Sam of God's favor.

Sam's adult vision of both this world and the next was shaped by this community in ways that can be measured by his external actions while he strove to become a rich man. In his last decade, though, he underwent a significant shift away from the legalism of his Protestant upbringing, exhibiting less rigidity in his ideas of the Sabbath and a greater understanding of the complexities that create the evils of this world. Despite this shift, much of his early religious teaching continued to support his reform vision of the 1890s—but with a new and remarkable intensity.

If the Calvinistic Methodist Church emphasized self-discipline and respectability, parishioners were "also highly democratic in their inner life." In Wales, democracy and the Calvinistic Methodist Church were so intertwined that Welsh politics has had deeply religious implications; political strength is measured by adherence to principles. All evangelical sects locate the center of religious life in interior experience and can be said to be democratic in a way that the hierarchical traditional churches are not. But the Calvinistic Methodist Church especially stressed equality and brotherhood: the creed recognized the experience of the individual as crucial. The denomination emphasized the parable of the Good Samaritan—yet another version of the biblical imperative upon which Sam Jones centered his reform life. Calvinistic Methodism taught that a humanitarian attitude toward one's fellow man was as important as one's own spiritual climate. Young Sam's church stressed that corruption in business was sacrilege "for the market-place is an outer court of the temple and never far from the Holy of Holies"—a conviction that resurfaced when he organized a factory on the principle of the Golden Rule. Thus Sam had learned the essential lesson of evangelism: Christianity is not doctrine; it is life.[29]

If clear connections can be seen between the teachings of his church and Sam Jones's political programs, there is a less neatly documentable, but more crucial, connection to be drawn. Sam Jones was raised in an intensely evangelical community and it shaped his view of himself and the world in inexorable ways. Because of the limitations of the sources, we must work backward from the reformer's turn-of-the-century feelings, beliefs, actions, and programs to make sense of the experience of his childhood. What we know of Sam Jones in the 1890s and what we know of the lessons learned by evangelical children make it clear that Sam Jones remained an evangelical in temperament, if not in doctrine, throughout his life. In fact, it is impossible to understand Sam Jones's remarkable yet desperate attempts to change both himself and his world without reference to his evangelical sense of self.

Young Sam's world was shaped by the Welsh Calvinistic Methodist Church, even in New York. The defining characteristic of the evangelical temperament is its persistent hostility to the self. The evangelical child is trained to be preoccupied throughout life with ways to abase and deny the self. Evangelical parents begin training children at the age of nine months or so to meet without question the demands put upon them. This training, begun the moment the child's will begins to emerge, was rooted in the conviction that only by destroying the self could a child learn to conform absolutely to the sovereign will of God.[30] We cannot document how Sam was disciplined as a child, but it is clear that as an adult he was perfectly willing to conform to God's will through self-denial. In 1899, Sam Jones wrote that the only real success comes from "the life of self-renunciation, a life in which you shall give yourselves up with a surrender as complete as was that of Jesus" (*NR*, 415).

Evangelicals are preoccupied with the idea of depravity. As a member of the Calvinistic Methodist Church, young Sam, in all likelihood, would have been taught that he must practice self-denial because of the doctrine of original sin. John Wesley would have agreed with George Whitefield when he said that men needed "to be pricked to the heart with a lively sense of their natural corruption." Consistently through three centuries, evangelical parents have sought to break the emerging will of their children. Self-assertiveness must be totally suppressed, it was thought, or the child would face eternal damnation. Wesley advised: "Break their wills that you may save their souls." He learned that lesson at his mother's knee, it seems. One of the clearest indications of the unnatural pressures put upon the very youngest of children comes from Susanna Wesley: "When turned a year old (and some before) they were taught to fear the rod and to cry softly, by which means they escaped abundance of correction which they might otherwise have had: and that most odious noise of the crying of children was rarely heard in the house, but the family usually lived in as much quietness as if there had not been a child among them."[31]

There is evidence beyond Jones's later conversion to Christian socialism to suggest that his parents had sought to break his childish will. The most revealing allusion Jones ever made to his mother came in an 1888 speech, urging Lima's citizens to support a YMCA: "I do not believe in wispy, waspy, milksoppy religion. We must have a YMCA to help the young man who thinks he must break away from his mother's apron strings."[32] This comment suggests there may have been tension in his relations with his mother and that he struggled to free himself from her control. This comment, the absence of the ubiquitous "sainted mother" passage in his autobiography, and a paucity of references to her in his voluminous correspondence suggest a relationship that was not particularly close.

An early life of shame, poverty, strenuous work, and isolation led to his tremendous need to be loved. Young Sam's early life was defined by his poverty. Not only had his family left Wales to escape poverty, but upstate

New York had not offered much relief. He was not sent to school even though New York offered free public schooling. At ten, Sam left home to do farmwork that he detested. He resented and was shamed by both his lack of education and his farmwork. Sam Jones lost his second home when still a child; he saw himself as a Dickensian orphan and was deeply ashamed of both his poverty and his exclusion from his family.

Shame seeks to maintain the boundaries of the self, preventing the loss of self that comes from external intrusion and the demand to merge with another—in this case, the parent. When one feels ashamed, the reaction is to hide. Thus shame, as a form of protection, can ultimately prevent the loss of self, allowing for individual growth. The propensity toward shame begins in childhood. When parents respond positively to the infant as he or she behaves spontaneously and begins to assert the self, the child grows up feeling unashamed. The child's sense of self as autonomous is not overly painful; the child does not fuse with the parents and the growing identity flourishes. If, however, parents see the child as an extension of themselves, they reject the child's autonomy and see to it that the child merges with the adults. Evangelical culture did precisely that so as to save the child's soul. Such a child grows up with a propensity to shame and self-doubt.[33]

In an evangelical family the father's authority was explicitly likened to God's, so Sam's view of God may suggest his feelings toward his father. "The will of a parent," wrote John Wesley, "is to a little child in the place of the will of God. Therefore, studiously teach them to submit to this while they are children, that they may be ready to submit to his will, when they are men." As a child, Sam feared God and perhaps his father as well. A child struggles to make sense of the idea of divinity by patterning his understanding of God on his own father. The Lord's Prayer invites such an identification, especially to a young child. Sam remembered learning the prayer at his mother's knee, though its essential message of brotherhood was not clear. As Sam knelt to say that prayer, beside Alice, John, Nell, and Mary, God would have taken on the lineaments of Hugh Jones in each child's mind. For years Sam carried with him the idea of a harsh, judgmental God; to the last days of his life he felt in some essential ways unforgiven—unforgivable. The extraordinary degree to which Sam Jones the reformer sought to deny the self suggests much, then, about his relations with his father. Was the Golden Rule reformer's ability to extend grace to others but not feel it had been extended to him—to feel convinced that prostitutes and saloon keepers were doing their best, but he had not yet done enough—linked to a troubled relationship with an exacting father? Unfortunately, there is no way to document his childhood view of his father. But Sam's two visions of God, first from the vantage point of a successful oilman and then as the Golden Rule mayor, make a compelling, if only suggestive, case for such an interpretation.[34]

Love and fear were the two poles used to mold the child's will to the parents.' Evangelical parents used the withdrawal of love to break the child's will and help to forge in the child's conscience an internal disciplinarian far stricter than either parent. The pattern was first to isolate the child physically and emotionally when he experienced parental disapproval; second, to allow the child to reearn parental love by insisting that he comply unconditionally to the parents' will.[35] Sam Jones's supreme confidence in the power of love ("Love is the true inner evolutionary force of the world," *NR*, 429) and the intensity of the shame and guilt he felt, even as he worked to divest himself of his personal fortune, argue more eloquently than Margaret's journal could—if one existed—that he was raised under such a regime.

Mayor Jones's single "solution" to social problems—the Golden Rule—raises questions about his early family life that cannot be fully answered. If brotherhood was Sam's reform ideal, what were his relations with his brothers? We know that Sam felt his elder brother John had killed himself with overwork. There seems to have been little contact between them before his death. Dan, who worked closely with Sam in his company, leading it when his brother became mayor, did not agree with his new reform agenda and made that quite clear. Without question, their relationship was strained. It seems likely that Golden Rule Jones sought to create familial relations as the basis of a new America because he felt the lack of a true family.

The Methodist doctrine of sanctification had an even more sustained role in shaping Jones's sense of himself. Methodism stressed man's immediate perfectibility and resulted in the intense focus on personal piety—a rejection of the sins of alcohol, gambling, and fornication. In his first life, the individualistic emphasis on sanctification allowed Sam to feel himself separate from political, economic, and social realities. Sanctification can produce a narrow legalism and hypocrisy. Later, however, this optimistic focus on individual responsibility led Sam Jones to a life dedicated to improving political, economic, and social realities. His belief in the Golden Rule depended on the assumption that men were perfectible. And his letters reveal that he judged himself harshly for not perfectly satisfying that test. It seems that in late life Jones lived out the logical implication of the standard Methodist doctrine: he held himself too accountable for his own failures. He seems to have thought that the road to perfection lay in actions, reasons, and education, rather than God's grace. Thus he placed the burden on himself. His exacting conscience produced great feelings of guilt and shame because he had not yet become perfect. One of Jones's most characteristic assertions in late life was the comment that he knew others were "doing their best." After stating that he was sure his friend William Cocolough was doing just that he went on: "An angel could do no more. I wish I could really be sure that I could live up to that high ideal myself."[36] In that comment lies the crux of his reform agenda and his personal unhappiness. He was confident that others were angels but had a clear measure of how far he alone still had to go.

There seems to be a pattern of Protestant evangelicalism in the childhood homes of men and women who became Progressive reformers. Not surprisingly, the childhood pattern of suppressing the self often led to a life of selfless activity. Teddy Roosevelt was proud that Jonathan Edwards's blood flowed in his children's veins. He had been taught from earliest childhood that social reform and charity were inextricably rooted in Protestant doctrine. William Jennings Bryan had a Baptist father and a Methodist mother and consequently he attended both Sunday schools. His family home had its own altar so it is hardly surprising that he experienced the standard evangelical conversion—though, because it took place at a Presbyterian revival service, it seems he asserted his own individuality to the extent of choosing the denomination. Perhaps no better proof of the pervasive lifelong influence of Protestant evangelical thinking can be found than to turn to a reformer who was not raised within it. In Terre Haute, Eugene Debs spent the Sunday nights of his childhood listening to his father read aloud from Voltaire, Rousseau, Dumas, Eugene Sue, and Victor Hugo.[37] Yet the rhetoric and style of the evangelists characterized America's leading socialist.

Both the need for work and fellowship in his church brought Hugh Jones to Collinsville, where he first found work in the stone quarries. He soon shifted from harvesting stones to harvesting food. The Joneses suffered many privations; life was not much different than it had been in Wales. The prices for farm produce were low which did not help matters. Hugh Jones did not have the capital to purchase farmland. He was able to rent land, but the increasing size of his family—Moses and Dan brought their number to nine—prevented him from getting ahead.

Sam Jones had little formal education—about thirty months, all told, as he estimated it. He had been permanently stuck at fractions and had no formal training in grammar—and for the simple reason that he was poor. When Sam was a lad of ten, a man asked him why he was not in school. The child replied that his parents needed him to work. The gentleman thought his parents could afford to send him to school because a new law had made education free in New York. His parents' decision makes little sense, especially given the educational statistics of the area: the Burned-Over District consistently sent more children to school than did counties in the eastern half of New York State.[38] The school year has always been arranged to suit the needs of the farm calendar; one wonders why he could not have been spared on the family farm in the winter.

His parents' decision is all the more surprising when one considers that they kept him out of the free public school and then paid a neighbor to instruct Sam and Nell privately in the winter evenings so that they could work on the farm during the day. They paid a small sum of money and brought with them a candle each evening: the neighbor and his wife would be sitting in the dark, waiting for the candle (*NR*, 40, 42). Whatever the intent of this decision regarding public school, it had the effect of isolating young Sam from the larger community and children his own age. Evangelical families kept children isolated from grandparents and even servants to increase their dependence on the absolute authority of the parents. Hugh and Margaret may not have consciously intended to isolate Sam, but his childhood years in New York are characterized by isolation, above all else.[39]

Thirty months of schooling provided him the opportunity to absorb the peculiar amalgam of democratic and capitalist values passed on through mid-nineteenth-century schools. Clarence Darrow, the famous lawyer, later Sam's friend, who attended the public school system in Kinsman, Ohio, a decade later, observed that schools stressed the cash rewards associated with virtue. By hard work the individual succeeded. Thrift or diligence could never spawn evil. The reward of virtue "was in no way uncertain or ethereal, but was always paid in cash, or something just as material or good." The first Jones, the successful oilman, would consider his wealth a sign of his virtue; it seems also to have been an effective mask to cover his shame.[40]

If wealth was a virtue, his parents taught Sam that poverty was a disgrace.[41] "We all feel poverty to be a disgrace," he wrote in the autobiography. As a child Sam questioned the way his church explained the Lord's work in this world. Young Sam asked his mother about the poor people he saw. He remembered asking the quintessential childhood question: "how God can be fair if he planned . . . that some are to be rich and others to be poor." His mother gave him the Calvinist answer that it was all part of God's plan. Much about his own life would have suggested to Sam that a fine line separated his family from those in the poorhouse. The idea of poverty and a God who could be satisfied with such a plan so disturbed Sam that Margaret had to tell him "again and again that if it were not so, God would not permit it" (*NR*, 455-56).

One of the few recorded memories of his childhood suggests how shame functioned in his community. Sam did not like farmwork; he could not remember a time when he had. His parents characterized him as "lazy"; forty years later the shame of that accusation still stung. The emotion of shame functioned to protect him from losing his own sense of himself. He knew he was not lazy, and shame kept him from merging with his parents' projection of his character. "This disliking [of farming] was called by another name by my family and the neighbors; they called it laziness." Notice the rhetorical strategy he used to distance himself from the charge: he began by being unable to say it ("called by another name"). The autobiography continues: "But I now assert that I have not now and never had a lazy hair in my head; it was simply the rebellion of a free soul against the injustice of the kind and quality of labor so sought to be imposed upon me." If one reads between the lines written by the adult reformer, the second Jones, "the rebellion of a free soul against the injustice," it is possible to see a child who felt misunderstood and silenced: "but I now assert." (*NR*, 40). Almost half a century later, he still felt the need to set the record straight. If shame protects the self by fighting for autonomy, shame also creates great fear. Shame is intimately connected with the worst fears of abandonment. Perhaps those feelings of shame were painfully intensified by the fact that he seems to have been abandoned by his family at just this time. As he sought to define himself in his own terms, his family rejected him, or so it could have seemed to him. He was punished for asserting himself by being left to himself.[42]

At the age of ten, Sam was sent to board at a neighbor's farm to work for him by the month. His autobiographical account suggests that he felt considerable anger and resentment. He stresses the rigor and deprivation of this life. The farmer got him out of bed at four in the morning; he could attend school only "in the winter, more or less." It was a "start for an education that I am still acquiring."[43]

Sam seems to have felt shame when his parents abandoned him. He handles this period obliquely in his autobiography. But it is the only recorded instance of the young child asserting his own identity, denying the charge that he was lazy, that at least in his account seems to have precipitated his removal from his own home. Jones begins his autobiography with a quotation from *David Copperfield*: "I do not know of what particular consequence it is to the people who read this book just when or where or why I was born, but, quoting from *Copperfield* and following the general custom, I will say that 'I was born, as I was told and have reason to believe,' on August 3^{d}, 1846" (*NR*, 40). It is a striking allusion, for Sam Jones seems to have been a kind of orphan himself. Like David, he lost a dear home in

Wales. Then, having found a new home, he was cast out of the house to board with a neighbor. By sixteen he was away from home for good. What is unsaid in the memoir speaks volumes. He takes time to comment about and show a picture of Ty Mawr but does not mention his New York home. Forced to leave it by age ten, he may have felt he had none.

At the beginning of his lifetime of work Sam struggled to determine how to give his considerable talents fair play. From about age eight to eighteen he constantly sought to find congenial work; at fourteen, for the first time he followed his own instincts away from the farm and toward machines: he secured a job at one of the many sawmills that had recently begun to dominate the Black River valley. He worked a twelve-hour shift sawing wood to make barrels. It was a monotonous, difficult, and potentially dangerous job for a young boy. One day he cut the little finger of his right hand with the saw (*NR*, 42).

While Collinsville had remained a hamlet in the ten years since the Joneses had been in Lewis County, the area as a whole had undergone significant change. Along the river, towns had sprung up in anticipation of the economic growth following the completion of the Black River Canal. Lumber from northeastern New York State had only recently been transported down to the Erie Canal and on east to New York or west to Buffalo and on to Detroit or Chicago. Boatbuilding enterprises, cider mills, sawmills, and hotels like Passengers at Bush's Landing in Watson, which sported a stuffed panther shot at Lock 44, suggest the frontier nature of this civilization.

Sam had a mechanical turn of mind. Soon after injuring himself at the sawmill, he realized his ambition: he landed a job on the steamer *L.R. Lyon.* In 1857, Lymon R. Lyon had built the boat, a stern-wheeler modeled after the famous Ohio riverboats, to tow boats from Lock 109 at Lyon's Falls upriver to the end of the canal at Carthage. Since the *L.R. Lyon* was the first steamer to be built for this stretch of the river, Lyon pioneered towing on the northern reaches of the Black River Canal. Lyon was the first person who could serve as a model: he was a pioneer, an entrepreneur, a man skilled at adapting equipment to meet new needs.

Further south, boats were pulled through the canal by horses, but at this section of the trip, thanks to Lyon's design, a steamer could do the work. Other boatmen followed Lyon's lead, but they found that steam towing was not without its frustrations. For the *Lyon's* first three seasons a steamer with even so light a draft (the *Lyon* drew but fifteen inches of water) had difficulty making the trip to Carthage. The Black River often dried up during the summer months, making the trip impossible for weeks at a time. The canal was plagued by "the breaks"; canal walls gave way, allowing the water to escape and creating a breach up to three hundred feet long. The steamers were stranded for days, sometimes weeks, at a time.[44]

It is not surprising that Sam found this work congenial; life on the Black River canal boats was often a family affair. The season usually lasted from at least April to the first of December. Wives often accompanied their husbands and brought the children along. Sam was employed as a "greaser and wiper" on the engine, which would have kept him belowdeck, but his interest in machines kept him happily engaged. And during a canal break or during dry weather when several boats waiting to get through a lock formed a stranded colony, Sam would be free to join the children in digging for worms or fishing. They hoped for trout but as often as not caught horned dace or eels.

Sam worked the canal on the *L.R. Lyon* for most of three seasons. He began as a youth of sixteen in the spring of 1863. While it is not surprising that a sixteen-year-old would have been free to pursue his own interests in the spring of 1863, it was unusual that he was not drafted by the war's end. Sam's brother John, five years older, did serve. The Civil War was the formative experience for many of Sam Jones's generation. He missed that experience—finding instead another in the oil boom town of Pithole—and this seems to have had a significant impact on his later life. Missing the horror of the war shaped Sam Jones's view of the world and human nature. The persistent idealism of his reform thinking came from spending the war years on the Black River and not at Bull Run, Gettysburg, or Antietam.

Abraham Lincoln serves as an ideal against which most Progressives defined themselves, and Sam Jones is no exception. Sam's lifelong allegiance to Lincoln and all he stood for is an early indication of his link to native-born Progressives. Unlike most immigrants, Sam Jones had been a Republican for just about as long as it had been possible to be one. The news of Lincoln's death early in the morning of April 15, 1865, was immediately telegraphed across the country. Improved technology made this the first "newsbreaking" event that virtually the entire nation learned of simultaneously. Sam would have known and been stunned by it, although his autobiography makes no mention of the news.[45]

As the country adjusted to a world without war and without Lincoln in the spring of 1865, Sam Jones's life was about to reach a major turning point. If the Welsh church was an essential building block in Jones's transformation, his experience at age eighteen in the oil fields was equally important. At the war's end Sam's one ambition in life was, like Samuel Clemens's, to work his way up to be a steamboat engineer. But during his third season Sam was befriended by a steamboat engineer who changed the course of his life. Sam confided his great ambition. The job did not seem so exalted to the engineer because he had spent the previous winter in the Pennsylvania oil fields. He said, "Sammy, you are a fool to spend your time on these steamboats; you should go to the oil regions; you can get four dollars a day there" (*NR*, 42-43). The lure of so grand a wage changed the direction of Sam's life. Suddenly, like many young men his age, he had "oil on the brain." Just a few days later, he was off to Titusville, Pennsylvania, the city at the center of the oil boom. Like this father before him, he was "stirred with ambition to try to better his hard lot."

2

The Only Problem Worth a Man's Attention

One Friday in the summer of 1865, Sam, not yet nineteen, reached Titusville, Pennsylvania, the headquarters for the oil region, on his way to Pithole, the nerve center of oil. Sam was dedicated to the pursuit of wealth. It seemed at the time "the only problem worth a man's attention . . . the attainment of the great American ideal—making money." That American ideal had utterly transformed western Pennsylvania, north of Pittsburgh. In 1859, Titusville had been the only village in the area, with a population between three and four thousand inhabitants. But when Sam Jones arrived, it had a population of ten thousand. Pastoral farmlands had been transformed—overnight it seemed—into a raw, foul-smelling frontier town dominated by oil. "Suckerod," a correspondent to the *Titusville Morning Herald*, described the "Oil Dorado" as an inversion of the natural order of things: "The atmosphere that hangs over this delightful spot, is composed of the vilest, the most villainous smelling gases that ever were inhaled by man. . . . The falling of what appears to be black snow, covering everything . . . with a thick coat of black soot, the product of a thousand and one furnaces. . . . All the mosquitoes that did not go to Cleveland are digging for oil here."[1]

In trying to make sense of his life, Sam Jones the autobiographer looked back to this experience in his first life as the source of his shame and guilt. He never saw that these feelings had roots deeper in the past, in his childhood religious training. Jones wrote his autobiographical memoir in 1899, when he was beginning his second term as mayor and contemplating running for governor of Ohio. Desperate poverty at Pithole is the experience Jones focuses on in most detail; for the autobiographer, the Pithole story functions as moral parable for Jones's 1890s reform social agenda. The autobiography takes up one chapter of more than seventy pages in his first book, *The New Right*. Because Pithole is so central to Sam Jones's late-life understanding of himself, it is essential to read his account with great care, seeing beneath the surface of the story crafted by the Golden Rule reformer.

Jones's autobiography is central to the phenomenological perspective of this book. It provides crucial information about the second Sam Jones's worldview, in particular the experience at Pithole, and the gubernatorial race so central to understanding his political failures. As we consider his perceptions it is important to stress that we are looking through the lens provided by the second Jones, the Golden Rule reformer. It is also important to stress that the autobiography is only a memoir chapter in *The New Right*. Therefore, it is important not to make too much of his strategies; nor are comparisons with other full-length autobiographies—Andrew Carnegie's *Gospel of Wealth* and Jane Addams's *Twenty Years at Hull House* come first to mind—specifically useful.

Though his account is brief, Jones's impulse to tell his life story connects him to other Progressive reformers. The autobiographical impulse was a dominant literary form for Progressives, not merely to communicate ideals—they seem to have taken those for granted—but to convey the spirit that permeated their careers as reformers. Because reform became a way of life, life-writing was the logical mode of expression.[2] Sam Jones believed it was essential for people to change in order for reform to succeed: what better way to make that case than with his own life story?

Pithole, as Jones casts it, is all about sin, guilt, and shame. The sin most likely to endanger a young evangelical's soul, of course, would have been sex. But the dynamics of his later life do not suggest that the account in the autobiography, with its focus on deceit, is a symbolic representation for the more obvious vices. The autobiographer was making atonements in every aspect of his life: for past poverty, for current wealth, for mistakes past and present. Atonement never dominates a life unless there is an urgent sense of sin. Something happened at Pithole for which young Sam never forgave himself. For a person raised in an evangelical household, the small offenses stressed in his account may have seemed grave sins at the time. In focusing on those deceits "that must have been damaging to my morals at that early period in my life," Jones claims for them a gravity that does not convince (*NR*, 47). Of course, to suggest that a young boy caught up in a capitalist get-rich-quick scheme endangered his young soul might have been useful political propaganda for the self-described socialist of 1899. There is another answer, though. The continual emphasis on the guilty actions at Pithole suggest that the Sam Jones of 1899 was struggling to understand the source of his overpowering feelings of guilt and shame. He was still searching, as if in a dark room, for an answer to the question, What is the cause of my feelings of shame and guilt? He came up with an inadequate answer, focusing on the guilt of *actions*, rather than the shame of *self*.

But there was no reason for young Sam in 1865 to think badly of trying to strike it rich. Everyone was off to make a fortune in oil, or so it seemed. The train to Titusville must have been quite an experience. At the shout of "train!" it looked as though a bomb had been dropped: the people stampeded, rushing toward it. One contemporary marveled: "They swarmed up the steps, into the baggage car, over the locomotive, everywhere but under the wheels, and how they escaped that was a mystery. . . . Men fought for precedence as if their lives depended on it. Women were rudely thrust back by anxious men who clung to the strap-rails and kicked off those who endeavored to climb over them. We were well on our way to the 'Oil Dorado.'"[3]

Sam got off the train, with a gripsack in hand and fifteen cents in his pocket. He made his way to Watson Flats, outside the city, on Oil Creek, and spent the afternoon running from oil well to oil well looking for a job as an engineer. He crossed and recrossed the Oil Creek footbridge, paying a five-cent toll each time. Before the day was over he was penniless. As night fell, he was still without a job and his heart was "as heavy as my pocket was empty." The dream of four dollars a day seemed elusive as Sam headed back to the city, possessed "with a feeling of utter desolation." He had no notion of how he could find a place for the night so he walked. The first thing the autobiography records is his isolation: he was "without the benefit of the acquaintance of a single individual in the city" (*NR*, 43).

His journey eventually took him through the mud and muck of the main street in oildom where, late that night, he found himself staring at the American Hotel, the finest in Titusville. He was inspired to stride boldly into the office. He asked for a room for a couple of days and politely asked the rate. "Two dollars and fifty cents a day," replied the clerk. Agitated, Sam said nothing but picked up the pen and signed the guest register. Asked if he wanted supper, Sam tried to reply calmly that he did. He went into the restaurant, feeling orphaned: "I remember it as though it were yesterday," he wrote thirty-four years later. "I had beefsteak and onions, and like Oliver Twist, after I had finished the first portion I asked for more and the girl brought me a second order" (*NR*, 43-44).

Refreshed but anxious, Sam got up early the next day to look for a job. He had brought with him letters of recommendation, which he was sure would immediately open up a job for him as an engineer. So he began this day with considerable hope for the future and pride in his own skills, despite the disappointments of the day before. But his feelings of hope were eroded all that long Saturday as he was turned down again and again. Years later, he described the experience as "one of the most disheartening of all that any child of God ever undertook, looking for a job among strangers . . . —the heartbreaking, soul-destroying business of begging for work" (*NR*, 43-44).

Utterly discouraged and disheartened, Sam spent the busiest three days of his work-filled life in a soul-destroying task in an utterly fantastic foreign world. Out of this experience came two distinct men. The fear first spawned a man who made a great success of himself in the oil business, who turned the American Dream into reality, becoming a highly successful capitalist. But out of this experience also came—thirty years later—that second self, the political reformer and autobiographer who wrote: "I shall never forget the busy scene Pithole presented in those summer days . . . whose streets were filled with a surging throng of people, every one, almost without exception eagerly engaged in a scramble to get something for nothing from his fellow-men" (*NR*, 50). Indeed, Sam Jones never forgot. This scene haunted him in the last decade of his life: it became emblematic of all that he felt was wrong with America.

The next day, Sam faced a moral dilemma, for it was the Sabbath. He had been trained to keep the Sabbath, but he knew that the search for work permitted no day of rest, not with a hotel bill racking up $2.50 a day. The Welsh observed the Sabbath fanatically: farmers did not milk their cows; drovers on their way to England with sheep would not travel; even at sea, Welsh captains forced their crews to a day of "contemplative sobriety" between morning and afternoon services; at Llanuwchllyn, Gwynedd, in the 1820s people did not even wind their clocks on Sunday.[4] Sam was breaking a law deeply embedded in his culture.

Sam met a man who became a model for his second self and his enlightened business practices in the 1890s. One of his stops that Sunday afternoon was in the office of the New York Oil Company. He asked for work as usual and was turned down as usual. But the man behind the counter was different. He was sympathetic. "He turned a kindly face upon me and said he was sorry that he had nothing for me to do." The man, Samuel Miner, got him chatting. He asked Sam where his home was, who his people were, what experience he had had. Then Miner put his concern into practice. He advised Sam to go to Pithole, twelve miles away, and wrote Sam a letter to help him locate work. With heartfelt thanks and a lesson he would hold dear to his heart as a reformer, Sam headed back to his hotel. "Perhaps," the autobiographer wrote in beginning his consideration of this episode, "the kind words of this sweet-tempered man have had their influence upon my life." Then the autobiography moved from planting a suggestion to a direct assertion: "At any rate, I have made it a point in my life . . . to try to find time . . . for a kindly word for the man out of a job"(NR, 45).

Sam felt disgraced by his poverty, and so he hid the truth behind deceptions. The day before he had lied to Miner, saying he still had money. It was only after writing a letter to his mother, hiding his dejection behind what he hoped was a "cheerful tone," that he realized he had no money to buy the stamp to mail it. Stumped, he noticed a gentleman nearby busily finishing up some letters, clearly getting ready to go mail them. He went up to the gentleman and asked, "Are you going to the post-office, Sir?" Upon being told that he was, Sam then said, "Will you have the kindness to mail this letter for me along with yours?" "Certainly," was the reply. So Sam fished in his pockets for the money he knew he did not have, "fully expecting that he would do just as he did, which was to say, 'Never mind, I will stamp it'" (*NR*, 46).

"We are reared up to the belief that poverty, deserved or undeserved, is a disgrace, deny it as we may, we all feel it when it comes home to us as keenly as I felt it on that desolate Sunday afternoon," wrote Jones. The aside about "deserved or undeserved" poverty reveals that even the Golden Rule reformer had not entirely shaken off the instructions of his childhood: even a reformer so sensitive to how external conditions shape a person could still speak of deserved poverty. More revealing still is "deny it as we may": clearly, Sam had spent emotional energy trying to deny the Calvinist injunction that to be poor was to be disgraced. He felt disgraced as he lied to get a room, to eat, to send a letter to his mother, and as he broke the Sabbath. "I was in no way responsible for the poverty and disgrace that were inflicted upon me, and certainly the deception that I practiced upon the hotelkeeper and upon the man who gave me the postage stamp must have been damaging to my morals at that early period in my life." Jones understood the Pithole experience in these terms, but Pithole seems rather to have been more damaging to his sense of identity than to his morals. "I do not believe," Jones wrote, "that a condition of life that would drive an honest boy to trickery of this kind to obtain a three-cent postage stamp is worthy to be called 'civilization.'" (*NR*, 46).

The "crimes" he committed—taking a room, eating, obtaining a stamp—are not, on the surface, serious enough to explain the shame and guilt he felt. Certainly, the lad must have been scared. He was all alone in a new state; Titusville was not much of a city, but it was the largest one he had been in since early childhood. And it was a city on the edge of an utterly unfamiliar world. He was flat broke and had been "buying" things he could not pay for. His explanation that his morals had been damaged does not account for the extent of the psychic suffering he felt. But if this experience caused him to confront the thing he feared most about himself—his poverty—his despair makes sense.

Young Sam Jones's feelings of shame at Pithole had multiple triggers, but all seemed tied to the connection between his fragile sense of self and his parents. On one level, his scramble for great wealth seemed an assertion of his own will against the combined will of his parents. The child who had long complied with his parents' projection now felt he was disobeying their injunctions in this wild city of greed. But on another level, he felt shame also because the desperate poverty seemed literally a descent into nothingness. He may have had the sense of slipping into the definition of himself as poor.

Sam's shame at Pithole signaled his psychic fight to save himself. Sam Jones was becoming that projection he most feared: desperately poor. The flush of shame was so powerful that he reexperienced it forty years later in writing the story. The Calvinist interpretation suggested his poverty was part of God's plan—and the eternal implications would have been unthinkable. The Methodist imperative made it even worse, if that were possible. If he was free to perfect himself, his poverty was *his* fault. The odds for a comfortable eternity were not improved in the slightest. But that youthful shame also enabled Sam to fight what he most feared becoming and allowed him to retain his identity.

Was Jones the autobiographical writer trying to reach the truth behind his feelings? He came close to the truth, but he seems not to have seen quite far enough. In the autobiography he masks his shamed self with expressions of guilt over things done. Guilt and shame are interconnected, but shame cuts much deeper: one is shamed of who one is but guilty over what one does. Guilt over things done often leads to a deeper sense of shame: clearly Sam Jones questioned both the things he did and the self who did them.[5]

Sam left his hotel early Monday morning with no word to his landlord and set off to walk to Pithole. He had to struggle to get through the twelve miles of mud, competing all the way with the horse-drawn wagons transporting oil from the fields to the train station in Titusville. People, horses, and wagons had been making a crush toward Pithole for a good six months before Sam made his way up that road. Pithole proved to be an apt name. Local legend tells of three tired hunters, who, early in the nineteenth century, paused to rest at a sandstone outcrop along Oil Creek. Their rest was disturbed by foul-smelling vapors that wafted up from deep fissures in the stone. The most intrepid of the three squeezed between the rocks and went down to explore. He found nothing of interest and came up to the surface. Suddenly, he fainted. When they later retold the story, perhaps by the warmth of a fire and with the aid of a drink, the three explained that they had discovered in this hole an entrance to "the Pit" itself, a gateway to Hell.

The name Pithole, proved prophetic, at least as Sam Jones cast his life into narrative form. For Sam, Pithole became hell. With the end of the Civil War and what was left of a generation of young men at loose ends, veterans from both sides of the war rushed to Pithole. Everyone suffered from the local complaint: "oil on the brain." Some met with success, many more with disappointment and despair. The city was a forest of derricks on a hill of mud and oil, a place unlike any seen on the face of the earth before. The way of life was so foreign that those who left spoke of returning to the United States.

By the summer of 1865, the entire countryside had been transformed. Pithole operated the third largest post office in the state—smaller in size only to Philadelphia and Pittsburgh. Only eight months earlier there had been no one within miles to receive mail. By September, Pithole was producing six thousand barrels a day—two-thirds of all the oil produced in the country. The roads were all but impassable that summer as Sam made his way through the mud to Pithole. "Never was such mud seen or felt before," reported the *Titusville Morning Herald* with Dickensian fervor. "Glutinous mud that defies the knife to cut away, wet mud which eats into the very texture of the cloth and defies the sponge, benzene, and every cleansing mixture! Mud that comes on the table with the pudding, that fills your finger-nails, grits your teeth! Mud everywhere! Everything wrapped in mud! Everybody lost in it."[6]

Sam had to fight his way through the mud, the oilmen, and the teamsters. The horses or mules, many of them, like their human counterparts, veterans of the recent war, had the worst of it: they lived in the mud. They pulled wagon loads of barrels of oil, sinking up to their chests in the mud. Sam passed horses stuck in the mud. Those that could not be extricated would be shot or simply left to die in the hot summer sun. A teamster could expect only a few months' use out of a good horse or mule. While they survived they presented an eerie sight: the combination of oil and mud formed a paste that destroyed their capillary glands. They completely shed their coats below the eyes. Many a hairless horse and mule worked the streets of Pithole looking like the otherworldly beasts they would shortly become. One reporter considered the venture from the animal's point of view, noting that it is "doubtful whether *he* believed in the benefits resulting from a blessed peace. And we are sure that his sensitive nature is touched when he thinks of the days when 'government oats' were plentiful and he was the *proud* mule that drew 'hard tack' . . . for 'Sherman's boys in blue,' instead of a degraded 'oil mule.'"[7]

When Sam reached the crest of the hill and looked down on the world of Pithole, it made an impression that lasted his entire life long. More than thirty years later, the vision of a long-gone Pithole was still tangibly present: "I shall never forget the busy scene Pithole presented in those summer days; the ceaseless din of hammer and saw and the swish of the carpenter's plane ring as clearly in my ears to-day as they did thirty-four years ago, as I stood on the hillside and looked down on this city of mushroom growth" (*NR*, 50). From that vantage point the young man trained to keep the Sabbath in the backwoods of upstate New York could have spotted the "Swordsman's Club" which boldly proclaimed its motto—"R.C.T."—rum, cards, and tobacco.[8]

Many of Pithole's residents were veterans accustomed to doing without the civilized amenities of life and determined to make up for lost time in enjoying its sinful pleasures. Before the year was out, the *Pithole Daily Record* printed a "Proclamation" by Alexander J. Keenan, the burgess, decrying that "houses for the encouragement and practice of vice, under various forms and disguises have been opened and the people have groaned under the unbridled tyranny of the most vicious in the community."[9]

Pitholeans were a hard-drinking lot. According to the reporter sent out by the *Nation,* "It is safe to assert that there is more vile liquor drunk in this town than any of its size in the world." Work was hard, and money, when one had it, seemed plentiful. And with water out-pricing whiskey, it is hardly surprising that Pithole residents had a reputation for liking a stiff drink. The *Nation* observed that "a person at Pithole is indeed placed between fire and water. To drink water is to drink a solution of salts. To drink whiskey is to drink poison. After every glass of water I took I forswore water, and every glass of whiskey, I forswore whiskey, and thus lived a life of zigzag perjury." One purveyor of bourbon advertised in the *Herald* the benefits of his product: "You will find it for your benefit as regards your health, especially strangers drinking the water in this country, who are apt to get the TITUSVILLE ITCH. My Liquors being Pure is a SURE PREVENTATIVE."[10]

The few women who were there, by and large, were motivated by the same impulses as the men: they wanted to make money. The *New York Herald* reported on the last day of July the summer Sam arrived that Pithole included "2,000 white males, eleven females, and one colored person." The condition of the streets alone was enough to keep respectable women out of Pithole. At many a street corner a bucket of water could be found on the plank sidewalk. To live in Pithole, a woman had to be willing to remove her shoes and stockings, raise her skirts above her knees, and, after making her way through the mud that endangered the lives of horses and mules, wash herself off before redressing—all to the admiring eyes of the idle males in town.[11]

Unaware of the world he was entering, Sam kept on. The growing desperation of those first three days on his own in a hostile, bizarre environment seemed a nightmare even thirty years later. Jones's later account suggests the fantastic and the bizarre: Pithole "reads like the story of the Lamp of Aladdin or some other Arabian Nights' tale" (*NR*, 43). Everything about Pithole was grotesque, exaggerated beyond recognition. The natural state of things was inverted everywhere: what looked like black snow fell from the sky produced by the area furnaces; hairless horses remained stuck in knee-deep mud until they died; a beautiful hillside had become a forest of derricks. As the *Morning Herald* put it, "The whole place smells like a camp of soldiers with diarrhea." There were few privies and those were badly maintained. People simply tossed garbage out of the doors of hotels and "free and easies." The United States Hotel alone served a thousand meals each day. The cost of drinking water rose from fifty cents a barrel to fifty cents a pitcher. Suddenly water cost more than oil; no one wasted any on bathing. The creeks in the area were so slick with oil runoff that they did not provide an option for bathing. Even with high wages, Pithole was an expensive town. For three dollars a night a man could stay at a boardinghouse and sleep in a bed much like a berth on shipboard. A dollar a day bought a bed of straw. While the East Coast panicked under the threat of a cholera epidemic that summer and the foreign press reported that people were dying in Pithole at a rate of fifty to eighty per day, visitors to Pithole responded to their situation with a gallows humor. The correspondent from the *New York Observer* noted that "no one has been buried in Pithole since my arrival (ten days ago) and but few deaths. It is said that the land being *too dear* to use for graves, is the cause of no one being buried, and as soon as the premonitory symptoms of disease are felt, the victim leaves town." Of course, not everyone could be expected to have such foresight. He noted that a contingency plan had been decided on: "It is proposed to start a cemetery on the 'Chocteau' plan of placing the coffins upon very high poles. This would enable the dealers in land to dispose of the land underneath." "Almost everyone here is sick," noted one resident, "and yet a sick man here works as hard as three well men elsewhere."[12] Young Sam's sense of being trapped in what seemed an endless search has the nightmare quality of repetition: "I remember, and shall never forget, the feeling of utter desolation that possessed me" (*NR*, 49).

At Dawson Centre, a "suburb" of Pithole, Sam delivered the letter from Samuel Miner to Captain E.D. Morgan, the superintendent of the St. Louis and Pithole Petroleum Company. His reception was considerably cooler than it had been at Miner's. Asked if he was an engineer, Sam said yes. He detected a sneer in the man's voice as he then asked, "A Sawmill engineer?" When Sam replied that he was a steamboat engineer, the superintendent seemed to take him seriously for the first time. He looked at his recommendations and murmured, "Well . . . you may be just the man we want; we have a lot of inexperienced men running our engines." He turned a keen eye on Sam and said, "What wages do you want?" In retrospect, Sam thought the answer he came up with was remarkably wise: he said he wanted the "going wages." In fact, he felt so desperate he would have taken the job at any wage. But the going wage was good—the lure that had brought him all the way from Lewis County, New York, $4 a day, was a reality. Just when he felt relief for the first time, Sam was brought up short. One last question: "Do you think you could pump an oil well?" His heart missed a beat: "I can run an engine, and I think I can pump an oil well" (*NR*, 47-48). Sam Miner's kindness had paid off: Sam had a job.

Within two hours young Sam was proving he could pump a well. He began that day with the noon-to-midnight shift. Sometime that evening his "partner," the man who would pick up the midnight-to-noon shift on the same machine, stopped by to chat. He asked the new recruit if he would be willing to work his shift for him—he would pay him $2. The partner had the opportunity to sit in on a poker game that night and expected it to be more profitable than real work, especially as he could "earn" $2 for not coming to work that night. Sam immediately accepted the offer and "sold himself" to his partner, thus completing his first "day's" work—twenty-four hours straight and $6 richer. Tuesday afternoon at lunchtime, Sam felt the night's lost sleep well worth it, for he had lost the "feeling of hopeless despair" that had daunted him all weekend. From the perspective of thirty years, the mayor of Toledo, who had made himself accessible to the perpetually out of work, looked back on his first day's work as a miracle. "I really believe," he wrote then, "that an inexperienced man, as I was in the oil business, would be more likely to get struck by lightning on a pleasant day than he would be to get a job today such as I found waiting for me on that Monday morning in Pithole" (*NR*, 48-49).

The St. Louis and Pithole Petroleum Company paid by the week; every Saturday the men came by to receive $24 for six twelve-hour days, a seventy-two-hour workweek. That first Saturday Sam picked up his $24. With the $2 "overtime," he had earned $26 for an eighty-four-hour workweek. He "hied" it back to Titusville to explain his situation to the hotel clerk at the American, pay his bill, and pick up his grip. Then he made his way back the twelve miles to Pithole with his debts, if not his conscience, cleared (*NR*, 48).

In the midst of this bizarre world, young Sam found at least one steadying influence. He, like everyone else, it seemed, was caught up in "the hopes and fears, the ambitions and aspirations, the scheming, conniving and planning . . . in the foolish scramble for wealth." At the time, the scramble did not seem foolish. Alex Kinnard was an exception; Sam knew he was different. Kinnard was one of a "few devoted souls who went to Pithole for a more noble purpose than money-getting." Kinnard, a Scot, was superintendent of the Blanc Farm Oil Company, but, more important, he was superintendent of a small Sunday school. In this role he proved to be a "friend to the 'boys,'" and Sam went to him for advice, for sympathy, even for tender nursing in illness (*NR*, 50-51).

Sam Jones was working harder than he had ever worked in his life, but it was not to last long. Sam had been drilling for only a few weeks when he and his fellow workers stopped by the company on Saturday afternoon to pick up their earnings. They found the office locked, the superintendent gone, and a sheriff's notice on the door. The company had gone bust. So it was back to the dreary tramp looking for work—young Sam joining thousands of others who had come to the oil region. Pithole was a highly transient community. Prother and Wadsworth, bankers in town, apparently could create feelings of confidence in their customers by advertising that they had been in business "since July 1." One reporter, after a stay of ten days, claimed that he was one of the residents who had been in town longest. Although that claim is hyperbolic, when the election of 1866 came around, Pithole had a real problem. By law a white man could vote if he had lived in Pennsylvania one year and the county for six months or if he had been a soldier who had made Pithole his first home after the war. Very few men met these requirements. And if legal voters were in short supply, candidates for office were nonexistent; the *Pithole Daily Record* bemoaned that even "the oldest inhabitant . . . has not been a resident long enough to qualify him for office."[13]

Sam hung on in this highly transient community. But as autumn deepened into winter, he still had found no work. With four other men he set up housekeeping in a shanty by the edge of Pithole Creek, and they "entered into a communistic arrangement to live through the winter, agreeing to share and share alike until spring should open." They all kept looking for work, walking many miles for the occasional job; they managed to bring in enough money to keep them in bread and beans three times a day. Years later he observed: "I can easily understand how Carlyle could say that a man looking for work, wanting work and unable to find work, is the most pitiable object that ever encumbered the face of God's fair earth" (*NR*, 44, 52).

Sam later doubted if they would have survived the worst of the winter if he had not stumbled upon a little capitalistic venture. Their shanty stood near an old dilapidated bridge that crossed the creek; Sam and his friends took some planks from an abandoned derrick nearby and repaired the bridge. They charged the teamsters ten cents for crossing. The group had made $27.10 before the teamsters banded together and demanded a free bridge (*NR*, 52-53).

If Pithole's creation was grotesque, its end had a natural logic. A reporter of Calvinist bent described one oil well fire in terms of Armageddon; it was "a teeming, seething cauldron of living fire," which made him "ready to imagine himself on the brink of the infernal gulf, and that the trembling multitude were the derelict of earth striving to evade the decisions of the scales of justice." The end came one cold February night in 1868, when a Mrs. Waring knocked over a kerosene lamp as she went to tend to her baby. Within two hours Main Street was a ruin: twenty businesses were demolished at a cost of $100,000. The *New York Tribune* described a desolate Pithole that summer: "The creek bottom filled with abandoned wells, the derricks lifted their black timbers like one of those dark, mysterious forests which Gustave Dore loves to draw." In 1870, 281 people lived in Pithole amid 250 empty buildings. By 1877 every qualified voter—all eight—served on the borough council. And in the next year, with no one living in town, the county commissioners sold the ghost town for $4.37; it had been worth $2 million in 1865.[14]

Sam Jones was caught up in the fever to get rich quick. He had seen that he could make the system work for him. The lad who had been called lazy had been tested and shown his strengths. His determination, quick wits, and willingness to work hard had seen him through a remarkable period. He was far from rich, but at eighteen Sam had discovered what he was made of. Looking back on these days, the adult reformer saw no inkling of the man he would become. At the century's end, then a vociferous advocate of the eight-hour day, Jones looked back to his Pennsylvania oil days: "As a boy of twenty-one," he admitted, "I heard the lecture about eight hours for work. . . . Apparently, it did not hit home: I went the next day to work twelve or fourteen hours and continued that way until I was able to enslave my men."[15]

The lessons of Pithole proved to be the formative experience of both his lives. At Pithole Sam found the best payoff of the American Dream—good wages, even the chance for great wealth. But also at Pithole he experienced the frustrating despair of a man willing to work but unable to find a job. That despair fueled his ambition for a good twenty-five years of his life; then, in his second life, the problem of unemployment stood at the center of his reforms. He continued to experience considerable guilt over the deceit this world seemed to require of him.

It is hard to imagine a more potent symbol of both the rewards and the hazards of capitalism than Pithole. Eventually Sam made a fortune in oil, but in this first experiment he worried that he might not survive the winter. For Sam Jones, then only eighteen, the "Oil Dorado" proved a nightmare. That nightmare vision ultimately defined the economic world as he later saw it. He understood neither the system nor his own behavior clearly. From his perspective at the century's end, the reformer criticized Pithole as a place where everyone scrambled "to get something for nothing." His early religious training merged with the American preference for hard money: spiritually trained to abhor gambling, he had absorbed the Jacksonian suspicion of people who make money in speculation. He saw himself as someone who had gotten caught up in the scramble to get something for nothing. This characteristic refrain indicts people—himself included—for seeking wealth out of all proportion to the work invested. Everyone at Pithole was a gambler, he thought.

The autobiographer's attitude toward his eighteen-year-old self is curious. The adult Jones blamed his young self because he had learned to cope, learned to survive, eventually learned to thrive. Pithole was a primitive boom town: an empty field had become the third largest city in Pennsylvania because people came there to make money. Sam bought into the ostentatious greed. He was earning more money than he had ever seen before. Yet amid the wealth being produced at Pithole he had managed to eke out only enough to live on bread and beans all winter. And he had done that by charging the teamsters for something that—it later occurred to him—he did not own. Thus, in writing his life story, he re-experienced a double dose of blame. As a reformer he blamed the system for its destructive cruelty; as a young man he blamed himself.

Now as a reformer he had come to see that it was the system that was at fault, not the boy, Jones felt shame because he had become a part of the system. He was actively engaged in an attempt to transform that system so one might reasonably wonder why he continued to feel shame. As a young man, struggling desperately to survive the winter, Sam had a purpose. Some of his later shame may have come from the fact that life had never again had such purpose.[16]

Proof that Jones recognized Pithole's importance to his own self-understanding can be seen in the relative space he allots it. He gives three sentences to the years 1867-70 but devotes almost twelve pages to less than a year at Pithole. Further proof that he engaged in some unnamed sin can be seen in the fact that, once he moves on to consider the subsequent years, the autobiographer does not chastise his earlier self for his attempt to get something for nothing.

The experiences at Pithole combined with his fundamentalist upbringing helped to create the advocate of brotherly love who could never do enough to satisfy himself. The correlation between a devout spiritual upbringing and the desire to create change seen in late nineteenth-century reformers suggests that Sam may have been psychologically primed to respond as he did in the 1890s. But, of course, not everyone raised in fundamentalist Protestant households turned radical reformer. Religious background cannot explain his later transformation, although it helped prepare the way for it. In his autobiography Golden Rule Jones locates the source of his guilt in Pithole. Without question, those months scarred his psyche. When he later began to question the way the business world worked, Sam kept returning to this period of his life. But just as his religious background alone cannot account for his transformation, neither can the traumas of Pithole entirely explain Jones's later thinking.

Freud would find Sam's feelings of guilt entirely logical. It is precisely those people who are most virtuous who feel chronic guilt. Whether Sam's aggressive impulse, which enabled him to survive in Pithole and later to thrive in the oil industry, was turned back and directed against himself or not, it is clear he turned on himself in his last years. Though he devoted all his energies to political and social reform and thereby probably shortened his life, he was not able to satisfy himself. The more he gave of himself, the more he felt a failure. He was driven by something larger and more ferocious than an honorable sense of justice.[17]

Sam Jones carried a religious burden that seems to have characterized most American reformers. The emotional demands he made on himself as a reformer were fundamentally driven by his own feelings of guilt; this response was typical of most American reformers. Guilt may be a necessary element in any reform movement, but American reformers seem to be uniquely characterized by guilt. Perhaps the American anti-institutional bias, which puts so much responsibility on the individual to create change, accounts for this pattern. Earlier in the century, transcendentalists and abolitionists did not see the value of working within existing institutions to effect change. Ralph Waldo Emerson dismissed the considerable contributions of his church, "this ice-house of Unitarianism, all external [and] corpse-cold." When institutions cannot be changed, reformers pay a terrible personal price. In 1898, Sam Jones wrote S.H. Comings, editor of *Commonwealth* and the *Social Gospel*: "I know that all of my life I have been so woefully in error that I feel the time has come when I do not want to continue mistakes due to the inexperience of past years."[18]

Sam Jones had been raised in a tradition that emphasized original sin. It was a conviction that shaped both his lives, tormenting him in his last years. But Jones's life as a reformer did not follow the plot that he had been taught to pray for as a child. Charles Wesley taught that spiritual awakening happens, if it happens at all, as a sudden revelation, like Saul's on the road to Damascus. Sam Jones's revelation, his conversion from capitalism to socialism, was possible because of his early Calvinist-Methodist training, but it was a gradual process that took years to bear fruit. Pithole was a crucial building block in Jones's acquisition of a radically new set of moral habits. Thus, as William James argued, Sam Jones's conversion was "gradual, and consist[ed] in the building up, piece by piece, of a new set of moral and spiritual habits."[19]

After the failure at Pithole, Sam rededicated himself to getting rich, and this time his perseverance and his mechanical intelligence paid off. The goal of making money led to a vagabond existence for the first year and a half after Pithole. He was totally anonymous in the oil fields of western Pennsylvania, following the trail of new oil wells from town to town: Petroleum Center, Petrolia, Oil City, Oleopolis. In his hopes to strike it rich, he managed to eke out a living, but he never secured steady employment. He took up a variety of trades, serving as a driller, a pumper, a tool dresser, a pipe liner, and a blacksmith (*NR*, 56).

Sam's position reflected the instability of life after the war, as the entire culture was forced to cope with the pressures that were transforming America. Sam was optimistic about his future, and there was good reason for optimism in 1870. Although gross national product statistics do not tell the whole story, those statistics for 1870-1929 do record real growth among capitalists, workers, and service employees. But even those whose lives were enriched by the postwar boom, including Sam Jones, paid a price. The great technological innovations combined with industrial expansion utterly transformed American culture. Within a generation citizens had to find ways to adapt to a radically transformed world, the new industrial age. Jones was not aware that any psychic price was being exacted. Nor was he inclined at this point to see that though the poor pay the greatest price, American culture as a whole pays a great price when self-interest defines the purpose of life: inequities are ignored, and the gap between rich and poor increases until violence calls attention to problems long suppressed.

Sam Jones subscribed to the prevalent assumption that the business of America was to create wealth. Out of that assumption came a complacent culture; even those who had fought slavery were largely quiet in this period. One has only to look back to the Civil War to understand that complacency, at least in part. In the years between the Civil War and the 1890s, middle-class America largely ignored the problem of industrial working conditions because no social problem was thought worth risking the tragedy of another war. During the post–Civil War industrial boom, the destruction of the dignity of individual workers could have been linked to slavery's destruction of human dignity, yet for the most part it was not.

At this point, Sam was understandably more concerned with finding steady work than with contemplating the degradation of it. He knew that he had to invest in an oil well to make any money, so he was intent on getting steady work and saving money. Sam spent the winter of 1867, when he was twenty-one, outside of Pleasantville, on the Cleveland farm. He had saved up enough capital to purchase a one-sixteenth interest in an oil well. He and his friend Johnny Mahan, who shared the shanty with him by the bridge, boarded at the farmhouse of the Widow Cunning. They tended the well until late, often coming home at midnight only to shiver in their beds as the snow blew through the cracks in the walls of their upstairs bedroom. In the morning they raced to see who could get dressed the fastest and make it to the well first. They shared a boyish enthusiasm for life, dreaming of fortune beyond measure. John constantly bemoaned a $5 investment he had lost earlier at Pithole. But Sam was more sanguine, knowing, perhaps, that looking backward was a fatal mistake for a man who wanted to secure a fortune in oil.

Even while working to get rich, Sam was an inquisitive person whose investigations often turned toward the spiritual realm. Johnny and Sam frequently tramped the muddy thirteen miles to Titusville to see "old Man Barnsdall, the spiritualist," who held regular meetings in his house. Sam longed to believe that the spirits of the dead walked the earth, able to communicate with the living.[20] Curiosity drew Sam; his need to believe in something beyond this world of mud, oil, and money prompted him to make those long treks to Titusville. This interest marks his having drifted away from the certainties of his childhood theology, seeking solace outside the church.

Once Sam had enough money to invest, the stresses became greater. But so did the hopes for success. His industry and his enthusiasm paid off—he scraped together enough money to invest in one-sixteenth of a "wildcat" well. Wildcat wells were drilled with hope, remembered one wildcatter so successful he later became president of Atlantic Richfield. "The wildcatter is to oil what the lone prospector with his burro, pick and pan is to gold. The wildcatter is the greatest risk-taker in the riskiest business ever. Indeed, the risks have sometimes been so extreme that the term 'wildcat' is often used to describe an undertaking which sensible men think unsound."[21] The impulse to do something sensible men think unsound was a characteristic that Sam Jones exhibited his entire life long.

That first investment was a bust, and so he retreated back to northern New York for about six months of work for the railroad.

Back in the oil region, he settled in Pleasantville, where he was finally lucky enough to land steady work. He "worked for wages," all told, for five years in the Pennsylvania oil fields. All that distinguished one day from another as one burrowed toward the earth's core was changes in the weather and the depth of the hole. The wooden derrick provided little shelter from driving rainstorms and sultry heat while it marvelously concentrated one's energies downward. The monotony was punctuated by broken sucker rods, hopes raised and dashed, washing days, and trips to Parker's Landing for the supplies and the news that entered the region by steamboat.

Terrible news from home added a new stress—one that was to become characteristic of the period. Death interrupted the monotony of those days in the summer of 1869. Moses, Sam's youngest brother, died on July 2, at the age of fifteen years and nine months. It was Sam's first experience of death. He was far away from home and of no use to his mother or his youngest brother. Sam's later descriptions of the terror death held for him in this period suggest that in the 1870s he questioned the possibility of life in a next world. But he had no doubts about life in this one; Sam's mechanical talents and his love of machines supported his dream.[22]

The isolation of his childhood continued as he tended wells. Sam turned to books for companionship. Charles Dickens's novels made "a lasting and permanent impression." *Nicholas Nickleby* and *Martin Chuzzlewit* were personal, and revealing, favorites. Sam had identified, it seems, with Nicholas, a high-spirited defender of the weak who emerges from poverty to success, and with Martin, an impoverished lad who crosses the Atlantic to find his fortune. Mark Tapply, Martin's lighthearted companion, "had a good deal to do in giving me so much of a cheerful disposition," he thought.[23] That cheerfulness seems the most striking characteristic of the young Sam Jones. A sensitive reader of these early novels of Charles Dickens, of course, would experience a world peopled with orphans, where good folk make a difference, transform lives, transform small parts of the world itself.

Sam seems to have been a man who tried to make a difference. He was an expert athlete who used his physical prowess to defend the weak. Bullies soon discovered that he was a "notable power in defense of the weak." In feats of endurance or games, "Big Welsh Sam Jones" was thought second to none. He was not a quarrelsome man, certainly, and was considered peaceful; at the same time, he was nobody's fool, as the rougher fellows soon learned. He quickly developed a reputation of being a dangerous man to trifle with. Sam Jones could eradicate the small inequities of his world with his powerful body. Throughout his life, it seems, Sam felt the need to defend the weak.[24]

At some point during this period, Sam met Alma Bernice Curtiss. Unlike the Joneses, the Curtisses were people of substance. The family had been in western Pennsylvania since at least 1824, when Alfred Curtiss, Alma's grandfather, had moved to Crawford County, Pennsylvania, from Washington County, New York. He purchased fifty acres of land in Randolph Township that year and, in 1826, enlarged his holdings by purchasing an additional five hundred acres. Alma's father, Henry, received one hundred acres of land from his father in 1842;[25] he married seventeen-year-old Varilla Waid in 1849. Alma was born September 24, 1854, the second of four daughters. Ida Evangeline, known as Eva, was two years her elder; Adelma Clarabell was two years younger. When Alma was five, Hattie May was born. Alma was going on nine in August 1863 when Hattie May died of diphtheria, not yet three years old.

By the time Sam met the family, Henry was a successful insurance salesman and was considered a prominent citizen in Pleasantville. By 1868 or 1870, the family had had plenty of opportunity to become thoroughly familiar with men with "oil on the brain." Most of what they saw would not have encouraged them to hope that one of their daughters would make such a match. Alma was twenty-one when she married Sam Jones.

Sam was deeply and passionately in love. The seeking, yearning side of his nature met his other half in Alma Curtiss. So, at least, we may infer. He felt so akin to this young woman that he felt married—"seriously and most religiously married—for several years before the ceremony took place." He discovered that it was the feeling each had for the other, "the union of two souls that have an affinity for each other," rather than the words the preacher says that performs a true marriage. The miracle of marriage takes place in the human heart. Alma was his kindred spirit. He felt for the first time a "consciousness of oneness, of unity," the sense that his life would be complete with her help. The intensity of his feeling came in part from years of isolation and his evangelical upbringing, which led him to feel deeply the need for unity.[26]

The love Sam felt for Alma is of crucial importance in understanding the second Sam Jones. The man who tried to live his life literally on the principle of loving others had known, in his first life, the peace, understanding, and union gained from loving another. It is hard to imagine a businessman and a politician basing his life on love as a practical philosophy had he never experienced deep and satisfying love. If his early religious training and his experience at Pithole did much to account for the later transformation of Sam Jones, his years with Alma were also of central importance. For his sense of self-worth probably was greatly strengthened by her love, especially if, as seems likely, his upbringing had made him feel unloved. Alma's pastor called her a "rare woman," who combined "clear intellect and natural goodness of heart . . . with the Christian graces." The result, he thought, was a "character of sterling worth and the highest beauty."[27]

Alma provided him with a purpose for his dream. With an investment of $700, he secured oil leases and set himself up in a small cabin on the Shoup farm half a mile outside Turkey City. The town, at a crossroad along Turkey Run in west Clarion County, was something of a regional center in the 1870s. It supported two grocery stores, two dry goods stores, two barbershops, a billiard hall, a cigar store, and a sucker rod shop. The one-room public schoolhouse taught children from first grade through eighth. Sam's cabin, named the Fort, was a windowless one-room shack with a front porch big enough to provide some shade from the midday sun while Sam leaned back in a chair to play the violin.[28]

By 1875, Sam's hopes, at least the most pressing ones, had been realized. He built an addition to the Fort, and on October 20 he wed Alma Curtiss. From the vantage point of 1899, Sam Jones looked back on the years 1875-78 as the happiest of his life. Their life was simple, hardworking, full of fun. While Sam dealt with his oil leases, Alma taught music to two of her friends and played the organ for the Sunday school. Sam and Alma tended the garden. Together they spent half a day each week doing the wash. They went down the hill to the boiler house, where Sam had developed a proto–washing machine; he had rigged a steam and hot water contraption to wash the clothes. It is interesting that even in this, the most idyllic section of his autobiography, Jones thinks in the economy of compensation: after detailing his functions in the family, Jones writes of Alma, "She repaid me by watching the engine while I was gone to town on necessary errands" (*NR*, 56).

Sam's marriage to Alma was a partnership that integrated domestic and economic life. Their lives were unified by a shared purpose. They did not suffer the strains of many of their generation, as work and domestic life became increasingly separated into distinctly male and female spheres.[29] Alma knew enough about wells, engines, pumps, and drills to look after things while he went to town on errands. "We lived," Sam remembered, "quite a natural life, comparatively free from the care and burden of 'things,' and being so, we were at liberty to contribute our share to the common welfare of the community, and we had the best kind of times in so doing" (*NR*, 56).

It was not simply a practical partnership; they shared the same interests—music, books, ideas. Sam joined the literary club; his reading over the past ten years had done much to continue the education that had been cut off in childhood. But it had been a fairly solitary endeavor. Sam wanted the guidance of other minds in the course of his reading. The Turkey City Literary Club provided a much appreciated outlet for a young man who loved to learn. Alma was also engaged in a systematic course of study.

But if Jones's life seemed centered, that was not to last long. Seven months after their wedding, Sam's mother, Margaret, died in Turin, New York, on April 18, 1876, at the age of sixty-six. There is only one clue to Sam's response to his mother's death. It is found in his copy of *Notes and Fragments of Walt Whitman*, his favorite poet. Some twenty years after his mother's death, Sam Jones, a rich man, signaled his interest by marking the following passage in the margin:

> When he arrived at his early home he found his mother dead. He stood and looked upon her face and then went aside, and many a time again approached he the coffin and held up the white linen and gazed and gazed. He came in the day when crowds were in the rooms—though all to him was a vacant blank—all but the corpse of his mother. And at last he came in the silence of the midnight before the burial, when the tired watchers were asleep. Long—long—long were his eyes riveted on the features of that dead corpse, with an expecting look, as if she wanted something. He bent down his ear to the cold blue lips and listened—but the cold blue lips were hushed forever. Now for two little words, *I pardon*, that proud, rich man would almost have been willing to live in poverty for ever: but the words came not.[30]

His attraction to this passage, compounded by his symbolic representation of his shame and guilt at Pithole, suggests that he felt his mother never absolved him from some sin. Perhaps it was the sin of rebelling against her authority or the sin of failing to love her completely.

If Sam was emotionally distant from his parents, he soon had the opportunity to help nurture his own children. By the summer of 1877, their happiness was complete: Alma and Sam were expecting a child. On February 6, 1878, Percy Curtiss Jones was born. The Fort must have seemed cramped with a baby, and new strikes in the Bradford field prompted the Joneses to move to Duke Center, several miles east of Bradford.

In Duke Center Sam actively began the kind of traditional Christian service that he rejected in his second life. Sam became the superintendent of the Sabbath school of the M.E. Church in Duke Center; he was a founding member and first president of the Social and Literary Association, which held weekly meetings in the Congregational church. Sam Jones knew the ideas found in books held truths to live by. He became involved in politics:

he was one of the six members of the Duke Center Borough Council, serving as treasurer.[31]

Sam Jones was comfortably part of a new conservative ideology that flourished throughout America after the Civil War. In a reaction against the federal government's intervention in the 1860s, moral and economic freedom became inextricably linked to the definition of democracy. Embracing the classical economic theory of laissez-faire upon which the United States had been founded, middle-class culture embraced the narrowest conception of Calvinist doctrine. Protestant religious doctrine contributed to that ethos. The accumulation of wealth, it was argued from pulpit to pulpit across the land, was an external gauge of one's moral capacities. Even Henry Ward Beecher, the famous abolitionist preacher, argued that "no man in this land suffers from poverty unless it be more than his fault—unless it be his *sin*." Beecher spoke for his culture as a whole in his unwillingness to see that poverty can have external origins.[32]

Protestant churches in this period endorsed the capitalist business ethic. The national religious mood can be measured by the subject matter and tone of the weekly and monthly periodicals published by the major Protestant denominations. The evangelism popularized by Dwight Moody argued that the problems of this world could not be solved until Christ's second coming. Thus evangelical Christianity endorsed the underlying assumption of laissez-faire economics: do nothing. The effects of this assumption were widespread, for evangelical Christianity was the primary force that shaped American culture.[33]

Even during this complacent period, a small minority argued that the church should seek to reform the world. The first Social Gospel journal, *EQUITY, A Journal of Christian Labor Reform,* published from April to December 1875, discussed labor issues "from the stand-point of the Bible." One of its editorials argued that Jesus was "the Supreme Reformer of all history" and that readers should seek to reorganize society into the Kingdom of Heaven.[34]

Proof that industrial and civic harmony was illusory came in the summer of 1877, when violence erupted all over the nation. Strikes of the Baltimore and Ohio Railroad in Martinsburg, West Virginia, spread to Syracuse, Albany, Buffalo, Pittsburgh, Philadelphia, Baltimore, Columbus, Cincinnati, Chicago, and St. Louis. President Rutherford B. Hayes called his cabinet into permanent session; an estimated sixty thousand militia were called out. Over the course of two weeks more than one hundred people were killed and at least a thousand were seriously wounded. A measure of the anxiety felt by middle-class Americans can be found in the *Independent,* an influential New York religious weekly: "Napoleon was right when he said that the way to deal with a mob is to exterminate it."[35]

Inner fears rather than concerns about violence in America sent Jones into a depression. He paid the price characteristic of virtually everyone who turned to reform late in the century: as a young man, he experienced deep depression. A series of deaths of close family members instigated a depression that lasted through most of the 1880s. Less easy to document but clearly relevant to the crisis was the psychic anxiety Sam felt from the conscience molded in the Calvinistic Methodist Church. It was, on some level, a religious crisis that sent him into a deep depression. In retrospect, Sam's years with Alma seemed perhaps the happiest of his life because the time was both brief and scarred with grief. Although Alma and Sam had each lost a parent suddenly, their own life together was filled with hope and happiness. In 1879, Eva Belle, named for Alma's sisters, was born. She was a delightful baby. They took to calling her Midgie. But then in 1881, Midgie became ill and died; she was two years and four months old. Sam's comment that Midgie "had somehow gotten nearer to my heart than any other creature" indicates his feeling of great loss. Alma had lost her sister Hattie at just about the same age; Sam had experienced Moses's death—from a distance. Nothing prepared them for this loss. Sam was devastated. Not only had he lost his favorite child, but her death caused him to question his assumptions about eternal life.

Soon another baby came: Paul Hugh was born May 11, 1884. Alma became pregnant within a month of the anniversary of Midgie's birthday. They had just observed the second birthday without her when both parents had to begin to adapt to the idea of a new baby. This child could not—did not—replace the one they had lost. Paul's birth apparently did not significantly alter Sam's black mood. Eighteen months later, as Christmas approached, Sam felt that "the cloud that obscured the sunshine from my sky" had just cleared away (*NR,* 54). Sam had become comfortably prosperous, but he was learning that money did not bring happiness. He was successful enough during this period to hire a Mrs. Thomas to help Alma care for the house and the children; Percy was a sturdy lad just entering school. But Sam's mood seems to have been grim.

Then came Sam's worst loss. Alma died at home on Christmas Eve 1885 at age thirty-two. The most likely cause of death would have been pregnancy or childbirth.[36] The funeral was held on Christmas Day. Sam later said he was terrified by Alma's death. The source of his terror seems to have been his religious doubts. "Then I believed, *or professed to believe,* in immortality, but my notions of it were vague and confused" (*NR,* 54, emphasis added). The distinction he made regarding immortality reveals a crucial difference between the private and the public self, between what one can safely assert and what one actually feels. If he only professed to believe in immortality, in the depths of his soul he doubted. For a year, and almost certainly longer, he was unable to find hope to balance this deep sorrow. The family moved soon after Alma's death to Bradford, Pennsylvania, but the change did not help. His melancholy overwhelmed him; his friends worried about his health. At their urging, he moved on again, late in 1886, to Lima, Ohio.

Sam Jones's religious doubts may be similar to those of other turn-of-the-century reformers. Washington Gladden, Jane Addams, and George Herron each experienced a severe depression before finding the profession that suited their sensibility. So did Sam Jones. Depression and self-doubt may have been the logical outgrowth of their evangelical religious training. Not only did Progressives grow up in strict Protestant households, but most also underwent a religious crisis because they had not yet found a satisfactory outlet for the demanding conscience their upbringing had formed. Sam Jones's religious crisis began in 1881 with his daughter's death; it was greatly exacerbated by the loss of his wife in 1885. During the same period, in 1883, George Herron, whose books Jones eagerly read a decade later, felt that he was groping "in that horror of darkness which settles upon a soul when it knows that there is no sound thing in it, and that it merits nothing but eternal death and endless night." Jane Addams discovered a career for herself when she created Hull House to serve the needs of others. Addams experienced her worst depression in 1885 and 1886. Then her religious doubts were exacerbated by grief over her father's death, resistance to her stepmother's pressure for her to marry, and her own yearning for some purpose in life: "For many years it was my ambition to reach my father's moral requirements, and now when I am needing something more, I find myself approaching a crisis and look rather wistfully to my friends for help."[37] Thus Addams was explicit about an issue that we can only infer in Sam Jones's case: that his depression was on some level linked with a perhaps as yet unconscious sense that he must find some socially useful occupation. These deaths emphasized that there must be more to life than Jones had yet seen.

The autobiographer does not tarry on the desolation and isolation he felt. It seems a characteristic strategy for nineteenth-century autobiographers. Henry Adams left a twenty-year gap in his life story to obliterate his wife's suicide. Not yet forty years old, with two sons to raise and two loved ones dead, the unity and connectedness Sam had found with Alma was gone. Leaving the community he had doubled his isolation. The only thing worth a man's attention was money, not love, not community, not hope of heaven.

After Alma's death, Sam managed to get through the details of daily life thanks to his sister Nell. Paul was only nineteen months old and something of a handful when his mother died. Percy was seven, old enough to experience the loss as terrifying. His father's melancholy would only have compounded his fear. Aunt Nell came to fulfill the quintessential role of maiden aunt. Nell had been keeping house in Turin, New York, but she packed up and moved to join Sam, Percy, and Paul. She "devoted many and many a sleepless night" to Paul.[38]

In his move to Lima, Ohio, Sam's devotion to attaining wealth, the "only problem worth a man's attention," finally paid off. Jones was the first person to strike a large oil well in the Ohio field. Only twenty wells had been dug in all of Ohio in 1886, when Sam leased land there. Standard Oil was the only company buying Lima oil at forty cents a barrel. In moving to Ohio he attained that ideal. He struck the first large oil well in the state—Tunget well, three miles east of Lima. It began bringing in six hundred barrels a day. But the Tunget strike serves as a reminder that making money was an ongoing problem. Overproduction was an issue for all national industries; as new technology made development attractive, more men increased output. There followed, as Adam Smith had predicted, a disastrous fall in prices. The pattern had been repeated in a variety of industries, not only oil but salt, sugar, cottonseed and linseed, cordage, wallpaper, and paint. By the summer of 1887, overproduction brought the price of oil down from forty to fifteen cents in less than two years.[39]

New York brought suit against Standard Oil for violation of the state's antitrust laws and won the case. Sam Jones had the opportunity to see the effects of industrial monopolies: in 1878, John D. Rockefeller controlled more than 90 percent of the oil produced in this country; by 1889, Rockefeller had acquired the company that made Sam Jones a wealthy man. Sam and a great many other producers faced the prospect of losing their entire investment. It was to be the last personal financial trouble he ever faced because the oil producers, including Jones, fought back—and won. In response to Standard Oil, they met on July 30, 1887, to pool their resources; they formed a corporation the next day which they named the Ohio Oil Company. Sam bought in with one hundred shares of stock and was elected to the eleven-member board. They banked on the future, having the foresight to see that eventually Lima oil would have greater utility. They purchased land with proven production value and gained new leases in the Lima field. Soon, as the Lima Board of Trade noted, the Ohio Oil Company was "among the heavy producers of crude oil," bringing in four thousand barrels a day.[40]

They were so successful that Standard Oil wanted to buy them out. In the spring of 1889, Ohio Oil sold out to Standard Oil for $650,000. Hindsight suggests that it was a mistake for the independent oilmen. In retrospect, Sam realized the company had the chance "to capture the Ohio oil field." In selling, however, Sam turned a tidy profit. It gave him enough money to live as he had always longed to live. He formed his own company and became president of the Geyser Oil Company.[41]

Nell, Sam, Percy, and Paul lived in the house of a successful businessman on West North Street. It was the grandest house that Sam had ever occupied. More than forty years after his death, Lima neighbors remembered Sam for his liberality and his love of learning. He exhibited a touch of the unconventionality that would come to characterize his new life in Toledo. Sam shocked his neighbors so much by letting Percy drive a girl in the family horse and buggy that they remembered it sixty years later. Sam could always be spotted around the oil wells "with a pipe wrench in one hand and a book in another."[42]

The life Sam led in Lima epitomized all that he later found wrong with conventional Christianity. He had, it seems, become a very self-satisfied Christian. The religion of his childhood had prepared him to believe that God's pleasure could be measured by one's worldly success. Sam Jones had reason to feel he was one of the privileged of "God's children, whom he was especially interested in." He was caught up in a life of good works for what he later believed was a very calculated, practical reason. Once he became a reformer, he saw the Calvinist doctrine in the most cynical light: his good works in the early years had been simply "a good bargain for me for a policy of future life insurance in the other world." His view of the good works he performed in Lima—that "future life insurance" policy—was later so distasteful to him that, when writing his autobiography, he omitted all mention of those good works from the Lima years. He had continued his work in Turkey City by becoming superintendent of the Trinity Methodist Sunday School; he made generous donations to his church; he helped create the YMCA in Lima, becoming one of its first presidents.[43]

He later may have sought to erase the YMCA from the story of his first life, but the institution would have been very appealing to the first Sam Jones, for the YMCA movement sought to provide young men new to the city and without the support of family with a strong sense of community. The explicit assumption of those building YMCAs throughout the United States was that the city was a dangerous place for a young man's morals. The YMCA worked to combat the city's tendency to undermine the social bond. Its mission was to provide a lifeline to isolated young men by bringing them into a support network. What is most interesting about Sam Jones's view of the YMCA, however, is that he thought it should not replicate the family but be a tool to break parents' stranglehold on their sons:

"We must have a YMCA to help the young man who thinks he must break away from his mother's apron strings."[44]

It would be a mistake, however, to see no links between Sam the reformer and the conventional Christian he later sought to deny. In the last year of the nineteenth century, Sam wrote to an old friend from Lima to reassure him that "since I became a 'crank' I want to tell you that I am just the same Sam Jones that I was in the days that you knew me, with the exception, perhaps, that those qualities of character that commended me to you have been developed, and I am more *Sam Jonesy* than then."[45]

Like most widowers of his day, Sam contemplated remarriage and found an apparent kindred spirit in Helen Beach. At the time they married, Helen was a thirty-five-year-old schoolmistress. She and Sam shared an interest in music: like Alma, she was a church organist. Like Alma's family, Helen's was prosperous. They lived in Toledo, where her maternal grandfather, Mavor Brigham, had been mayor in 1853. Her father, William A. Beach, had managed the Western Union telegraph office. Eventually, though, Helen achieved considerable independence for her day. Recognizing their daughter's talent, her parents sent Helen first to Cincinnati and then to Chicago to study music.[46]

Helen was anxious to return to Toledo. Sam had good reason to make the change as well. He had begun to experiment with improvements in oil equipment while at the Geyser Company. Since his partners refused to allow him to experiment with their equipment or wells, he began to look for other opportunities. He had great faith that things could be done better. So he planned to wed Helen and move to Toledo.

Sam and Helen were married on August 24, 1892, at her father's home on Huron Street in Toledo, the Rev. S.G. Anderson of Westminster Presbyterian Church and the Rev. O.D. Fisher of Washington Street Congregational Church presiding at the noon service. Afterward a wedding breakfast was served to one hundred guests. After an extended wedding trip, Sam and Helen moved into a house on Huron Street in Toledo near her family. Percy and Paul, now fourteen and eight, joined them, while Nell remained in Lima.[47]

At first, life did not change markedly after the wedding. Despite his Toledo home, Sam spent most of his time in the Lima oil fields in 1892 and 1893, where he worked on improving the drilling process. Sam was approaching oil drilling now as a challenging technical problem: he sought improvements that would increase drilling efficiency. This work paid off in a series of inventions, the most important of which was his sucker rod.

In 1894, Sam Jones secured a patent on an improvement of this device crucial to the oil industry that would transform his life. He did not invent sucker rods; they had been used since the first days of oil drilling in Titusville and Pithole. Early in the industry, sucker rods were a series of hickory rods strung together for twenty-five or thirty feet connecting the engine on the surface with the pump at the bottom of the well. Over the past thirty years, however, oilmen had been drilling deeper wells, which put a greater strain on the wood than it often could withstand. Sam Jones invented and patented the first all-metal sucker rod and thereby transformed the industry. The invention was crucial to his own transformation for it both brought him out of the oil fields into an urban setting and provided him with the fortune with which he began experimenting to create a more just industrial environment. Money would no longer be the center of life; Sam would discover far larger problems worth a man's attention, and he would radically redefine himself once he faced that truth.

3

The First Radical Move

Sam Jones had the experience that transformed his life during the devastating depression in 1894. Confronting desperately poor men, he came to the conviction that everything he had hoped for, worked for, and come to believe was false. As he sought to understand how to live in this new world, he fashioned a tin sign on which he inscribed the Golden Rule and hung it in his new sucker rod factory. It was, he later said, "the first radical move" of his life (*NR*, 64), and it would, to quote William James, form "the habitual centre of his personal energy."[1] In making the sign, it turned out, he was reforging a new self. That tin text declared his contract with the world: a compact of perfect reciprocity. He became a dedicated student of the important reform writers of the day, especially George Herron, Henry Demarest Lloyd, John Ruskin, Leo Tolstoy, and Giuseppe Mazzini. He created his own syllabus in "applied Christianity," books that kept him turning back to the New Testament Gospels. What he saw in industrial Toledo and what he read in the texts pushed him to make changes in the way he ran his business. He recreated his small part of the world and, in doing so, recreated himself. He had the courage to reconsider everything that he believed about Christianity. It is a measure of his inner strength and the seriousness of his intentions that he carefully analyzed his own feelings in light of the Gospels, contemporary social reformers, and the "pathetic" men looking for work on Segur Avenue. Sam Jones had been taught that poverty and suffering were part of God's plan. In 1894, he rejected that facile argument: he had come to recognize that the poor were his brothers.

The experience was, in one sense, the conversion his church had taught him to expect. As he put it in 1899, "I cannot but believe that thus far I have been divinely led in the crusade for social justice." Jones's conversion came not in adolescence, as is normally the case, but when he was almost fifty; so did his revered Tolstoy recreate his life at the same age. But it was the U.S. economic environment, not Jones's age, that was significant. In retrospect, it seems clear that if Jones were to come to such conclusions, it would happen in 1894. But his past provides the answer to why those conclusions prompted him to go so far, to become what one historian has termed a "religio-philosophical anarchist."[2] Had the U.S. economy sustained a boom in the 1890s, Sam Jones would never have become Golden Rule Jones: it took a confrontation with his former self to awaken Jones's social conscience.

As recently as 1892, when Jones first had moved to Toledo with Helen, the city had been enjoying great prosperity. Toledo seemed the ideal industrial city for an Ohio oilman intent on expanding his fortune. It was so central an east-west rail connection that it had become a transportation center: 140 trains came through each day on twenty-three different tracks. Twenty-five miles of docks along the Maumee River served coal, lumber, grain, and ore shipments from the Great Lakes. By 1900, Toledo had become an important oil center where crude oil was refined, stored, and shipped and oil well machinery and appliances were produced. There were 950 factories providing jobs for Toledo's growing immigrant population in 1892: in addition to oil, glassmaking, shipbuilding, and bicycle manufacturing had transformed Toledo into an industrial city. Perhaps even without industrial Black Friday, May 5, 1893, when 500 banks and nearly 1,600 businesses failed, it should have been clear that the prosperity would not last. An estimated additional 10,000 immigrants arrived in the two years after the 1890 census. The city had been largely foreign even before the latest influx: in 1890, out of a population of 81,434, 65 percent were either foreign or first-generation Americans; 4,386 could not speak English.[3]

Toledo's economic prosperity was short-lived. Many of those 950 factories went under when the depression hit with full force in 1893. By the time Sam Jones sought a factory, the Segur Avenue area, like much of industrial Toledo, had been hit hard by the national depression that would affect the economy until 1900.[4]

Statistics on unemployment vary considerably, but it is clear that it was a terrible problem at the time Sam Jones was establishing his factory. The *Commercial and Financial Chronicle* noted in August 1893: "Never before has there been such a sudden and striking cessation of industrial activity. Nor was any section of the country exempt from the paralysis. Mills, factories, furnaces, mines, nearly everywhere shut down in large numbers. . . . And hundreds of thousands of men thrown out of employment." Samuel Gompers estimated that three million were unemployed, and the economist Richard Ely put the figure as high as two million; *Bradstreet's* surveyed 800 companies from 210 places around the country and found 8,000 to 9,000 out of work. Police figures in New York recorded 67,280 unemployed, plus 20,000 homeless. In Illinois, Pullman normally employed 4,500; as early as November of 1893 only 1,100 had Pullman jobs. Chicago had an estimated 100,000 unemployed when the World's Fair opened in May 1894.[5]

When Sam Jones purchased and converted an empty factory on Toledo's south side, he experienced what can only be termed a religious conversion. Establishing his factory was the keystone to the building blocks that William James identified as essential in creating a new set of moral and spiritual habits. It was at that factory that Jones had an ethically inspiring experience. As soon as life appeared around the old factory, men started showing up looking for work. Desperate men, some of them homeless tramps, demeaned by days of wandering the streets in search of work and nights sleeping in empty railway cars, saloon basements, or outhouses, showed up on Segur Avenue. At first, Jones had believed what his business associates told him: suffering was caused by something mysterious called "the times." Nobody could explain good times or bad, and nobody was responsible for the times. Each manufacturer dismissed the "hard luck stories." The most sensitive told him it had always been this way. More cynical men assured him that the poor only pretended to look for work while they prayed they would not find it or easily dismissed the whole lot as drunken, worthless, and no good. But this comfortably impersonal view of economics could not insulate Sam Jones from the men who begged for work at his new shop. He was deeply shaken by what he saw, so shaken he transformed his life. Jones felt an intensely personal response to the stories men told him. How could his friends dismiss these men so cavalierly? Jones observed that his friends had shut themselves deep in inner offices and paid employees to listen to the hard luck stories and turn the men away. As added insurance, they placed "No Help Wanted" signs on the wall so that they could turn their eyes away. Jones had not shielded himself from the sight of those desperate men. As a result, the right to work became one of his guiding principles for the remainder of his life.[6]

The assumptions of Jones's manufacturing friends were shared by a significant number of America's upper middle class. One Chicago newspaper sought to instruct William T. Stead, author of the popular Social Gospel novel *If Christ Came to Chicago!*, in his mistaken compassion: "The American tramp . . . would not work if work were offered him. . . . The toe of a boot by day and a cold stone floor by night—these be the leading courses in the curriculum by which we would educate into self-respect such tramps as are capable of it."[7]

Self-respect was the issue as Jones began to see it—both that of the unemployed and his own. He believed that work gave people a sense of dignity and self-worth, probably because that had been such an important aspect of finding himself on the *Lyon* on the Black River Canal as a youth. But he did not romanticize the power of work as the Social Gospelers tended to do. Washington Gladden spoke of conscientious employers as chivalrous knights and the men in their employ doing heroic service.[8] A life in the oil fields made such fulsome language impossible for Jones.

Sam Jones had been a fairly successful oilman for nine years now; why did this situation suddenly shock his sensibilities? Part of the answer lies in the fact that the time, the place, and the conditions were totally unlike his business dealings over the past two decades. Jones had weathered the severe 1873 depression in the small-town safety of Turkey City, Pennsylvania. He had never seen how devastating a depression could be for urban workers. Here in Toledo, he met for the first time "a new kind of man." Jones had not had occasion to think about it before, but life in the oil fields inevitably had led to a measure of equality between the masters and men. Primitive field conditions tended to level the difference between those who had money and those who did not. Jones had always believed in the equality that the Declaration of Independence promises, but he had never had to test that belief, nor had he ever seen anything to shake it. These men startled him so much because they apparently did not share his belief in equality. To them he was literally a master of their fate. For the first time, Jones "came into contact with working men who seemed to have a sense of social inferiority, wholly incapable of any conception of equality." Jones thought these men pitiful and pathetic as they begged for work. They "stirred the deepest sentiments of compassion" within him—a feeling that remained for the rest of his life (*NR*, 62).

What Jones's friends and the Chicago newspaper would not see, it seems, is that the depression was having a disastrous effect even on those who kept their jobs. Those out of work suffered the most, of course. But even those who had jobs suffered wage cuts in the early months of the depression. Real earnings declined an average of 18 percent from 1892 to 1894, and, though consumer prices would decline (11 percent from 1892 to 1896), they did not keep pace with falling wages in the early months of the depression.[9]

As Jones began converting the factory in 1894, he toured the Toledo factories run by his fashionable friends. What he saw, both in the manufacturers and their factories, distressed him greatly. He entered the factories by the workers' entrance and was stunned by a "string of rules a yard long . . . at the tail of every one of which was a threat of dismissal." He went home that day and said to Helen that there would be only one rule in *his* factory: the Golden Rule. He got to work right away, fashioning a tin sign that read "THE RULE THAT GOVERNS THIS FACTORY: 'Therefore Whatsoever Ye Would That Men Should Do Unto You, Do Ye So Unto Them.'"

Jones considered placing the Golden Rule in his factory the most radical decision of his life. As he saw it later, "It was not any belief in my own goodness of heart or my ability to reach the lofty ideal of doing to others as

I would be done by" that prompted his decision. Rather, it was the simple recognition that laborers were "abject slaves": posting the Golden Rule was Jones's reaction to contemplating "the outrageous injustice that was practiced upon my fellow-men by the iron-clad rules to which they are made abject slaves in order to gain the right to a bare living." He thought his decision radical for three reasons: it acknowledged "a basis of equality" for everyone at the company; "it ignor[ed] the time-honored precedent of 'doing as other people do'"; and it assumed "that this fundamental rule of conduct, given us by the founder of Christianity, was a livable and practical thing" (*NR*, 64).

At first, he thought there was only one root problem: the "purely arbitrary" arrangement of the "'going wages.'" Jones considered it wrong that a man who had nothing to sell but his labor had no real choices: he could work twelve hours a day, seven days a week for life, or he and his family could starve. Jones decided that the "'going wages' rule should not reign supreme in the Acme Sucker Rod Company." He was determined to organize his company on the truth that men are entitled to a share in the profit from their work so that they might live decently. It was for the good of the individual *and* the country, for Jones felt that only under these conditions would the men and their children "be fit to be citizens of a free republic of equals" (*NR*, 62).

If the problem was as discrete as wages, there were fairly simply ways, Jones thought, to correct the problem; he posted the tin sign, paid a minimum wage of $2 a day, gave each employee a week's paid vacation, at Christmas gave them a bonus equal to 5 percent of their wages, and urged his men to join a union. Employees received the bonus whether or not the company turned a profit. Luckily, there was such a provision, for had he instituted a stricter form of profit sharing, no one would receive anything. Jones did not turn a profit. By December 1895, he had come to the radical belief that profit itself was wrong. Toledo businessmen could not begin to fathom such thinking. One needs access to Jones's inner life even to begin to understand his reasoning. Jones was confident that he had seen the heart of the problem and that his solutions would reap remarkable benefits. With time, he would come to see that the problem was far larger than the wage system. Looking back in 1899, he wrote: "At that time I did not realize the limitations that are placed upon our better natures by the economic conditions that surround us. I did not know that the competitive system of industry was calculated to bring out everything that is bad and to suppress all that is good in us, as I now know that it is" (*NR*, 64).

Once word got out in Toledo that a fellow named Jones over on Segur Avenue was paying a wage of $2 a day when the going wage was $1, sometimes less, the Acme Sucker Rod Company must have been swamped. He read Washington Gladden's *Tools and the Man* before becoming Gladden's friend. His notes in the margins of Gladden's book signal his remove from Social Gospel thinking. He questioned whether "the market rate" was "the correct way to scale wages." On the next page, Gladden argues—and Jones underlined—the "laborer is not merely the embodiment of so many foot-pounds of muscular force; he is a human being; with hopes and fears, affections and ambitions; and the efficiency of his work, in the great majority of callings, greatly depends upon his state of mind." Sam wrote in the margin, "And the only right way to test your wages and your treatment of the worker, is to put yourself in his place and say, 'how would this work, this wage, these hours, etc. suit *me*?'" Jones always went further than did Gladden, as the next marginal comment suggests. After Gladden observes that better relations with employees make for a better annual balance sheet, Sam wrote, "But he ought to establish right relations even though he *fail* [financially] on account of it."[10]

Jones soon went from deciding to create a more humane work environment to being willing to lose his entire investment in the service of that idea. Within a year, perhaps two, Sam Jones became convinced that business competition was a synonym for war, that property is theft. Why? The answer, as far as it is recoverable, takes us beyond the harsh economic conditions of 1894. It is necessary to consider how his past led him to his striking emotional response to those out-of-work men. This uncanny ability to identify with other people—to feel their pain—would be his great power as a campaigner, if not a politician. He identified with unemployed men in 1894 because the emotions he experienced at Pithole came back to haunt him. He witnessed the same shame he had experienced personally in Pithole when he felt disgraced by his poverty. What is perhaps most interesting is that he felt shamed once again, this time, apparently, of his wealth. Now the positions in Pithole were reversed. Samuel Jones, not Samuel Miner, was the man behind the counter, the man with money, security, and a roof over his head. "Without knowing why or how," Jones remarked in the autobiography, "I began to ask myself why I had a right to be comfortable and happy in a world in which other men, by nature quite as good as I, and willing to work, willing to give their service to society, were denied the right even to the meanest kind of existence" (*NR*, 62). Because of his own experience of poverty and the sensitivity of his nature, he could not return complacently to the comfort of his home after having seen such poverty and despair without questioning his position in life. The answers he found led him to turn his back on his past.

Jones's business reforms, his generosity, and his charity all seem to have been compensatory acts. Large gestures such as Rockefeller building the University of Chicago or Carnegie endowing libraries all across America certainly function as monuments to the builder, but they also may be seen as compensatory gestures. As Sam Jones divested himself of his wealth, he rejected the idea of building monuments. On one level he was simply compensating men for work done, returning some part of the profit to the men who earned it for him. There was no reason to be praised for this act; as he saw it, "Most manufacturers keep about eight out of every ten dollars which their employees earn for them. I keep only about seven and so they call me 'Golden Rule' Jones."[11] On another level, as both his speeches and his actions over the next seven years document, he seems to have felt the need to atone for his wealth. His deeply personal reaction to the unemployed men suggests that he wanted to make recompense for the sin of having beaten the odds in the capitalist system. He needed to make amends for damage he had done others: he won at their expense, so now he owed them all. On certainly the most complex level, his financial strategies, played out in the context of the Golden Rule, were gestures of compensation to himself. Everything he did for others was what he wished had been done in the past for him.

Sam Jones adopted what would become a holy cause, an attempt to institutionalize selflessness in his business, at the precise moment when he began making the most money. A commitment to a holy cause can serve as a substitute for lost faith in ourselves. Exchanging a self-centered life for a selfless one permits a person to gain self-esteem.[12] Jones began rejecting the self he had become; he sought to merge with a New Testament projection. Over the years he was so successful in taking on this new identity that he became known as Golden Rule Jones. The new cause and the new name gave him a sense of pride, worth, and a new purpose in life. He was no longer interested in making money. Instead, he defined his company by the Ruskinian value of making men.

Sam Jones paid a great emotional price for his second self. On the streets of Toledo, as he faced those desperately poor men, he responded with shame because he knew he could lose himself in their eyes. He could see in them the young man from Pithole, grossly distorted into something hardly human now. It was an awful feeling: the successful and wealthy businessman disappearing into the nothingness of the tramp.

If Jones's childhood determined to an important extent his response to the economic crisis, he was not alone. The severe suffering during the winter of 1893-94 elicited an unprecedented outpouring of public relief.

Henry Adams, ever the cynic, observed: "We are now in a spasm of virtue, the outcome of hard times." William T. Stead, the Social Gospel novelist and reformer, organized prominent Chicagoans into the Chicago Civic Federation, which offered an eclectic group of reforms: unemployment relief, improved garbage pickup, and a campaign against prostitution and alcohol. While municipalities struggled to respond, this depression raised for the first time the larger issue: did ultimate responsibility for relief of unemployment reside at the municipal, state, or national level? There was no consensus; Governor Roswell P. Flower of New York argued that, unlike Europe, "in America people support the government; it is not the province of government to support the people." Toledo, however, had adopted the "Indianapolis Plan" of offering food in return for a day's labor.[13]

Two incidents do much to suggest the limited success of any relief efforts: Coxey's Commonweal Army and the Pullman strike. So-called industrial armies of ragged, hungry, homeless people, much sensationalized in the press, marched on Washington in the spring of 1894. Rain diminished the symbolic effect of "General" Jacob Coxey's arrival at the Capitol, but Coxey's arrest on the Capitol steps—for trespass—offered a different, perhaps more powerful, symbol. The Pullman strike was the most famous, but hardly the only, strike of the period. *Bradstreet's* reported some 750,000 workers on strike nationwide. Coal miners, iron miners, brickmakers, shoe workers, and western railroad workers went on strike in reaction to wage cuts. Of course, it was the Pullman strike that aroused national attention. Illinois governor John Peter Altgeld was denounced as a European anarchist because he supported the striking Pullman workers.[14] Eugene Debs, sitting in a jail in Woodstock, Illinois, changed his vision of himself and America the same year that Sam Jones did, and the two would share an uneasy friendship for the rest of Jones's life.

The panic of 1893 and the subsequent depression pushed Detroit's mayor Hazen Pingree on the same political path that Jones would follow in Toledo later that decade. The parallels between Jones and Pingree are closer than those between Jones and Debs. But the fact that these three reformers were shaped by this economic crisis illustrates how important the events of 1893 were in creating a reform agenda that would define the next political generation. Pingree, already an advocate of municipal ownership of utilities, began to identify with his foreign and working-class constituents in 1893. Already distanced from those in the business community who had supported him, Pingree responded to the impact of the depression on the city's poorest residents. With about twenty-five thousand men out of work in Detroit and a poor commission supporting six thousand families with alms, religious, ethnic, and social prejudices flourished. Pingree found the ethnic and class-based attacks repellent and became one of the most successful middle-class reformers who championed the working class.[15]

Setting up the factory and meeting those who needed work awakened Jones to the reality of an unjust social system. That revelation led him to adopt the Golden Rule as a business maxim. It would be a mistake, however, to locate Jones's philosophical conversion in this one event. William James explains that the volitional stage of conversion consists of the significant events of life which constitute the "gradual . . . building up, piece by piece, of a new set of moral and spiritual habits. But there are always critical points here at which the movement forward seems much more rapid." This was the critical point when the movement seemed so rapid. Seeing those desperate men was the stage of conversion where the unconscious mind took hold. Sam Jones was psychically ready for the conversion to Christian socialism at the factory on Segur Avenue, but there was nothing sudden about it: his moral regeneration came out of his evangelical training, his youthful isolation, the devastating experiences at Pithole, his love for Alma, and the religious crisis of the mid-1880s. All had made him susceptible to respond personally to the sufferings brought about by great urban poverty.[16]

Sam Jones's marginal markings and notations show that *The Varieties of Religious Experience* was a book he held dear. William James's insights can help make sense of Jones's changing view of himself and the world:

> Let us hereafter, in speaking of the hot place in a man's consciousness, the group of ideas to which he devotes himself, and from which he works, call it *the habitual centre of his personal energy*. It makes a great difference to a man whether one set of his ideas, or another, be the centre of his energy; and it makes a great difference, as regards any set of ideas which he may possess, whether they become central or remain peripheral in him. To say that a man is "converted" means, in these terms, that religious ideas, previously peripheral in his consciousness, now take a central place, and that religious aims form the habitual centre of his energy.

In the last ten years of his life, the "hot place" in Sam Jones's consciousness, "the habitual centre of his energy," was the religiously informed social consciousness that had previously been peripheral to his life.[17]

Charlotte Perkins Stetson Gilman's *Woman and Economics* seems to have described Sam's painful response to social problems. In his copy of the book, he underscored in red pencil and drew a hand with finger pointing to the passage in blue, suggesting his emphatic agreement: "In the course of social evolution there are developed individuals so constituted as not to fit existing conditions, but to be organically adapted to more advanced conditions. These advanced individuals respond in sharp and painful consciousness to existing conditions, and cry out against them according to their lights." As the passage continued, Sam marked the margin: "The heretic, the reformer, the agitator, these feel what their compeers do not, see what they do not, and naturally, say what they do not." His sensibility and his exacting conscience, both formed by the expectations of the Welsh Calvinistic Methodist Church, led Jones to feel what others generally did not. He talked with the unemployed, which his friends refused to do; thus he saw what they did not. He later came to earn nationwide fame by saying what others did not. His words carried weight because as a man, as a manufacturer, and as a mayor, he was doing things that others did not.[18]

Although Jones never referred to his experience as a conversion, his reading of James suggests he may have understood it, on some level, as such. Religious sentiment integrated the self, providing him with a greater sense of direction, a clearer purpose in life, and an added awareness of the complexity of his own motivations. Sam's experience gave him a new purpose in life around which he created a new integrated identity. By the time he was Toledo's new mayor, he expressed a sense of having lived two lives: "I am the same Jones [from the Pennsylvania days] but am not the same man. . . . The Jones you knew . . . has become quite another man."[19]

The unemployed workers led him to feel "keenly the degradation and shame of the situation." Thus Jones's conversion came under conditions of degradation and shame, rather than sin, the concept often at the center of religious conversion. Sam Jones, who had been a fairly strict employer just the year before, the man who would dismiss employees for drinking, began to take in anyone—on principle. He and his brother asked no questions of prospective employees: nothing about their past, their habits, their morals, or their religious beliefs. Such an open policy inevitably led to problems. Jones remembered that they got "men who had been victims of all sorts of injustice from their infancy up, and, as a consequence, many of them were far from perfect." Men might disappoint him, they might not function well in the relative freedom the company offered, but the fault was not theirs: "I think it is well for us to remember that the best of us have our faults, and if our opportunities had been the same as those of our brothers and sisters whom we criticize as 'worthless and drunken' etc., there is sound reason for believing that our characters would not have been any improvement upon theirs" (*NR*, 64). Every time the Golden Rule manufacturer made a statement about others, he was also making a statement about himself, as this remark suggests. He never saw it in these terms, but it is clear that the tremendous number of compensatory remarks he made about others signaled his own need of atonement. Pithole and a thirty-year scramble for wealth now seemed a defilement. The remainder of his life was, on one level, a series of compensatory acts. Beginning with the fair wage he paid his men, losing money because of his business experiments, and donating his mayoral salary, Sam Jones compensated for organizing his first life around money.

The self-suppression and the impulse to compensate for his former life made him ill. Sam suffered from asthma for the first time, beginning a pattern of illness associated with the emotional stress his exacting standards created. Unable to sleep, he woke in terror three or four times a night, unable to breathe. He felt as though he was being strangled.[20] And that seems close to the mark: asthma attacks the central nervous system, the endocrine system, both sides of the brain, and the lungs. Doctors do not yet know why asthma is so frequently a disease of the night. His chest tightened unbearably, and he could not stop his hacking cough. He struggled to get enough air—gasping, he could not get enough. He stumbled up out of bed, struck a match to some jimsonweed. The smoke from dried jimson, a poisonous plant, is particularly vile, but it at least temporarily allowed him to breathe.

Some theologians suggest that the Sermon on the Mount can plant a seed of permanent dissatisfaction in the soul. The compulsion to resist what is natural and meet the demands of the spirit can create pain and great tension. His first asthma attack was the signal that this happened to Jones. The Golden Rule had inspired him, but now he could not breathe. His asthma was a sign that he could not reach what was most life-giving. His distance from the Golden Rule translated into his inability to get enough air. These feelings of inadequacy could not be entirely repressed: they emerged in his nightly fight for air. Asthma has long been considered an illness tied to the patient's emotions. By the nineteenth century, at least some members of the medical community thought the passions of anger and grief played an important role in the timing of asthmatic attacks. In 1864, Dr. Henry Salter's classic text defined this disease of "direst suffering" as "essentially a *nervous* disease." By 1873, "the neurotic character of the complaint" had been identified.[21] Sam began suffering from asthma in 1893-94, just as he began rethinking what it means to do as Jesus would do.

In 1903, Jones wrote Bernarr MacFadden, the publisher of *Physical Culture,* to say that his recent illness was a result of "a mixture of causes—physical, mental and spiritual. I was sort of out of harmony. . . . I am myself again. When a man is sick, he is away from himself; when he comes to himself, then he is well."[22] Thus Jones's continual battle against ill health, waged in response to the pressures of his principles, created a feeling of division within himself. "I am myself again" are the poignant words of a man who often felt other than himself. Jones's bouts with illness reveal the great psychological costs his new life exacted.

If he sufered serious health costs, Jones also experienced growth in self-knowledge and social awareness. He sought to build community where there was none because he had come to understand himself in terms of society. Psychologists suggest that when a person experiences a conversion, the pronoun "my" carries a weighted meaning it did not previously hold. The convert's conduct becomes attached to the person more consciously: *my* beliefs, *my* words, *my* actions have a powerful purpose associated with the new cause. For Sam Jones this certainly was true as he came to recognize the primacy of the commonwealth over the Gospel of Wealth: he argued that society must uphold moral judgment based on universal ethical principles and that people must be taught to see that doing so is just. "I am not one of those," he wrote in the *Independent,* "who believe that the Kingdom of Heaven—that is, a just social and political order—can be established on earth by merely passing a law. My hope of improvement rests upon the belief in the development of a better citizenship through the gradual operation of the forces of evolution and education that are slowly but surely bringing mankind to understand . . . in the fundamental principle of unity or oneness."[23]

What would Jesus do? The most popular Social Gospel novel of the nineteenth century, Charles Sheldon's *In His Steps,* got Americans asking that question. Golden Rule Jones transformed his own life and much of Toledo by repeatedly asking the question. There is a scene in Sheldon's novel that may shed light on Jones's response to the unemployed: a tramp listens to a sermon in a fashionable church about the need to follow Jesus. He speaks up, confronting the complacent congregation:

> I've tramped all over the country trying to find something. There are a good many others like me. I'm not complaining, am I? Just stating facts. But I was wondering as I sat there in the gallery, if what you call following Jesus is the same thing as what He taught. . . . I've tramped through this city for three days trying to find a job; and in all that time I've not had a word of sympathy or comfort except from your minister here, who said he was sorry for me and hoped I would find a job somewhere. . . . I understand you can't all go out of your way to hunt up jobs for other people like me, I'm not asking you to; but what I feel puzzled about is, what is meant by following Jesus. What do you mean when you sing "I'll go with Him, with Him all the way?"

Like the fictional tramp, young Sam Jones had wandered about Pithole for three days without a word of sympathy from anyone except Sam Miner, who not only hoped Sam would find a job but helped him to get one. Because of this experience, the question, "What do you mean when you sing 'I'll go with Him, with Him all the way?'" had a painful resonance that Sam Jones could not ignore. Just before the tramp collapses in the church he observes: "It seems to me there's an awful lot of trouble in the world that somehow wouldn't exist if all the people who sing such songs went and lived them out. I suppose I don't understand. But what would Jesus do?"[24]

Sam Jones became a radical businessman in 1894, when he began asking "What would Jesus do?" He institutionalized selflessness at the Acme Sucker Rod Company factory when he decided to conduct his company on the principle of the Golden Rule, offered higher wages, and began working toward equality in his factory. Jones struggled with the disparity between his own life and the lives of his men, for he sought help in coming to terms with what he saw. He turned to contemporary writers to help him make sense of the world and his new self. Sometime in 1894 or 1895, while he was establishing his factory and struggling with his first feelings of personal discomfort, Jones encountered five authors who would change his life: Henry Demarest Lloyd, George D. Herron, John Ruskin, Leo Tolstoy, and Giuseppe Mazzini. Reading their works seems to have been another essential building block in the creation of his new set of spiritual habits.

Jones once said it was Henry Demarest Lloyd who made him "a Golden Rule" man. Jones met Lloyd, the leading reforming journalist of the day, in 1893. Lloyd, who had studied at Columbia University with Francis Lieber, the leading free trader, had come to see that capitalism corrupted both those it enriched and those it impoverished. Jones became his most famous convert on this point. Lloyd had said: "The Golden Rule is the original of every political constitution ever written or spoken." Although palpably untrue, Lloyd's words hit Jones forcefully. He had been raised a good Christian, but that meant only, it seemed to him after talking with Lloyd, that Christ's teachings were to be saved for "some impossible millennium or heaven in the dim and distant future."[25]

After their meeting, Jones eagerly took up Lloyd's *Wealth Against Commonwealth,* a dense, carefully argued indictment of Standard Oil. Jones differed with Lloyd about Standard Oil's responsibility for the wrongs in the social system, but he found the source of his own philosophy in the final two chapters. Lloyd's words changed Jones's view of the world. Jones, then Toledo's mayor, spoke at the memorial service for Lloyd in Chicago in late November 1903. A crowd of five thousand listened to speeches by Jane Addams, Clarence Darrow, and Cleveland's Tom Johnson. Then Toledo's Golden Rule Jones spoke: "'Love they neighbor as thyself,'" he told the crowd, "is not the phrase of a ritual of sentiment for the unapplied emotions of pious hours; it is the exact formula of the force today operating the greatest institutions man has established. It is as secular as sacred. . . . Only thus is man establishing the community, the republic, which with all its failings, is the highest because the realest application of the spirit of human brotherhood." Lloyd's words struck a chord from Jones's childhood. Golden Rule Jones remembered being taught to "lisp his prayers at [his] mother's knee," learning there that Jesus expected us to live his philosophy daily. Lloyd "so effectively clinched" that childhood lesson that Jones told the crowd a "new world opened before me and I saw, as I now see with a more clarified vision, that the only hope and all the hope of the realization of the American idea of equality lies in the breeding of a race of strong men and splendid women who will make this simple philosophy the rule and guide of every transaction in life." In the midst of his first election campaign, in 1897, Jones would write Lloyd, "I have been especially fortunate in coming in contact with one who has already proven of so much benefit to me as you have."[26]

Jones was inspired by Lloyd, but he knew he could not be a practical model for a Welsh immigrant. Henry Demarest Lloyd was a member of the privileged class and looked the part. In his later years he had the look of Mark Twain: a sweeping mane of thick white hair, a bushy mustache, and deep, thoughtful eyes. Jones appealed to the working-class crowd in Chicago mourning Lloyd's loss by describing himself as the "son of Welsh common labor parents" who fought the political battles he did because of his birth. "A fighter in the French Revolution was asked," Jones told the crowd, "why he was fighting in the place where he was found, and he replied, 'I was born on this side of the barricade.' That describes my condition exactly." It is one of Sam Jones's most revealing comments, affirming that everything he did as a reformer—and much of the personal discomfort he felt—was rooted in his deep personal identification with the working poor. His working-class background distinguished Jones from virtually every other reformer of the period, and it accounts, in large measure, for his unique ability to reach the working class.[27]

Jones argued vociferously against a class-based view of society. He considered the word "scientific" an adjective for "socialism" in *The New Right:* "With regard to the term 'scientific socialism' of course, I do not want to use it, if it is to be taken to mean the socialism of the extremist Karl Marx school." Unlike the Marxists, Lloyd (and later Jones) argued for a Christian socialism which denied the importance of class-based struggles. Jones explained to the editor of the *Coming Nation,* "I see myself as a mere atom in the human Whole. I have no desire to separate myself from the Whole and become an atom of a class. I could not so separate myself, if I could. Society is an organism, not a congregation of individuals." When Jones suffered, it was because he felt divided from the "Whole." The passion of his later commitment to nonpartisan politics rested on this heart-felt belief in social union. If Jones learned from Lloyd, Lloyd also learned from Jones. Lloyd wrote in *Men the Workers*, a book that was first published posthumously in 1909, that labor is "the most religious movement of the day, for it carries the Golden Rule into the Market."[28]

George Herron's "Philosophy of the Lord's Prayer" was especially important to Jones as he began the process of redefining himself. Jones wrote his closest friend, Nelson O. Nelson, that Herron "more than any other man has been useful in bringing me from the darkness of economic ignorance to the measure of light that I now possess." George Herron, the Congregationalist minister who argued more passionately than anyone else for early Christian socialism, seems first to have set Jones on the path of finding an intellectual basis for reform. Although Sam Jones would have close connections with the Social Gospel movement—Washington Gladden delivered the eulogy at Jones's funeral—his religious thinking became every bit as radical as Herron's. Herron distanced himself from the term "socialist" in a way that Jones did not, but only because for Herron the term was too conservative. "I object to being called a socialist," Herron wrote in *Between Caesar and Jesus*, "not because socialist is too radical, but because it is too wholly conservative." Even Karl Marx would be deemed "a rude and conservative pioneer on the social frontier," thought Herron, once the new Christian order had begun.[29]

Herron was simultaneously convinced of his own innate sinfulness and the divine mission of the United States. Through his endowed chair of applied Christianity at Iowa College in Grinnell and through his fifteen books, Herron sought to teach the "redemptive power of sociology." At the time Jones began his experiments in reforming working conditions, Herron first taught his course in Christian sociology in the 1893-94 academic year; the rigorous year-long course relied on one hundred lectures and twenty-six texts, including Georg Hegel's *Philosophy of History*, Frederick Denison Maurice's *Social Morality*, Ruskin's *Unto This Last*, and Mazzini's *Duties of Man*. When Jones turned to texts to make sense of the world he saw, he devised a kind of independent study in Christian sociology. The first author on his "syllabus" was George Herron; Ruskin and Mazzini also became crucial to Jones's intellectual development. The course of studies would continue for the rest of his life, but at first he consumed, as he told W.T. Stead, in addition to "everything . . . Herron has ever written," the works of Lloyd, Ruskin, Tolstoy, and Mazzini.[30]

Herron is doubly important to our understanding of Sam Jones's life as a reformer. Not only was he instrumental in setting Jones on the path of reform, but George Herron, more than any other reformer, clearly distinguishes just how healthy Jones's complex emotional response to the world really was. The personal doubts Jones began experiencing in 1894, as he first faced the inequities dividing him from the workingmen around him, deepened over the next decade into a continual self-questioning. As he gave more of himself, he became more critical, more convinced that his response was inadequate. But the course of George Herron's life in the 1890s suggests a self-destructive element absent in Sam Jones, however critical he was of his own inadequacies. Herron argued in the early 1890s, when Jones first encountered him, that the Kingdom of God was at hand in this world. His thinking would become more radical as his own life became more controversial. As early as 1890, Herron wrote, "It would be a joy to be pilloried and disgraced before the world." That martyr impulse was soon to be fulfilled. After Herron separated from his wife of fifteen years, she sued him for divorce and support of their children. Despite the services of Clarence Darrow, Herron lost the suit. His do-it-yourself "marriage" just two months later to Carrie Rand, the daughter of his benefactress, shocked both the Christian and reform communities and cost him his job in Iowa; he lived the rest of his life in self-exile in Europe, far from the reform movement he helped to initiate. Characteristically, Jones was one of the least judgmental: "He is sound as a bullet and quite indifferent as to whether he stays in Grinnell longer or not," Jones wrote. "I told him I thought he ought to stay and let them kick him out, so to speak; that would help the cause of education along more than to have him resign. He thinks the kick will come some time next year." Sam's embrace of Herron distinguishes him from many reformers, for Herron truly was outcast. Josiah Strong called his conduct and his letter repudiating the sanctity of marriage—written the day he married Carrie Rand—"despicable and a crime against society."[31]

George Herron left the country and the socialist movement just when it had its greatest chance of success. Jones, too, would suffer many failures, some linked to his inability to free himself fully from the evangelical impulse to suppress the self. His vitality did not require failure to feed itself, nor would Jones retreat from his work—although the temptation would be very strong.

The idea of sacrifice, the ultimate compensation, fascinated Jones. The sacrificial theme takes up much of Herron's *Christian State;* Jones underlined many of those passages when he read the book. Herron wrote and Jones, the new student of Christian socialism, underlined in his copy, "the law of sacrifice [is] the fundamental law of society."[32] Led by Herron, Sam Jones now believed in sacrifice, which would lead to considerable self-doubt. The greatest struggle of Jones's life, which came to a head in 1902, centered on the question of how much sacrifice was required—by Jesus, by society, by himself.

To follow Jesus literally requires that one at least contemplate the ultimate self-sacrifice. Jones underlined Herron's words that we can be true to the past and the future only "through the sacrifice of our present life in bearing away the sins of the past for the deliverance of the future." Jones's discomfort at the sight of human suffering did not, even by 1897, when he read *The New Redemption*, prompt him to sacrifice his present life. Herron ends his chapter "The Coming Crucifixion" by discussing the truth of Christ's love at the heart of society. He writes: "The joy of seeing this truth with a clear eye and believing in it with all one's being, and proclaiming it with a doubtless faith in its ultimate triumph, is worth any crucifixion the wrath of selfishness is able to devise. To such a joy, to such a faith, to such a cross, to such a glory, the Son of man now summons you and me. Arise, and let us follow him." Sam wrote immediately after those lines, "I *will.* S.M. Jones, Toledo, Ohio, Jany. 1897."[33]

Sam Jones's dawning belief in the economic philosophy of socialism linked him not only with many intellectuals of the day but with ordinary citizens as well. The pages of turn-of-the-century magazines such as *Arena* and *Outlook* dealt regularly with socialist theory. *Arena,* under the editorial control of Benjamin O. Flower, who would become Jones's friend, discussed not only political theory but prostitution, birth control, and socialized medicine. Even *World's Work,* normally an optimistic apologist for current business trends, ran an article sympathetic to socialism by Upton Sinclair.[34]

Even before he became mayor, Jones sought to awaken the citizens of Toledo. In the winter of 1896-97, he organized a series of sociological lectures open to the public to expose more Toledoans to the theories he had embraced. Jane Addams, Washington Gladden, and Henry Demarest Lloyd spoke in the series. Lloyd arrived in Toledo in February to give a speech titled "uses and abuses of corporations," a subject Jones thought was "the best calculated to educate a Toledo audience." At Jones's suggestion, all the members of Toledo's city council received special invitations to the lecture.[35]

Although sociological reform texts had great influence in shaping his new response to the world, Jones always believed it was God's "holy spirit" that brought him to those texts. He wrote, "Thanks be to God, I have been led by His holy spirit until I now 'stand fast in the liberty wherewith Christ hath made me free.' SMJ. 1895," in the margin of Washington Gladden's *Ruling Ideas of the Present Age.* The lessons he was learning in his factory and in the reading of "applied Christianity" all turned him back to the Bible, which had been a part of his life from childhood. But he saw the book and its teachings with new eyes in the 1890s. Sam Jones owned his 1891 Oxford edition of the King James Version from 1898 on, so there are no marginal markings from this early period. The New Testament is so central to Jones's changing worldview and his role in it that his response should be considered here. Not surprisingly, of all the books in the Bible, Jones was most drawn to the Gospels. Matthew and Luke seemed to interest him most, judging from his marginalia. These two books (like the reformers he was attracted to such as Herron and Mazzini) emphasize the need to change the world *now*. The words of Lloyd and Herron would have drawn him to Luke 6:27-28. Sam wrote "Our Rule" in the margin where he read: "But I say unto you which hear, Love your enemies, do good to them that hate you, bless them that curse you, pray for them that despitefully use you. To him that smiteth thee on the *one* cheek offer also the other; and from him that taketh away thy cloke [*sic*] withhold not thy coat also. Give to every one that asketh thee, and of him that taketh away thy goods ask them not again. And as ye would that men should do to you, do ye also them likewise."[36]

Jones saw the example of Jesus' life in new ways after reading Herron and Lloyd. He realized, apparently for the first time, that Christians only *pretend* to believe Jesus lived a perfect life. "We are exhausting ourselves in either striving to lay up treasure, or in formulating rules to guide our children in so doing. . . . We have written upon our door-posts,—'It is more blessed to receive than to give,'" he observed. "We have turned the law of Christ upside down" (*NR*, 463, 470).

Jones's correspondence and that of his friend Ernest Crosby reflect Tolstoy's importance to Sam Jones. In March 1898, Crosby wrote Tolstoy about Jones: "A few years ago he became the head of a manufacturing company in the city of Toledo, and ran the business on the basis of the so-called 'Golden Rule,' and is known to everyone as 'Golden Rule Jones.' The population elected Jones mayor against his own desires, even though 'respectable' people considered him a 'crank' or a fool. . . . He is one of the best people, is very well known, and is constantly mentioned as a candidate for President." Jones wrote Crosby to ask for Tolstoy's address because he wanted to "write to him and tell the dear old man for myself how much good his books have done me." He was not to write until the autumn, but Crosby kept Tolstoy up to date on Jones's career. In April Crosby wrote the Russian about Jones's reelection, adding, "As you know, he shares our views completely. . . . This [his reelection] is a great political event in the interests of socialism."[37]

There is only one extant letter from Sam Jones to Tolstoy. Jones sent the Russian a well-received speech he gave to 170 mayors and wrote: "You know that as they are elected by the votes of the people in our country, they must represent public sentiment to a very great extent. And I know it will encourage you to know that here, where we are credited with having more political corruption than in any other country, such sentiments could be received by city officials with favor." Jones informs Tolstoy, "It gives me great pleasure to say to you, my friend, that your books and sayings that I have read for many years have been a great help to me, and as best I could since I came into public office as mayor of this city, I have tried to hold up the doctrine of overcoming evil with good as the only scientific doctrine that we could . . . expect anything from."[38]

Jones was to become such a devotee of Tolstoy that he proudly included one of Tolstoy's letters (one that had arrived collect in Toledo with three cents postage due) in *The New Right* and he commissioned a Hull House artist to paint a portrait of Tolstoy for his mayoral office. Beneath the portrait, he had placed Tolstoy's words: "Men think there are circumstances when one may deal with human beings without love, and there are no such circumstances. One may deal with things without love, one may cut down trees, make bucks, hammer iron, without love, but you cannot deal with men without it." He envied Jane Addams and Ernest Crosby their pilgrimages to Tolstoy's home and hoped that he, too, would have the opportunity to meet the man who lived the simple life the Gospels advocate.[39]

Jones's practical application of Herron's and Lloyd's ideas aligns him with the Russian master. At this point, Jones did not worry too much about the disparity between his own comfort and that of his men—he built a larger, grander house on Monroe Street in 1896—but he would chafe in later years at the burden his wealth put upon him. Those feelings had their source, in part, in the example of Leo Tolstoy, who gave up everything and took on the life of a peasant. That vision of Tolstoy was for Jones the most powerful condemnation of his own life in his later years.

If Tolstoy would later prompt Jones to consider even more personal forms of sacrifice, it was from Ruskin that he learned how to adjust the relations between himself and his men. Ruskin helped Jones develop his idea of cooperative economics, for Ruskin, more than any other reformer, focused on the just relations between employer and employee. Sam read *Unto This Last* with great care, as his heavily marked copy attests. Ruskin dismissed the "science of political economy" because it reduced human beings to parts of scientific models. The models do not work because they do not allow for individual human response; Ruskin admired Dickens's *Hard Times* because it dramatically destroyed the illusion that people can be programmed in response to facts. *Unto This Last* charged classical economic theory with negating the soul. Jones not only underlined Ruskin's advice, he actively followed it. Ruskin cautioned against being good to one's employees for one's own benefit, the same philosophy that informed Gladden's *Tools and the Man*: if you "treat the servant kindly, with the idea of turning his gratitude to account, . . . you will get, as you deserve, no gratitude, nor any value for your kindness." Ruskin continued, "But treat him kindly without any economical purpose, and all economical purposes will be answered; in this, as in all other matters, whosoever will save his life shall lose it, whoso loses it shall find it." Sam underlined that passage in Ruskin and also in his own Bible: "He that findeth his life shall lose it; and he that loseth his life for my sake shall find it" (Matt. 10:39) is underlined and in the margin he drew a hand, with the first finger pointing to the verse. Clearly, it was an idea from his evangelical youth that Sam Jones had come to believe in fervently.[40]

Ruskin's view was paternalistic. Sam marked the passage in *Unto This Last:* "In his office as governor of the men employed by him, the merchant or manufacturer is invested with a distinctly paternal authority and responsibility. In most cases, a youth entering a commercial establishment is withdrawn altogether from home influence; his master must become his father, else he has, for practical and constant help, no father at hand."[41] As a Golden Rule manufacturer, he adopted Ruskin's paternalism wholeheartedly; it suited his personality and his own experience, for the world of work had taken him away from Hugh Jones's guidance, first at age ten and then for most of the next decade. Jones often talked of men as his brothers, but he dealt with his employees as his sons. "We were going along in a sort of free and easy way," he wrote of the time of the founding of the Acme Sucker Rod Company, "occasionally giving the boys a word of caution, perhaps printed on a pay envelope, or a little letter expressing good will and fellowship, and a word of friendly advice" (*NR*, 63). He later formalized that practice, including letters in pay envelopes, published as *Letters of Labor and Love,* similar to Ruskin's letters to English workingmen in *Fors Clavigera.*

After reading Ruskin, he decided that "by far the more important work" than making money at the Acme Sucker Rod Company was "making men" (*NR*, 64). This phrase became a refrain in his speeches and his correspondence throughout the rest of his career: making men quickly became a sacred calling. In response to Gladden's *Ruling Ideas of the Present Age,* on the sacred nature of work, Sam quoted George Herron in the margin: "Work is worship, I am excited to more reverence when I stand in the workshop or factory amidst the work of men's hands, than when I stand before the cathedral." It is a measure of his conviction that he carried

Herron's exact words in his head. The *Los Angeles Herald* would say of Jones in 1902 that "there is probably no employer in the country who stands in closer personal relations with those who work for him than Mr. Jones."[42] If the *Herald* was right, it was because Sam Jones lived John Ruskin's ideas. At Ruskin's death in 1900, Jones was so saddened that he delivered a talk on the English reformer at Golden Rule Hall, reading from *Unto The Last* to his employees.

Jones was also a student of Italian Giuseppe Mazzini, the Christian collectivist who spent most of his life in exile planning to overthrow the Austrian Empire and the papacy. He championed the working classes, worked for the unification of Italy, and ardently believed in the unity of humanity. Sam Jones was primed to respond to this belief because the Pithole experience had prompted him to see himself in those out-of-work men who came to the Acme Sucker Rod Company. Herron and Lloyd, both admirers of Mazzini, led Jones to read his works. Mazzini was to become such a constant inspiration that Jones kept a copy of Mazzini's biography on his desk at home. Later, Mazzini's emphasis on duty would inform Jones's sense of his own role and his message. After publishing *The New Right,* Jones regretted its title, believing that he was really talking about new duties as Mazzini did. He prefaced the final chapter of that book, "The Brotherhood of Man," with an excerpt from Mazzini's *Faith and the Future* which reads, in part: "We believe in the people, one and indivisible; recognizing neither castes nor privileges, save those of genius and virtue, neither proletariat nor aristocracy, whether landed or financial; but simply an aggregate of faculties and forces consecrated to the well-being of all. . . . We believe in the people bound together in brotherhood by a common faith, tradition, and the idea of love. * * * Equality, liberty and association: these three elements constitute the true nation." Sam Jones was not dealing with the broad national and international concerns of Giuseppe Mazzini, but he did take Mazzini's ideas for a true nation—equality, liberty, and association—and make them his founding principles for one factory that employed fifty men on Toledo's south side. He also absorbed Mazzini's vision of the Kingdom on Earth, but, like George Herron, envisioned it coming to being in the United States. "There is," Sam Jones believed, "a heroic and spiritual core to our national life. . . . We are developing a free-spirited, tolerant robustness of character which will set us free from small and petty conceptions of life. We shall yet have *men to match our mountains, rivers and prairies*—large-natured men, too generous to be tyrannical and too strong to be selfish." Not surprisingly, then, Whitman soon became Jones's favorite poet (*NR,* 472).

Sam Jones dedicated his later life to ideas he internalized from texts. He was concerned with the core values of society. Lewis Coser suggests that "men of ideas" have an "unusual sensitivity to the sacred" and are the "descendants of the biblical prophets, those inspired madmen who preached in the wilderness far removed from the institutionalized pieties of court and synagogue. . . . They question the truth of the moment in terms of higher and wider truth; they counter appeals to factuality by invoking the 'impractical ought.'" Sam Jones had just begun to invoke the "impractical ought." He would become a striking anomaly because he would take his "unusual sensitivity to the sacred" and his invocation of the "impractical ought" to the center of Toledo's government. Sam Jones is unusual in that he brought the discussion of justice and truth to the marketplace and the seat of municipal power.[43]

Clearly, Sam Jones carried explicitly religious ideas with him to the marketplace and the mayor's office. George Herron was the only cleric who directly influenced Jones's thought, but his career must be seen in the context of the Social Gospel movement. It was a minority movement in the liberal Protestant churches, but it became so vocal it helped define Protestantism for a generation. By the time Sam Jones met him, Washington Gladden had become its most articulate spokesperson. Like Jones, Gladden had come to a new vision of Christianity in response to the harsh urban conditions of Cincinnati. Walter Rauschenbusch, the movement's most systematic theologian, also came to reunderstand Christianity when faced with the terrible poverty in his Hell's Kitchen parish.

It was not until after Sam Jones began implementing his new experiments in industrial righteousness that the movement became known as the Social Gospel. In February 1898, a Christian communal community in Georgia, influenced by Herron, published a magazine, the *Social Gospel,* that gave a name to the movement that had been stirring in liberal Protestant circles. The first issue declared that the journal's purpose would be "to inspire faith in the economic teachings of Jesus, and courage to put them into life. . . . The Social Gospel is the brotherhood of man and the fatherhood of God. . . . It is the proclamation of the kingdom of heaven, a divinely ordered society, to be realized on earth. It is the application of Christ's Golden Rule and Law of Love to all the business and affairs of life." By the time these words were published, the sentiment was being used to govern Toledo, Ohio, as well as Commonwealth, Georgia. The Social Gospel was the most significant change in Protestant theology since the Second Great Awakening. It redefined salvation, the nature of God, and religious commitment. Salvation was no longer seen as a private individual concern but as a social question. Jones shared with this movement the conviction that the Kingdom of God was not something to look forward to in the next world but to work for in this one.[44]

Sam Jones shared some of the basic assumptions of the proponents of the Social Gospel. Influenced directly by Herron, he was friends with Gladden, W.D.P. Bliss, and Rauschenbusch. The movement can be seen as a complex response to late nineteenth-century American culture: the violent labor conflicts of 1877, 1886, and 1892-94; America's religious pluralism; the absence of a state church; and a characteristically American hopefulness and feeling of liberation which overshadowed the pessimistic perspective.[45]

Sam Jones's reading brought him to the convictions shared by many in the growing social Christianity movement. Over the course of the next several years he decided that the social order needed to be entirely reconstituted, which is to say that Sam Jones was becoming a Christian socialist. Jones eventually went further than those who advocated the Social Gospel. Christian socialism takes as its starting point an idea essential to the Social Gospel, the unity of humankind, but moves beyond that assumption to argue against private property. Property should not be privately owned because land and resources belong to God. As W.D.P. Bliss put it, Christian Socialism "is not one reform. It is many reforms on one *principle*. Perhaps most important of all is land reform. Christian Socialism would revert to the Bible principle, that God is the owner of all the earth, and men only entitled to its use." Its advocates argued that society has a responsibility to care for the poor and supported the eight-hour movement, direct legislation, and municipal socialism. As Jones came to see it, "Municipal ownership and home rule will lead us to see . . . that city is not truly rich that has a single pauper within its limits. It will teach us that we can only be truly patriotic when we study the welfare of all. It will teach us that if there is a single man within the limits of our city denied the right to work and to enjoy the fruits of his toil in bringing out the best manhood and citizenship that is in him, every man and woman who is enjoying reasonable comfort is morally guilty of the injustice done to the man denied the right to work." Christian socialists went further than the advocates of the Social Gospel in arguing that competition is the anarchy that destroys society—and Sam Jones would come to argue precisely that.[46]

Sam Jones never looked to the institutional church as the force that could implement change, and he was in good company. His friend Benjamin Flower's rhetoric was harsher in attacking the church than Jones's would ever be, but he agreed with the sentiment that urban churches were places of "cowardice and lethargy," "rich in gold but poor . . . in moral energy." Reformers as diverse as the philosophers John Dewey and Josiah Royce, the sociologist Franklin Giddings, writer-reformers William Allen White and Frederic Howe, as well as Jane Addams, all raised in evangelical Protestant households, looked to other solutions than the church to solve the problems of urban America. Like Bliss, editor of the *Dawn* and founder of the Society of Christian Socialists, as mayor Jones published as regularly as his schedule allowed; both men remained enthusiastically committed to the belief that people needed to be educated by a unified reform movement for the new social order to be realized. Even Stead and Gladden, both ministers, moved beyond the church, turning to fiction and politics respectively to transform America. Gladden was more interested in the redemption of social institutions than he was in personal salvation. Nevertheless, the various reforms of all were rooted in a vision of community inspired by the Bible.[47]

Early in his reform career, when still an advocate of social Christianity rather than Christian socialism, Jones would seek to reform two institutions: the workplace and the city. Sam Jones would first seek to institutionalize selflessness in business. His reforms would give him a unique opportunity, first as a manufacturer and then as mayor, to put into practice the ideas of Lloyd, Herron, Tolstoy, Ruskin, and Mazzini. He set about proving that the Golden Rule could work in this world. Washington Gladden thought that "a fierce egoism has dragged the industrial world to the brink of chaos." Sam underlined the following sentence: "The want of a Christian temper has brought us into this trouble; and the cultivation of a Christian temper is the one thing needful to bring us out of it." Gladden ends the paragraph and the chapter "The Labor Question," underlined by Sam: "Thou shalt love thy neighbor as thyself." Sam writes, filling the page: "THEREFORE ALL THINGS WHATSOEVER YE WOULD THAT MEN SHOULD DO UNTO YOU, DO YE EVEN SO UNTO THEM." THAT WILL SOLVE THE WHOLE PROBLEM. AT ONCE."[48] He scrawled those words early on, before coming to see it might not be as simple as that.

PART 2

Factory and Municipal Reforms

4

Produce Great Persons, the Rest Follows

Sam Jones's strategies to institutionalize selflessness in business were the immediate outgrowth of his reading and his new religious self-consciousness. He had every confidence that the men, his factory, and the neighborhood—perhaps even the industry—could be transformed. Having placed the Golden Rule at the center of his business and his personal life, he turned next to reordering the environment. He wanted nothing less than a reconfiguration of space and time, but he knew an ethical and just working environment would require Americans to rethink their assumptions about the values of space and time and their commitment to the community. At the expense of his own profits, he created a space for the surrounding community to enjoy itself: he called it Golden Rule Park. Among oilmen, he became a vociferous advocate for the eight-hour workday. He had expanded his scope, seeking to influence the surrounding neighborhood and the power brokers in the Western Oil Men's Association. Jones proclaimed his new intent to the neighborhood community, inscribing a Whitman text for all to see on an exterior wall at the Acme Sucker Rod factory: "Produce Great Persons, the Rest Follows." People needed space and time to breathe and to think, to know their own value in order to become great. Sam Jones was enthusiastic about Golden Rule Park and an eight-hour workday because these reforms connected with his own deeply felt personal needs. His entire life story made the idea of creating community not only intellectually but emotionally compelling.

Community is not a given, it is a task. His factory reforms sought to build community, to bridge the gaps of language, religion, and traditions among his workers. Personally, Jones found he also needed to bridge the gap his wealth created, separating him from his employees. Being a member of the upper middle class, Jones now discovered, had cultural and ideological as well as economic dimensions. His money provided him with the status he had long been seeking, but it made him terribly uncomfortable. He quickly learned he was much more comfortable with working-class culture and ideology. His own sense of identity and his personal charisma enabled him to relate to workingmen. He had a smoother transition in adjusting the system within his factory than in adjusting his relations with the world of wealthy businessmen.

Looking back on his decision to run a factory on the Golden Rule and writing to someone living the great communal experiment at Commonwealth, Georgia, Jones realized it had not been well thought out: "We simply made an attempt to love [the men] and act about as we would want them to act toward us, if our positions were reversed." It was, he thought, "a crude idea of the Golden Rule and it is not at all in harmony with the radical views that I now hold, but. . . . I unhesitatingly say that there has been a complete moral transformation not only in the lives of the men, but actually in the neighborhood where our factory is located."[1]

There was considerable need for both economic and moral transformation in Toledo. The oil industry played an essential role in the economic transformation, which, in turn, heightened the need for moral transformation. While Jones was at work on Segur Avenue, oil was bringing prosperity back to Toledo, but with prosperity came difficult social problems. Frederick Law Olmsted, who designed Central Park, thought that the central moral problems of the rapidly expanding American cities were not vice and crime but the "erosion of the social bond, the deadening of human sensitivity, and the loss of opportunity for reflection and repose." Cities were, he thought, "enervating" places where selfish interests were pursued with "devouring eagerness." Sam Jones had some sense of this as he surveyed the streets surrounding his factory. Toledo was not a single-industry town: Libbey glass, railroads, and urban rail lines all contributed to the city's rapid demographic growth. Toledo was home to 50,000 people in 1880, 81,000 in 1890, and nearly 132,000 in 1900. With eighty-seven churches and more than twenty languages and dialects spoken and the transient sailors, stevedores, and oilmen, Toledo was a diverse, often rough, town. The "tenderloin district," down by the Maumee River, covering Summit, St. Clair, Superior, and Lafayette Streets, offered the enticements of houses of prostitution, saloons, faro banks, poker rooms, and crap joints.[2] There did not seem to be much to bind Toledo's people together into a community. Experiments on a small scale were taking place on Segur Avenue, but they were not yet attracting the city's attention.

Sam Jones worked alone at this point, but others, such as Olmsted and Jane Addams, were already arguing that the city was an alienating force. Addams's autobiography suggests that she experienced an isolation that may well have been comparable to Jones's feelings when she first went to the city, feeling forlorn as a stranger in an unfamiliar place. Addams felt the "quick sense of human fellowship" when the hotel waiter brought her breakfast. Quickly she realized that "it would be grotesque to claim from him the sympathy you crave because civilization has placed you apart, but you resent your position with a sudden sense of snobbery."[3] It was worse for Jones because, unlike Addams, whose life was nothing like her waiter's, he felt "civilization" had separated him from his own kind. The natural bonds of community had been broken by his great wealth so he sought to recreate human fellowship.

Creating true community was, for Jones, a religious avocation. The "religious condition of working men" Jones argued, was a direct result of the connection between employer and employee. "It follows that my religious condition will be reflected in the condition of those most closely related to me"—his employees. He thought that "it is as certain that the immorality which I am practising by using my fellow men as mere instruments to gather profit will be reflected in their lives as the virus of small-pox is certain to show itself when injected into the human body."[4] For Jones, then, traditional "vices" reflected badly on the wealthy industrial class, not the laborers.

As Sam Jones rejected the exploitation of his men, he was less successful at rejecting the trappings of Gilded Age America and living a selfless life at home. His discomfort with his own wealth is clearest in two upper-middle-class gestures: international travel and a grand new house. To soothe his reform conscience, he balanced the traditional tourist destinations with research about factory and municipal reforms. In his first trip, to Mexico with Helen and Paul, he was impressed with the wonderful social life he witnessed in Aquas Calientes, where free public baths were available to the thirty-five thousand inhabitants. In contrast, Toledo's population, which was four times larger, had no public swimming pool and citizens who sought relief from Ohio's summer heat by swimming in the Maumee River were arrested. On a European tour the next year, he balanced traditional stops, such as St. Mark's Square, Venice, with a carriage trip out to the Romanian oil fields to witness pumps operated with horse power. Jones was sufficiently interested in public policy issues that he investigated the municipally owned transportation services in Glasgow. Even the most emotional aspect of the trip, a triumphant homecoming to the village of Beddgelert, Wales, became, at least retrospectively, a lesson in socialism. (*NR*, 74-76).

Sam Jones was sufficiently romantic about his own past to return not only to Wales but later to Collinsville for a reunion with family and friends and to Pithole to see the ghosts of a town that once was. In Wales he saw his birthplace through the eyes of a reformer: his autobiographical handling of the trip does not mention reunion with family and friends but records only sources for despair. The visit to Beddgelert was good, but it was "marred by the contemplation of the same wrongs I look upon in this city . . . the social injustices that doomed my ancestors, my father and my mother, to a life of bitter hardship and toil for the benefit of the privileged classes."[5] This is one of the rare examples when he cast the problem in class terms; it is also one of the rare instances when Sam considered not his own suffering or that of Toledo's unemployed but the plight of his own parents. Jones was very conscious of them, of his own upbringing, of his place in the world.

On his return, at the train station, he met with the rewards of his community-building experiments. Only his brother Dan was expected to meet them, but when Helen, Paul, and Sam stepped off the train, they saw all the men of the Acme Sucker Rod Company there to greet them. Waving hats and hands they shouted as a chorus, "Welcome home, Mr. Jones!" "You don't know," he told Gladden, "how that went through me! It did me more good than it would to have all the owners of bob-tailed horses in Toledo there to meet me."[6] More comfortable with his men than in the trappings of a gentleman, he rejected the waiting carriage and took the streetcar home with his employees.

Jones would turn his attention to space as an agent for community reform, but he remained in the traditional mode at home. The Joneses built a new house on Monroe Street, a grand three-story house with a large front porch extending over the face of the house. In an attempt to mask his embarrassment, he gave a party for the men and their wives as soon as the family was settled. In 1898, when the country was pushing to control Cuba and expand its territories into the islands of Asia, Sam cast himself as the victim of his architect, who "in spite of me, built a big house that is not in harmony with my idea of a home, aesthetically or artistically, but it is in perfect harmony with the prevailing ideas among people who believe in 'expansion,' and want to make a display. The best apology that I can make for being led into such an error was to have carved on the door sill this inscription, 'A wide house to lodge a friend.'" Sam also etched into the horse block in front of the house the Welsh words "Tan y Dderwn," or "Under the Oaks." His inspiration was Ty Mawr, the house he had been born in, which was known as "Tan y Craig," or "Under the Rock."[7]

Visits to Henry Demarest Lloyd's house, the Wayside, sheltered in Hubbard's Woods in the town of Winnetka, north of Chicago, may have been a model for what such a house could become. Lloyd had remodeled an old inn on Sheridan Road so it continued the purpose for which it was built—hospitality. In its new life it became a salon for all sorts and conditions of reformers. Sam Jones frequently visited the Wayside, joining congenial guests around the table—union and labor leaders, settlement house residents from Chicago, New York, and Boston, sweatshop workers, farmers, mugwump journalists, clerics who preached the Social Gospel, Fabians, and single-taxers. His own house came to share something of this ambience. Over the years, speakers at Golden Rule Park would lodge with the Joneses. The home was scarcely ever without a guest. "I learned to expect," remembered Helen Jones, "that Mayor Jones would announce a luncheon guest with so little as a half hour's notice, and it could be any person from one of his oil workers to a New York lawyer."[8] As that implicit class-conscious comment suggests, Helen looked at the world in traditional ways. Sam was far more likely to have been hostage to Helen's wishes than those of his architect. There is considerable evidence to suggest that there was increasing marital tension. The evidence of Helen's social philosophy is more elusive, but still suggestive, during Jones's life, but after his death, the record is clear: Helen Beach Jones was no socialist. She lived until 1939 and remained a prominent member of Toledo society. The facts of her final thirty-five years are utterly at odds with the life she shared with Sam Jones for twelve years.

The structure of Sam and Helen's marriage differed from that of his marriage to Alma. He was now a successful businessman whose business was no longer centered in the home. Helen could not watch a well for him or tend the boiler as Alma had for the boiler and the wells were far removed from her front yard. Helen and Sam did not share domestic tasks or devote a day to doing the wash together—they had no need to because he could afford to hire servants so that Helen was free. Helen and Sam had a marriage unlike his first and unlike his parents'. It had become the new model for middle-class marriage, but from Jones's perspective there may have been some dissatisfaction because it was foreign to his experience.[9] Even if Helen had shared his philosophy, the changed nature of middle-class marriage meant that she was not a part of his life as Alma had been a part of his first life or as his mother, Margaret, had been a part of Hugh's life.

These frustrations, if present, probably remained unconscious, but they were not the only problem. There are strong suggestions that fundamentally Helen did not agree with the philosophy of selflessness her husband now advocated. In one of the most poignant revelations that suggest the tensions in their marriage, in 1899, he wrote to his eldest sister, Alice: "My own dear wife sometimes, I think, half fears that I am loving the poor so much that she will be robbed of the portion that is her due."[10]

In the years after his death, Helen Jones became Toledo's preeminent club woman. Her picture frequently appeared in the Society section of the

Blade in later years. In 1908, under such a picture ran the caption: "Mrs. S.M. Jones: Director of the Eurydice Club, who has recently returned after a summer in Europe." Perhaps the most suggestive statement Sam made about his relations with Helen was the comment in 1899 to his sister Nell that "those nearest me cannot see but that I am making a mistake; they considerately call it 'going too far.'"[11]

The Acme Sucker Rod Company prospered; Jones's patent provided him a monopoly that secured his success and tormented his conscience. From the start, it seems, his great wealth was a serious burden. To a startled friend he once said, "If I don't look out I'll become a millionaire, and what should I do with a million?" Jones seems to have been haunted by the story in Matthew of the young man who had always kept all the commandments and who asked what must *he* do to be saved; Jesus replied, "If thou wilt be perfect, go and sell what thou hast, and give to the poor, and thou shalt have treasure in heaven." As Jones saw it, Jesus did not mince words; Jones wrestled with the realization that "like all worshippers of Mammon, I soothe my conscience with honeyed words, and try to believe that I can 'do so much good' with private property, that I know in reality is the fruit of other people's toil." His friend Arthur Henry felt, after three years' intimate acquaintance, "that the rapidity with which his wealth increases, and his inability to use it for the real benefit of either himself or mankind, is a constant and deep distress to him."[12]

As Jones's political ideology developed, he instituted other important reforms among his employees, all geared to create community: a settlement house, a free kindergarten, and co-operative insurance. He was always willing to underwrite such reforms; they were only the smallest gesture of abiding by Jesus' admonition to the young wealthy man. The first essential reforms belonging to this prepolitical period attempted to create an atmosphere that might foster more humanity in the lives of the poor by providing working people with space and time to enjoy life. Sam Jones was one of the earliest municipal reformers to improve urban life by creating recreational parks to improve the environment. Within a few years the park movement was seen as one of the most forceful and successful social reform programs of the era.[13]

Jones's thinking was far ahead of that of the Toledo electorate on the importance of public parks. In 1887, the Toledo park commissioners had observed that the public was not ready to support a park system. As early as 1884, a special bond issue that would have used $250,000 to convert the old canal bed into a park was rejected by the voters. The *Blade* blamed the city brewers who controlled the "bummer" vote for the rejection—perhaps they feared that parks would lure people away from their beer gardens. A second bond was defeated—7,372 to 2,040—in 1886, which would have placed the money in the hands of a board appointed by the governor. Toledoans seem to have feared that too much land would come off the tax rolls, thus increasing the city's debt and decreasing its future ability to pay it off.[14]

Jones's interest in parks began simply and seems to have been something of an afterthought. Business was progressing very satisfactorily at the Acme Sucker Rod Company, and the management looked around for a place to build a foundry. At first, Sam intended to purchase the lot adjacent to the factory and erect the foundry there. Instead, he decided to raze the dilapidated buildings and transform the land into a park and playground. Golden Rule Park occupied nearly an acre along Segur Avenue. The Acme Sucker Rod shop wall, with flowers planted at the base, and a high wall with Whitman's words—"Produce great persons, the rest follows"—edged the park on the other two sides. There were no ornamental bushes or a fountain: it was a park to be *used*. Benches placed under shade trees provided a place for friends and neighbors to visit while little boys in knickers and girls in long dresses whirled by on the swings or the maypole. Neighborhood children could be seen there at almost any time of day. Frank Carlton, professor of economics at the University of Wisconsin, accompanied Jones to the park and thought it a little oasis in the industrial desert for the neighboring families.[15]

On Sunday afternoons adults gathered to listen to music or to speakers who came from across the country. Here Jane Addams of Hull House, Eugene Debs, soon to become the perennial Socialist candidate for president, Dr. John H. Kellogg of Battle Creek, Michigan, and Dr. J.D. Buck, the "eminent theosophist," talked on subjects ranging from "brotherhood" to "direct legislation" and "the union label" to sympathetic crowds. An estimated twenty thousand people attended Sunday afternoon meetings during the first summer alone. Jones tried to make it an ecumenical forum. An estimated 3,000 gathered to hear Toledo's first free outdoor music concert in 1897, when the Toledo Musicians Union gave a band concert. One summer afternoon in 1897, the people listened to an agnostic, a rabbi, and a Protestant minister speak about the Golden Rule. The atmosphere was unusual for such talks, what with the squeal of streetcars scraping by on one side and the sound of children laughing on the other. Often when Jones spoke, young children would leave the swings or the sandpile and crowd down front, hanging on to the edge of the platform. From Jones's vantage point, the first thing to be seen was a row of faces looking curiously up at him and a border of little fingers all along the front of the platform. The factory wall served as backdrop: on it was painted: "Every Man who is willing to work has the right to work. Divide the Day and Give him a Chance. S.M. Jones" All this cost Sam Jones about $500 a year.[16] The park, like the crowds content to spend a Sunday afternoon thus, is long gone.

Golden Rule Park covered only the lot adjacent to Jones's factory, but it offered the residents of Segur Avenue's working-class neighborhood many of the amenities larger, grander parks offer—fresh air, recreation, amusement, relaxation. The idea for the park had its origins in Ruskin, who argued that "wealth" is not money, it is life. Golden Rule Park enriched the lives of those who played there, rested and relaxed there, listened to music or to new ideas there.[17]

Many American cities preceded Toledo in recognizing the importance of public recreation. The year Jones became mayor, the Board of Park Commissioners reported that Toledo spent $5 per capita on parks: only five other cities of the twenty-seven studied spent less. That was true despite a major parks campaign in the 1890s, led by Sylvanus P. Jermain, secretary of the successful Woolson Spice Company. Jermain, like Olmsted and Jones, believed that parks were essential for the sake of both beauty and sanity. A grand plan for what was called the Toledo Boulevard had been proposed during Jones's first term: a one-hundred to four-hundred foot-wide parkway would connect all the parks with a paved path "for man, beast and bicyclist" in a circle around the entire city. As mayor in 1899, Jones drove the horses and plow that began the pathway connecting Ottawa Park to Walbridge Park as the first step in creating the Toledo Boulevard. Jermain (appointed to the board by Jones in 1897) became chairman of the Board of Park Commissioners, but he and Jones together could not sustain this ambitious plan. The pathway completing all the parks was never finished.[18]

Perhaps it was his trip to California in 1895 that convinced Jones of the importance of public recreation. Nothing he ever saw elsewhere in the world stirred his soul as did Yosemite Valley; he hoped that someday government ownership of the railways would bring the cost of the journey to Yosemite within "the reach of multitudes of our people." As it was, they had no more hope of seeing its "incomparable beauty" than if they lived on the moon (*NR*, 74-75).

Creating Golden Rule Park led Sam Jones to producing playground equipment, in particular maypoles. He was in the forefront of a movement embraced by the Progressives. While today we assume that parks are places where children play, the original impetus for building parks was rooted in a Wordsworthian conviction that contact with "Nature" would ennoble the soul. Those who argued, like Joseph Lee, known as "the Father of American playgrounds" and President of the Association of American

Playgrounds, that "play is the intensest part of the life of a child and it is therefore in his play hours that his most abiding lessons are learned" had a very different assumption about the use of parks. The two perspectives clashed with an intensity we would find surprising. The depression of 1893 virtually stopped the creation of playgrounds, but by 1897 and 1898, they were introduced, or reintroduced, in Chicago, Philadelphia, New York, and Baltimore. Jones sold the playground equipment he produced to public institutions at cost. Jane Addams wrote him about the maypole he sent to Hull House: "We are greatly pleased with the Giant Stride. It is the finest piece of apparatus that we have, and the children are filled with pride and pleasure with its possession."[19]

Playgrounds were an urban reform strategy that evoked great enthusiasm in the Progressive era. Jacob Riis, whose photographic documentary *How the Other Half Lives* shocked middle-class sensibilities, thought that playgrounds were among the most "wholesome counterinfluences to the saloon, street gang, and similar evils." More than a decade after Jones's death, the rhetoric still was enthusiastic and the idea had gained more prestigious supporters. In 1916, Jane Addams joined W.D.P. Bliss, the Social Gospel leader, with the U.S. commissioner of education and former president Theodore Roosevelt in support of city playgrounds. The president of the American Civic Association spoke for all of them in arguing that playgrounds provide a "powerful tool against the forces of evil."[20]

As mayor, Jones brought in an expert to create a thriving park system in Toledo. Stoyan Vasil Tsanoff had established the Culture Extension League in Philadelphia, which had established fifty playgrounds. He went on to have a similar influence in Manhattan before he came to Toledo at Mayor Jones's invitation. Two playgrounds were established by the Children's Playground Association, with Tsanoff as director: Smokey Hollow on Canton Street and one in City Park on Nebraska Avenue. Mayor Jones spoke at the opening of the playgrounds. He observed that it had taken Americans too long to realize that open areas where children could play ball in a corner of a park were not sufficient. They needed play equipment because play is as necessary to a child's proper development as is work for a man or woman: "No child can be a natural, healthy, hopeful, happy, useful child without opportunities for play, for vigorous, inspiring, exercise." He thought that Toledo should have one hundred playgrounds for its estimated twenty thousand children and hoped that soon playgrounds would be seen as essential to the municipality as the streets or parks because "they are equally important, equally necessary."[21]

Under Jermain's leadership and with the mayor's enthusiastic cooperation, a greenhouse and a zoo were constructed at Walbridge Park. Electric lighting was added to all parks. In 1900, Toledo opened the first public golf course west of New York City so that adults could benefit from park exercise as well. Ottawa Park's golf course had the mayor's support because it was free.[22] Clearly, Jones's success with parks and playgrounds first improved the lives of those in Segur Avenue's working-class community and then inspired changes in Toledo as a whole.

The Golden Rule factory owner sought to shape space in other significant ways. A trip to Hull House in Chicago in early 1896 had impressed Jones with the impact a settlement house could have on the city's poor. Jones seems to have impressed those at Hull House as well. The secretary for the Social Science Club remembered that the only speaker they had ever had who "had been able to overcome all [the members'] dogmatic differences" was Samuel Jones. In 1898, he purchased a house across the street from the factory at 621 Segur Avenue, which he named Golden Rule House; he brought his sister Nell up from Lima to run it. Nell Jones became a friend of Jane Addams's, and she ran the Golden Rule House along the principles of Hull House. Nell lived at Golden Rule House and ran a kindergarten there until the public schools took over the work. That same year, on Thanksgiving Day 1898, Jones opened Golden Rule Hall, a room above the factory, where people could meet or listen to visiting speakers to study the idea of brotherhood. In 1901, Jones built a dining room to bring the men in closer relations with one another; the company operated the dining room, offering a hot meal for fifteen cents. All these initiatives were the logical outgrowth of his Ruskinian conviction that making men was as important work as making money. Nell managed the dining hall, the company lost about $60 a month subsidizing the meals, and the Golden Rule mayor bicycled over from his downtown office every day to eat with his employees. He tried to convey how important all this was, "how much like men it makes us feel," knowing that part of their time was devoted to learning how to help one another.[23] Sam Jones rearranged both space and time and in so doing made a more livable environment.

Sam Jones's name is closely associated with the eight-hour-day movement, the most important reform regarding time in the progressive period. Jones was the first mayor in the country to establish an eight-hour day for city servants such as firefighters and police. Providing space for relaxation and refreshment was simple compared with the struggle to provide workingmen time off from work. American factory workers characteristically put in twelve-hour shifts, seven days a week, with only the Fourth of July off as a holiday. Jones rejected outright the Malthusian notion that subsistence wages were essential for the good of the global community. He paid his workers higher wages while offering shorter shifts in the belief that these were their right. As early as 1896 Jones instituted an eight-hour day in his oil fields at the Acme Oil Company. He also avidly promoted the idea among other oilmen before he became a political figure. Although he was slower to institute the eight-hour day in his factory, there is no doubt that he saw it as a reform that would simultaneously improve an individual's working conditions and alleviate the unemployment problem. He wrote the pamphlet *The Eight-Hour Day in the Oil Fields* to distribute among oilmen. In the thirty years he had been in the oil business he had seen technological improvements, but "there has not been one particle of improvement in the condition of the oil well worker. . . . All of the benefit arising from the introduction of machinery goes to the owners of the machine," none to its operators. According to Sam Jones, "there is no justification for this condition whatever in the domain of *right* and *wrong*." His pamphlet asked a Ruskinian question: "Why should there not be improvement in the methods of distributing the earnings of the machine?" Answering that question accounts for all of Jones's reforms: he attempted to improve the distribution of the earnings of his improved sucker rod through his investment in Golden Rule Park, Golden Rule House, better wages, paid vacations, a 5 percent bonus, cooperative insurance, and his decision to "divide the day."[24]

Sam did not just appeal to manufacturers on this subject, he reached workers directly. In 1897, he copyrighted a song, "Divide the Day—A Practical Reply to the Question 'WHAT SHALL WE DO FOR THE UNEMPLOYED?'" He wrote the words; Helen wrote the music. It was frequently heard at his public appearances, first as candidate and later as mayor. The words to "Divide the Day" are corny, certainly:

> Divide up the day, and it soon will be found
> That there's plenty of food to reach all around;
> When father has work, there'll be no lack of bread,
> Nor innocent children go hungry to bed.

But the corniness is a measure of how Jones could appeal to his men. Unlike George Herron, Henry Demarest Lloyd, John Ruskin, and Leo Tolstoy, Sam Jones could appeal to workingmen because he was one of them.

By Christmas 1897, after the eight-hour day had been tried in the oil fields for a year, it could hardly be deemed a success: it cost the Acme Oil Company money. But the company's president, now Toledo's mayor, was unwilling to go back to the old ways. Jones wrote in his annual Christmas message to the workers of the Acme Oil Company that 180 men were employed whereas at twelve hours a day 120 had been employed. In the first year thirty wells had been drilled: "The Acme Oil Company will never go back to the twelve-hour plan. There are 100s of drillers who can't find one hour's work. Why should we *ask* or *allow* others to work twelve hours? . . . The Acme Oil Company has not made *any money. We may never make any.* No matter, we will continue to *stand flat* on the Golden Rule."[25]

Sam Jones always would be a vocal advocate of the eight-hour day; he seems not to have appreciated that others would resist institutionalizing selflessness in business. He frequently told oilmen who were churchgoers that "they might as well quit praying and going to church, and quit saying complimentary things about God" unless they put the eight-hour day into practice and provided jobs for more men. One friend thought Jones had written him with "a bad spell on" when he received a letter from Toledo's mayor saying that he would pay all the extra costs that might be involved should Jim Harrison switch to the eight-hour day. Even that offer to underwrite the experiment found no one willing to take the chance. Sam would write in late 1898 that for two years he had been "pleading for the eight-hour day, both by precept and by example, and so far not one operator, in the church or out, has joined me in it. I have written hundreds of letters and made personal appeals, but all in vain."[26]

Business owners were not the only ones who resisted Jones's ideas. He met resistance in his own company. In trying to make "great persons," Sam Jones did not make it easy on himself by actively seeking the best men. In fact, he seems to have preferred to pass those men by. Forgetting, it seems, how much his own desperate hopes had depended on a letter of recommendation at Pithole, when men applied to him for work with such letters, he refused to look at them, saying, "If you have recommendations, anybody will help you to a place. I must help those who have none." The business end of the factory, as opposed to "producing great persons," was largely in the hands of his brother Daniel, who did not share his elder brother's perspective. There were weekly complaints about problems resulting from slackers—or worse. A drunken employee injured a company horse by driving it into a telephone pole; he received no reprimand from Jones, who got his Bible and read the story of the woman taken in adultery to whom Jesus said, "Go and sin no more." With that, the interview ended.[27]

His factory reforms required a certain selflessness from his employees and Jones sometimes encountered resistance from the people most likely to benefit from the cooperative ventures. Jones encouraged his men to join a trade union because it was a cooperative venture. While men at other factories all across America were being pressured to stay out of unions, Jones pressured those who resisted to join. He never spoke more sharply about what he expected of his employees than when he ardently supported a shop organizer trying to sign up recalcitrant workers: "We do not want any one to stay around us who is there simply and solely for himself."[28]

The company insurance plan deducted 1 percent of a worker's wage, which was matched by a deposit from the company. The fund was managed by the employees for use in sickness or injury. In urging the few men who remained outside the cooperative insurance program, Jones stressed that they must participate in cooperative ventures to help improve social conditions. Supporting Bryan or McKinley or Debs would not bring about better conditions; the men themselves must act: "How can you ever expect better social conditions unless you are willing to practice them? Suppose the thing is not managed to suit you; it cannot be improved by staying outside. YOU, everlastingly YOU, must do something yourselves, if we are ever to have better conditions." On some occasions Jones had to dig deeper into his pockets because the men would not embrace the level of selflessness required. The hot lunch was a case in point. When the program was set up, Jones had expected it to provide neither profit nor loss to the company or the employees. The company paid for the equipment, Nell Jones's management, and fuel; each employee was to pay fifteen cents to cover labor and food. They soon found it cost more than twenty-one cents. When Jones tried to get his men to increase their contribution to twenty cents, they refused. Jones suggested that they think of twenty cents as the price of five glasses of beer or five cigars; however, from the employees' perspective it represented 10 percent of their daily wages. The price remained fifteen cents. Jones willingly concurred. The $60 monthly loss was "well invested," he thought.[29]

The Golden Rule had become, to use William James's words, so fully *"the habitual centre of his personal energy"* that in two years, Sam Jones's ideas about business, the economy, capitalism, and himself had been transformed. He had become so convinced of the necessity of selflessness in business that he was willing to forgo profits in order to make men. Space and time were reconfigured so that the lives of working people could improve. Golden Rule Park brought fun to the neighborhood; Golden Rule Hall provided space for intellectual inquiry; the dining room allowed for fellowship and the opportunity to break bread together. Sam noticed a moral transformation of the neighborhood. Many of his employees felt it as well. He had not only transformed his thinking, he had transformed their lives. In hindsight, we can see that his reforms at this point were only partial, but already he experienced tension between his ideals and the combined force of his own limitations and the burden of guilt laid on him by family members.

Like Ruskin and Tolstoy, Samuel Jones believed that reform must come from within individual human hearts rather than from institutions in the form of new laws enacted or a new political party in power. His own heart had been changed, and it seemed clear to him that other hearts needed changing before oilmen would allow institutional change. Although his changes at his factory were institutional, he began them to reeducate his workers who did not believe in their own worth. That the men resisted co-operative benefits proved that their hearts needed changing too. Yet because his experiments with social reform were just beginning, Sam still believed that improvements could be made in institutions.[30]

His belief in the efficacy of systemic change was at its high point in 1896-97. He believed that as Toledo's mayor he would be able to change the institutions of government and so improve people's lives. He still believed that charity really helped people, and so he gave generously from his own fortune.

In political office, Jones would come to see that his first impulse was correct: changing things did not help; people needed changing. In holding that belief, Jones was heir to a long tradition of social reform extending throughout the nineteenth century. Although Sam Jones was a direct heir of recent American reformers, his impulse to reform the human heart aligns him with many English reformers. In England the Industrial Revolution altered landscape and lives beyond recognition long before it did so in America; those who believed in the need to reform the human heart fought the economic theories of David Ricardo, whose work provided the standard argument for free trade and the utilitarian formula of Jeremy Bentham. Not surprisingly, the reformers who took this position tended to be writers rather than politicians. Sam Jones is something of an anomaly when compared to those in the tradition who sought to reform the human heart: Samuel Taylor Coleridge, Thomas Carlyle, Charles Dickens, George Eliot, Frederick Denison Maurice, John Ruskin, and Leo Tolstoy. Unlike these writers, Sam Jones was in a position to deal with institutions. His later despair would come from the disjunction between his political position and his philosophical beliefs: as mayor he could legislate political reform, but no one can legislate the human heart. Like these others, Sam Jones was dismissed as a sentimentalist who did not understand the complexities of social problems. From Jones's perspective, this had nothing to do with sentiment; if he was wrong, then Christianity itself was wrong. In Herron's *The New Redemption* Sam had read and underscored: "If Christianity cannot be applied to the actual life of men, if the Golden Rule cannot be practiced in the market . . . then God has not spoken his truth and revealed his life in Jesus Christ."[31]

Mayor Jones demonstrates the High Kick.

Cartoon depicting Mayor Jones's morning exercises. Courtesy of *Toledo Blade*

Mayor Jones in casual conversation. Below, the mayor exercises at the Congress Street School.

The Jones home, Monroe Street, Toledo. Below, Sam Jones and Brand Whitlock in Whitlock's office

THE RULE THAT
GOVERNS THIS FACTORY
Therefore Whatsoever Ye Would
That Men Should Do Unto You
Do Ye Even So Unto Them

The Golden Rule at the Acme Sucker Rod Shop. Courtesy of Jones family. Below, children enjoy the playground at Golden Rule Park. Courtesy of Drake Well Museum.

S.M. Jones and his two sons, Percy and Paul. Courtesy of Toledo-Lucas County Public Library

S.M. Jones and second wife, Helen. Courtesy of Toledo–Lucas County Public Library

Holmden Street in Pithole. Below, Pithole despair: "For Sale Cheap." Courtesy of Drake Well Museum

"Ty Mawr," Samuel Jones's home in Wales. Courtesy of Marnie Jones. Below, view of Pithole, Pennsylvania. Courtesy of Drake Well Museum

Jones and the Gamblers and Saloon-Keepers. Courtesy of *Toledo Blade*

5

I Will Not Be the Mayor of Any Ring or Faction

On a blustery March night in 1897, fifteen days before the election, Sam Jones, dark horse Republican candidate for mayor of Toledo, strode into Felker's Hall at the corner of Hawley and Vance Streets half an hour late. He strode on stage, ignoring the podium. Jones told the crowd he felt uncomfortable standing high above them; after all, he had been down among the people all his life—that was where he belonged. The fifty-year-old candidate then sprang nimbly from the stage to the floor of the hall. The crowd shifted back and forth, craning to get a look at Golden Rule Jones. The people were on his side immediately because he had, quite literally, made his side theirs. His words only emphasized that connection. He "had done nothing in politics in this city," he boasted. He had not been in council, had not been a ward committeeman, and had "not even the honor to be a ward heeler." A voice blurted out, "More glory to you!"[1] Virtually no one in Toledo, at the start of the new year, could have imagined such a candidate.

Two months earlier, the Republican *Blade* had asked for just such a candidate, actively stirring up sentiment against Mayor Guy Major. The paper wanted a successful businessman, "not . . . a politician. . . . He should not be a member of any ring." The *Blade* continued the plea on Lincoln's birthday: "If ever Toledo was in need of a Moses to lead it out of the wilderness of municipal mismanagement, the time is now. For years it has been bound in the iron fetters of politics, politics for the furtherance of personal ambition." There was, it seems, little hope that a Moses was to be found: "From present indications history is about to repeat itself . . . before the Ides of March, the meek, humble, supplicating taxpayer will wake up, cautiously poke his head from beneath the bed covering, and wonder what has happened." It was, it would turn out, the people's plea too. Ironically, Jones's nomination, which seemed to be the answer to just those pleas, was the product of strident infighting among machine power brokers far removed from the newsroom of the Republican newspaper or the crowd at Felkers' Hall. The people might elect Jones their mayor, but the machine would make him its nominee. It was the greatest irony of a bizarre political convention.

While Sam Jones was working alone with little support from family and close friends, major movements were at work in the world attempting to respond to the new challenges of industrial life. To appreciate Sam's surprising appearance in the political arena, it is necessary first to consider both the political and the reform contexts. The Social Gospel movement was one response to the massive problems created by the chaos of life in newly industrialized cities. Political machines were another response. Neither was without its dark side, but in the age before the New Deal the machine provided important welfare functions in the immigrant communities. It set itself a more basic task than producing great persons. Machine bosses came to power because cities were structurally unprepared to deal with the huge influx of immigrants: eleven million between 1870 and 1900. City services could not deal adequately with the burdensome numbers so the machine stepped in. The Protestant church failed to meet the needs of the urban immigrants, inculcating the prejudice against the poor, who were often Roman Catholic or Jewish.[2] The *Toledo Blade* was so strident in its call for a reform-minded mayoral nominee because the city's Republican machine under the control of then mayor Guy Major was not likely to convince a dispassionate observer that his machine was good for the city. Reform had become the political rallying cry for both parties.

Reform in Toledo was made more difficult by the huge and unwieldly governmental structure. Toledo's original charter, in 1837, had provided the city with a mayor and an elected council of six. All other officials were appointed by the powerful council. Thirty years later, this system seemed to put too much power in the hands of a few. In 1870, prompted by the fundamental American distrust of government, the Ohio General Assembly had passed a charter that gave Toledo for the first time a two-house legislature: a board of aldermen, one from each ward, and a board of council, two from each ward. Toledo had fifteen wards during Sam Jones's tenure, which gave the city a common council of forty-five men. In addition, there were fourteen boards and commissions (from three to fifteen members each); six were elected; all were autonomous. In 1899, the *Blade* reported that 120 men legislated for Toledo, which came close to the number of legislators for the entire state. Clearly, by century's end, power had been dispersed among too many.[3]

Two years before Jones surfaced as a political force in Toledo, when the mayoral election of 1895 got under way, at the center of the scramble to control Toledo's mayor's office stood Guy Major, just completing his first term as Republican mayor. He did not hold much power because the bicameral city council oversaw the board system. Major tried to initiate reform, and the impulse ended his political career. When he searched out the inefficiencies in Toledo government, people held him responsible for the corruption uncovered.[4]

Toledoans bore the burden of an abnormally high tax rate; laborers and the middle class were taxed at the rate of 3.10 percent, in an effort to reduce the city deficit of almost $7 million. Toledo supported six thousand paupers the year Sam Jones became mayor. Meanwhile, Major's machine had bought votes with patronage, received kickbacks for city contracts from textbooks to sewer lines, and profited from prostitution and gambling. Looking to the future, political factions struggled for control of Toledo because huge profits could be made from city services. Technological breakthroughs such as electrifying the street railways and laying natural gas pipelines provided new opportunities for graft. The franchises for gas and electricity originally had been given to companies on generous terms so a great deal of money was being made by the utilities and the politicians. Workers began looking to other institutions for support: Toledoans had joined fifty to sixty labor unions and a Labor Union Party.[5]

Hazen Pingree's attempt to institute reforms in Detroit at the same time that Toledo began to consider reform helps make sense of Sam Jones's career. Pingree, born in Denmark, Maine, in 1840, had been a poor lad who had little education. A Union veteran who fought at the Battle of Second Bull Run and spent five months in Andersonville prison, he went to Detroit after the war, hearing of economic opportunities there. By the time Pingree attracted the attention of the important local Republican power brokers he was a wealthy man, running a successful shoe factory. He became a proponent of reform when a strike at his company in May 1885, led him to confront the reality of industrial problems. He agreed to arbitration and became a champion of that approach to ending labor-management conflicts.[6]

Pingree transformed the Republican Party to make it efficient, reform-oriented, and strong in the ethnic wards. His successes stand in contrast to Jones's inability to transform the Republican Party in Toledo. Pingree managed to turn the party's nativist and business biases into a useful tool for reform. Like Toledo's Mayor Major, Pingree had attempted to centralize municipal control by charter reform. He also was far more successful than Major in using his patronage power to achieve the central control necessary for a strong mayor. He succeeded in incorporating the strengths of the business world into his municipal administration.[7]

The depression of 1893 refocused Hazen Pingree in much the same way it redefined Sam Jones. Pingree began to identify himself and his administration, just as Jones was identifying himself, with the foreign-born urban working class. A new understanding of the plight of the unemployed prompted him to criticize those who had built their wealth on the backs of the laboring classes: "The vast accumulations of wealth," he wrote in 1895, "are more dangerous to the liberties of our republic than if all the Anarchists, Socialists and Nihilists of Europe were let loose on our shores."[8]

Guy Major was no Hazen Pingree. He won re-election in 1895 without the support of the Republican newspaper. The *Blade* endorsed the Democratic nominee, Parks Hone, under the slogan "Down with the Gang!" Walter Brown, a Harvard-trained lawyer, and Robinson Locke, editor of the Republican *Blade*, led an attack on Major, accusing him of "boodling" and inefficiency. Brown, who would control the Republican machine during Jones's mayoralty, and Locke, who would write searing editorials against Jones in the pages of the *Blade*, would support him in 1897 only to become his staunchest local enemies. Brown and Locke began their apprenticeship in frustration in 1895. Even against such opposition, the Major machine produced a victory, though by only sixty-seven votes.

Sam Jones was wholly dedicated at this time to forging community and "making great persons" at the Acme Sucker Rod Company. There was no reason in 1895 for Jones to see mayoral politics in nearby Detroit as a foreshadowing of his future. Nor was there any reason for the Toledo Republican regulars to worry that Major's narrow victory signaled the end of their control of city administration. But 1895 was the last election in a decade which Sam Jones did not dominate. And the Republican Party would flounder until 1913. The experiments on a small scale in one factory would, in the next two years, come to the forefront of municipal politics and policies.

As the mayoral campaign of 1897 approached, Toledo politics for the first time caught the interest of the national Republican machine. Ohio's William McKinley became president on March 4, 1897, midway through the Toledo campaign, and everything political in Ohio took on a new importance. Once in office, McKinley appeared weak; to some it seemed that Marcus Hanna, the Ohio senator, was all but running the country. The Spanish minister, Enrique Depuy de Lôme, who left Washington in diplomatic disgrace after disparaging McKinley just six days before the *Maine* exploded in Havana Harbor, observed: "For a long time past, I have not understood whether I was accredited to the government of the United States or the state of Ohio. There is the famous Mark Hanna, McKinley, Secretary Sherman, and the Honorable Mr. Day, all from Ohio. Some of you that I leave behind ought to investigate and determine whether Ohio runs the

United States or has merely annexed it as an outlying province. Possibly that is the reason of the annexation of Cuba."[9]

Ohio's fortunes were linked inextricably with the Republican Party: the Republicans had benefited in Ohio for years from the moral virtue associated with saving the Union. To hear Senator Joeseph B. Foraker campaign, one would have thought he had led the Army of the Potomac. Ohioans had voted Republican in every presidential election from the Civil War to the most recent election of their native son. Republicans held both U.S. Senate seats, a majority in the House of Representatives, the governor's mansion, and a majority of state legislative seats. Although it was somewhat unusual for an immigrant to have lifelong affiliation with the Republican Party, Sam Jones had been a Republican for as long as it had been possible to be one. Impressed initially with the party's stand against slavery, he continued until 1899 to believe it to be the party of the people—against all the evidence.

Two factions of the Republican machine were engaged in one of the most extraordinary fights in American political history. The Hanna-Foraker split influenced all Ohio politics until Hanna's death in 1904; Hanna's biographer calls it "one of the most extraordinary factional fights offered by the history of American politics. It . . . was notorious."[10] Mark Hanna was at odds with Senator Foraker, who was paid by Standard Oil while in the Senate to protect its interests. The local version of the fight resulted in a deadlocked convention and the turn to the dark horse candidate, Golden Rule Jones.

The statewide rivalry between Senator Foraker and Mark Hanna created the chaos that led to Sam Jones's surprise candidacy. Because of their power struggle, there was no clear mayoral candidate as the Republicans geared up for the primaries in late February. Neither Hanna nor Foraker had a comfortable hold on politics in Toledo, hence the statewide and even national attention. During Major's tenure, Colonel George P. Waldorf controlled the Hanna machine, while Major headed the Foraker machine. Major was so ineffectual, even though a Foraker man held city hall, that the Hanna machine did more to run Toledo. Each machine, therefore, had great interest in making sure it held city hall with a strong leader. The Hanna machine chose James Melvin, a seventy-year-old businessman of considerable integrity. Major went against his own machine to endorse Melvin.[11]

Republican businessmen actively sought a candidate to serve their interests rather than the interests of either machine. "No class of men should be as deeply interested in the spring election as the business men," wrote the *Blade*. "The future of the city depends largely on the selection of a mayor this spring." The Republicans were faced with a complicated race:

reform-minded businessmen supported John Craig, a Great Lakes shipbuilder. He also had the support of the politically astute Jim Ashley, son of a noted local abolitionist, a Hanna chieftain. Thus the Hanna machine was divided between the aging James Melvin, who had the primary machine support, and the reformer John Craig, supported by Ashley. Lem P. Harris, city clerk under Major and seen by some as his political heir, received some support from the Foraker machine. But because some thought Major would enter the race, elements of the Foraker machine did not support Harris. The week before the convention, the liquor dealers admitted that they would vote for Melvin, "but every one of us stands to switch to Major the moment the word is given."[12]

No one seemed to be speaking for labor. One day Sam Jones strode into the office of William Cowell, the editor of the weekly *Toledo Union*, wearing a large sombrero. He said he had a small shop on Segur Avenue. He had been greatly struck with a recent article and abruptly ordered forty subscriptions of the *Union* to be sent to his employees. Cowell was stunned: the paper had been struggling to survive so this was no small sale. Grateful, he offered Jones a discount. Jones turned the offer down immediately: he saw no reason why he should pay less than anyone else. Thereafter, Jones took to dropping in on Cowell and his partner, Mason Warner, on a regular basis. One day he took out a subscription for all of Toledo's Protestant clergy. His gift did not greatly increase the *Union*'s circulation; the news-paper seems to have outraged most of the ministers. But there were at least a few converts. Several sent money to Cowell and Warner to pay for their subscriptions themselves. The newsmen tried to repay Jones, but he told them to use the money to purchase subscriptions for others who might benefit from reading the *Union*. During one afternoon's visit as Jones was speaking, Warner passed a note to Cowell, suggesting that he would be the ideal mayoral candidate.[13]

The *Blade* wrote before the convention, "There are just two men in Toledo who don't want to be mayor—S. M. Jones and Frank L. King." In a small column in early February, the *Blade* noted that "very little had been said" about Jones as a candidate for mayor. The paper noted that workingmen and organized labor were pushing for his nomination: "Mr. Jones is well known throughout the city as president of the Oil Men's association, but is, perhaps, better known on account of his sociological views. As a sociologist, Mr. Jones practiced what he preached, as his employees will testify. All his men are devoted to him by reason of the fact that all are treated as brothers."[14]

On Thursday, February 25, the convention took place in Memorial Hall. The hall was packed—280 delegates, onlookers, the press, and the occasional Democrat—eager to find material to use in the campaign. The frustrated candidates and their "lieutenants," trying to shake as many hands as possible before the first ballot, had to fight their way across the room. Sam Jones was in the squeeze as well. It was so chaotic that it was not the ideal atmosphere for orderly business, but the chaos suited a private deal. Just such a deal would put the unsuspecting Sam Jones before the crowd as their mayoral candidate before the afternoon was out.

When the Toledo convention got down to the business at hand, the rousing nominating speeches somehow did not rouse the room. The result of the first ballot surprised the pols: the first surprise of a surprising day. The three top candidates were the Hanna machine's Melvin (123 votes), the Foraker machine's Harris (73), and the reformer Craig (56). Conventional wisdom had it that Melvin would be stronger and Harris weaker based on the strengths of the respective machines. On the second ballot Craig and Harris were the gainers—but not by much. Melvin remained locked in place on the third ballot, Harris lost three votes, and Craig gained two. No one had any momentum. By the fourth ballot, with the delegates bored and ready for lunch because it was 1:30 P.M., Melvin came within eleven votes of the number needed to win the nomination. In retrospect, there was one surprise: from the tenth ward, came one vote for Sam Jones.[15]

Sam Jones was the unexpected beneficiary of the stop-Melvin movement. While the ballots were being counted for this round, a deal was struck among those who did not want to see Hanna's man, Melvin, take the prize. Harry King, a prominent lawyer, suggested Jones. Police Commissioner John B. Merrell instructed King to do whatever was necessary to stop Melvin. King approached one of Harris's managers, William Fellows, in the aisle. With Harris losing strength, Fellows was willing to deal:

"We must down the ripper[16] gang," King said tersely. "We must do something promptly or Melvin will win out," King said.

"I think so, too. What shall it be?"

"Spring a dark horse."

"Who?"

"Any good man at all."

"Name him," said Fellows.

"Sam Jones," replied King.

"He will do for us, but you get Ashley. . . . Ashley must lead the way," Fellows warned. "We are afraid Jim might give us the slip if we flopped first.'"[17]

While all this was going on behind the scenes, Jones received 6 votes on the fifth ballot. Melvin had picked up some votes to reach 132; Harris and Craig dropped to 69, and 50 respectively. As the results were announced and the Melvin crowd cheered their candidate, occasional shouts for Jones could be heard. All this was backdrop to the conversation between King and Ashley. With his nominee, Craig, falling far behind, Jim Ashley was ready to deal. He went to the Craig forces in the ninth ward delegation, but the ninth ward delegates, led by Noah H. Swayne, a leading lawyer and son of a Supreme Court judge, were hard to please. Ashley finally asked a question he came to regret heartily over the next seven years: "How will Jones do?" Those who handed Jones the nomination thought him a sound party man with some useful eccentricities that would attract the labor vote.

Jim Ashley went before the convention, calling for order. He withdrew Craig's name, the delegates listening in tense silence to his words, and he offered to substitute in its place the name of a man "upon whom the party could unite and who could be nominated without leaving any sore spots to be healed over," a "sterling business man, the friend of labor, the friend of the poor, and a self-made honest man—the noblest work of God." So saying, he put before the convention the name of Samuel M. Jones, which was met with a great shout. Delegates from all of the wards jumped to their feet, yelling, throwing hats and tickets into the air: the noise was deafening. Cowell, sitting next to Jones in the tenth ward delegation, said that the new nominee stood up upon hearing his name to withdraw it, but he was pulled back into his chair by his coattails. Elsewhere on the floor, someone was heard to ask: "Who the hell is Jones?"[18]

The sixth ballot—Jones's first official ballot—went easily his way: Jones 168, Melvin 103. The *Bee* reported that "the look of blank amazement on Major's face was interesting. A moment before it was wreathed in smiles for he saw victory within his grasp." It was, the Democratic paper suggested, "a miniature reproduction" of Bryan's nomination for president the previous year; it was "just as impromptu and for the size of the crowd as wildly enthusiastic." Jim Ashley had successfully stampeded the convention. A year later Negley Cochran wrote in the same paper: "Jim Ashley is still entitled to much of the credit for being the discoverer of Sam Jones. Keep your distance, though, if you go remind Jim of it."[19]

Sam Jones tried to make his way from the tenth ward delegation up to the podium to speak to the crowd. Throughout the hall were heard shouts of "Jones, Jones!" The nominee, clearly emotional, began by telling the crowd he had been approached earlier in the winter to be a candidate but had turned all offers down. Now he saw it as a call of duty. He approached the prospect as "the greatest responsibility of my life." He prided himself, he told them, on being "the friend of the laboring man; I am prouder of

[that] distinction than of any other that could come to me. And I will not be the mayor of any ring, or faction, but of all the people, if at all."[20] He would keep that promise, much to Jim Ashley's chagrin.

The Republican *Blade* stated that "never in Toledo's history has there been such spontaneous enthusiasm over the nomination of a candidate for mayor." The triumphant headline announced: "Sam Jones Winner, A Splendid Man Nominated for Mayor, Good Dark Horse Defeated All Entries." For the next few days it looked as though he would be the candidate of all the people—including the politicians. Melvin, Harris, and Craig took their defeats with good grace; all said, to the press at least, that they thought the nomination of Jones a good one. All the political factions were pleased with Jones, at least for twenty-four hours, simply because though they lost, no one who mattered had won. Outgoing Mayor Major said, "If Jim Ashley can get any consolation out of it, he's welcome to it."[21]

Sam Jones profited by the political infighting in his own party though he never clearly saw it that way. He was such a visionary idealist that he could not work within the system. He was blind to the reality behind his sudden rise to political power—and he remained largely blind to political realities for the rest of his life. He cast his nomination as an exercise in democracy: the three candidates were deadlocked, he said, but "the people said they would nominate a rank outsider." Nothing could be further from the truth. Jones understood it as a result of his work at the Acme Sucker Rod factory: "It was all due to a little effort put forth to deal justly with our fellow-men" (*NR*, 81). Jones's nomination had nothing whatsoever to do with justice or brotherhood. The great irony of the election was that the machine had operated on the principle of undemocratic self-interest and had come up with a powerful symbol of selflessness—a man who lived brotherhood and empathy.

Sam Jones was a great campaigner because he had such tremendous empathy he could speak to the people from their own perspective. He generally scheduled three meetings a night because the party had ceased to perform this function. Because he was making the decisions he covered the whole city—all the wards, all the ethnic pockets.

Sam Jones's campaigns revealed his greatest talent: he knew naturally how to meet people on their own terms. He possessed tremendous energy and unflagging enthusiasm. Jones rode to his various campaign stops in a little buggy drawn by a white mare named Molly. After covering Molly with a blanket to keep off the chill night air, Jones hurriedly brushed her white hair from his chest with his large hands and bounded up the stairs into a dimly lit hall in Toledo's Polish neighborhood. The men, huddling about a stove in the middle of the hall, their caps on, their pipes going furiously, dressed in clothes from their native land, set up a shout when they saw him leap onto the stage. He did not wait to be introduced but called out: "What is the Polish word for liberty?" The crowd shouted out, "Wolnosc!" Jones listened, cocked his head, wrinkled his brow, and asked:

"What was that? Say it again!" Again they shouted—"Wolnosc!"

"Say it once more!" he worked the crowd. It came back at him louder still: "Wolnosc!"

"Well, I can"t pronounce it, but it sounds good, and that is what we are after in this campaign."[22]

The *Blade* got just what it had asked for—a candidate who was not a politician. But he was a great campaigner who was a natural orator with empathy for everyone. He campaigned so energetically because it gave him the opportunity to advocate his heartfelt personal beliefs.

Most important, campaigning provided him with a heady sense of connectedness to others, the feeling of brotherhood he needed. The campaign expanded the opportunities to express his contract of the heart: now he could articulate his faith in equality not just with his own employees but with all of Toledo. Sam Jones loved campaigning; the crowds energized him. He had advocated love as the operating principle of the world, and he had sought to build community at the Acme Sucker Rod Company for three years now. He met with some successes, but love in daily life is always complicated. On the campaign trail it was not. When he spoke before a campaign crowd, the love he felt came radiating back at him. Both speaker and crowd felt the common bond, the unity that made them a community, if only for an hour. No wonder he loved it so. It helped heal the childhood hurt, it provided him the reassurance he sought at home, and it seemed to demonstrate the truth of the principles he argued.

Jones's campaign meetings always had an educational as well as a religious aspect. His speeches covered themes with titles such as "The Right to Work," "Abolition of the Contract System," "Public Ownership of Public Utilities," and "The Golden Rule as Against the Rule of Gold." The meetings were frequently laced with quotations from his favorite authors or verses and songs written by the candidate himself. After one speech in the 1899 election a gentleman observed, "This seems more like a University Extension lecture than a political rally."[23]

He determined not to build a political machine. In speaking to a crowd in the third ward, the home ward of his Democratic opponent, Parks Hone, Jones said, "Some thought I ought to have a campaign manager to steer me as to what I should say and what I should not say, when I should rise up and when I should sit down, but that wouldn't work. I thought the only way to do would be to get out and get acquainted with the people." There were clues from Jones's acceptance speech at the convention through his early weeks of campaigning that he would be his own man and neither machine nor party would control him. Party leaders grumbled that Sam Jones never applied the Golden Rule to them: he did not do unto them as they wished him to do.[24]

Perhaps the best indication of his political independence at this stage of his philosophical development was his forceful advocacy of the Golden Rule. He had so completely refashioned himself that by fall the *Blade* would note that Sam Jones was becoming known by his nick-name—Golden Rule Jones—all around the country. "The cognomen is applied in some cases in approval of one of his distinctive ideas—the practical application of the Golden Rule to the everyday affairs of life. In other cases it is used in a semi-humorous way, implying that he is a theorist or dreamer. Both of these views regarding the mayor find advocates here in Toledo."[25]

Jones's identity had fused so seamlessly with the image of a Golden Rule reformer that, within the year, it became the talk of the town. The Current Topic Club heard a paper by Rev. F.L. Wharton on the subject close to Christmas Day. The meeting "discussed a question which has of late claimed much attention on the part of people of Toledo—'Is the Golden Rule Practicable?'" without any indication of the seasonal irony of such a question. An advertisement for the Model Clothing House suffered no doubts about the question that interested Rev. Wharton. The ad begins: "SKINNING CATS has become a very large industry inasmuch as the hide is extensively used for making furs, muffs, and other like articles." Having gotten the reader's attention, the ad continues: "SKINNING CUSTOMERS Is no new innovation in trade circles. In fact, if we are to believe the doctrine that the golden rule cannot be safely applied to business, there being so many successful businessmen today, they must have been skinning customers all these years. . . . Our business experience demonstrates that to 'Do Unto Others as You Would that Others Would Do Unto You,' is the only safe, sure, and successful plan for building an enduring business."[26]

Unlike the Current Topic Club or the retail clothing store, Sam Jones struggled with the practical ramifications of his philosophy. As mayor, Jones would receive thousands of applications for aid: for money, work, a place to live. He responded to many of them, supplementing the welfare function of the local machines, turning over his mayoral salary of $800 a month, and when that ran out, turning again to his own private fortune.

Over the years people would raise Sam's ire by claiming their rights based on his advocacy of the Golden Rule. Jones wrote back to one supplicant to say: "You must have a singular conception of the 'Golden Rule' if you think that in so doing I can send money to everyone that should ask for it." That irritation, normally kept in check, was let loose on a lawyer who demanded payment of a bill from the Acme Sucker Rod Company that Jones thought was a mistake. He began his letter by acknowledging the lawyer's legal expertise: "I suppose I ought not to question your statement that 'the law would require us to pay this bill.'" But he then disparaged E.W. Tolerton's professional ability to understand the Golden Rule: "But I am not prepared to accept your interpretation of the Golden Rule as being final, for as a lawyer, I do not believe you come into contact with it sufficiently to be able to say very much about that sort of ethics."[27]

Sam Jones had been coming to terms with these radical ideas—radical to Toledo's elite and to his own way of thinking—for fewer than five years. They were by no means solidly formulated as he went about the city campaigning for the first time. The campaign provided him the luxury to begin working out his ideas; the next seven years of his life allowed him to develop them further. Sam saw that himself, as he wrote to Henry Demarest Lloyd: "It was because I was yet in the callow days of sociological study that I wrote the golden rule on the wall of our factory."[28]

The Republican Party found the candidate deeply disturbing. Jones met formally with a gathering of Republicans to become acquainted. Aware how much his independence must rankle, he offered to resign. It would have been well for the party to have taken him up on the offer. Jones wanted to focus on local issues. Toledo had been growing at an alarming rate: the influx of immigrants—Germans, Poles, Bulgarians—gave it the greatest population increase of the thirty largest U.S. cities. Local issues—taxes, jobs, housing, streets, sanitation, public transportation—were the compelling issues of the day.[29]

Nevertheless, discussions about parties and vice dominated the campaign. The Republican regulars could not have liked what Jones said later about political parties. He took that as his subject when he went to speak to the fourteenth ward Jackson League Club, the Democratic ward organization. Jones thanked the club for breaking from past traditions. His entire speech made the case for the abolition of political parties on the local level.

Political parties at the local level serve no real purpose, he argued with staggering naïveté. Cities, Jones told the Democrats, do not have to deal with the great regional differences, nor do they arrange finance or tariff systems: "No reform is more urgently needed at the present moment than an absolute divorce of our municipal from our State and National politics." Sam Jones found it surprising that in 1897 people thought they must oppose a local candidate "without any reference to his qualifications for the position—merely because he is associated, even remotely, with the wrong party in National politics." Jones wanted these listeners to look at his qualifications and those of his opponent, Hone, and then make a decision. "It is a betrayal," he reminded them, "of a sacred trust for any man to vote for me in the present contest for mayor of the City of Toledo, when he knows or believes that my opponent is by reason of his experience, his training, or his knowledge of the people of the city, better qualified to fill the place."[30]

Sam said to Helen one morning late in the campaign that he had done nothing that he regretted, nor had he said anything he would prefer unsaid. The Republican newspaper felt that left much for it to say: "Mr. Jones has been accused by those who did not know him, of having horns and a cloven hoof, of stealing about dark alleys to close the back doors of Saloons on Sundays." "In sheer desperation," according to the *Blade* a few days later, "the opposition have misrepresented, vilified and maligned him, yet there has not escaped from his lips one unkind word against the opposing candidates." In fact, he had been called insincere, dishonest, a crank, a lunatic, a charlatan, a demagogue, a socialist, an anarchist, dangerous, and in league with the saloons and the criminals.[31]

Pithole, which constantly haunted his imagination, was the source of his empathetic identification with his working-class crowds, as he made explicit one night late in the campaign when he spoke before the Good Government Club, a black organization: "I know what it is like to walk the streets without money," he told his audience. "On one occasion, I landed in a strange city with but fifteen cents in my pocket and it was three days before I could get work." Sam Jones would later argue that work was the "new right." That night's campaigning ended with the Toledo Colored Band playing to a pleased crowd, smoking cigars, and socializing.[32]

The *Blade* identified his final stop of the campaign in the fourteenth ward, which housed the Acme Sucker Rod Company, as his "best." The meeting, held in Scharff's Hall at the corner of Western Avenue and Langdon Street, brought the crowd to a frenzy of rousing cheers. "The men in his employ," noted the *Blade*, "fairly idolize him, and their enthusiasm last night was unbounded." He campaigned, as always, on the need for scientific administration of city affairs. He spoke of the need to improve living conditions. His speech was repeatedly interrupted with frequent applause. At his conclusion a shout went up: "Who's all right?" "Jones!" shouted the throng. "Mr Jones," concluded the *Blade*, "has conducted a fearless and manly campaign. . . . His earnest words spoken during this campaign, backed by the eloquence of his private life, have made a powerful impression on the people of Toledo."[33]

Monday, April 5, saw the results of Jones's independent work and the Republican machine's lukewarm support of this political orphan. The election was close. It was after 11 P.M. before it was clear that Sam Jones would be the new mayor of Toledo. Of the 20,614 votes cast, 10,566 were for Jones, 10,048 for Hone. Golden Rule Jones won by a margin of 518 votes. Although Jones did better than Major had two years earlier, the lack of machine support is evident in that the Republican Party did far better than the head of its ticket. Only one Republican, Police Commissioner Judd Richardson, against whom Major had actively campaigned, won by a smaller majority than Jones; five won by a margin of more than 1,000, four won by 2,000.[34]

When the Republican victory was clear, however slight some of its margins, the machine celebrated at the Law building. Jones spoke briefly, suggesting that the saloons were not the places to go to get the best election "tips": "We tried Lincoln's advice to stick close to the common people and the dinner bucket carried the day." Tired, in all likelihood, from the strains of the day and speaking to Republican Party officials and friends rather than the common people, Jones kept his comments brief and went home to his wife and family. The *Blade* was satisfied that "the mayor will no longer be the head center of a political machine."[35]

The next day he met with a problem that symbolized all he stood for. A man, a woman, and their two children had come to him early that morning desperate because they had been thrown out of their home. The man was unemployed and could not find work. Mayor-elect Sam Jones referred to that family when he spoke to a crowd at his own factory later that morning. His employees had decorated all the machines with American flags and bunting. When he arrived, they tried to lead him up to a makeshift platform, made from a barrel, but he remained on the floor, wanting "to stand down with the people." Jones claimed his win as a victory for the Golden Rule. At that phrase the men put up a cheer. But his speech to his own men, where he was most likely to be candid, was anything but triumphant. While he had been restrained about his opposition in public speeches during the campaign, here he let his disappointment, his hurt, and his anger show through: "As Mayor of Toledo I shall endeavor to work along the same old plan as here. I have no definite plans; I will continue to urge that a man, who is willing to work, has a right to live. . . . The most pitiful part of the whole thing, however, is to see how the head of the ticket was knifed in the ward where the good people live. I think that if the people of Toledo knew the truth as you boys know it, the ticket which stood for this idea would have swept the city by six thousand instead of 600." The lack of support among Toledo's well-to-do and respectable citizenry would rankle for his entire mayoralty. Jones spoke of the malicious lies and misrepresentations that had circulated about him. He told his men that even the eight-hour day had been used against him—to workers. The Polish workers who presently earned a dollar for a ten-hour day were told that the eight-hour day would reduce their daily earnings to eighty cents, thus misrepresenting Jones's philosophy. He took some solace in the outcome: "Despite widespread misunderstandings, the campaign has demonstrated that men will respond to the touch of a brother's hand, and that men are not dead to their instincts of honor and right." Sam Jones's wounds are apparent in telegrams he sent to Washington Gladden and Henry Demarest Lloyd: "Am elected in spite of 600 saloons, Traction Co., and the devil."[36]

Several weeks later, the *Blade* reported on Lloyd's recent article on Jones in the London *Review of Reviews* with considerable pride but some concern as well. The newspaper was pleased that the international community would now look to Toledo as a model for municipal reform. Jones would initiate an "evolution . . . along right lines—not a revolution, turning everything topsy-turvy." If the *Blade* had seen the letter Jones wrote to Lloyd after publication of the article, the newspaper's editor would have had cause for great concern. Sam wrote: "I really feel that you are laying out a larger contract for me than I shall be able to carry out. As the field opens out before me, I am feeling more helpless (and I was about to say hopeless) than ever. The increasing strain and the injustice of the present social situation is forcing itself upon my attention more and more vividly each day, and sometimes I think that perhaps the quickest way out of the wrong and injustice that surrounds us is by the way of revolution. That word does not alarm me as much as it used to."[37] It is important that Sam Jones saw his responsibilities as a "contract"—one that began at this point to seem "hopeless."

Thus, within just a few months of his election, Jones was beginning to receive national, even international, attention. B.O. Flower, hyperbolic editor of *New Time, Arena,* and *Coming Age,* wrote that Jones's election was "one of the most important and encouraging events of the closing years of our century. It is a positive step toward a truer democracy than the world has yet known." In the London *Review of Reviews,* Lloyd had characterized Sam Jones as "a dangerous man, in the best sense of the word, and it will pay you to keep your eyes on him. He might make a good Vice President for your Presidential Candidate, Pingree."[38]

Sam Jones exasperated and frustrated those Republican Party regulars for the next seven years—all the way up the power line to the president's friend, the closest this country has ever seen to a national "boss," Marcus A. Hanna. Sam Jones failed politically in part because, with complete naïveté, he took on the toughest political boss there was. Behind the scenes Mark Hanna would work hard to stop Sam Jones: he found Jones a dangerous man because he believed what he said.[39]

6

The Time to Think about Someone Besides Self

Samuel Jones's greatest interest always had been the problem of unemployment. As he took on the responsibilities of governing Toledo, he considered the right to work essential to the health of the city. Work had for him a larger meaning than merely a job and a salary. He believed that honest, useful work suited to the person was essential to the development of a healthy personality. Sam himself finally had found *useful* work that would tremendously develop his ideas and his unique talents. His mayoralty, defined by the Golden Rule, gave him the opportunity to think consistently about others, to conceive plans, and to begin working to implement them.

He began without a formal plan. Within a year of his death Golden Rule Jones reflected back on his experience as mayor: "I have never had a program; I have never planned a campaign to reform society, the city, or the world." Echoing William James's idea of a defining "centre of personal energy," Jones said, "I have simply tried to keep at peace with the eternal hammering within my breast."[1] He took the oath of office as Toledo's mayor with no prescribed program and no concrete plan in mind to reform the city. If Sam Jones's municipal policy was not particularly well defined when he took office, his first term would crystallize the "hammering" of his heart into a political philosophy that was the logical extension of his personality.

There was a logical connection between his experiences at the Acme Sucker Rod Company and his early thoughts about governing Toledo. As an employer, all he would claim was that he had adopted strategies that distributed the wealth created by his employees a little more equitably than did other manufacturers; as mayor, the fundamental conflict between Jones and his opponents was cast as a question: "Who shall the government of Toledo serve: all the people or special groups?"[2] As mayor, Jones conscientiously strove to serve the needs of all the inhabitants.

Halfway through his term as mayor, he came to a point where he could articulate his reform philosophy and his municipal policies. Politics, he had come to see, was the science of doing good for all the people through government. He dreamed of a city that was a true community: no one would make money at the expense of others; people would be willing to contribute more than taxes to the "commonwealth" of the municipality. He advocated building a city hall, increasing appropriations for streets and parks, and establishing public swimming pools, playgrounds, kindergartens, and better market facilities. He urged adopting the merit system in all city departments. He also recommended that the city own and operate the gas and electric plants in Toledo. Not all of these proposals would make it through the intensely partisan political process in Toledo, but in his first term, Mayor Jones would have real successes because he was working in concert with others. The official messages to city council, in which he laid out his vision of a municipal commonwealth, were another manifestation of his contract of the heart.[3]

His greatest success in his first term was reforming the police department. Jones's early reforms were successful because he was able to work with the Police Board: he proposed that the department function under civil service rules; he heartily approved the recommendation to provide policemen with walking sticks, not heavy clubs; he instituted an eight-hour day for policemen.[4]

Jones experienced sufficient successes that he seems to have remained optimistic about the possibility of transforming Toledo through much of his first term, despite a major crisis in the police department that was orchestrated by those with local political ambitions of their own, both to test and to weaken his power. On April 15, 1897, Jones went to the Valentine Hotel to take the oath of office, and within the week he confronted a political problem that would emphasize his Golden Rule thinking. The first crisis reveals just how independent a reformer Sam Jones would be. His passionate faith in absolute democracy extended beyond the understanding of even his closest friends. The reform mayor would find himself at odds with the reformers, Police Commissioner John B. Merrell, and the recently elected commissioner Judd Richardson, who wanted to clean up the police department. Merrell charged Chief of Police Ben Raitz with drunkenness on duty.[5]

Ben Raitz, two years older than Jones, was a man of small stature but large girth. His pale blue eyes looked worn by 1897; his hair, now gray, was receding. The chief suffered from the diabetes that would kill him in 1902,[6] although his men would not have known it from the way he lived his life. A native of Switzerland, Ben Raitz had served in the Union army during the Civil War and still had something of the air of a Union soldier about him. An urban police department, after all, replicates some of the rigors and much of the camaraderie of a military company.

"The Old Man," as his men fondly called him, courted danger at the hands of Toledo's criminals as well as its politicians. He seemed to need to live at the high end of the emotional register. He personally took on the most dangerous cases, escaping death on several occasions. One time Raitz decided not to kill an armed man holding a woman hostage. Raitz called the fellow by name, but the man pointed his gun at the chief and fired point-blank. Just as the gun fired, the chief caught the man's wrist, and the bullet knocked off his hat. The chief detective remembered, "The whole thing was done so quickly, that, when the man fired, I believed that Raitz had been shot, and I don't believe that one man in a thousand would have taken the chance that he did simply for the sake of capturing this poor wretch without hurting him."[7]

Ben Raitz seems to have needed danger, and when criminals did not provide it, he sought it out. His fondness for a drink was also a product of his culture and his military experience. Like a soldier twenty years younger, the chief enjoyed carousing at the end of the day. The problem was that he had a habit of carousing *before* the end of his workday. A Major appointee, Ben Raitz had been chief of police for five years, but he seemed compelled to break the very laws he was hired to enforce. Raitz's pattern of drinking suggests that he no longer could control his dependence on alcohol, but the particular occasions on which he drank to excess indicate that the chief needed to be on the edge, if not of losing his life, of losing his job.

The Raitz issue was the center of attention—it seemed all Toledo wanted to know how the new mayor would respond. The case provided the perfect test of the mayor's attitude toward liquor. Ben Raitz was nothing if not intemperate. The charges brought against Raitz went back three years to 1894. The chief prosecuting witness, Ed Kimes, was a sorry specimen. He, like most of those testifying against Raitz, was a "knocker," a man dismissed by Raitz who was seeking reinstatement. Those gathered in the room listened eagerly as Kimes testified that during a streetcar strike he and the chief met about midnight and, over the course of the next four hours, had several drinks together before heading down to deal with traction company strikers. In response to pointed questions from Raitz and from Commissioners Charles Stager and J.A. Bartlett, the two board members who supported the chief, Kimes grudgingly admitted he had been drunk on duty many times before he was dismissed from the force. Kimes was also forced to admit that Merrell had sent for him recently and had repeatedly met with him about the case.[8]

Much of the testimony against Raitz was very damaging. The new mayor heard tales of the chief drinking whiskey at fourteen different saloons one night, having to be half carried home. As the *Bee* noted, the "testimony is neither edifying nor instructive, but it illustrates the fact that whatever the police force may be at present it was, generally speaking, a disgrace to the city during the years 1893 and 1894."[9]

It was clear from the start that Police Board commissioners Merrell and Richardson would vote to replace Raitz and that Stager and Bartlett supported him. Because a majority was required, Sam Jones faced the prospect of casting the deciding vote. As the *Bee* noted, the deadlock placed the entire responsibility on Jones: both factions seemed to delight in putting the mayor in "a tight corner." "As a matter of fact, if the department is ever to be resurrected from the chaotic condition in which it is at present Mr. Jones must do it single-handed and alone." The mayor supported Ben Raitz, arguing that the charges were from a previous administration.[10]

Why did Sam Jones keep a man on as police chief who clearly seemed unfit? Even a person who enjoyed a good drink would have been persuaded by the evidence against Raitz. But for the abstemious Welshman, brought up to fear the evils of alcohol, one would think this would seem an open-and-shut case. Within six months Raitz was found drinking in a saloon after closing hours—which he clearly had not enforced. Again Jones supported Raitz. One must ask why. To some extent Ben Raitz's actions make more sense than Sam Jones's. Clearly irritated that the issue had arisen again, the mayor fell back on his standard Golden Rule reasoning: "I will not condone in any member of the force a habit of frequenting saloons while on duty or habitually drinking to excess. I think the chief feels that he has offended. But I do not think the offense warrants summary dismissal. That would not be doing as I would be done by."[11] For many in Toledo it seemed a disturbing application of the Golden Rule and a violation of the public trust.

If the Golden Rule cannot fully explain Jones's actions, power politics and the nativism that supported temperance help make sense of his first crisis. Raitz was the victim of political infighting among the Police Board members; perhaps the circumstances surrounding Jones's nomination made him all the more likely to empathize with a man caught in such a power struggle. Jones's motives make more sense when one turns to John B. Merrell. If Ben Raitz was to some extent self-destructive, he had in Merrell an enthusiastic assistant. There is a certain irony to the fact that Jones's first political battle was with Merrell: he had instigated the stop-Melvin movement at the Republican convention. King, Merrell's intermediary, first suggested Jones as the compromise candidate. Merrell resembled the Sam Jones of the 1880s in many ways, but he was as interested in wresting power from Jones as from Raitz. Merrell, a second-generation Welshman, was a manufacturer of agricultural tools. He was a devout member of the

First Congregational Church and had served as superintendent of its Sunday school and as director of the YMCA[12] Thus his tolerance for drunkenness was constitutionally thin.

The Christian intolerance of liquor did not stand well with Sam Jones for it simply hid a more despicable intolerance. "In my opinion, both Merrell and Richardson are members of a very prescriptive Order—the APA [the anti-immigrant American Protective Association], and much of the warfare that has gone on in the Board has been due to the spirit of bigotry and intolerance that exists between the two organizations." Therein lies the answer to Jones's vote: he hated the bigotry against Raitz the immigrant. He saw that the temperance issue, particularly when used by the APA, appealed to nativist prejudice: "I want to say that all our effort at *separatism* shown by continual digging at the whiskey men, is to my mind unchristian." It was an issue that emphasized how such prejudice was used to stir political fears, and it reminded him how isolated he was from his respectable neighbors: "You do not know how bad I feel to have respectable people and preachers call this kind of talk an 'apology for the saloon,' and 'a bid for the saloon vote' and in addition to have it [the occasion for] ostracism from certain respectable circles."[13]

For Sam Jones, Ben Raitz's drinking problem translated into a political and moral problem. Jones was presented with a situation that pulled him in two directions. The politically responsible action would be to replace Raitz and perhaps send him to an asylum to dry out; yet the ideal of brotherhood as Jones had conceived it required him to support the chief.

Tensions between his job and his ideology that would become everpresent emerged in this crisis. Ultimately they left him a man divided. This duality was seen in his lifetime only by his closest friends—N.O. Nelson and Brand Whitlock especially. They could see beyond the surface of the successful businessman turned charismatic leader to the troubled, tortured, self-doubting soul who was never satisfied that he lived by the ideal he symbolized to others.

Living the Golden Rule immediately took its toll. One night in early May, just as the Raitz affair was heating up, Sam woke up with a start. He had been suffering from a cold, but he knew what was coming. His chest tightened unbearably, and he could not stop his hacking cough. Gasping, he stumbled up out of bed, struck a match to get the relief the jimsonweed brought. He had suffered problems with asthma since he began living by the Golden Rule, but it had never been debilitating and it never had lasted for more than a couple of days. He was suffering as he had never suffered before, getting up as often as four times a night. Asthma had long been understood to have a connection to anger: Hippocrates is said to have warned, "The asthmatic must guard against anger." Dr. Salter, in the mid-nineteenth century, noted that sudden emotional outbursts could bring on an asthmatic attack.[14]

What did Jones understand about this illness? He was not surprised that asthma might be connected to his emotions. His doctor told him his asthma was caused by nervousness, so he he gave up caffeine. In the last years of his life, he was absorbed with unconventional remedies advocated in Dr. Edward Hooker Dewey's *The No-Breakfast Plan and the Fasting Cure.* Jones came to believe in the systemic nature of illness and health. Dewey wrote, "The contagion of health is a power no less than courage or fear." In the margin, Sam added "and good—goodness, and good health are contagious as surely as evil and disease or ill health." His own experience suggested that his goodheartedness was not always contagious. And it often made him angry, it seems. To be angry at another person violates the moral code by which Sam Jones defined himself—to be angry is to hurt someone else. Sam noted a line in Harry Gaze's *How to Live Forever: The Science and Practice*: "Every change of emotion is accurately registered and science demonstrates that grief, anger, hatred, love and joy have each a specific chemical effect upon the blood." At the bottom of the page, Jones wrote: "My own experience has proven this true, I would rather lose $100 than lose my temper. SMJ." Intent on keeping his temper, he lost his health instead. [15]

What did he fail to see? Sam was so intent on suppressing his anger because in Protestant America and in evangelical cultures in particular anger is the forbidden emotion. Suppressing anger was so central that it had the powerful effect of shaping life. The evangelical child felt anger when parents began to break his will, and he learned to express it at his own peril.[16] That suppressed anger intensified when the child naturally resisted being broken. He learned quickly that anger led to pain, punishment, isolation, and shame. It threatened his inner security. Sam was so intent on suppressing his anger because he had been taught that anger was shameful; it was a loss of control and it violated the moral code: it hurt someone else.

During the Raitz affair, Jones controlled his anger, but it could not be entirely repressed: it emerged in his nightly fight for air. The word "psyche" means "breath": the asthmatic attacks were the physical manifestation of the conflict at the center of his psyche.[17] The inability to catch his breath signals the most egregious instance of his internal disharmony. The Sermon on the Mount had planted the seed of dissatisfaction in his soul. His public persona gave no sign that the demands of the spirit caused him such pain. Yet his distance from the Golden Rule was translated into his inability to get enough air. He felt powerless. Feelings of power stem from the sense that one has control over one's own life. That is precisely what Jones lacked in those nightly attacks—the power to control the essence of life. Powerlessness in any significant sphere, one's job, one's family, one's health—and Jones had reason to feel powerless in all three—reactivates the feelings of childhood helplessness. And with powerlessness comes shame. As his struggles with poor health intensified, Jones became ever more ashamed of his lack of control because he took it to be a spiritual failure.

Sam Jones recognized that physical, mental, and spiritual stresses combined to make him ill, or "out of harmony." Business concerns exacerbated the pressure he placed on himself. Throughout the spring and summer, business in the oil industry was so "dull" that the company did not make enough to pay its stockholders a dividend. Nevertheless, Jones decided that the smaller stockholders ought to receive their share. Things were so bad that he worried that his company, now in the hands of his brother Dan, might fail. Even though they were losing between 10 and 15 percent on each engine produced, Jones was unwilling to lower wages and extend work hours, as his chief engineer advised. He instructed him to find another way to produce the engines more economically or "we will simply quit making engines." He felt a deep personal responsibility. To one person critical of his management of the company, Jones revealed his essential lack of harmony: "I do not expect to please everybody. I am unable to even please myself."[18]

Despite his self-doubt, Jones approached the task of learning the job of mayor as he had all the others; he rolled up his sleeves and went to where the problems were. "Jones' Move Against Gamblers," read a two-column front-page *Bee* headline on Easter Sunday. Three of the city's faro banks were closed. Featuring faro tables, poker, and roulette, they could be found in the heart of the downtown business district in the eleventh ward. At the Toledo Turf Exchange at the rear of a saloon on St. Clair Street, Mayor Jones watched young men not old enough to vote placing bets on horse races run in the Deep South and Far West. The *Bee* characterized them as boys "actuated by the desire to get something for nothing." Clearly, Sam Jones did not like what he saw: "the desire to get something for nothing" had characterized everyone in Pithole, himself included. By now Jones saw it as a reprehensible motive. Jones told the proprietors of the Turf Exchange and Harmon and O'Day's poolroom on Summit that he would not tolerate public gambling as long as he was mayor. They took him at his word, chose not to contest his ruling in court, and the poolrooms and faro banks were shut down by Raitz. The whole affair gave the *Bee* every reason to believe that "Mayor Jones has backbone and will enforce the law." Nothing would dumbfound respectable Toledoans more over the next seven years than to learn that the *Bee* was wrong.[19]

After dealing with the gamblers, Jones turned to the poor. The mayor appointed a special committee to devise innovative measures for poor relief. Rev. S.G. Anderson, of the Westminster Presbyterian Church at Locust and Superior Streets, Helen Jones's pastor, the man who had performed their wedding service, was named chairman. The committee found that in the past year, 1,301 men and 84 women had been unable to get work. Its recommendation surely must have disappointed the mayor, for it clearly did not see unemployment as the effect of large social inequities. The committee strongly endorsed "men's rights": "It has been shown that where women take men's places, the wages go down, while the man is thrown out of work."[20]

While others comforted themselves with explaining away poverty by turning it into a woman's problem, Sam Jones continued to struggle with his feelings about his own wealth. The discomfort that pained him shortly after setting up the Acme Sucker Rod Company intensified; Jones told Helen he would find it a "relief" to be poor. This must have concerned Helen, who was now expecting a child, at age forty, in the autumn. There was nothing in her background or her current situation to prompt her to sympathize with Sam's compulsion to free his conscience from guilt by opening his wallet. Perhaps in response to her pressures, Sam reconciled his feelings with the thought that perhaps he should try to do his best in his place. But this did not placate his feelings. He realized that "to do that, runs directly counter to Christ's injunction to sell your worldly belongings and follow him." He found himself "very much perplexed . . . to know what to do." William James accounts for Tolstoy's melancholy as a "clash between his inner character and his outer activities and aims."[21] Sam Jones's new inner character clashed with the fortune he had dedicated his adult life to procuring. He was at war with himself.

If he was unsure what to do with his own wealth, he was very sure of himself when he sat in as acting police court judge for the first time in June 1897. Toledo's charter allowed the mayor to appoint someone in the judge's absence. Jones chose to sit in as judge. But when Jones availed himself of this opportunity, no mayor had done so in ten years, and no one who had taken that seat had ever used it to mete out the radical goodheartedness of the Golden Rule. Jones's philosophy as judge was to do as he would be done by. His first case was not serious. Nine blacks were brought before the court on a charge of disturbing the peace near a saloon in the early hours of a Monday morning. Recognizing several of the men, Jones spoke to them by name, saying he was surprised to learn they had been out on the street at such an hour. He dismissed them without a fine and with instructions to be better citizens. Over the course of the next seven years, he would take every opportunity to mete out such justice. The charges would not always be so harmless, but his response was always the same. When arraigning himself before the court of his conscience, however, he became ever less inclined to temper his judgment with mercy.[22]

If political crises and the struggle to know what to do drained him, Jones found sustenance when he spent a week in late June at Crosbyside, New York. Ernest Crosby, a lawyer and an international judge in Egypt, experienced a conversion to reform during his 1894 visit to Tolstoy at Yasnaya Polyana. Like Sam Jones, Ernest Crosby was a man of considerable wealth, which he used in the service of reform. On his return from Russia, Crosby turned his seven-hundred-acre farm near Rhinebeck, New York, into a Progressive conference center. Crosby thought Jones so effective at putting the principle of love into action that he seemed "a sort of visitor from some other planet where brotherhood and harmony have been realized in the common life, dropped down here in a semi-barbarous world and calmly taking his place in the midst of its crude and cruel institutions." Brand Whitlock shared the feeling that Jones was utterly foreign, but for him, the Golden Rule mayor seemed from some future time, not some distant planet: "He was an odd man, born so far ahead of his time that the sins of others never troubled his conscience."[23]

Those who knew Jones best saw what a remarkable man he was. Perhaps he seemed so extraordinary to the likes of Crosby and Whitlock because he lived more fully than they the implications of the convictions they all shared. The comparison to Crosby makes the point. However great Crosby's admiration of Tolstoy, he never renounced the life of the master for that of simple peasant. What most disturbed Ernest Crosby and many of Jones's contemporaries was a kind of political paralysis, a spiritual torpor.[24] Sam Jones, in contrast, committed himself wholeheartedly to active plans to change the nature of the business and political worlds.

It was at the Crosbyside conference that Crosby introduced Jones to the poetry of Walt Whitman and to Rev. Benjamin Fay Mills. Crosby and Mills agreed that Sam Jones "was about as nearly Whitman's ideal comrade-man as could be found." Whitman, in *Song of Myself,* called himself "no stander above men and women or apart from them," and, in "Sing of the Broad Axe," the poet observed, "A great city is that which has the greatest men and women." A group of about a dozen reformers attending the Crosbyside conference gathered to take the funicular railway at the top of a nearby mountain. There, surrounded by beauty, looking down on a spectacular view, Mills asked Crosby to read Whitman. Crosby read aloud for half an hour, "ostensibly for the general benefit, but really with a solitary eye to Jones." When Crosby finished, Jones laconically remarked that he didn't call *that* poetry.[25] If Crosby and Mills were disappointed, it was to be only temporary. Whitman soon became Jones's favorite poet.

Whitman said of his most famous poem, "I know very well that my 'Leaves' could not possibly have emerged or been fashion'd or completed, from any other era than the latter half of the Nineteenth Century, nor any other land than democratic America." The same is true for Sam Jones. He may have seemed out of this world to Ernest Crosby and Toledo's politicians, but Sam Jones could not have been "fashioned" or "completed" from any other era than the second half of the nineteenth century or from any other place "than democratic America." Whitman's poetry celebrated freedom, emotion, personality, and, above all, democracy. Sam Jones's goodheartedness celebrated individual freedom and democracy in daily life with all the strength of his considerable personality.[26]

Both men spoke for the individual life in language that can only be called (however secular a poet Whitman was) spiritual. Horace Traubel, Whitman's "second son," inscribed for Sam Jones the *Complete Poems and Prose of Walt Whitman* with the words: "You may be a man without a party, Sam Jones, but you are not a man without a heart." He repeated the same phrase in a letter, adding, "But I am glad that it is within my power to send one of these books to a man whose practical democracy goes to confirm all the exultant prophecies of Whitman's Exile." "Statistics will not save the world," Traubel wrote Jones the next year, "only a radical good heart will save the world. Sweet comrade, you have a radical good heart in abundant degree. You will save the world you and yours."[27]

Sam Jones firmly believed that Whitman was right in seeing that "our American superiority and vitality" came from "the bulk of our people, not in a gentry like the old world." He also believed with Whitman that "our leading men are not of much account and never have been, but the account of the people is immense, beyond all history. . . . We will not have great individuals or great leaders, but a great average or bulk, unprecedentedly great." Why did Sam Jones respond to Whitman more than to any other poet? Whitman himself provided the answer in a manuscript "Notes on the Meaning and Intentions of Leaves of Grass": "Every page of my book emanates Democracy, absolute, . . . without the slightest compromise, and the sense of the New World in its future, a thoroughly revolutionary formation to be exhibited less in politics and more in theology, literature and manners." Sam Jones's politics crossed the boundary into theology and in doing so advocated absolute democracy. It was thoroughly revolutionary. Whitman also believed that "no one will perfectly enjoy me who has not some of my own rudeness, sensuality, and hauteur." Jones underlined those lines (as he underlined the other Whitman quotations in this paragraph) and in doing so acknowledged his own sensuality, rudeness, and hauteur.[28]

Jones's membership in a growing national community of nineteenth-century reformers was, as Whitman had prophesied about the culture at large, based on literature and theology rather than hard political strategies and complex economic visions. Sam Jones, and the reform community as a whole, would probably have accomplished more had politics and economics dominated literature and theology. Yet would they have captured the enthusiastic interest of the people at large? Much of the interest, then and now, in these larger-than-life charismatic reformers who energized the country—Jane Addams, William Jennings Bryan, Eugene Debs, and Sam Jones, different as they were—lies in their vision of what America should be.

In the autumn Sam Jones extended his connections with the body of national reformers when he attended, along with three hundred participants, Dr. Kellogg's economic conference at Battle Creek. Jones felt himself to be "among some of the brightest minds in the country," but he was more impressed by the living conditions than by economic forecasting. "We were all entertained at the sanitarium and lived on the saw-dust and hay of vegetarians," the mayor told reporters on his return. Despite this description of the menu, Sam Jones was the perfect guest: he was deeply impressed by this experiment in living and later became a vegetarian. Kellogg ran his large residence without servants; the work was done by his twenty-two adopted children, who were trained for medical missionary work and sent out to improve the world. Sam Jones was struck with Kellogg's communal world: "If the workings of that sanitarium were written up after the style of Bellamy, they would be regarded as highly improbable as some of his imaginings," thought Jones. Yet Sam Jones was enough of a "character" to fit in well in this improbable utopian oasis that seemed, even to him, to be out of the pages of fiction.[29]

Back in Toledo, buoyed by the Crosbyside conference and the support of reformer friends, Jones became concerned with a nationwide crises that seemed to symbolize society's selfishness. In July, the soft coal miners struck for better wages, arguing that improvements in mining machinery were displacing men in the mines. Union representatives estimated that miners had earned $7.60 a month before the strike. In Toledo, one hundred people signed a petition calling for a mass meeting on the subject, which the mayor gladly called, but only seventy-five people attended. A discouraged Sam Jones opened the meeting. The small turnout spoke to the "selfishness" to be seen everywhere, he said. The evangelical politician who sought so hard to suppress the self observed: "That is the trouble with all of us, with the miners, the operators and all classes, but I am optimistic enough to believe that we are passing into the time when men find the time to think, two to three times a day, about someone besides self." Those gathered had pledged $221, of which $100 came from the mayor, who told the group he would donate the last $100 of every $5,000 raised. The group applauded, but Jones stopped it, saying, "I am not generous. I don't have to starve; I don't have to have children about me starving. I've been barefooted myself and my friends say I'll go broke again, but there's nothing startling about that."[30]

The miners were eventually victorious but not until mid-September and not without tragic loss of life in Hazelton, Pennsylvania. As the sheriff read the riot act to the men, most of whom did not understand English, they gathered around him, pushing and shoving in their attempt to understand whether he was arresting them. As the sheriff left, thinking himself in danger, his deputies opened fire at his call. Jones responded to the twenty-two deaths with horror: "To call such a civilization as that which tolerates the outrages inflicted upon the unoffending miners Christian is blaspheming the sacred name of Christ."[31]

To Sam Jones the Hazelton incident revealed both the worst and the best of American society. Jones faced the deep injustice in his culture—not only were the men who fired the shots guilty, but society at large shared the blame for tolerating such inhuman treatment. But he found good as well: the assembled miners, in concert, won their fight. Sam Jones deeply believed in "union." He gathered a mayor's council, sure that together they could do much, whereas alone they would do little. He watched as the miners' union won against the spirit of competition. He spoke to a group of Sabbath schools, including Congregationalists, Baptists, and Methodists, gathered for a Grand Union Picnic: "I like the word union," he told the appreciative listeners; "it expresses so much. When we realize its real meaning, we will have solved many of the great problems of the day, we will have eliminated and wiped out the word which Moody is pleased to call 'denominationalism.' Denominationalism misleads us. It is not Christianity. . . . We don't do half enough of this union work. If we did, we would become more interested in doing things outside ourselves and would work more for the good of others."[32]

Sam Jones would have accomplished more despite his political naïveté and the enmity of Hanna had he continued his early successes and worked more consistently in concert with others. Eugene Debs tried energetically to persuade him of this. Unions—political or otherwise—could do much good, but while Sam Jones saw the value of group effort, he remained essentially a lone man, fighting the considerable power of others working in concert, often against him. The Pastors' Union, a gathering of Toledo's clergy, organized to fight back against the mayor. Perhaps the most disquieting means was the one Rev. Anderson, Mrs. Jones's pastor, chose. He provided religious-cum-political instruction from the pulpit of the Westminster Presbyterian Church. "The saloonkeeper is my brother," admitted Rev. Anderson in his sermon, and everyone in the congregation must have known who he was quoting, "but when he ruins my sister's children, and breaks my sister's heart by debauching the husband and the father, he has dishonored the Divine relation of brotherhood. He must be compelled to respect the relation. My sister and her children must be protected, and it is somebody's business to see to it that she is." Clearly, Rev. Anderson thought it Mayor Jones's business.[33]

"The Church, as it exists at present, is not Christian, but merely engaged, like the rest of humanity, in saving itself," thought Jones. When the Golden Rule mayor invited the radical minister George Herron to town, the clerics felt besieged. They responded by answering Herron from their pulpits, and the mayor was outraged. He thought that nothing so completely revealed "the utter stupidity and servility" of the church as the "monstrous savagery" of the recent sermons. The newspapers were no kinder to Herron, it seems. One reporter confided to the mayor "I wish I could write up the lectures as I want to, but I was told to THROW it to him."[34]

Proof of Jones's alienation from the Protestant church was poignantly evident in the autumn of 1897. There was great cause for happiness at home: on the evening of October 3 Helen delivered a ten-pound baby boy. Because she was forty, the birth of such a large baby was not likely to have been easy. They named the baby Mason Beach Jones. Jones was so alienated from the institutional church by this time that he determined not to have Mason baptized. Whatever consternation this caused Helen remains unknown, but it was likely to have been considerable. Sam Jones's decision not to baptize the baby speaks more eloquently to his rejection of the established church than any other fact. Sam certainly must have come to believe that a just and loving God would not doom a baby who had not received the Church's first sacrament. Six weeks after the baby's birth, Jones wrote that he "used to believe in the Church," but that it seemed to replicate society. The church was "engaged in the selfish business of looking out for number one. I have lost much of my faith in the Church and have become a great believer in Christianity."[35]

Once again, it is clear that the second Sam Jones defined himself in terms of quintessential American texts. Sam Jones had a strong antinomian streak, cultivated in part by his reading of Whitman and Emerson. But if

Jones was a quixotic reformer, his antinomian impulse was deeply embedded in American culture. As Whitman put it, in *Democratic Vistas,* "I hear it was charged against me that I / sought to destroy institutions, / But really I am neither for nor against institutions." In rejecting the church, Jones had links to the American Revolution as well as the democratic Protestant revival of the early republic. By the end of the eighteenth century there was a deep heritage of attacking religious authority and celebrating the persuasive talents of individualists who "chose to storm heaven by the back door."[36]

Jones's antinomianism contained the old Puritan refusal wholly to accept the church's laws. But the tradition had been transformed in the intervening years into a mode of assent by both populist preachers and writers. Jones's rejection of the church had become an affirmation of self and community. Like Whitman or Emerson, Jones saw himself as an Adam, at one with God and certainly at one with all humankind. Of course, such a view put a tremendous burden on the self. One had to be self-reliant, rather than God-reliant. In Puritan New England antinomianism was seen as a potent threat with the power to destroy the community. For Whitman or Emerson it seemed the only possibility for community. And Whitman, Jones's favorite poet, expressed it most clearly. He celebrated individuality and democracy en masse.[37] If Whitman's antinomian vision offered Jones a kind of community, his stand outside the church and against it led to a feeling of isolation that undercut the Whitmanesque community he experienced in the campaign.

Events during the winter months crystallized Jones's understanding of social problems and his reform philosophy. Eugene Debs was at the heart of it all. As Christmas approached during Jones's first year in office, he invited Debs to speak at Memorial Hall. The invitation created a furor. Debs had risen to natural prominence in 1893 when he organized the American Railway Union, but he had not caught the attention of the people until his role in the Pullman strike of 1894 brought him a six-month jail term for conspiracy to obstruct the mails. If George Herron made the clergy uncomfortable, Debs unnerved the entire community—or so it seemed. On the evening of December 22, as Jones was on his way out the door to meet Debs, a telephone call stopped him. An irate T.P. Brown had phoned to plead with the mayor not to introduce Debs. "It will be the mistake of your life," warned Brown. Far from being the mistake of his life, Debs's speech that night shaped the way Jones made sense of his own life.

Jones knew it was important that the people hear Debs and he tried to make Brown understand his contractual obligation. He tried to be conciliatory, keeping his own views of Debs out of the discussion: "I have promised to do so and I generally carry out my contracts." "Don't do it," insisted Brown. Then, trying another tack, he said: "Get up on the platform and tell them you don't want to do it. It will be more to your credit. He is a dangerous man, inciting the poor against the rich." Sam Jones did introduce Eugene Debs to a large crowd, most of them workingmen, without any apology. Beginning that night, the two men developed what Debs's biographer called a "warm personal friendship."[38]

The crowd looked up at the stage where a Yuletide banner proclaimed "Peace on Earth, Goodwill to Men." F.L. McGuire introduced the mayor. Unlike Brand Whitlock, McGuire did not think Sam Jones was ahead of his time; he thought he was *behind* it by about eighteen hundred years. Sam Jones, he said, was "a man who thinks the Teacher was in earnest about what he said in that day and who is trying to live in accordance with those teachings." When Jones got up to speak, he defended himself against the objections of men like T.P. Brown by observing that he served the people when he attended such public meetings. He estimated that he had done so twenty or thirty times—at religious meetings, temperance meetings, and socialist meetings. If that sounds apologetic, his next words were not: "I hear a good deal about 'dangerous men' in these days. Indeed it has been intimated that I am a dangerous man. Perhaps an era of peace on earth would be dangerous to some men." He then turned the podium over to a man many who were not in the hall that night considered truly dangerous.[39]

Eugene Debs's talk, "The Evolution of the Tramp," was to be the most important speech Jones ever listened to for it resonated within him, connecting his own experience to the social problems he worried about. Debs told the crowd that the economy was not good: business failures totaled almost 14,000, up 12 percent from the previous year; one man in every 357 was in jail; one out of 443 lived on charity. How does that happen? asked Debs. Unlike Jones's committee that saw the answer in women taking jobs, Eugene Debs blamed competition. "Under the competitive system a man must become a millionaire or a mendicant, with the chances a million to one that he will be a mendicant." Sam Jones listened intently to Debs's words. His own experience confirmed Debs's message. He had, of course, beaten the odds. But as he thought back to the young man struggling to survive the winter of 1865 in Pithole, Pennsylvania, he knew that Debs was right. He had been well on his way to becoming a tramp. Debs's words clarified the reason people must "think about someone besides self." The most compelling evidence that Debs's words shaped Jones's view of capitalism can be found in Jones's 1898 St. Louis address "Our Brothers: The Millionaire and the Tramp."[40]

The criticism from all sides that followed Debs's appearance solidified Jones's convictions. Rev. D.M. Fisk, who had helped Jones organize the series of speakers that brought both Henry Demarest Lloyd and Jane Addams to Toledo, wrote to criticize his friend for introducing Debs. Thus even friends who shared Jones's views brought to his attention the errors of his ways: "I realize that you have a peculiarly hard place, and need great sagacity, and a wise but stiff back-bone, or the artful will weave their nets around you [in] spite of vigilance. . . . I earnestly beg you to take wise stands, and to hold a firm rein on local evils." Sam clearly was disturbed by Fisk's letter; his earnest response was five and a half pages long.[41]

Jones wrote Jane Addams to tell her that the Current Topic Club of one of the local churches "thoroughly roasted" him for introducing Eugene Debs. As a result of the attack, the clergy found themselves on the receiving end of some secular sermonizing. In his Christmas Eve editorial, Negley Cochran criticized the clergy who attacked Jones: this is a country, Cochran reminded his readers, where speech is free. "When he deserves criticism," Cochran said, "the *Bee* won't be behind-hand in giving it to him and straight from the shoulder or hot from the griddle, but there's no sense in jumping on everything he does just because Jones does it. There is danger of the men who want to down Jones overdoing the thing." Writing to thank him for his Christmas Eve editorial, Jones said that he believed Cochran "to be my brother, you know. I wanted to thank you for it."[42]

Cochran's plump good looks, with the hint of a double chin and the start of a receding hairline, belied his inner strength. He was every bit as independent as was Jones. Raised a Republican, he was trained in the newspaper business at the *Blade* when it was under the control of David Ross Locke. Cochran became a "rip-snorting Democrat" because of the Republican position on the tariff. An Ohio native, he had graduated from the University of Michigan, but his journalistic style was hardly academic. As Clarence Darrow saw it, "There are few men who write as well as Negley Cochran does. . . . Neg had a college education but it didn't last long enough to hurt him much."[43]

Support from the Democratic *Bee* was all the sweeter because the Republican *Blade* was no longer particularly supportive. The *Blade* was under the editorial control of Robinson Locke, a man of great wealth and strong partisan loyalties. Locke was classically good-looking, with a strong, straight nose and the requisite mustache. He wore his dark hair as current fashion dictated, parted in the middle with a curl on either side of his forehead. His father's generation had considered this an affectation: Ulysses S. Grant is said to have disliked a man on sight who parted his hair in the middle. But at century's end, Robinson Locke was not a dandy. Locke's penchant for satirical attack, exercised with increasing regularity over the remainder of Jones's tenure, seems to have been in the blood. Locke's father, David Ross Locke, his predecessor as editor and publisher of the paper, had become famous during the Civil War as the Copperhead "Petroleum V. Nasby." Abraham Lincoln had so admired these satiric attacks on Democrats and slaveholders that he read the latest Nasby letters to his cabinet before signing the Emancipation Proclamation.[44]

In the early weeks of 1898, Toledo had the opportunity to see that the Golden Rule mayor was thinking about "someone besides self" as he sought to defend absolute democracy against the issue that most dismayed the middle class: liquor. Gilbert J. Raynor, district superintendent of the Anti-Saloon League, revealed how rancorous the rhetoric could become when he wrote in a letter to the editor of the *Toledo Bee,* "It's too bad Mayor Jones has not an educated head to match his magnificent heart. A little knowledge has always proved a dangerous thing, and never so much so than in the realm of sociology. . . . [Every] sot and bum of the slums, . . . gamblers, bawdy house keepers, and anarchistic discontents," he wrote, were happy with the mayor. They "dance with fiendish delight, intoxicated with unrestrained lawlessness."[45]

Whether or not fiends were to be seen on the streets, Toledo was an "open city" and the perfect site to test local prohibitionist sentiment. Republican police commissioners John Merrell and Judd Richardson, still outraged about Jones's handling of the Raitz case, initiated a push to enforce the blue laws. Originally passed in 1864, the blue laws had not been enforced for some time. As a result, Toledo was the only place for miles around where one could get a drink on Sunday. Liquor was the issue, but Commissioner Richard Kind saw to it that all of the blue laws were enforced as a calculated strategy to defeat the antisaloon politicians at their own game. Everything was shut down. It was a gamble. Would public sentiment accept open saloons in exchange for open plays, concerts, and restaurants?

By the time the blue laws went into effect on Saturday, February 5, at 11 P.M., most of the state legislators had fled town. The Sunday newspapers reported that everything had been orderly late Saturday night, though "the streets were made lively" by "young men who had provided themselves with generous sized bottles just before eleven o'clock and paraded the city well-pleased with their independence of the actions of the city leaders." Not everyone had such foresight, apparently. One man, a representative of human nature, wistfully told a reporter that he "had not been thirsty till the time came when he could not get a drink." The saloon keepers were almost universally compliant, but some found creative ways to let their displeasure be known. Two Adams Street saloons were reported to be selling beer in teacups, and the Hockenberger saloon had carefully left its curtains open, hoping patrolling policemen would peer in to see the flock of chickens roosting in the bar.[46]

The quiet lasted for only a very few hours. Sunday afternoon the Marine Band was scheduled to give a concert downtown at the Valentine theater, in the building that housed the mayor's office. The owner of the theater had decided that the show would go on, regardless of the blue laws. The press speculated that the band would be arrested and all thirty-eight musicians would request separate jury trials. Some thought the audience would be arrested as well. To make matters more interesting politically, the lawyer representing the Marine Band had been Jones's unsuccessful Democratic opponent for mayor, Parks "Punk" Hone. Women and children and "many of the best of Toledo's citizens" showed up, not out of love for the Marine Band but to protest. It was a jovial protest; friends greeted one another in the lobby, stopped for a moment to chat, and parted, saying, "Well, so long. I'll see you at the [police] station." Outside the Valentine, a crowd of thirty-five hundred, which the *Bee* carefully described as more "mixed" than those who had paid for the concert, had gathered in the streets to see all the fine people get arrested. When Company A, with fife and drum corps, marched from the armory to the theater a wild rumor circulated that the militia had been called out. Although the show went on as scheduled, the crowd was not to be entirely disappointed. As soon as the curtain went down after the last number, Chief Detective "Silver Jack" Carew placed Charles Strobel, owner of the company, under arrest. As soon as the detectives and Strobel appeared on St. Clair Street, the crowd spotted them and shouted, "Strobel's pinched!" The three had a large escort to the station. Tuesday's *Bee*, under the headline that made its position clear, "Changed Social Conditions Call for New Laws," reported that the city council had begun to dismantle the blue laws.[47]

If that was the mayor's intent, the gamble had paid off, though, apparently, the city paid a price. The state legislators chose Cleveland over Toledo as the Centennial City; Toledo was to have only one dry Sunday in the mayor's seven years in office. The Golden Rule mayor naturally outraged the Anti-Saloon League, the clergy, and many among the middle class because he did not seem to share their concern with vice. The very people who had been most distressed by his election seemed to profit most by his stand. A little over a year later, as the 1899 mayoral election heated up, the Republican paper ran a political cartoon that spoke for many who were disappointed in the mayor. "United We Stand, Divided We Fall," it read. The cartoon caricatures Sam Jones in the middle, ears at right angles to his head and a badge over his heart that reads "G. Rule," his arms around the shoulders of a fellow on each side. To his right stands an unsavory-looking, mustachioed character, leaning on a gambling table with a hand of cards at his feet; to Jones's left stands a saloon keeper, squinting into the smoke from his own cigar, supported by his bar, with a bottle by his side and a spittoon at his feet. It reads, "Jones with the Gambler and the Saloon Keeper." The message could not be more explicit: Sam Jones is almost literally supported by his two cronies. The fight against the blue laws is the most dramatic example of Jones's inclination to seek to legislate Whitman's belief that "American superiority and vitality [is to be found in] the bulk of our people, not in a gentry."[48]

During his first term in office Sam Jones conceived his program and began working to implement it; the principle behind all his practical programs was to defend the public interest against private interest, to enrich the value of the commonwealth, and to govern so that all of Toledo might benefit. The man who had made his wealth in oil and kept it under the advantages of the patent system believed that natural resources properly belonged to the people. He had become known as a "gas and water socialist." He believed that municipal ownership would lead to public ownership of all utilities, "which in turn will lead us to see our common origin and our common right to the natural resources of the earth." No city could be considered rich "that has a single pauper within its limits." He wanted the voters to grant the city franchises to control public transportation and power—gas, water, and electricity—rather than let the city council make a closed back-room deals.[49] He sought to protect the rights of the city against the state legislature by ardently advocating home rule—and would have some success in the Ohio Supreme Court with Brand Whitlock's legal help. His interest in penal reform would later lead to changes in the Ohio penal code. He began pushing for public kindergartens, convinced of the value of early childhood education; the school board established them in February 1901. He improved the life of the city by instituting an eight-hour workday for municipal workers and by instituting civil service reform. Civic-minded citizens helped Jones expand public playgrounds. The city council was persuaded to fund many of his ideas: public parks, the zoo, swimming facilities, playgrounds, free concerts, municipal sleigh rides, and a free golf course. These additions transformed the city and offered new pleasures to its inhabitants. While the Brown machine planned to oust him from office and the Toledo clergy fumed about vice, Sam Jones was making Toledo a more livable city. The people had noticed and heartily approved.

7

Like Christianity, Democracy Has Never Yet Been Tried

In the early spring of 1899, the considerable force of Sam Jones's personality would see him through a bitter fight with the Republican Party, a near-riotous nominating convention, and a triumphant reelection as a political independent. Jones had so fully fused his second identity with the Golden Rule that he gloried in the challenges of the fight. Brand Whitlock thought that "the mere force of [Jones's] own original character and personality compelled a discussion of fundamental principles of government."[1] The 1899 Toledo mayoral election came closer to true democracy than anything Mark Hanna or the Toledo Republican convention had in mind, but it had a dark side Sam Jones never acknowledged.

Before the Republican convention in 1899, Jones outlined his contractual obligation to the citizens of Toledo. He published a letter to the people to let them know that he sought another term as his party's nominee "as a Lincoln Republican. I believe in the people as he believed in them, and trust them as he trusted them. I have been the mayor for all of the people, high and low, rich and poor, black and white, employed and unemployed. My experience in the office has served to strengthen every conviction to which I have ever given expression regarding the brotherhood of all men." He closed his lengthy letter by asking "all who believe in the principles that I have outlined and who trust the justice of the golden rule and the Declaration of Independence to assist me with their support for the nomination." An outraged *Bee* subscriber wrote: "Is Jones the only man in Toledo who believes in the Golden Rule and the Declaration of Independence? Has he any patent right on either of them? . . . Does the Golden Rule depend upon Jones's election for its existence? Is the Declaration of Independence in danger if some Toledo man should happen to be elected instead of Jones?" Negley Cochran bridled at Jones's comparisons to Lincoln, Thomas Jefferson, and Christ: why not, he asked, seek help from those "who believe in cow's milk, fresh eggs, good air, sweet children and restful sleep?"[2]

Sam Jones's repeated references to Christ, Jefferson's Declaration of Independence, and Abraham Lincoln understandably irritated men like Cochran and the disenchanted Republican Party officials. Jones repeated this litany to create his own "party." Throughout his political career, he turned to Christ, to Jefferson, to Lincoln, and most recently to Bryan to place his political philosophy within the ideals of Christianity and the founding principles of the country. He needed to do that more than others, perhaps, because he functioned outside the comfortable confines of political labels.

Sam Jones found no safe, easy answers by looking to the founders of the country. He saw clearly, as Josiah Strong did not, that the wisdom of the Founding Fathers would not suffice as the country struggled to meet the problems of the twentieth century. "Their kind of wisdom," scrawled Sam in the margin of his copy of Strong's *Twentieth Century City*, "wouldn't help us—They never saw a R.R. trust, never sent a telegraph message, never talked to a telephone, never saw an electric car. How could stage coach methods help us today?" "Ours is a democracy only in name," his marginal note instructs his friend Strong. "Evidently democracy in our larger cities has failed," wrote Strong, to which Jones retorted with antinomian fervor, "*Like Christianity*, Democracy has never yet been tried."[3] Jones was correct that democracy was not being tried, and Mark Hanna proved it. By conscious design the Constitution had created a republic. Mark Hanna was in office because the country had not yet moved to direct election of senators.

Emerson's texts helped bring Jones to this conviction, had Hanna's example alone not sufficed. John Dewey called Emerson "the Philosopher of Democracy." "Against creed and system, convention and institution, Emerson stands for restoring to the common man that which in the name of religion, of philosophy, of art, and of morality, has been embezzled from the common store and appropriated to sectarian and class use." Jones shared that intention: he helped to restore the country, or his city at least, to the common people. Emerson argued that the source of truth was accessible to all. That conviction led him to consider religious and political authority as fictions.[4]

In 1901, Jones formulated his thoughts on the subject in an article for Benjamin Flower's reform journal *Arena*. "We are not yet a democracy," he argued, though most people assumed that we are. They assume we have a government of the people. Our government is in the hands of a very select few. "One-half of the race, the women, are yet declared politically and socially unequal, and both men and women accept this as being divinely ordained." He argued that partisan politics limits democracy not because of political corruption but because of "the undeveloped state of mind" of both politicians and people.[5]

Proof that democracy was not being tried in Toledo soon came. Sam Jones had been causing the Republican officials considerable distress since his nomination, but in the fall of 1897, nine months after his election, he went too far. He would not support Mark Hanna in his attempt to retain his Senate seat. Party officials decided to bring their mayor into line. They instructed him to support Hanna publicly. His discomfort can be seen in the way he handled his assignment. Speaking to a small group, mainly Germans, some of whom did not understand English, Jones sidestepped Hanna completely.[6]

As Sam Jones saw it, there could hardly be a more striking symbol that democracy was not being tried in Ohio than Hanna. In the privacy of his correspondence, Jones did not hesitate to express his feelings about Hanna. He found his party "hopelessly split by the injection of [Hanna's] vile personality and impious money into it." To another correspondent, he wrote of the "selfish greed of our Ohio autocrat Mark Hanna."[7]

"Mayor Jones may have many admirable traits, but political courage doesn't seem to be one of them," wrote Neg Cochran. "We want to see Jones do one of two things, either come out for Hanna, or against him. Nobody loves a coward." Privately, Sam considered the clash between his principles and politics: "I am more ready to step down and out when the question of surrendering my self-respect shall be the only alternative of remaining in politics."[8]

In his next political speech Sam seemed to be working out his position: "Every man should know his own mind and vote according to its dictates; not stoop to barter and sale of a vote. It is simply throwing away the God-given right of suffrage. I believe that to be good Republican doctrine, and if it is not, I am not a Republican." It was a public declaration. He was speaking as much to Jim Ashley and William Tucker as to those listening to him at the railroad switching yard. Four days later, Jones couched his discussion of what it meant to be a Republican in theoretical terms: "I have held to the theory that the Republican party is the one to bring relief to the common people, and when I find that it is not I am as ready to repudiate it as were the Republicans to repudiate the Whig party in '56."[9]

An outraged party executive committee called Jones to meet with it. Chairman William Tucker, Jones's recent campaign manager and a staunch Hanna partisan, began the proceedings. Tucker's Quaker background, it seems, had influenced him only enough to give him a pious appearance. Looking through his gold-rimmed spectacles, so small they did not cover his eyes, he began by reading aloud the accounts of the Jones-Hanna controversy from the *Bee* a week earlier, including a private conversation between Colonel Waldorf and the mayor. In the article, Cochran sought corroboration from Jones: he instructed readers who doubted the story to ask Jones himself. Tucker did exactly that: he asked Jones if the story he was about to read was true. Waldorf apparently had come to see Jones, and as the *Bee* had it, before Waldorf could open his mouth, the mayor said, "I know what you are here for. You want me to endorse Hanna and I can't do it and I won't do it. I had thought seriously of coming out openly against him, and the only reason I don't is because while holding the office of mayor I consider myself the guest of the Republican party." When Tucker finished reading, Jones said in his own defense: "You have known where I stand for some time. I will not vote for or support the Republican legislative or senatorial ticket. I am not for Mark Hanna." Charles Griffin defended Jones by saying that he had not endorsed either party's platform in the mayoral election but had run on the people's platform. Jones and Griffin left the room. The meeting concluded with a vote to read them both out of the party. Sam Jones was officially independent at last. Mark Hanna had made the inevitable happen.[10]

Neg Cochran gloried in it all. "Griffin and Jones Fired, Sizzling Seance at Republican Headquarters: Mayor Jones Hurls Defiance into the Teeth of the Dictators—A Hot Old Time," read the *Bee*'s headline account of the fight. Still, Cochran did not let up. Reporting Jones's removal from the party, the Democratic editor wrote, "If some one will kindly hand Mayor Jones a pneumatic saddle he will find the wear and tear of sitting on the fence less painful."[11]

Sam Jones seemed to have won nothing by his handling of the Mark Hanna incident. Eltweed Pomeroy, in the *American Fabian,* compared Jones to Hazen Pingree, Michigan's reform governor, noting that they shared the enmity of the churches, the respectable people, and the Republican machine, but they differed in approach: Pingree was depicted as a fighter, a "political tactician of a high order"; Sam Jones was "a big, bluff, hearty Christian gentleman who would rather efface himself if he could, but whose burning love for his fellow man forces him into the arena. He would prefer to persuade rather than to fight, to win over rather than to conquer. . . . He may have the far-sighted general in him, but as yet he has not shown it." Jones would lose many a fight because he was not a political tactician of any order, as his first run-in with Mark Hanna at year's end showed. He took the opportunity in the coming months to state his opposition to Hanna clearly—and made a potent enemy.[12]

Two months later, Jones was ready to go on the attack. He wrote Governor Asa S. Bushnell, praising his courageous repudiation of Hanna as "an act of genuine heroism . . . [since he was] called upon to consider principle more sacred than loyalty to mere machine-made party domination." Cochran was so delighted that he placed the letter on the front page of the *Bee*. The *Bee* embraced Jones's stand with the headline: "Mayor Jones All Right."[13]

Jones traveled to Columbus and was introduced to a political arena where, as the *Blade* put it, "The Golden Rule in politics down here is 'do everybody or they'll do you.'" "They laughed at him," explained the *Blade*, because of his political naïveté. Sam Jones circulated through the Southern Hotel with a Hanna button pinned on his coattails without realizing it. Finally, a friend, observing those laughing at Jones, helped the mayor remove the button.[14]

The anti-Hanna forces, motivated as much by self-interest as was Hanna, lost their fight. Sam Jones watched as seventy-six legislators voted to reappoint Hanna to the U.S. Senate; Republican state senators jumped on their chairs and shouted themselves hoarse at the news. The next day, the Ohio legislature formally elected Mark Hanna to his first full term as a U.S. senator. Sam Jones's political future was effectively curtailed. Hanna would do everything he could to stop Sam Jones.[15]

"Life meant war to Mark Hanna," observed Frederic Howe, "war on his business associates, on his employees, on the state itself. And he made war, not to bend men but to break them." The *Bee* commended Jones: "Toledo's golden rule mayor was on the scene and attracted considerable attention. He was wide open against Hanna from the day he wrote that letter to Governor Bushnell." One *Bee* headline, however, ought to have been a warning to Sam: "Hanna to His Enemies, 'No Traitors Are Wanted in Our Camp,' Says He. Admits He Seeks Revenge." In the article, the *Bee* quoted Hanna: "I have a desire to visit upon every man the fruits of his own sins when he sins against our party."[16]

On the train home to Toledo from Columbus, William Tucker, the man who evicted Jones from the party, confided to Neg Cochran that Sam Jones's career was over: he never again would be renominated for mayor by the Republican Party. Or, as Tucker put it, "There wouldn't be a grease spot left of Jones when the Hanna men got through with him." Cochran dutifully reported all this in the *Bee* as Tucker had surely intended him to do. The editor doubted the party's ability to stop Sam Jones: "I'm betting on Jones, no matter what game they play."[17]

In early January 1898, two weeks after Debs's Toledo appearance and a few days after the statewide stop-Hanna fiasco fizzled, Sam Jones took a trip to Texas and California. Sam looked in on his oil interests in Texas, visited friends in Los Angeles, and stayed with Nelson O. Nelson while in

St. Louis. On his return to Toledo, Mayor Jones was elected to the League of Ohio Municipalities, where he eagerly took up the question of home rule.[18]

While local politicians were concerned with replacing Mayor Jones, the larger world impinged on many Toledoans, including Jones. In 1898, that larger world seemed a most unstable place. Newspapers across the country reported the rumblings of war between the Japanese and the Russians. The Toledo newspapers reported insurgents at work in Nicaragua and the assassination of Guatemala's president; by year's end there was an uneasy truce in the Philippines. These crises paled, however, compared with the question of Cuba.

If Sam was sure democracy had never been tried, the Spanish-American War was further proof that neither had Christianity. Few people believe that the world can do without war, but he was one of those few, as he told a volunteer disgruntled with what he had seen of the Spanish-American War. Others argued "that [war] is a necessity, and that it has done a great deal of good for the thing we call civilization, etc., but I seem to find confidence in relying wholly upon the fundamental truth expressed in the quotation . . . 'love overcometh all things,' . . . as well as in what seems to me to be the plain teaching of Jesus which, as I understand it, is all against war or fighting of any kind."[19]

Jones's anti-imperialism and his pacifism were integrally connected to his Christian socialism. Like many anti-imperialists in 1898, Jones saw this war as a mistake. But Jones went further than many—to him, all war was wrong. By 1903 he was actively antimilitary. "I am for the abolition of the army and navy," he wrote. "We have no need of them except to the inhuman poison of hatred that yet rankles in our bosoms. I am doing all that I can to abolish [the army and navy] by trying to keep young men from enlisting to be soldiers."[20] Jones did not live long enough to test his pacifism during World War I, but the vehement consistency of his intensely antimilitary comments and his dear friend Nelson's passivism throughout the Great War suggest he would have remained faithful to his position.

Once Congress had declared war and Toledo was sending troops to fight in Cuba, Sam Jones could not share in the general euphoria. Reports of the fighting deeply concerned him: "The reports that are coming from there today are perfectly dreadful, yet I am afraid that the whole truth is even worse," he wrote during the last month of the brief war. The attitude of those at home was equally disquieting. While Sam was riding the streetcar one sweltering July day, an elated friend rushed on board, sat down next to him, and said, "Well, Santiago is ours!" "Is it?" inquired Sam. "Yes, Sir," was the gleeful reply. "Well, you can have my share of it."[21]

The war was over by August. Jones argued in support of international disarmament at a local Baptist church. While Americans all across the country were buoyed by victory over Spain, Sam Jones tried to convince the Baptists that the czar's peace proposals formed "one of the most important documents in history since the signing of Lincoln's emancipation proclamation." Sam Jones's response was in tune with the European assessment; the Belgians, for example, saw it as an act "of colossal importance," while the Italians saw it as "one of the great documents that honors its century." Of the Baptists' response there remains no record.[22]

If the war did not bode well for future resolution of international issues, closer to home Jones saw reason for optimism. In January 1899, he stood at the podium of New York's Grand Central Palace, looking out over an enthusiastic crowd of four thousand members of the National Association of Letter Carriers. "I believe in people and all of the people," he told them, echoing Lincoln and Whitman. The crowd roared its approval. If Hanna and Toledo's local power brokers thought Sam Jones an irritating fool, the people he believed in believed in him with a passion. In 1899, Sam Jones saw his greatest triumph because of that mutual love. Golden Rule Jones reached people because he spoke the language of democracy. He struck a chord in people. A man who had heard him speak wrote Toledo's mayor: "Your voice, and principles enunciated there made me start, it was the old call of my soul, and the call of the soul of the world."[23]

He preached brotherhood to the letter carriers and distanced himself from the term "socialist": "I believe in human brotherhood," Jones went on. "Some people call this socialism. I don't care what you call it. I have tried to see socialism become a respectable word and a socialist a respectable person." He was heartily cheered throughout the speech. Those close to the platform interjected questions. One man shouted out that Jones seemed a socialist to him: why wasn't he affiliated with the Socialist Party? Jones said it was a good question: "As I understand it, the Socialist party arrays class against class. I don't believe in that doctrine." One woman started shouting, "The New Right, the New Right," and those around her took up the chant. Before long four thousand voices echoed throughout the hall.[24]

Sam Jones brought democracy to life for those who followed him. His reformer friends, such as Crosby, thought he put democracy in action. He never thought he was doing anything so grand. "To say that I have put the Golden Rule into practice in the conduct of the private business with which I am connected is to overstate the truth. To say that I have put it into practice in the city government of Toledo is a greater exaggeration." Nevertheless, he did distance himself from the normal workings of business and municipal government when he added: "I am in an unjust, unrighteous, and unfair social order, but while I am IN it, I am not OF it."[25]

In retrospect, the oddest aspect of Jones's second election campaign is that he ever wanted the Republican nomination. Perhaps he thought it possible to be *in* it but not *of* it. He had been read out of the party in November 1897; he apparently realized that his philosophy was too extreme for the party. But since the break in 1897, both Jones and the party officials had behaved amicably, acting as though there had not been a break. And it would not have happened, at least not that year, if registered Republicans rather than party leaders had had their say. He was willing to continue in the party, it seems, because he had not yet thought beyond the two standard parties: "Just now I see no high moral standard in either party," he said, in sharp contrast to his comments in the spring of 1897. "I don't see any reason for leaving my party for another that may offer no higher motives." He would not join a separate party, he told a correspondent, "just as I won't leave the church, though it doesn't seem particularly Christian." One party politician had told the *Blade* that "no sane man will claim for a moment that the mayor is a Republican." In January, the mayor's friends circulated petitions to put his name on the ballot as an independent candidate. As it turned out, it was well that they did.[26]

In late January or early February, some one hundred of the city's Republican businessmen met to discuss how to stop Sam Jones. They selected Charles E. Russell to run against the popular mayor. In response to the rumors that Jones would start a new party, they determined to oppose his reelection bid. Ironically, their decision brought about the very result they most feared.

Before the February convention, Sam visited Walter Brown to request that the primaries be held under the straight Baber Law. The Baber Law, passed in 1871, made it possible for either party voluntarily to hold a direct primary. Because the current system, the modified Baber, had been abused, Jones asked for a straight Barber primary so Republicans could vote directly for the nominee, avoiding a convention. Both Jones and Brown knew under that system Sam Jones would be the party's standard-bearer. He made his request, then he added a threat. If the straight Baber were not used, he would feel free to put his name before the people, but if Brown agreed to the straight Baber and he lost, Sam would be out of politics. Brown refused and went with the modified Baber that had nominated Major in 1895: he hoped to win the convention fight and a three-party race in March. Given Jones's great personal appeal and Toledo's past history of supporting third-party candidates, the odds for Brown were not good: in 1879 and 1881, Toledo elected Jacob Romeis of the Nationalist, or Greenback, Party mayor; in 1877, the entire Nationalist Party slate from state senators and congressmen to the surveyor and county commissioners was elected.[27]

Meanwhile, the Democrats met in their city convention on February 25. It was rare for them to convene first, but Walter Brown delayed the Republican convention to make it more difficult for Sam Jones to run a successful independent campaign. Neg Cochran chaired the convention—a fitting symbol of the symbiosis between press and party typical of the period. P.H. Dowling won on the first ballot and received, for the first time, the support of Cochran, who said he would be the "ideal mayor" because he would offer a centennial exposition "run on a business basis instead of on wind. The greatest problem is to get a mayor that will run matters in the interests of the people, and not as an advertising billboard for one individual."[28]

Sam Jones kicked off his reelection bid on a cold, wet night to a group that only half filled Golden Rule Hall. Sam went up to the podium. He believed that "each person could reach a kind of perfection," he told those gathered, drawing on the Methodism of his youth, "just as plants reach perfect beauty" living under the proper conditions. He saw municipal government as the means for fostering those conditions. He then outlined his specific plans: municipal ownership of the lighting, telephone, and streetcar systems.[29]

The next night Charles E. Russell declared himself a candidate for the Republican nomination in a speech that made his allegiance to the Republican Party clear. Russell, seventeen years Jones's junior, was a Toledo native who had made money in real estate and a building and loan business. His political experience was limited to his service on the board of education and as an alderman.

On March 2 the Republicans held their primary to elect delegates to the convention under the auspices of a committee of five headed by Judge John H. Doyle, former justice of the state supreme court. Even the *Blade* was concerned that this was not the best way to promote a fair election. Sam Jones was convinced of it. In a speech to a crowd of three thousand or more at Memorial Hall the night before the primary, Jones told the enthusiastic audience that the word "socialist" is not nearly as bad as it sounds: "A socialist is for everybody, while the anti-socialist is for the individual—for self only. Just now, a few of the people," said Jones, holding up the five fingers of one hand, "seem to take it upon themselves to run matters for all the people." The crowd, catching the allusion to the committee of five, laughed and cheered. "Divide Up the Day" was sung. Governor Pingree spoke, enthusiastically endorsing Sam Jones: "You now have a mayor whom you cannot afford to retire to private life," he told the crowd.[30]

The outcome of the modified Baber primary guaranteed a convention fight: 134 Jones delegates and 139 Russell delegates were elected to the convention.[31] The day before the Republican convention Sam wrote a friend to say he did not know whether he would be nominated and "did not care very much, for I shall be a candidate even if turned down by the machinists of the party."[32] But as it turned out he was to care—deeply and passionately.

The convention began Saturday morning, March 4, and a near riot broke out before business could get under way. The large crowd gathered at the doors of Memorial Hall found them barred. The executive committee decided that at this convention only delegates would be admitted—a formality that the party had had no need to turn to in past years. This outraged Jones's supporters, who found themselves, for the first time in their political experience, being denied access to the party convention. The crowd had been trying to force the issue by the strength of their numbers and the sound of their voices for about half an hour when, at 10:30 A.M., Sam Jones, a delegate to the convention from the tenth ward, arrived. He found an angry crowd.

They peaceably made way for him as he moved up the steep steps to the hall's door, suggesting that the events of the next hour—in fact, the next two years—might have followed a different course if Jones had controlled his supporters. But he did not control them; he might even be said to have kindled their anger. As the mayor arrived, the doorkeepers were struggling to keep the crowd outside the hall. "Cooney" Sherman, an Acme Sucker Rod Company employee, grabbed a chair, held it over his head, and threatened one of the doorkeepers. Luckily, those in the crowd closest to Sherman intervened and saved the doorkeeper from a nasty bash on the head. At that point, Sam Jones calmed the crowd. "Don't punish these men," he told his supporters, "they are only paid employees." By the side door, a group effectively "punished" another doorkeeper, who fled his post as a crowd of cheering men stormed the hall. Then Reynold Voit, the mayor's secretary, appeared with a police escort. Sam Jones appropriated Sherman's chair, standing on it to address the crowd. He reminded them to act like gentlemen. Probably relieved at the mayor's pacific influence, the doorkeeper let Jones in the front entrance. But at that point Sam Jones deliberately choose to be inflammatory. At the doorsill, he turned to the doorkeeper and said, loud enough for the crowd to hear: "Why let me in and not the people? I claim equal rights for all: special privilege for none." The crowd cheered and with the aide of Chief Raitz's men pushed into the hall. No one was hurt; the doorkeeper must have had the good sense to retreat. But the excited Jones supporters moved with such force that they pulled the inner doors off their hinges. A Russell Republican accused Jones of ordering the police to break down the doors. "No sir, no sir," said Jones, and, looking toward Walter Brown, he said, "If you fellows attempt to saddle that on me, we will place you in a warmer position than you are now."[33]

Walter Brown took the podium shortly before eleven. Boos and hisses echoed throughout the room. Looking as though he might drop from apoplexy, he banged his gavel, threatening to clear the room. "Try it, try it," shouted some, while others dared him, "you can't do it." Somehow Walter Brown and Jim Ashley put T.P. Brown, the railroad president, forward as convention chairman; the Jones forces put forward Harry E. King. The scene was 1897 revisited, but this time Ashley and King did not work together to bring Jones the nomination. "Jones is my personal friend," Jim Ashley shouted to the crowd, "but I do not agree with him in his conduct of municipal affairs." The rest of his speech could not be heard, drowned out by the vocal disapproval of the Jones delegates. If Brand Whitlock was right and Jones's legacy to Toledo was that he "compelled a discussion of fundamental principles of government," there was to be no discussion of those principles that day.

Ballots were finally cast for the chairman. Out of 253 delegates to the convention Harry King received 126; T.P. Brown received 125; two delegates, it seems, were out of the room. King began to mount the podium but was pulled down to learn that Walter Brown was declaring no winner. It took a full majority, King heard him say, of all delegates—present or not—so 127 was the number needed to elect. Many in the crowd were outraged. In fact, Walter Brown was abiding by the laws of the convention: the rules read: "Necessary to a choice, 127." Brown at the podium was trying to control a room full of passionate, angry Republicans, unable to call them to order. So desperate was he to gain control that he broke his gavel: its hammer flew into the crowd hitting one delegate in the head. A second vote began, but the Jones wards refused to participate until their man got up on the platform and asked them to let the vote be taken. This time Harry King lost to T.P. Brown 120 to 133. The first battle had gone to the Russell men.[34]

Jim Ashley attempted another speech, which no one was able to hear, putting Charles Russell's name before the delegates. "Let us not go after strange gods, and untried experiments," exhorted Ashley, "let us stick to the Republican party." Sam Jones's name was put forth, but a Russell delegate reminded the chair that the committee of five had resolved to require any candidate to pledge his support to the entire Republican ticket. The ruling meant that as a candidate Sam Jones had to pledge his support of the Republican nominee in advance, thus eliminating any third-party attempts.

It was a patently anti-Jones move. Ashley pledged Russell's support of whoever won the nomination. Jones spoke for himself. He did so at great length, as was his wont, so T.P. Brown reminded him that he was supposed to be answering one specific question. Jones began again, getting no closer to a simple yes or no. He affirmed once again that he was "a Republican, a Lincoln Republican," and went on to warn the party professionals that what they had witnessed this morning was "but the murmurs of a storm that will break and sweep away all opposition to the popular form of government and give us a government for the people and by the people. The question is not shall you turn Jones down, but the sentiment Jones stands for—principles that I stand for, will live for, and will die for." These last words were met with a tremendous ovation. When the crowd was somewhat quieted, an exasperated Waldorf called out to the mayor, "Will you be loyal to the ticket?" Jones told him he would answer the question when he was through speaking, but the rest of his impromptu address was met with catcalls. Finally, the Russell supporters were doing unto others as they had been done by: "Get to the point. Answer the question," the Russell delegates shouted. Jones did finish speaking, but he never answered the question.[35]

The first ballot provided 125 votes for Russell, 124 for Jones, and 2 for John D.R. Lamson, who had not been nominated. A second ballot changed virtually nothing. The din was so loud that at one point the convention chairman turned to Jones's ward and asked, "Will someone from the Tenth who loves the Golden Rule please secure order?" On the third ballot Russell received 130 votes to Sam Jones's 123—Charles Russell was the Republican nominee. But the loser took the podium. "All the dishonorable means known to politicians" had been used against him, said Jones, therefore he would not accept the decision. At 3 P.M., he got down from the podium and left the hall.[36]

The Republican Party was "like the Sampson of old," Jones wrote Pingree within forty-eight hours: "In the victory they won, they pulled the structure down upon their own heads. In order to accomplish my defeat they resorted to ballot box stuffing, fraudulent counting, and open and unblushing bribery on the floor of the convention; even at that they had a chairman whose arithmetic showed that 126 did not beat 125."[37] Even if Jones's charges are false—and there is no way to prove them one hundred years after the fact—Jones's analogy still holds some truth. There does seem to have been an inherent weakness in the Republican organization. Despite being so sure of its own strength and power, the party was "brought down" by the forceful personality of one individual who seemed to threaten it. It is also true that the Party, like Samson, did not take proper measure of its opponent; as a result, the Republican organization in Toledo was effectively emasculated for the remainder of Sam Jones's life and a decade beyond his death.

That is not, of course, how the party viewed the situation. If Sam Jones was outraged after the convention, Walter Brown was beside himself. Brown castigated Jones for a multitude of sins, the most grievous being that he had not been a Republican. Brown repeatedly charged him with responsibility for the actions of "a mob of hoodlums which have been gathered together by your devoted friend Captain J.B. Luckey." Brown began with the perfect opening: "I note with regret your determination to end your affiliation with the Republican Party. That determination costs the Republican Party your vote." If his opening was disingenuous, his conclusion disclosed his true outrage: "If your doctrines of government by love, universal brotherhood, the golden rule, the declaration of independence and Lincoln Republicanism, as you have been preaching them of the last two years, have had any influence whatever upon your employees and followers, the acts of violence, committed in your presence, at last Saturday's convention, make it extremely easy to locate the 'dangerous men' in our community. In one of the intense moments of the convention, you and I agreed that we should not be able to agree until the millennium." Brown signed the letter, "Hoping that the millennium may soon come, I am, Very Truly Yours."[38]

Apparently without any consciousness that his actions deviated from the principles of the pure democracy he advocated, Sam began his campaign as an independent with a speech called "Opening of the Campaign of Education." Drawing a parallel between himself and William Jennings Bryan, Jones noted that Bryan's recent defeat had been worth the effort despite the loss to McKinley because the election had effectively broken down party lines and "revealed to the people the utter silliness of the spirit of partisan hate." In the future, it would be "harder for unscrupulous or bigoted leaders to make them respond to the crack of the party whip."[39]

Jim Ashley, who had placed Sam Jones's name before the 1897 Republican convention, let the Golden Rule mayor know in no uncertain terms that he considered him misguided, foolish, and ambitious—a dangerous combination: "Your ardent temperament, the school of philosophy to which you suddenly turned after years of successfully chasing the nimble dollar, an amiable eccentricity which most of us have taken and suffered from years ago as we did from the measles and other ills of childhood, together with your impatient ambition, have led you astray."[40]

By mid-March Sam Jones was luxuriating in the freedom he found outside the party. "If it did not smack of superstition," he told a friend in Chicago, "I would call it . . . providential." Jones's actions to extricate himself from the party may not have been much better than the actions of the men who tried to stop him, but they finally freed him from the political pressures that had been hampering him ever since the party insisted that he publicly endorse Mark Hanna. "I do feel a sense of freedom to have taken off the straps of partisan politics," he told another correspondent. "I honestly pleaded with them not to destroy the Republican party," he continued: "no crocodile tears rolled down my cheeks as I contemplated their determination to commit political suicide in this city."[41]

The conflict between Jones and middle-class moralists got particularly virulent during the mayoral race. Toledo clergy brought another Sam Jones to town the month before the election: Sam P. Jones, a dark, wiry fundamentalist preacher from Georgia who affected a coarse "down-home" style, though his opening prayer was always rendered in perfect English. His presence in Toledo revealed the close connection between politics and religion, two opposing agendas for social reform, and the stake the clergy felt they had in this election. Although his supporters denied that the timing of his revival meetings and the extension of Sam P. Jones's Toledo stay had anything to do with the April election, the *Bee* wrote, "The preachers may pretend what they please but we have positive proof that Evangelist Jones was brought here to affect the spring election." If that was the purpose (and Sam M. Jones believed for the rest of his life that it was), his message reached huge numbers of people. Sam P. Jones packed them in at the armory—three thousand went to his first meeting—to hear a very political sermon. Eight days later he was still drawing crowds; the *Bee* headline read: "Many Hear Jones; Last Night's Sermon Blanched Faces in Crowd; It Was on Sudden Death: The Revivalist Predicted That Many Lives Would Go Out Like a Flash." Although he did not make the connection explicit, the revivalist's constant reference to the number of drinkers in town certainly implied that the danger of spontaneous combustion went up in direct proportion to the number of beers consumed.[42]

The Republican paper, both angered and threatened because the mayor was seeking reelection as an independent, printed the headline "Evangelist's Hot Shot; Jones Batteries Turned on Municipal Authorities; Declares If the Devil Were Mayor He Would Not Change a Thing." In likening Mayor Jones to the Devil, the other Sam Jones established the line of attack that the clergy would take for the rest of the mayor's life. On his last night in town, Sam P. evoked the image of a mad dog on the attack, heading toward his own wife and children. "Do I say I believe in the Golden Rule for that dog?" he asked rhetorically. "The mad dog in this town is the saloon and the shameless houses. I don't believe in the Golden Rule for that mad dog. . . . I say the way to meet a mad dog is with a shotgun."[43]

Golden Rule Jones was concerned about the attacks; just a week before the election, the mayor wrote to another Georgian, complaining about his treatment and seeing his own story in terms of Christ's. He consoled himself, saying: "I know that in His day the Christ, whom he [Sam P.] professes to preach, was counted a 'wine bibber, a gluttonous person and the friend of sinners' by the same class that Sam P. Jones now belongs to." He knew that if Sam P. ever preached "the real religion of Jesus," then "the respectable, the well-to-do, and particularly the rich who contributed to pay him for his service here will withdraw their support, and when he preaches the real gospel of love instead of the gospel of hate, the 'hickory club and the shot gun' gospel, he will have to be as Jesus and his disciples were, content to be poor." The respectable people lost both fights, the blue laws controversy and the attempt to defeat Sam Jones. New York's reform mayor Seth Low's experience in 1902 may suggest that Jones took the politically wise stand. Low lost reelection largely because of his opposition to Sunday liquor sales. At least one reform politician agreed with Jones on the issue. Detroit's Hazen Pingree argued that the saloons and dens of iniquity were not the most dangerous enemies of good government.[44]

The other Sam Jones's attacks hurt, but more substantive charges did not. The Russell campaign attacked Jones's administration as incompetent and extravagant. Sam, however, remained unruffled. His reactions were much different from the previous election. Why? Because he had found his true platform, he was serious about the educational value of the campaign, and it was clear he was winning. The support he received from traditional Republican quarters touched him deeply. He replied to Dr. J.P. Haynes, a black man who described himself as a "Jones man," that "the action of the colored man in this city has moved me more than anything else that has taken place since the campaign began. It seems to me an act of pure heroism for colored men to break away from party bondage." He considered his opposition to be both party machines, the press, corporations seeking franchises, and "a considerable element in the protestant church, some of whom have classed me as a 'moral leper' because I have not waged war upon" vice.[45]

Shame-filled though Jones was, these attacks did not dismay him; rather, they proved the validity of his views. But Helen saw it otherwise. Thirty-three years after his death, she reflected on those turbulent times. They were "interesting but sad years, too, in some ways. The people who misunderstood my husband brought about the unhappiness which came in those years." The attacks of others surely brought her unhappiness, but for Sam the sharpest criticisms came from within.[46]

The press did not support Jones. In response, perhaps, to his recent New York speeches, the *New York Times* called Sam Jones "one of the most interesting of all the dreamers who are now dreaming" but undermined an apparent compliment by asserting that his "schemes are a good example of the result of the attempt of a third-rate, uneducated, well-meaning mind to improve upon the laws of nature." The *Blade* was so pleased that it reprinted the *Times* comments. In the same issue, in fact on the same page, the Republican paper acknowledged that Sam Jones "has made a very good mayor." Nevertheless, the paper endorsed Russell because of the mayor's support of public ownership of utilities.[47]

The support of traditional Republican groups, even with the endorsement of labor, could not have guaranteed Sam Jones's reelection, at least not with such striking results. The split within the party worked for Jones. Foraker's Toledo supporters saw in Sam Jones the perfect tool to wrest power from the Hanna organization of Jim Ashley and Walter Brown. Important Foraker men such as Lem Harris and Charles Griffin actively worked for Jones. Harris was his campaign manager; Griffin made a series of speeches, as did George Herron, in support of Jones's reelection.

Afterward, Sam Jones remembered his reelection as an example of the "spontaneous uprising and manifestation of the noble spirit of patriotism," rather than "a tribute to personal popularity." The reality was considerably less noble. Throughout the campaign the Republicans found it almost impossible to hold campaign meetings. Jones supporters used the "heckler's veto" to drown out Russell's speeches. The police never intervened even though some pro-Jones groups broke into closed meetings. It was the *Blade*'s opinion that a good many of the Jones men did not "understand his fine-spun theories, except this far: they are told by the Mayor that somebody is making money which ought to be theirs. . . . With the feeling that they are being robbed thus indoctrinated by Jones, they are intolerant of all speech-making against him." "Jones probably doesn't realize it," granted Locke, "but his speeches directly inflame his hearers against all men who are prosperous."[48] The facts clearly show that the Golden Rule campaign, which Sam Jones tried to elevate to a higher plane of political discussion, had another, much darker, side. It was a side that Jones never acknowledged.

There were, of course, positive political demonstrations. But the people's patriotism seemed directed toward Sam Jones the man. On Saturday night, April 1, sixteen hundred people marched in a parade for Golden Rule Jones. The turnout was nothing short of remarkable: the next day was Easter Sunday and the parade was conducted in a swirling spring snowstorm. Five bands, two drum corps, twelve mounted parade marshals, a contingent from the Newsboys and Bootblacks Union carrying a sign, "We do not vote, but our Dads do"—sixteen hundred people struggled through the quickly falling snow.[49]

Easter Monday was election day. Probably few people in town thought Russell had a chance. Dowling clearly was not in the running. But no one, including the candidate, realized that Russell was not in the running either. Sam Jones received just under 70 percent of the votes cast: 16,733 to Russell's 4,266 and Dowling's 3,148. Some 7,000 people voted for Sam Jones and no one else on the ballot.

That night, a crowd confidently awaited the good news outside the Valentine building. Lem Harris worked the crowd by using a "magic lantern," or stereopticon, to flash the election returns onto a screen the crowd could see. As they waited for other precincts, Harris fashioned sentences onto the screen. "What's the matter with the Golden Rule?" the magic lantern asked. "Nothing!" roared the crowd. "Big Jim says it's a shame. Is it?" "No!" they bellowed. An emotional and drained Jones spoke briefly from the second-story window to thank the crowd and then left for the night with Helen.[50]

After his triumphal reelection, Jones almost seemed to gloat at the opposition of the Protestant clergy. "I know it will grieve you to learn," he wrote Josiah Strong, "that there was one union in Toledo that did not endorse me or the independent movement; on the contrary it stayed by the republican machine and the corporations"—the Toledo Ministers' Union. "When I reflect that of the seventeen ministers in Springfield when Lincoln was first elected only three were for Lincoln, I am led to think that maybe the Toledo Ministers may be wrong in this instance." Negley Cochran was "quite certain" that "Brother Jones didn't practice the Golden Rule [on election day]. . . . Certainly, he wouldn't want anybody to do unto him what he did unto the rest of us at the polls."[51]

Ernest Crosby, who continued to keep Leo Tolstoy abreast of Jones's career, reported his victory. It was, he wrote, "a great political event in the direction of socialism, and they are already talking of making him Governor of Ohio." Six months later, when Jones ran for governor, Crosby mused in a letter to Tolstoy, "It puzzles me to know how he will combine the Golden Rule with the Constitution and the laws of Ohio."[52]

PART 3

Political Defeats and Personal Victories

8

That I May Rid Myself of Guilt and Complicity

The spring of 1899 would be the high point of Golden Rule Jones's political career because his personal needs pushed him to make politically untenable choices later that summer. In the months between his triumphant reelection in April and August 1899, when he decided to run an independent campaign for governor of Ohio, Sam Jones took stock of himself and engaged in the greatest political gamble of his life. In the weeks following his reelection, Jones felt supremely connected to the people and confident about reform. The temptation of becoming Ohio's governor was irresistible: how could he not run? In fact, he almost seemed willing to be the Republican nominee; when that option was eliminated by Mark Hanna, Jones required the people to entice him into the race. His actions are incomprehensible when examined only in the political realm. They can be understood only by the religious injunction to deny the self.

In retrospect, the 1899 mayoral campaign seems to have been a catalyst; the great defeat of the Republicans, who so condescendingly handled his first campaign and then had ejected him from the party, was a heady affirmation of his own personal power. There was great satisfaction to be had on that level. Perhaps more important, he reveled in the people's love for him. The victory gave him fame of a higher order; the love and the national attention felt so wonderful, so seductive, that his childhood distrust of self became the major force of his inner life. He needed to run for governor, but he could not seem to need it. Writing his autobiography, which he began as he struggled to decide his political future, intensified his shame and guilt and his feelings of complicity with the system. Repeatedly, Jones spoke of an overwhelming compulsion to shed his intense feelings of guilt. It is striking how quickly his euphoric sense of connection faded into intense self-criticism.

The essential paradox of reform lies in the fact that the existing order of things is an integral part of the reformer. Emerson understood the reformer's complicity with the system he seeks to reform: "You are yourself the result of this manner of living, this foul compromise, this vituperated Sodom," he wrote in "The Conservative." He foresaw Sam Jones's problem: "You are under the necessity of using the actual order of things, in order to disuse it; to live by it, whilst you wish to take away its life. The past has baked your loaf, and in the strength of its bread you would break up the oven." Emerson knew how impossible the situation was. Raised on the bread of Methodist sanctification, Jones would, as he put it, "pour out" his life "in a continual protest" until his last breath. To a close friend he wrote, "The iniquity and injustice of the present situation is becoming clearer and clearer as the days go by, and I am striving as fast as I can to understand the truth in order that I may rid myself of guilt and complicity in it." His sense of complicity with the system made his failure to disconnect from it all the more unbearable.[1]

Jones took personal responsibility for the system and blamed himself harshly not just for failures to improve the system but for things "left undone." "I feel," he wrote his men at Christmas 1902, "that it is a scientific fact that it is absolutely impossible for me to know perfect happiness except as I shall, to the extent of my ability, put myself into just relation with my fellow-men." Jones went on to say that "therefore, I get each time a larger and ever larger grasp on happiness . . . because of the consciousness that I have done my utmost to make happiness possible for all." Perhaps, had Jones stopped there, he could have found some measure of happiness and peace. He went on to say, "But while I leave undone one thing that is in my power to do to enhance the real happiness of the least or lowest man or woman on the planet, my own claim to happiness is defective, *and I shall be miserable and I ought,* for the same law that entitles me to share in the happiness that I produce condemns me to share in the unhappiness for which I am responsible, whether it be caused by what I have either done or left undone."[2]

To take full measure of the shift from heady confidence to complicit guilt, one must begin by considering the euphoria Sam felt in the spring of 1899. Golden Rule Jones's contract of the heart offered to others a passionate commitment to the idea of brotherhood to which the people responded with a passion that matched Jones's own. His triumphant reelection proved that the passion and the faith in equality Jones articulated were reciprocated. So, too, do the thousands of letters written to Jones from anonymous people who have no claim to history's attention, no tie to Toledo. They wrote to thank Sam Jones for what he stood for. The tone and tenor of these letters are striking; they measure both his political strength and the tremendous personal burden he carried. Harry N. Robins, on the editorial staff of *Arena,* wrote, "I want you to know that I (and, of course, many others) are looking to you to exemplify and carry forward what MUST become the regenerating principle in American, and all, life." No wonder Jones felt his position a burden. "There are millions watching you," wrote another who would only intensify the burden, "hearts your words will cheer with hope, souls of men whose intelligence and mentality is failing, because of oppression, the time is now most opportune, every auspice favorable to their redemption through your energetic work and truthful words. God bless the day my friend that brought you to light, made your undying principles new to a despairing people." Another correspondent wrote, "I think if you could realize the incentive your life is to others for them to try and make the world better for having lived in it, it would help sustain you in the arduous duties."[3] Clearly, the recipient of these heartfelt endorsements felt a tremendous personal responsibility to his correspondents.

In the months leading up to Ohio's gubernatorial race, Sam Jones's political ambition collided with his Calvinist distrust of self. What is most striking about his decision to make this campaign is his almost complete passivity. He sought to cover his ambition under the ideal of remaining subservient to the will of the people. Hence he claimed he did not respond to the dictates of his own heart or to the sage political advice of Debs and Nelson. He convinced his evangelical conscience of his utter passivity: "I can truthfully say that I have not done one thing to help it forward. I have felt all along that it ought to be understood that the movement came *to* me rather than *from* me." The *Cleveland Leader* noted that "Mayor Jones has decided to put all the responsibility upon the people. If they want him to run for governor . . . he will consent." The editor misjudged both the people's response and the politician's urgent needs when he concluded, "That settles it. Jones will not run." The internal "requirement" to remain passive set the pattern for the future.[4]

The tension between Sam Jones's political goals and his personal needs was perhaps never clearer than in the race for governor. The gubernatorial campaign is essential in understanding the trajectory of Jones's political career. Clearly, the evangelical imperative to deny the self does not suit the political profession. Had he exerted his energy to fulfill his ambitions, Golden Rule Jones's career might have more nearly paralleled Hazen Pingree's. Sam Jones stood in position to become Ohio's governor. His refusal to organize an independent political party certainly cost him votes; it may have cost him the election. Personally, however, Sam Jones thought it his greatest triumph. He felt more connected to all of the people than he ever had before or ever would again.

Jones's potential political power can be gauged by the fear he seems to have struck in some prominent Republican hearts. Sam Jones was seen as such a powerful threat that some Republicans contemplated making him the Republican gubernatorial nominee. The talk was so widespread that it made its way to the White House. Mark Hanna reasonably said, "I don't see how Mayor Jones could run on a Republican platform." President McKinley asked Clarence Brown and Senator Foraker about Republican politics in Toledo. His concern is hardly surprising. He "spoke kindly" of the mayor, said Brown, and "said that he inferred from what he had heard of Mayor Jones that he was a man of accomplishments, positive convictions and of great personal popularity and kindness." But, according to Brown, the president also thought Sam Jones a concern only to the local party. Subsequent events suggest otherwise; even McKinley campaigned for the Republican nominee in the three-way gubernatorial race.

If President McKinley was not yet interested in Sam Jones, Governor Bushnell was because Jones might help him undermine Mark Hanna's power. Asa Bushnell hated Mark Hanna. "As sure as there is a God in Israel," he said that summer, "the people of Ohio will rise up one day and rebuke that man." In the spring, Bushnell seems to have thought that Sam Jones might incite Ohioans to do just that by beating the Hanna man, Judge George Nash, for the nomination. Bushnell distanced himself from Jones's ideology: "While I do not agree with all of his theories, I know I could live under the administration of Governor Sam Jones, for I believe him to be an honest, sincere man. He has always been my staunch friend and supporter."[5]

It is not at all clear why Jones might have been interested in the Republican nomination. He later said that he had wanted only to bring in sufficient delegates to the convention to make things interesting. But Mark Hanna intervened; as a result, Sam Jones would have no power in the Republican Party. Lucas County Republicans had agreed to abide by the straight Baber Law for the May primary, which would, among other things, elect delegates to the Republican state convention. Had Hanna not intervened, the combined forces of Toledo Republicans, so shaken by their defeat, and the machinations of Asa Bushnell and the Toledo Foraker men could easily have handed the Republican nomination to Sam Jones without his doing a thing. That Hanna did concern himself proves how real the Jones threat was. Speaking of Jones, Hanna told the press, "When I learned that he and his fellows were candidates for delegates to the state convention I told some of our timid people down that way that they must make a fight against him." Hanna said of Sam Jones, "He is simply a crank, but he is a moral crank, and that makes the thing worse, for he believes what he says."[6]

Whatever the Foraker machine was planning behind the scenes, the senator himself repudiated Jones. Foraker, now publicly accused of taking bribes, predicted that Sam Jones was politically "on his last legs." "Here he is, a man whose political stock in trade is a theory and a total lack of knowledge of practical politics, and the hallucination that he has no need of a political manager." Although Jones's political legs would support him longer than Foraker's would, he was right about Jones's "hallucination," if for "political manager" one substitutes "organization." Foraker considered Jones's suggestion that he would run only if the party accepted his platform "grotesque."[7]

While Jones repeatedly denied that he was interested in higher office, the people—at least a vocal minority of them—treated him as though he already were the candidate. At an American Federation of Labor speech in Columbus to a crowd estimated at four thousand, people kept up a cheer to "the next Governor of Ohio, the next Governor of Ohio." Addressing the crowd on the topic of politics and labor, Sam Jones sounded very much the candidate. He hit hard at the party system: "I deliberately charge failure against the present social order known as competition. Until we shall speak of competition by its shorter name of WAR, we shall not be able to properly appreciate this statement." Continuing, Jones argued for the "absolute destruction of party machines." It was the principle he would advocate for the rest of his life, the conviction that social problems could be solved if only the party system were destroyed. He sought an explanation for the disjunction between his belief in people and the daily examples of suffering. If people were innately good, something must be to blame. Focusing on parties as the problem provided an explanation that allowed him to find no fault with people.[8]

He rejected parties to defuse his guilt. He wrote the Rev. George Candee, who tried to persuade him to join the Union Reform Party: "Together we must share the guilt or the glory of the condition that our fellow men are in. I . . . *will pour out my life as a continual protest* from now until my last breath against any conspiracy of a few of the people to assume the governing of the rest of the people."[9] It had been six years from the moment he experienced the "shame and degradation" of those desperate men seeking work; he had been mayor of Toledo for more than two years so he bore the burden of complicity. He had made his wealth from a natural resource that, as he saw it, rightfully belonged to the people; his self-interest was protected by a patent. As mayor he now knew he could not transform the institutions of municipal government. Because his evangelical religious training connected to Methodist perfectionism taught him to assume that success lay within himself, he equated municipal failure with personal failure. Neither Hugh nor Margaret Jones had envisioned their son defining success or failure in terms of transforming the entire culture.

This "pouring out" of his life as a continual protest was not compensation enough to satisfy the demands of his Methodist conscience. He thought often about the requirements of martyrdom. "I often think that what the world is in need of," Jones had written Lloyd in 1898, "is not men who feel that they 'must live,' but men who are willing to die for the truth, if that is the way that the interests of truth are to be best served. Certainly there is nothing inconsistent with Christ's idea in this position. . . . He willingly laid down his life in the flush of early manhood for the sake of a principle." In a letter to his closest confidant, Nelson O. Nelson, he wrestled more personally with the question of sacrifice:

> I think it was Mazzini who said, "We admire martyrdom but do not adopt it," and I think it is the contemplation of that truth as it has been revealed in my progressive experience that discourages me more than anything I know of. . . . In the little I have done, I have not suffered anything that could be called martyrdom in the mildest sense. It is true that to some extent I am ostracized from polite circles for the opinions that I hold, and in the Church even "all men do not speak well of me," in fact I am not thoroughly respectable, but I have made no sacrifice; I have lived well, had all and more than I needed, and it might, I suppose, be said that I have had a good deal of newspaper glory.[10]

As Emerson had written, he was living by the current order of things while he sought to destroy the current order. He was discouraged because even his admirers had not adopted his ideas of reform, while "those in the church charge me with being a crank, and those outside of the church repeat the same thing, only varying it by saying 'damned crank.'" What disturbed him was that everyone—those moved to admiration or profanity—agreed that "social reform 'is a good thing.'" His inability to get support for his ideas led Sam Jones to criticize himself more harshly than even his most vociferous critics could do. If *he* would only do more, sacrifice more, perhaps then great good would be done. It is the most striking dimension of his deep compensatory impulse. Perhaps he would need to lose his life to improve the world.[11]

Henry Demarest Lloyd was "startled and dismayed" by Jones's discussion of sacrificial compensation. "There are many reasons for not making a martyr of one's self; one of the most cogent is that one's duty is to save himself to fight another day. . . . We must not only love as doves, but be as wise as serpents. . . . One of the troubles with our side is that our men, in the spirit of Mohammedan self-abnegation, are continually destroying themselves."[12] Despite Lloyd's advice, the guilt-induced feelings of martyrdom disturbed Jones for the remainder of his life.

Jones's feelings of guilt had become centered on the uses of his own money. He was attempting to better distribute the profits he earned, convinced they were not his by any right; he was daily giving away his mayoral salary and regularly dipping into his fortune. But these actions did not satisfy him. He wrote to S.H. Comings, editor of *Commonwealth* and a proponent of the Social Gospel: "I know that all of my life, I have been so woefully in error that I feel the time has come when I do not want to continue mistakes due to the inexperience of past years. I am trying to evolve a plan for work, and as soon as I see my way clear, I shall adopt it." Sure that he was not on honest terms financially with those who worked for him, his family intensified his feelings of guilt by telling him he was making a terrible mistake: "My own relatives, especially those whom I have helped from poverty to a reasonable degree of comfort" say I am "going too far." They felt he went too far—he knew he had not gone far enough. Saying no to relatives was far easier than the intensely painful task of turning down the desperate appeals for financial help or for work. He was overwhelmed with such requests, receiving from twelve to fifty a day. "The appeals for help that come to me from all over the country are simply overwhelming, and to answer them in the way expected would bankrupt a Carnegie or a Rockefeller in a year," he told a woman committed to charitable philanthropy. To a petitioner he wrote that same day, "My dear boy, You do not know with what a heavy heart I try to reply to your letter. I have had an unusually severe drain upon my sympathies this morning by the letters and appeals that have come to me, and so I think of the vast army of people, like yourself. . . . I sometimes get depressed almost to the point of despondency." His inability to respond to their need only intensified his feelings of guilt and inadequacy. In a letter to the editor of the *Christian Endeavorer,* written for publication, Mayor Sam Jones wrote that the competitive system was fit only for wild animals; he was able to run a Golden Rule shop "for the reason that we have a patent which, of course, you understand is an unfair advantage over other people."[13]

One of the most extraordinary features of his mayoralty was Jones's compulsive need to write personal answers to the letters sent to him. He felt so connected to those whose need he could not meet that he must make a heartfelt response. Toledo's city government was structured to afford its mayor little real power, it is true, but that alone does not explain Jones's daily commitment to his correspondence. For he went far beyond letters dealing with municipal affairs. The great bulk of his letters concern reform questions. They created a vital connection to others in the reform movement: Debs, Addams, Lloyd, Herron, Pingree, and Steffens, to name but a few. Letters to his closest friends, such as Nelson and Ernest Hammond, allowed him to work out the complexities of his situation, his growing sense of inadequacy in the face of an overwhelming burden. This correspondence served as working notes for his contract of the heart.

It was here, primarily, in the words searched from his heart and composed into letters that Sam Jones struggled to make sense of himself and the needs of this world. Herron, Gladden, and Rauschenbusch used sermons and books to accomplish the same end. Debs and Pingree used political speeches. Jones made speeches as well and published articles and two books. Significantly, the last book is a collection of his letters to his employees: *Letters of Labor and Love*. But the letters written to friends—"brothers" known and unknown—were the first drafts in his attempt to come to terms with what was expected of him. He had defined himself by posting the Golden Rule text in his small factory. He had turned to the written words of more accomplished writers, Tolstoy, Ruskin, Herron, and Lloyd, and to the words of Jesus in the New Testament to gain a better understanding of what the imperative to "Do Unto Others" in the workplace actually meant. Through a quirk of political infighting, he had come to a place where he could try to make a city function as a living embodiment of brotherly love. Now he had the opportunity to look to the future to consider how the entire country could make Jesus' ideas practical realities. By the summer of 1899 he was far less sanguine that these ideals could be realized.

He wrote thousands of letters, committing time each day to the task, because such writing provided a venue to understand himself and his world. He could compensate strangers with his loving epistolary attention, if not the desperately needed job. In his letters he could perhaps love his correspondents more easily than in daily working life. He took the time to struggle to make himself clear to those who disagreed with him—Walter Brown is an example—opening his heart as best he could as a daily exercise in brotherly love. Writing letters dominated his daily activities because it offered a means of entering into that contract of the heart, a compact of absolute reciprocity with political foes, those most concerned about "vice," well-meaning friends, well-wishers from across the nation, and those seeking help. He was writing as much to himself as to them, representing his intentions and ideas. The act of writing internalized his reform intentions.

His feeling of complicity had haunted him for several years now. Since 1897 at least, Sam Jones was radically at odds with his culture. He acknowledged, "I am doing my best to destroy a social system that makes millionaires out of a few and paupers out of many." He worried, in a letter to James L. Cowles, whom he had met at Crosbyside, about the "one thing that really troubles me: Will I be able to conceal my discontent with the societal injustice that I see around me, or must I break forth and cry out against it in such terms that will lead me to be characterized as an anarchist and a crank? It seems that to keep silence is to share in the societal guilt. I do not keep silence, but assure you I keep as nearly silent as I can, and even then, perhaps, make more noise than I should." Jones suffered from a double-edged guilt: when he remained silent, his silence signaled his complicity with society's crimes; when he could not help but speak out, he felt guilty for speaking.[14]

The mail also brought criticism that must have intensified his feelings of responsibility. Consider one exchange with an irate man who was outraged over Jones's political passivity. Jones defended himself by discussing the dread he felt at the task he faced. T.J. Dawson wrote on the Dawson Dental Company stationery, complete with an illustration of an upper and lower jaw displaying a fine set of teeth. The letter begins formally; in fact, the ceremonious formality of the whole makes the writer's true feelings, expressed in the last sentence, so amusing. The missive is addressed to "the Hon. Mr. Jones, My Dear Sir. The opportunity awaits you. The people crying aloud with their wrongs and burdens, appeal to you as their modern Moses. It would be impossible for man to shape political matters more to your benefit than the present. Circumstance has placed the Governor's chair before you. You make no effort to sit down in it. Mayor Jones, you are a chump—Yours very truly."[15] This outrage reveals the depth of passionate response Jones elicited in people; clearly, Dawson felt the reciprocal contract was being broken by Jones.

Even though Sam Jones was extraordinarily self-conscious about the meaning of his life, the ways he represented his intentions to himself do not tell the whole story. Jones saw clearly enough that he dreaded becoming governor because it would broaden his responsibility. He could not presently meet the needs of people who sought his help, and it grieved his "radical good heart" greatly.[16] The contract of the heart he had entered into with his employees and the people of Toledo to seek absolute fairness and Golden Rule reciprocity held him to a standard he could never satisfy.

Because of this self-imposed standard he regarded the governor's office with a great deal of dread. He wrote Dawson that the dread was rooted in "the injustice of the present system and my absolute inability to right thousands of wrongs that I see daily before my eyes." But he did not explicitly recognize the degree to which his own feelings of ambition pained him. He tried to deny his personal ambition because it seemed self-seeking. But he was no more successful than the alchemist in transforming base personal ambition into that Golden Rule contract that would allow his political position to become the people's political power. He liked the attention and acclaim; he needed to feel connected to the electorate. His evangelical background made him uncomfortable with these feelings, so he defensively took exception to the idea that he could possibly *want* to be governor: "I suppose if I am looking for personal advantage, your charge that I am a 'chump' is true; but, my friend, I am after larger gain than merely to get the governor's chair, which you say is waiting for me."[17]

The tension between the political pressures to run for governor and Jones's personal feelings of responsibility can be seen in an extraordinary interchange between Jones and Eugene Debs. He turned to Debs for advice, inviting him to come to Toledo so they could discuss his decision about the gubernatorial campaign. Jones wrote to Debs:

> I can regard [this] undertaking in no other way than with great dread on account of the great mental and physical trial that is involved. The innumerable army of submerged and disinherited that swoop down upon one who is brought into prominence as I have been, make a burden that well might make the stoutest heart quail to think of bearing. Because I plead their cause, they fancy I have some magic way of administering relief, and this, you know, is a simple absurdity. But much as I dread it, if the sentiment becomes so pronounced as to convince me that it is a matter of duty, I shall make the undertaking, and this is one particular thing I would like to talk with you about and get your view on the question.[18]

The image of the disinherited "swooping down" on him comes from a man who felt overwhelmed at times. Writing to Debs, who had faced greater notoriety and greater mental and physical trials than he had, Jones opened his heart. In asking Debs to visit him in Toledo Sam Jones exhibited his need to be persuaded to do his "duty"; the letters of spring and early summer suggest a man who is fighting both against what he feels is required of him and what in his innermost heart he wants.[19]

Debs's own later history would suggest his answer to Sam Jones, if we did not have his lengthy response, written in late July. Debs, who would go on to be the unsuccessful Socialist candidate for president of the United States five times and who could garner 919,799 votes while serving time in the Atlanta penitentiary for having violated the Espionage Act, had perhaps the clearest eye of any of Sam Jones's advisers. Debs thought Jones was merely the tool of subversive capitalist interests. "An Independent Party," he wrote,

> has been persistently boomed, with you as its candidate for Governor by such capitalist papers as the *Cincinnati Enquirer*, in which I have no faith whatsoever, and as you may rest assured, with no honest intention to advance the cause of socialism. Nor, to be candid with you, have I been pleased to see such a paper as the N.Y. *Journal*, another capitalist publication, utterly destitute of conscience or moral char-

acter, cover you with fulsome flattery. Were you an avowed, clear cut and uncompromising Socialist, the *Journal* would have no such interest in you and would drop you with amazing suddenness. The fact is, that the common enemy, with its sentinels on the watch towers, ever on the alert see and *clearly* see, what is coming and are quick as lightning to discover a leader or an element that bids fair to assume decided proportions and are as quick to make pretended concessions and by fawning and flattering recognition lay their plans to sidetrack or swallow up or otherwise dispose of the threatening leader or element. Your own Ohio movement is in this danger today. Of course, I have full faith in your integrity nor do I underestimate your judgment and your intelligence but you are dealing with the slickest politicians and tricksters that ever enlisted in the service of the devil for his dirty gold.

Debs's suspicions seem more well founded than Jones's optimism: the *Cincinnati Enquirer* was a Democratic organ owned by John R. McLean, who had hopes for the Democratic nomination. This paper had good reason to give Jones positive coverage: a viable third-party candidate would split the Republican Party and perhaps hand victory to the Democrats. Debs's letter is a passionate attempt to educate Sam Jones. But an independent party would be "neither fish nor flesh," and Debs predicted that it would fail as all its predecessors had. "I am a Socialist and being a Socialist, *I am a partisan*. I have said and say again, that at this stage there are but two kinds of politics—viz: Capitalist and Socialist and there can be no sort of compromise between them. Every 'step at a time' movement will go to pieces." Debs continued, "The fight will be fought out and socialism realized on the basis of the class struggle, without reference to what our wishes or preferences might be." Jones argued the evils of capitalism but denied it was a class-based struggle. Debs argued his case so passionately, it seems, because of Jones's potential importance to the party: "I do not hesitate to say that I know of no man I would rather see President of the United States than yourself, provided only, you are the candidate of a Socialist Party and stand squarely on the platform of International Socialism, through which alone, in my judgment, Socialism can be realized." That is a stunning affirmation of Jones's stature, coming the year before Debs first became such a candidate.[20]

Many of Jones's public pronouncements about socialism reveal that he knew that the people feared the term. Yet he was convinced that the people he trusted so much did believe in its essential concept. On the cover of a campaign brochure, produced later that summer, was a quotation: "I claim no privilege for myself or for my children that I am not doing my utmost to secure for all others on equal terms." It was the articulation of his contract of the heart, and Jones considered it a "definitive and comprehensive declaration of socialism." The people believed in this, but they would "reject it in toto if I were to preface the statement with the words 'I am a socialist.'"[21]

His friend Nelson, whose sensibilities were closest to Jones's; agreed with Debs: Sam Jones should not run for governor. In early May, Nelson, thinking, perhaps, of James Bryce's assessment that "the government of cities is the one conspicuous failure of the United States," said "there is more to actually do in a city . . . getting something actually done is more important than the approval of theories by a popular vote."[22]

Jones wrote so often about the great dread he felt—it appears in virtually every letter dealing with the question—that he seems to have already committed himself to the task. "I really dread it," he wrote Nelson in July, "and yet I do not feel that I have a right to say positively that I will not go into it." He had convinced himself, it seems, that he did not want to run but that he could not refuse the people who demanded it of him.[23]

Jones could not be utterly passive, and the Ohio press detected hypocrisy. Sam Jones crafted a letter which invited the public to petition him to run. The *Tiffin Tribune* thought Jones had "grown weary of waiting for the demand of the people for him to run for governor and has come out in a letter practically requesting the people to call him. . . . He need not worry about the people of Toledo—Toledo people would be glad to get rid of him, but the people of Ohio are not ready to take Jones off their hands." The *Cincinnati Times-Star* took a jab at both Jones and the Democratic contender McLean: who owned the rival *Cincinnati Enquirer*: "'Golden Rule' Jones has lost the support of the *Enquirer* as a gubernatorial candidate. There is a rumor afloat that the paper has flopped to McLean." Even the *Washington Post* criticized Jones's need for attention: "Possibly it will eventually occur to the press agents at Toledo, Ohio, that the country doesn't care a rap about the political plans of Hon. Sam Jones."[24]

The people responded positively, however, and he was able to disclaim his own ambition. To Nelson he said, "I am really afraid we shall have to go into the campaign." His evangelical conscience quieted by this passive and dutiful acceptance of the people's need, Jones set his sights on becoming Ohio's governor. Under the protective shield of the people's need of him, Jones devoted himself energetically to the task: he opened his campaign headquarters in the Valentine. William Cowell sent petitions to people throughout the state who had expressed support; in the first week of August they had received more than the nine thousand signatures needed to place Jones's name on the ballot. Jones convinced himself it was democracy in action: in late August he "accept[ed] the nomination thus tendered direct from the hands of the people through the long established sacred right of petition. . . . I believe in all of the people and am, therefore, a *man without a party.* I believe in the people as people, not as partisans, not as Democrats, not as Republicans, not as Populists or Prohibitionists or Union Reformers, but as people." He went on, "Believing this to be a foundation of truth I, therefore, declare that I will never again wear the label of any party or claim political loyalty to anything less than *All of the People.* In this way I shall always be free to vote and act for *principle.*"[25]

Jones's internal demands to suppress the self led him to decry not only parties but any political organization. Jones was met with scores of requests that he establish an organization. In all cases he did nothing; he asserted no control. He felt his position demanded it: the nomination, like the people, must come to him. Thus he cast his psychological need to suppress the self in terms of the democratic ideal. As a matter of principle, he would have no organization.

The rejection of any organized structure limited his political effectiveness, as one curious incident at Uhrichsville, Ohio, suggests. Sam Jones, independent candidate for governor, strolled into a street fair going full tilt in Uhrichsville. He was surprised to find a fair at all. He had been scheduled to speak at the fair, but his supporters had contacted him, saying that bad weather had caused its cancellation. Since he was on his way to New Philadelphia anyway, he had decided to look in on the men working for his campaign. He made his way to the office through the crowd, strode into the office, and introduced himself to the "Jones man" for Uhrichsville, J.H. Bartley. Bartley was dumbfounded, greatly embarrassed by the Republican Nash button he was sporting prominently on his lapel. Jones did not spend time with Bartley—there was no point. He went back out to the fair to take advantage of the clear skies and the people gathered. He found a patent medicine salesman willing to lend him his platform and began speaking. A sizable crowd gathered to hear the Golden Rule mayor of Toledo.[26]

Jones never allowed himself to see that *he,* not his principles, was the force that made the movement. He could not let self intrude so he repeated the refrain, "Jones is not the issue." He did not permit himself to see that he could have given the movement more momentum by the forceful use of his own personality. Jones feared that any organization would lead to the corruption of the ideals he advocated. "Somehow I feel somewhat afraid of organization," he admitted.[27]

Sam Jones's passivity during the spring and summer of 1899 and his fear of organization had unfortunate consequences for his reform agenda. Clearly, in retrospect, the April 1899 reelection was the high point of Jones's political life. The high point of his personal life, however, was the call from the people in August 1899. His deeply divided self can be seen in the disjunction between these two points. The mayoral election was a practical *political* triumph. In April, having pulled off what to many seemed a miraculous triumph over seasoned political professionals, Sam Jones could have done what he wanted in Toledo. But he never translated his impressive victory into political programs. Instead, he reveled in his personal triumph—the feeling of complete brotherhood outside political parties that gave him the heady sense that he was in harmony with the world. During the campaign in the autumn of 1899, Sam Jones experienced oneness with the people.

While considering his political future, Jones made a commitment to write a book, and this experience deepened his feelings of guilt and shame. *The New Right* contained his autobiography. Writing his life clarified and intensified his understanding about the feelings of shame and guilt that he suffered. It was another essential experience in the development of both his spiritual and reform lives. It helps explain the growing despair of his final four years. For several years he had thought it would be a "relief to be poor." He had felt he needed to keep silent about "societal guilt," but now he knew to do that was "to share in the guilt."[28] Writing the autobiography made him understand that truth and thereby served to intensify the guilt.

As Sam Jones wrote his life, he reexperienced it. In 1899, he gave it shape and meaning that had not been clear in the living of it. We cannot recapture his feelings in reexperiencing the past because his letters make no specific reference to that aspect of the task. That he re-tells his story from a distance, never bringing to life the feelings of the past (with the notable exception of his shame and guilt at Pithole) suggests that he may never have felt comfortable with the task. But it seems he did become comfortable with the past: he tamed it to meet his needs in the present.

Sam Jones reconciled the central inconsistency of his life—how Golden Rule Jones could once have happily lived by the rule of gold—by casting himself as the guilty innocent of Pithole. In writing his autobiography he found himself to be a person who lived what he had been taught was a Christian life. But it was, he had discovered in 1894, a lie. In devoting himself to business, he had not recognized brotherhood as the inevitable human condition. "Brotherhood *is,*" he told those attending commencement at Iowa College that summer, "and the mere matter of whether we believe or disbelieve it does not change the fact in the slightest."[29]

Jones made a useful moral parable out of his life. Unlike the admired Tolstoy, he had no great sins to repent. He had always been "good." And that is just the point. The problems of society, as Sam Jones saw them, stemmed from the blindness and guilt of the "good" and not from the sins of the "lower depths." The problems were to be found in the churches, not in the saloons.

The writing process presents a key to understanding the trajectory of Jones's political career. He did not write the book to become a candidate, but once having written the book, he was simultaneously able to take on the larger challenge and restricted in his political options. Sam Jones's autobiography becomes a moral parable in *The New Right: A Plea for Fair Play Through a More Just Social Order.* Deciding to run for governor while writing his memoir, Sam Jones, like Janus, simultaneously had to confront the future as well as the past. His political anxieties concerned how best to use his talents. He was a man tormented by feeling he was not doing enough, not sacrificing enough; he was deluged with mail from people sure that he had the power to transform America. Both his authorial and his political anxieties emerged in his effort to come to terms with his past. Andrew Carnegie wrote *The Gospel of Wealth* to reconcile the discrepancy between his own rampant capitalism and the radical thinking of his grandparents.[30] Sam Jones had precisely the opposite problem: he had to reconcile his own early capitalist fervor with his new radicalism. But this problem allowed him to use his life to convince others: his confidence that people can change their nature was based on his experience of his own radical transformation.

We must be careful not to make too much of what Jones omits from the story of his life. Keeping in mind the necessary compression involved in writing a memoir chapter, it is still possible to see that composing his life was an essential step in Jones's spiritual and political lives.

Sam Jones had two questions to answer: Who was he? Where was he going? When our lives play out so that we must simultaneously determine the answer to both questions, it is exceedingly painful, often resulting in paralysis. That is doubly true when one has been raised in a denomination with strong Calvinist leanings. At this critical juncture in his political career, Golden Rule Jones was undermined by the Calvinist call to examine the self and to deny it. When he turned to a consideration of his past, the childhood culture that shaped him seems to have reexerted its hold. Samuel Jones wanted to run for governor, but he had to create an elaborate charade of self-denial. The people must want him as governor; he could not want it himself. His unwillingness to declare himself a candidate made it seem as though he was serving the will of others, not answering the dictates of his own heart.

Sam Jones never recognized how his political career was shaped by the conflict between self-examination and self-denial: his letters and the autobiography show how well he learned the lesson of self-reflection, but he could never free himself from the Calvinist imperative to suppress the self. He would have been far more successful as a politician and a reformer if he had.

This intellectual understanding of his past actions and present pain brought little relief, though, because his position increasingly put him at the center of attention. He found himself needing to shun the personal adulation that was so nourishing. He was afraid that "Jones" had become the issue (and he had) because he so clearly saw his own inadequacies and he was so distrustful of the impulse to put self forward. The selflessness of this period—the unwillingness actively to seek the governor's mansion—indicates a preoccupation with the self that must be denied. His attempt to live his life according to the Golden Rule required him to suppress the self in the act of considering it. One must constantly monitor one's treatment of others in terms of the self; one's consideration continually shifts to the self. As he sought to deny his personal desires, self continually intruded. As a result, his feelings of failure intensified.

Jones's letters dealing with the book reveal more sustained frustration on his part than any others in the seven years of his mayoralty. Jones had secured the services of Herbert Casson to edit his messages, letters, and speeches for the book; Casson was to work with him in Toledo, but ill health and an obligation at Hearst's *Journal* kept him in New York. In one sense, Jones was frustrated by having his editor function independently in New York. Whatever reasons persuaded Jones to begin the book, by midsummer they paled in comparison to the folly he was committing. Jones wrote that he had "been persuaded into the folly or unwisdom of undertaking to write a book." In letters to close friends Henry Demarest Lloyd and Nelson O. Nelson, Jones called up a biblical parallel: "I fell into the position," he wrote Lloyd, "that Job wished for when he said 'Oh, that mine enemy would write a book.'" Clearly, Jones felt over his head.[31]

Editing frustrations alone do not account for this personal anxiety. This task, taken on out of duty at the behest of others, made Sam Jones an author for the first time in his life. He had given speeches before, he had seen his words quoted in the newspaper, had even written short pieces for reforming journals, but now he was a *writer* and he experienced the feeling of vulnerability familiar to all writers. He wrote Nelson: "I want your Introductory to be a very good apology for what might be a very poor book . . . [then perhaps] the people will feel that they have the worth of their money anyhow." It was the autobiography that made this writing different from his past experience. The man who never accepted the power of his own personal charisma was clearly uncomfortable with placing his life story before the world. It placed too much attention on the self he sought to deny.[32]

When the Democrats convened in late August, they nominated John R. McLean on the first ballot. Cochran wondered what would keep the Democrats loyal to their ticket with Jones making it a three-way race: "Will you say to them that democratic principles are safer in the hands of Nash or McLean than in the hands of Jones? If the three candidates go before the people, which will be nearest to them?" Cochran did not even feel the need to answer that last question; he thought the answer was Sam Jones.[33]

McLean campaigned on a platform that favored a law requiring the eight-hour workday while declaring itself "radically and unalterably opposed to imperialism." But Jones's nonpartisan platform measured just how far he had moved away from the standard liberal position. His platform endorsed the abolition of all political parties, public ownership of utilities (specifically mines, highways, steam and electric railroads, telegraphs, telephones, and water and light plants), union wages and eight-hour days, abolition of the contract system and use of prison labor, and a promise that the state legislature would find work for anyone willing to work. But Toledo's mayor turned it into a single-issue campaign: the need to abolish political parties.[34]

Governor Asa Bushnell, who had said in May (when it served his own interests) that he could live under a Jones administration, now seemed to have become aware for the first time of just how far Jones had moved out of the political mainstream. The governor, according to the *Bee*, spoke with "unusual emphasis": "I want to tell you that he has changed wonderfully. He used to be a good Republican, you know, but he has drifted off up in the air. He is a visionary and a dreamer. He talks the Golden Rule a great deal, but he has no practical plans." If the governor considered his plans impractical, then, retorted Jones, his quarrel was "with Christ and not with me."[35]

Earlier that summer Jones had high hopes for his campaign: "If we go into it I want it to be a campaign for a revival of real religion, a religion that will bring fellowship to every human heart," he told Nelson. In many respects it was just that. But as Eugene Debs had foreseen, Sam Jones was up against adversaries with powerful resources at their disposal. If Jones was afraid of organization, McLean, a newspaper owner, was not. The editors of Democratic newspapers across the state received a letter from the Democratic press bureau "urg[ing] them to refrain from mentioning anything about the Jones movement in their columns, as it is believed such publicity is doing great harm to McLean." McLean effectively controlled the Democratic press throughout the state with the exception of the recalcitrant *Bee*. In seeing to it that these papers did not cover the Jones campaign, McLean wielded a most powerful campaign weapon—it is hard to image a more potent one. Cochran broke ranks with the state's Democratic editors; he sent a newsman to stay with Jones and cover his campaign.[36]

Since Sam Jones would do without organization, he had to do all the work himself. "No trip is too long for him, no place too far out of the way for him to visit, and no crowd too small for him to talk to," wrote E.F. Kemp, the on-the-scene *Bee* reporter. Leaving Toledo at 9 P.M., after a full day's work, Jones boarded a train for Mansfield. He arrived at midnight, slept three hours, and got on another train at 4 A.M. to be in Zanesville for a breakfast meeting. Jones traveled 275 miles in one day. In one four-day period he spoke to six gatherings in four different towns, addressing ten thousand people. He often spoke for ninety minutes, and Kemp reported that the audiences listened to him with great care. Primarily, he concentrated his efforts on the cities of Cincinnati, Cleveland, Columbus, Dayton, and Lima. Since he did well on election day in urban areas, a well-organized campaign that covered rural Ohio might have carried that success throughout the state.[37]

The *Philadelphia North-American* considered him "an aggressive fighter, the style of man to inspire confidence and impress himself and his cause upon the public mind by sheer force of zeal." He certainly did not need an organization to turn out large crowds. In Akron he addressed fifteen hundred while hundreds, including the parade that had escorted him, were turned away from the hall. He spoke to a thousand in Bushnell's hometown, Springfield, but the newspapers did not print a word of his engagement—the *Republican* even refused to accept it with advertising rates. For his last speech in Cleveland to a crowd of eight thousand, he drew twice as many people as the combined oratorical talents of Mark Hanna and Joe Foraker could gather at the same time on the other side of town.[38]

If a lack of organization and the powerful opposition of the regular parties worked against Sam Jones, there was a wonderful anything-can-happen feel to the campaign that was a direct result of the absence of political organization. This spontaneity suited his own vital energy. Impromptu Jones meetings were held wherever the candidate went: on trains steaming through the Ohio night, on street corners in small towns. Standing on the steps of his hotel one day in Findlay, while he talked to a friend, a few people stopped to listen to "Toledo Jones." Before long there were so many people listening that the street was blocked. This won't do, he told the crowd, let's go over to the square. In Mansfield that October he became his own advertising agent. One morning he saw an opportunity to schedule another talk: he personally saw to having three thousand handbills printed, found and paid boys to distribute them, and then returned to town that night, traveling eighteen miles in two hours on two different freight trains.[39]

Sam Jones was perceived as a real threat despite his makeshift operation. Both the Republicans and the Democrats on the national level saw the 1899 gubernatorial contest in the president's home state as a preview of the 1900 national election. While Nelson, George Herron, and Clarence Darrow worked the campaign trail for Jones, the Republicans brought the big guns to Ohio. Governor Teddy Roosevelt, in the speech that opened the Republican campaign, told loyal Republicans that "we recognize throughout the nation that the contest this year in Ohio is not, and cannot be anything but a national contest." Speaker of the House David Henderson, President Pro Tem of the Senate William Fry, and both of Ohio's senators spoke on behalf of Nash. So did President McKinley, who, three years earlier, had not campaigned for his own election. "What office is William McKinley running for this year?" wondered the *Bee.*[40]

Both major party candidates took the same line in speaking about Jones. Neither wanted to alienate voters who responded deeply and personally to this man so they argued that to vote for Jones was to throw away a vote. McLean told listeners that if they did not vote for him, they should vote for Nash. Mark Hanna took the same position the next week, recommending McLean as the next best choice if voters could not see their way to supporting Nash. It is hard to conceive of a greater compliment that Hanna could pay Sam Jones.[41]

Hanna took more active steps than recommending the Democratic Party. Seated at dinner one night in Lima, an East Coast financier told Hanna, "President McKinley is anxious about Ohio." Hanna retorted, "He has damned good reason to be! . . . Whenever I have been in the smaller towns and cities, I have called together the leaders, and have personally given out the necessary funds, one hundred dollars here, one hundred dollars there, and so on." He was off, he said, to Toledo the next day: "I am going to follow the same tactics which I used to beat Jones in the Convention—to get the delegation,—do you remember? They sent word to me a few days ago that if they had five thousand, they could buy up all of Jones's lieutenants."[42]

In the final vote, Nash won with 417,000 to McLean's 368,176; Golden Rule Jones trailed with 106,721, far ahead of the Union Reform candidate, Seth Ellis (7,799), the Prohibitionist, George Hammell (5,825), and the Socialist-Laborite (2,439).

That night at election headquarters was another defining moment for Golden Rule Jones. Because Jones truly was interested in the long, slow process of education to transform the culture, he saw victory where seasoned politicians read only defeat. As the returns came into election headquarters at the Valentine building, the mayor looked calm and unmoved.

He accepted no condolences, claiming it a "moral victory." For Jones this victory was much more important than his win in the spring. Even from the political perspective there was reason for optimism: his nonpartisan candidacy polled more votes than any third-party candidate for governor of Ohio had ever received. Toledoans seemed to prefer him as their mayor, however: he polled just under 10,000 votes, almost 7,000 fewer than he had in April, carrying his county by a plurality.[43]

A closer look at the election results suggests his political loss was linked to personal issues. Had he an organization in place, he might have had great success with a developed, statewide plan. He bragged to Nelson that he had carried Toledo by 2,270 votes without a formal organization and by spending no more than $250. His results were even stronger in Cuyahoga County, where he received 54 percent of the vote; he carried Mark Hanna's home ward and precinct in Cleveland. Jones received the largest plurality a head of the ticket had ever earned in Hanna's county. Jones cherished these numbers. The win in Cleveland was "enough alone to have lived for," he admitted publicly. Privately he spoke of Hanna's "humiliating" defeat in his own ward.[44] The results should have shaken the Republicans. Sam Jones won the state's largest county, Cuyahoga (Cleveland); received enough votes in the second largest, Hamilton (Cincinnati), to give the county to McLean by a small plurality; and won the third largest county, Lucas (Toledo). Thus he sent a message to the Republicans: they may have won the election, but they lost their three most populous counties. More people voted for McLean and Jones than for Nash. Sam Jones received votes from 39,171 people who voted for no one else on the ballot. Imagine what he might have achieved with some organizational structure.[45]

A statewide organization would have developed a strategy for rural Ohio, where Jones did very poorly. Surprisingly, Jones never expanded his concern for urban workers and the urban poor to the debilitating problems farmers faced in the 1890s. Had he done so with sufficient political organization to run an effective campaign, he would have presented a serious threat to the major parties. Before the election, no one knew how to estimate the Jones vote: the *Washington Post* predicted anything from 25,000 to 125,000 votes. As 80,000 people had signed petitions for Jones to run, and as those petitions included a statement that the petitioner intended to vote for Jones, fewer than 30,000 additional voters cast ballots for him; it is clear that Jones did not greatly expand his original base of support. The next year, in his campaign for president, Eugene Debs would speak to packed, enthusiastic crowds but, like Jones, had few votes to show for it. "Thus closes the campaign," said Debs, "—and the results show that we got everything *except* votes."[46]

After the loss, he did not analyze it or rail against the wrongs of the system as he did after losing the Republican nomination in the spring. In fact, he wrote one correspondent, "No enterprise that I have ever engaged in in my life has afforded me so much satisfaction as the campaign that we have just begun for this larger liberty." He repeated the same feeling to George Herron, adding, "The world is full of the idea that to gain a victory some one must suffer defeat. You know that I had no such groveling thoughts, and as best I can, I am saying publicly and privately that ours is a great victory."[47] This is the first significant indication that Jones could find personal victory in political defeat.

Sam Jones had found temporary peace. Even though his closest friends disagreed with him, he felt connected to all. He thrilled at the experience of unity and freedom. "The feeling of oneness that has taken possession of me, of unity with all humanity, has separated me effectually from all parties and at the same time united me to the entire race," he wrote a week after the election. For the first time, he contemplated leaving the political arena: "It may be that I may never again run for office. Personally, my own inclination just now is that I would like to be free from all entanglements, free to go out as a mere preacher in the new crusade for equality."[48]

If Jones is considered in the context of the reform community, his passionate cry for unity was the voice of wisdom. Reform was being paralyzed by factional fighting among disparate groups, each of which had found the one—different—way to transform America. In 1901, in the first issue of *Social Unity,* W.D.P. Bliss had "rejected the growing movement for socialist unity in the form of a new party and urged instead the unity of all people."[49] But the life of working people in America might have been improved had the socialist laborites, social democrats, Christian socialists, single-taxers, Populists, and trade unionists worked together; the political arena requires structure.

Jones's opposition to political parties was a commitment to the principle of brotherhood, but his rejection of any form of organization clearly was a political mistake. The wisdom of Nelson, Debs, and the Union Reformers, combined with the telling lack of organization in his campaign, surely suggests that while he was right in separating himself from both major parties, he needed an organizational structure to advance his ideas. He was never able to see it this way. He wrote Pomeroy: "You say you must have organization. We have the organization of the state of Ohio; all of us are citizens of the state and of the city of Toledo, and every other political division. For my part, I claim the right to be free from any minor organization of wheel within wheel that proposes to capture the larger organization and coerce it into righteousness." When Jones wrote John McLean after the election,

"Above all things, I disclaim leadership," he articulated that deeply held evangelical injunction to suppress the self. He did not recognize it as that, so he cast it in terms of pure democracy. Without thinking, it seems, of the examples of either Jesus or Lincoln, Jones wrote: "No one leads the people. They know intuitively about how things ought to be, and all humanity leans in the right direction." Jones's response to Nelson was the most telling. His letter begins, "Nothing could grieve me more than to feel that separating from party and machine methods of even righteous people and uniting with the entire race, has somehow seemed to impress you that I have gone wrong. If I am wrong, I can only assure you that I am hopelessly wrong."[50]

9

I'm a Man Without a Party and I'm Lonely

Sam Jones's second term as mayor gave him the opportunity to test the limits of his political power in the "freedom" of his political independence. He learned quickly that alone he could not transform his political landslide into public policy reforms. His isolation intensified as Democrats courted him, as the citizenry in Toledo disappointed him, and as socialist supporters around the country called him a traitor. The great surprise of 1900 and 1901 was that Samuel Jones, "the man without a party," a nonpartisan mayor, seems to have denied his cardinal principle by working closely with the Democrats. Close consideration of Jones's thinking and his positions reveals, however, that, far from denying his political ideal, Jones established a strong but short-lived connection with Democrats as he sought to find his way. If he must reject his own political organization, perhaps established political structures could help him effect real change in Toledo and in the country as a whole.

William Jennings Bryan came to town in early May 1900, in preparation for his second run for the presidency. The Republican showing in the gubernatorial election the past autumn had made Bryan's prospect of winning McKinley's own state seem a real possibility—especially if Golden Rule Jones were to endorse the Democrat. "The surprise of the evening," wrote the delighted *Bee,* "was the mayor's presence on the platform." Jones introduced Bryan at what he called "a monster meeting" in the armory. He went up to the podium and welcomed the huge crowd: "I feel very much at home among you. I'm a man without a party and I'm lonely for everyone is against me—except the people." The crowd erupted in applause. When Bryan took the podium, he turned to consider Sam Jones, then scanned the crowd. While Toledo's mayor had been called "a man without a party, I have been accused of having three, so I can divide with him." The crowd was clearly willing to share. Bryan went on to argue that the Democrats, silver Republicans, and Jonesites were branches of the same party. Jones could hardly be expected to share that view and discerned "a real lack of enthusiasm" among the crowd. As he sat behind Bryan, looking out to the five thousand listening spectators, the mayor read his own views into their reactions: "I thought I could discern a real look of disappointment as the speech progressed—not but that Mr. Bryan is a good man, for he is, but his plan, his programme, is only a partial one, a party one."[1]

"I'm lonely." The feeling of peace and oneness had not lasted. His family thought he was "going too far"; he knew he was not going far enough. And all sides, it seemed, wanted him to join *their* party.

His complete political independence doomed his most practical political program—municipal ownership of utilities. He had fought for it unsuccessfully in his first term. In 1899, he failed to keep the city-owned gas plant and could not persuade the city council to a plan that would make electricity a municipal utility in five years. The city council seemed to enjoy thwarting the mayor. The council even was willing to lose money to stand in the Golden Rule mayor's way. It greatly angered and frustrated him. One night council began its session, while a boisterous crowd watched, by discussing the sale of the only municipal utility, the city-owned gas plant. The council seemed about to accept an offer for the gas plant of $228,000, although the mayor had earlier brought an offer of $300,000. The mayor was, understandably, incensed. Sam Jones took to the floor to argue vigorously that the city was, in effect, throwing the gas plant away. The council was doubly irresponsible in willingly accepting a $72,000 loss. The large crowd gathered in the lobby cheered him. But he had few supporters in the council: the vote was twenty-six to three. Next came the question of extending Consolidated Electric's lighting contract, which would eliminate the possibility of the city owning the electric utility in the foreseeable future. The city council spent no time discussing the subject. Councilman John C. Coleman asked the mayor if he had a check accompanying the Arbuckle-Ryan bid. Jones replied: "I will give you a check that can be certified in this room to-night. You should know that I am not running a game of bluff." "Judging from the past," said Coleman, "I don't know." Jones reddened at the attack on his personal integrity. The council refused to allow him to present the alternate Arbuckle-Ryan Company's proposal. It went on to give unanimous approval of an extension of the Consolidated Electric Light Company's contract for another five years. The council had virtually delivered the city to the utilities, Jones told Hazen Pingree. It was inconceivable. He had had "no more idea that votes could be secured to sell the plant than I had that votes could be secured to sell the public library or the High School building."[2]

At the century's end, the mayor proposed to turn the financial liability of the gas company into a profitable municipal venture by building an artificial gas plant. Sam Jones fought the sale of the gas pipelines, but legal battles slowed the fight. In May, the Court of Common Pleas rendered the sale to the Kerlin Company void; in July, the Circuit Court of Appeals granted the pipeline outside Toledo's city limits to Kerlin but left the city in possession of the inside pipeline. Of course, the inside lines alone did the city no good. Finally, more than a year later, the mayor signed the lease for the inside pipeline. The city was out of the gas business.

When the aldermen had met after approving the sale of the gas company, they could vote for an extension of the lighting franchise comforted with the thought that the public, which had voted overwhelmingly for Sam Jones on a platform that included a municipal light plant, no longer seemed committed to the change. Jones spoke that night and read the Arbuckle-Ryan offer, which gave the city the option to buy the light plant for $150,000 at any point after the first five years. But because city law required that no lighting contract could be approved without having been put before the people for a vote, the council had no choice but to accept the offer of Consolidated Electric. On one level, then, Jones's defeat seems not to have been a personal one. He had tried to get the question on the April ballot, but the aldermen had turned him down the previous February. Given his landslide reelection, however, it would seem that Jones could have better prepared the way for the consideration of this issue.[3]

The board of aldermen met again the day after the Christmas holiday. The mayor attended to present his "Christmas present": a veto of the lighting contract. He read the lengthy veto to the aldermen, who were stunned, not by his action but by his words. The veto was full of choice quotations from Whitman. One councilman, Henry A. "Sport" Ryan, got up to say he thought it a "lovely literary effort," but "Who was Whitman? He was nothing but a literary hobo and travelled around the world like a tramp. His writings . . . are only fit for degenerates. You do not find anything like his stuff in the works of Longfellow, Tennyson, or Bobby Burns." The mayor could not resist responding to this newest of literary critics by quoting Burns.[4]

In early January first the council and then the aldermen met to pass the lighting contract unanimously over Jones's veto without discussion. It was hardly an auspicious start to the new year. It appeared that Jones did not control a single vote. The mayor demurred that he did not want to control votes, but these municipal fights clearly reveal just how isolated Sam Jones was locally.[5]

This was a politician's failure, and Sam Jones the visionary was playing a different game. As a visionary he remained an outsider. His passivity was the logical result of his vision. Writing to Clarence Darrow about his dealing with the council, Jones said, "Every move convinces me of the utter hopelessness of the '*fighting*' policy."[6]

He saw himself as an educator, conducting election and municipal campaigns of education, rather than as a politician. Golden Rule Jones believed in the principles he advocated so wholeheartedly that he saw no reason to act politically. Toledo did not have a practical manager, it had a visionary. Proof that Jones never saw the world in political terms can be found in his assurance to Lloyd as he looked back over his own actions: "I know of nothing that I can do that I have not done, or that I could do, had I the time and experience to live over again."[7]

The fight over municipal ownership was an important turning point for Jones: he now saw that the people were not ready for democracy. "Nothing stands in the way," he wrote, of municipal ownership of utilities, "but the people themselves." Until people have "learned . . . their real relation to each other is that of friends, of brothers, municipal ownership will fail." To Tom Johnson he wrote in 1903, "I find now that I did not place sufficient emphasis upon the fact that the failure of the gas line is due to the mischievous interference of the legislature in denying the cities of Ohio Home Rule; for it is perfectly plain that if the cities had Home Rule they would be as free to finance such enterprises as our natural gas plant or electric light plant as a private corporation. . . . Nevertheless, it is true, as I say, that in the last analysis it is the people's fault. They are yet dreaming of democracy but not practicing it."[8]

The experiences of losing the municipal gas plant and failing to guarantee future ownership of a municipal lighting plant did more than anything else to convince Jones that the people he believed in were not yet ready to change the status quo. A tired and disappointed Jones confessed to Henry Demarest Lloyd that the pipeline and lighting controversies had confirmed his conviction of the past three years "that the social conscience of but very few people is yet sufficiently awakened to understand the only philosophy that will save them," the brotherhood of the Golden Rule. The controversy strained the emotions of a man who would rather lose $100 than lose his temper. It greatly wore down his confidence in the people, frustrating his most practical hope for urban reform. Jones argued in the *Bee* that "the only failure that can be proven by the history of the plant is that, not municipal ownership but municipal government is a failure."[9]

In Jones's second term, there were plenty of Democrats willing to befriend and assist him. Brand Whitlock was perhaps the only one who did not want something from him. Whitlock had come to Toledo shortly after Jones became mayor in 1897. From the start, he heard a lot about the mayor—everyone had something to say, and it all seemed disparaging.

"The most charitable thing they said was that he was crazy." It seems Whitlock did not meet the "crazy" man who would become his mentor until 1900. Whitlock, then a Democrat, was to become Jones's closest friend in Toledo.

One day the door to Whitlock's law office burst open and the mayor he had heard so much about entered, sporting a large cream-colored slouch hat and a flowing cravat, the kind worn by artists and social reformers. The reformer, Whitlock later decided, "must be an artist of a sort, else he could not dream his dreams." Jones wheeled a chair up to Whitlock's desk and sat down abruptly. The younger man felt that the mayor's eyes looked right into the center of his skull. Without preface, Jones said: "I want you to come out and speak." "On what subject?" asked the startled Whitlock. "There is only one subject," was the expansive reply, "life." The lawyer noted that Jones's face radiated a smile beautiful in its warmth and humor. When Whitlock murmured something about needing to prepare, the mayor interrupted. "Prepare! . . . why prepare? Just speak what's in your heart."[10]

That Whitlock was Jones's closest friend in Toledo suggests much about how isolated the mayor remained. After the mayor's death, Whitlock was most struck that living by the Golden Rule, the law of love, Jones "became finally a free man, free from the slavery of prejudices and mean passion, from the imprisonment of superstition, of conventionality and of formalism." He was largely free of these things, but the assessment tells us more about the urbane and fastidious Whitlock than it does about Jones. But it also alerts us to how unwilling Jones must have been to share his most painful doubts. Whitlock knew that he could not be as completely free as his mentor. What he did not know, it seems, was that Jones was hostage to his unrelenting evangelical conscience.[11]

Whitlock was a Democrat who would do more than anyone else to help Jones implement his dreams. Later mayor of Toledo as head of the Independent Party, he did not urge Jones to join the Democratic Party. Others, however, were as anxious as Bryan to bring Golden Rule Jones into their fold. Neg Cochran wanted Sam Jones to run for Congress as a Democrat and was worried by the evidence that Jones contemplated making a nonpartisan run for Congress. In July, Jones thought that the Democrats might well endorse his nonpartisan congressional campaign. There he was, one year after the gubernatorial defeat, again contemplating the possibility of another campaign. Lem Harris was beginning to get a petition drive started, but it seemed too much for Jones. He wrote Harris: "I want to be honest with myself first, and that once gained, I am pretty sure of being honest with everybody else. This feeling compels me to say that I really shrink from the question of making another campaign so soon."

Although publicly he remained a contender throughout the summer, privately he was troubled. First, he had the struggle of being honest with himself—he never could face his ambitious feelings.[12]

Perhaps Jones thought he could use the Democrats to build a larger independent movement. For, while Sam Jones continued to denounce parties, Cochran used his considerable power to force the state party to make no Democratic nomination for Congress, thus allowing Jones to be petitioned to run as an independent. It was a remarkable scheme for the hotly partisan Cochran to envision, much less accomplish. As Cochran himself noted, "Nobody has fought him [Jones] harder than we have for partisan reasons, but we are tired of it, for Jones doesn't represent a single vicious thought or principle in politics." Why, then, did he support Jones? In an earlier editorial, Cochran noted: "It is generally conceded that if Jones runs as an independent candidate he will easily defeat Mr. Southard and that Bryan and Stevenson will not only carry the district, but possibly the state of Ohio." Neg Cochran thought, much as the Union Reformers had thought in 1899, that Sam Jones could rejuvenate his party. "It is," he reminded his Democratic readers, "principles were are fighting for, anyhow. . . . And on principle Mayor Jones is as near a true democrat as any man in public life."[13]

William Randolph Hearst was so interested in Jones as a Democratic congressional candidate from Toledo that he sent a reporter from his *New York Journal* to Toledo to report on Jones. The reporter exhorted the *Bee*'s readers to take heed of the fact that "Mayor Jones is attracting much attention all over the country and Democrats everywhere are hoping and praying that you Democrats will send him to Congress from this district." If it was hyperbolic to suggest that all Democrats hoped for Sam Jones in Congress, it is clear that Hearst saw moving a Jones pawn to Washington as important in checkmating McKinley's bid for reelection. That winter Hearst instructed Arthur Brisbane to write an editorial praising Jones. Under a boxed headline, "Here's a Mayor Who Might Make a Good President," the editorial reads: "We don't . . . know whether he is a Republican, Democrat, or betwixt-and-betweener. But we do know that Mr. Jones has brains, for we have read with care his annual message, and we congratulate the citizens who knew enough to select such a man for Mayor." While in New York, Jones gave an interview to the *Journal* in which he said: "Wall Street is a synonym of selfishness. It is the one place in this country where we can see the soul-destroying game of grab-all, get-all, keep-all and devil-take-the-hindermost in all its hideousness."[14]

The presidential race tested Jones's position on political independence. He had spoken with Bryan; would he support him? Some newspapers tried to force Jones's hand by reporting that the nonpartisan Golden Rule mayor had endorsed William Jennings Bryan, but he wrote a member of the Arkansas Democratic State Executive Committee to say, "I have not announced that I would support Bryan, although it has been widely published that I have." Jones conveyed his discomfort to Clarence Darrow; though neither party offered a program that he, Jones, agreed with, "I feel that in order to give expression to the best that is in me, I must be with those who are *nearest the truth, nearest the center of life.*"[15]

The need for political comrades who were nearest the center of life may have been so compelling because Jones felt his family had strayed from that center. Helen did not share his views. There was no one to talk to about his increasing feeling of inadequacy: his family thought he was doing too much, not too little. And now his middle son, Paul, seemed entranced with everything he thought false and frivolous. He felt utterly alone, like the Old Testament Abraham, wrestling with God for Paul's soul. He wrote Nelson, "It is a battle for a soul that I am now in." Percy, now twenty-two, seemed settled, working responsibly in the family oil business, spending most of his time in Texas. Paul, however, had turned sixteen in May 1900 and was a source of great concern to his father. Jones had worried for at least the past two years about the effect his wealth was having on both his sons. In 1898, Jones had written Nelson of his concern that Percy "is filled with the ambition to make money and, like all the rest, he must be born again, made over with new purposes and new ambitions."[16] Jones now thought Percy seemed to have those new purposes and new ambitions. Paul had no memory of his mother, who died when he was nineteen months old; he had no memory of a life other than one of considerable luxury.

"The fraudulent, feverish, frivolous life, the red lights, the tinsel, glitter and glare of it all have simply got the poor boy's brain bewildered . . . and his better nature seems to be entirely subjected to it," his father wrote to his longtime friend Ernest Hammond. He remarked to another correspondent, "No boys ever had more sterling training so far as fundamental truth is concerned," but he was no longer surprised that this did not inoculate against the frivolous life.[17]

Paul had not done well in school in Toledo or Ithaca, New York. Jones had brought him back to Toledo to work in the mayor's office, where he could keep an eye on him, but this experiment failed also. So Jones had his son try his hand at real work—at the Acme Sucker Rod shop, scraping castings, work Paul found "monotonous." When both Jones and Percy were out of town, Paul quit without telling anyone. At a loss, Jones contacted Ernest Hammond in Corry, Pennsylvania, to ask him if he could send Paul out to work in the new municipal light plant that Hammond was building and Jones was financing. Jones thought it good for Paul to escape the city. In all likelihood, his experience with Paul would have led his thoughts back to his own childhood and his father's considering him a "lazy" worker. Jones assured Hammond he had every confidence that "if he once gets started on the right road, there will be no trouble."[18]

Eventually, the Corry municipal light plant turned out to be personally more distressing than either of the Toledo municipal projects because it revealed the limitations of charity—and friendship. Jones had originally agreed to lend Hammond $2,000 to start the plant, but more money was needed. Jones continued to finance the plant over the course of the next year, lending Hammond more than $8,000. The experience convinced him that private property was "an unmitigated evil from top to bottom." He told Hammond, "Had it not been for this cursed stuff there would be no question as to the friendship between you and me; but because I used this private poison, as I innocently believed, to try to help you, the effect has been to raise a suspicion and doubt in your mind as to the integrity of my purpose." The division between the external and internal Jones is nowhere more clearly expressed than in a letter to another correspondent: "I have reached the point where I am willing to lose not only what I have put into the Corry lighting plant but all that I have on earth in the way of property or material possessions, *but I am not willing to lose my soul or my peace of mind.*" When he came to write his life, he looked back on his desperate unemployment at Pithole as having "endangered" his soul; now, thirty-five years later, his wealth undermined his peace of mind and threatened his soul. He gave his fortune away in an attempt to save his soul while he watched Paul lose his soul to the "fraudulent, frivolous" life.[19]

Jones's concerns about Paul give us insight into his conviction that middle-class life was a corrupting influence. To his dear friend Nelson he wrote that he had been dismissing "success" for six years, claiming there was nothing in the success the world admired. Paul proved it was worse than that—success was dangerous. He now was dealing with a very real price that success exacted: "The distress, the trial, the sore agony that I endure for my boy is a part of the price that I pay for the possession of the Moloch that the world is today worshiping—the Moloch of 'success.'" It is a telling image—Moloch, the deity who could be appeased only by the sacrificial burning of children. Jones sought courage as he contemplated this sacrifice by looking to that most prominent Old Testament story of paternal sacrifice. He admitted to Nelson "all the pain and sorrow and agony" he felt but had faith "that in some mysterious way the sacrifice that I appear to be called upon to make just now of my beloved boy will prove to be a contribution to the common good; and I also have further faith to believe that . . . like Abraham of old, who God called to lay his son upon the altar, if I am true to the truth that is within me, God, in this instance as in the fable of the Bible, will 'provide me a lamb', and my dear Paul's life may be spared to make his contribution to the common life." To Hammond, who had day-to-day responsibility for Paul, he was considerably more philosophical: "He is a marked illustration of the failure of success and a living witness to the truth that I have been proclaiming, as best I knew how, that there is no success for some without success for all."[20]

Paul's experience confirmed the insight Jones had found in writing his autobiography. It was Pithole revisited. Paul, like his father before him, was becoming tainted by the culture. "Why can we not learn this simple truth," he asked Hammond, "that certain causes produce certain effects, certain social and political conditions produce certain characters in men and women; that if the smallpox is in the city and we are indifferent to it, we have no need to complain if it breaks out in our own family. Poor dear Paul!" Shortly after creating a useful moral parable out of his own experience, Jones had to watch Paul live out the same plot. "In a certain sense he is only in a measure responsible for the distressed condition into which he has fallen; and yet, as I have told him, he alone can will to get out of that condition." It was painful indeed. He was not at all sure that Paul would be able to "get out."[21]

Jones saw it as the classic case of second-generation wealth. He wrote his mother-in-law, Paul's grandmother: "I literally and truly think that I had a great advantage over Paul when I was of his age, because my parents were very poor, and therefore I stood a better chance of leading a useful life." His despair emerged: "I know that the world worships wealth and 'success', which they say I have attained; but if I have success, I do not know what I can do with it. I do not know how I can convert it into a beautiful human life in my own dear son."[22]

Jones went to Corry to see about the lighting plant and, more important, to see about Paul. Together, they took the opportunity to "slip over" to Grandma's for a visit. While there, Jones took his son to his old boyhood "stamping grounds" at Oil Creek. They "had just the best kind of time." He introduced Paul to some of his old friends and told him stories from those days. It seems likely that the Pithole story, with its moral so appropriate to young Paul's confusion, was retold. Jones thought it all very hopeful: Paul showed signs of hard work; his body had developed; he had a pride in his work. Jones felt delighted with the improvement.[23]

The worry over his son's moral health took its toll on Jones in a now recognizable pattern. He wrote Paul in late May, "I was not exactly myself today," because a severe attack of lumbago was making all movement very painful. As spring deepened into summer, his asthma returned; the attacks were so bad he feared traveling at night, having been stricken with a "dreadful" asthma attack on a train. He would later look back to this as a time when he was "considerably overweight" at 5′10 1/2" and 200 pounds.[24]

In September it was not yet clear whether he would run for Congress or would endorse Bryan. There was also the prospect of Eugene Debs' candidacy; were Sam Jones to endorse the Socialist candidate for president, the Democrats would be badly hurt in the Midwest. Jones was in desperately bad health while trying to come to terms with these questions. In 1900, for seven straight months, he had to resort to burning jimsonweed two or three times each night so he could breathe as he struggled with his personal and political isolation and his despair over Paul. Throughout the difficult fall and into the winter, Jones felt weak. Finally, with less than two months to the election, Sam Jones, nonpartisan, announced that he would vote "in favor of equality and against war" come November and "vote for William J. Bryan as the best way that I know of for giving expression to these sentiments." Jones had explained to the letter carriers in New York early that year why he would not vote for a Socialist for president: it was not yet time. So his rejection of Debs' campaign was not surprising.[25]

But in 1900, there was a major party nominee who shared many heartfelt beliefs with Toledo's Golden Rule mayor. Without question, though, William Jennings Bryan and Golden Rule Jones were an odd couple. Aside from decidedly different views on the institution of the political party, Bryan was not the radical that Sam Jones was. His belief in free silver did not reflect a distrust of wealth in and of itself. Jones had always thought the free silver men were grasping at the wrong solution to the problem. He also felt that his own wealth was not really his—an idea that Bryan would have found alarming. Bryan believed in competition, which Jones saw as a polite synonym for war. He was on the wrong side of the old "saloon chestnut" as Sam Jones saw it; in fact, he worked hard for passage of the Eighteenth Amendment, which Jones would not have endorsed had he lived that long. Most significant, the Democratic candidate was uncomfortable with the industrial world that Jones as a manufacturer had helped to create and now as a mayor was hoping to make human. Bryan was a backward-looking agrarian radical who distrusted and disliked the cities and, as a result, failed to do well outside the South and the West. Jones's failure to concern himself with farmers had been vividly demonstrated in the gubernatorial election results. Bryan's agrarian roots drew strength from a deep belief in individualism. Sam Jones, with his reliance on the Golden Rule as a practical political "platform," valued community over the individual and was a part of the communitarian tradition. "There is no doubt," he had told B.O. Flower, "but that we are better collectively—as a whole —than we are individually."[26]

Despite these differences, Bryan took the stand against imperialism that Sam Jones thought so important. Bryan's anti-imperialism outweighed questions of liquor or monetary policy for Jones in 1900. Jones spoke throughout Ohio in late September, keeping to the theme of his opposition to the Philippine war and steadfastly endorsing Bryan from his own nonpartisan position. Although Bryan was not yet a pacifist (and would never be in Sam Jones's lifetime), the mayor supported him "because he is against one war, the Philippine War, and that, I consider a step towards doing away with all war."[27]

Both men were driven by a mission to purify politics. They were champions for the people; Jones felt that "the right of the people to govern themselves is again on trial, or to say the least, it is questioned by President McKinley." This, he said, "was the real issue" of the campaign. Bryan and Jones spoke the same language: their rhetoric was moral and spiritual in tenor. Both men were charismatic leaders who emphasized their principles. In his famous "cross of gold" speech to the Democratic convention in 1896, Bryan had distanced himself from the other contenders for the nomination: "I would be presumptuous, indeed, to present myself against the distinguished gentlemen to whom you have listened if this were a mere measuring of abilities; but this is not a contest between persons. The humblest citizen in all the land, when clad in the armor of a righteous cause is stronger than all the hosts of error. I come to speak to you in defense of a cause as holy as the cause of liberty—the cause of humanity."[28] Sam Jones spoke with the same fervor, the same religious conviction, and for the same cause. Neither man, it seems, fully realized just how important his own person, clad in that righteous armor, was to the cause. While Bryan sought to place principle before person, like Sam Jones, he waged exhausting personal campaigns, essentially working outside the political organization. Bryan's failure to win the presidency, like Jones's failures, was in part owing to his weak organization.

Bryan touched the same nerve that Sam Jones touched—in both his adherents and his critics. The *Toledo Blade* had hoped for a Moses to lead the city out of the quagmire of machine politics as it searched for a reform candidate in 1897; William Jennings Bryan had been hailed in the press as a David fighting Goliath, a "Young Moses" leading the people to freedom, as early as 1895. Bryan's aspiration to national office made his political-cum-religious fight seem considerably more threatening to the Goliaths and the pharaohs of the Republican Party than Sam Jones's local career did. To

Teddy Roosevelt, Bryan had launched "a revolt aimed foolishly at those who are better off, merely because they *are* better off," which was precisely the criticism leveled at Sam Jones. Roosevelt scoffed, "It is the blind man blinding the one-eyed."[29]

To Bryan, Sam Jones's decision seemed natural and inevitable. He responded to the news of Jones's endorsement by publicly "welcom[ing] the Mayor into the party," while he told Jones privately that his "cordial" endorsement was sure to "have great weight with the 100,000 who voted for you."[30]

Others thought it a shameful betrayal. Supporting the Democrat eventually made Jones even more lonely because it emphasized the peculiarity of his position. While Jones was inundated with requests from various Democratic central committees and Bryan clubs to speak on the question, many of his former supporters considered his doing so a heretical act. An Indiana tailor, who had used his own money to advertise Jones's gubernatorial candidacy, wrote a letter that must have been painful to Jones. It likened him to Judas: "I held you in estimation second to none but to use a little slang you are a dead one among the Socialists. . . . Shame. Shame. . . . What you have done simply is enough to make one cry aloud, My God who can we trust? But we must console ourselves with the fact that even one of Christ's disciples has played traitor and we must console ourselves once more." A Cincinnati Socialist wrote, refusing to credit the newspaper letter published above Jones's signature which endorsed Bryan and offered to stump for him: "I lost my position, (I worked for a Democrat) upholding you last fall. I spent my saving, am now still without employment, without money. All for a principle I worked for night and day, do you blame me for not believing the papers?" Jones admired Debs and valued his friendship and advice, but he could not support him. He spoke of his unwillingness to support the Socialists as a party, yet he supported the Democratic Party nominee. He argued with Debs that it was a mistake to see things in terms of class. What he never said, but may have had much do to with his distrust of the Socialist Party, was that he disapproved of its irreligious connotations. Ever the Christian socialist, he could not possibly support the Socialist Party.[31]

After making the Bryan endorsement, Jones said repeatedly: "I have not joined the Democratic party," and "I always expected to be Free to vote for the candidates that I believe to be the best in line with my conception of liberty, Democracy and Equality without any reference to their party name or label." Jones was exercising his liberty in turning to Bryan and clearly resented those who instructed him to do otherwise: "The highest conception of duty that I have is to be true to my own soul; to be true to the truth (the

God that is in me). I think that a person who votes in a way to violate his own conscience simply because some one advises him or thinks he had better, defiles his own soul." "The important question," he wrote, "is not *who* one is for, but *what* one is for."[32]

On the local scene, the Democrats actually did follow Neg Cochran's plan of endorsing Jones as a nonpartisan candidate for the Ohio Ninth Congressional District seat. Someone rushed to the mayor's office and brought him back to address the convention. The rambling speech led the Democrats for more than an hour to expect that Jones would run under these conditions, but he ended the speech by saying he would not run. Jones refused to make this partisan campaign, which surely would have sent him to Congress, because he did not want his critics to impugn his support for Bryan as a trade for a seat in Congress and he wanted to remain free to work for higher things. After Jones finished speaking, the stunned Democrats gathered their collective wits to nominate Neg Cochran, who said he had been "under the influence of Jones just long enough to make me promise to be Congressman for all the people."[33]

Eugene Debs, who had determined to run for the presidency, was deeply disappointed in Sam Jones: the man Debs thought should run as a Socialist for president was willing to work for Bryan. True, Debs himself had voted for Bryan in 1896, but that did not ameliorate his view of Jones's apostasy. "Moses was not for all the people; Jehovah himself, if he is correctly quoted, was not for all the people. They smote their enemies and they smote them hard. Only Mr. Jones of Toledo is for 'all the people' and being for all the people, as a matter of fact is for none of the people." Therein lies a significant difference between the two: Eugene Debs was an Old Testament prophet who worked to smite his enemies hard; Sam Jones was a New Testament prophet who abjured having enemies. Clarence Brown, a Republican who had been an avid Jones supporter in the 1899 campaign, broke with the mayor because he could not be a New Testament politician: "I don't know much about the Golden Rule," admitted Brown; "I don't love my enemies. I have trouble getting along with my friends."[34]

But there is another way of viewing the situation than from either Debs's or Brown's perspective. Jones was looking for ways to cut across party lines to find agreement about specific reforms. His connection with the Democrats gave him the opportunity to present his ideas to a much larger audience. In one sense, Jones did a skillful job using the enticements of the Democrats so that he could participate in a dialogue with people beyond his steadfast followers. Certainly, the Democrats—Bryan, Hearst, and Cochran—were eager to use Jones to benefit from his one hundred thousand votes. But just as clearly, they did not "get" anything from Jones, while he got what he wanted: the opportunity to discuss ideas that mattered.

On September 20 Jones made his case for Bryan at a Detroit rally. Jones focused on prosperity when he was not dealing with the issue of imperialism. He attacked the "full dinner pail" argument used by Republicans to convince voters to stick with the party. He did not agree with the Democrats on Negro suffrage, nor did he agree with Bryan on the question of trusts, but ever since he had become mayor he had fought the Republican argument that the country was prosperous. There was no real prosperity while so many people sought work. Jones found the Republican argument "insulting": did they, he asked the gathered Democrats, assume that human beings were all stomach and no soul? Jones took the opportunity to retell the story of Christ's temptation in the wilderness. He reminded his audience that the Devil challenged Jesus to turn stones into bread:

> Here, boys, is your "full dinner pail," argument; you'll get it—if you obey orders. (Cheers and laughter)
>
> The great teacher said: "It is written that man shall not live by bread alone." Today another kind of devil, that thinks man is all stomach, is tempting you. If the man who conceived the "full dinner pail" had but read the holy writ, he would have learned that God blew into the nostrils of man and man became a living soul. If you're a starved soul, it doesn't make much difference what the condition of the body is. (Applause.)

Bryan wrote Jones after the speech: "Your answer to the dinner pail argument was very effective." Meanwhile, William Randolph Hearst had personally wired and written Jones to ask that he speak to the national convention of Democratic clubs. Sam Jones shared the platform with Bryan on that occasion and accepted an invitation to accompany the candidate on a tour through New York the next month.[35]

On a chill dawn in early October, Bryan's special train stopped in Toledo to take the Golden Rule mayor on board. Bryan greeted Jones, who exhorted the candidate to speak to those who had waited with him in the dark. Clearly surprised that anyone was there to greet him, the Nebraskan went to the caboose and quickly warmed up to his theme. But his engineer seems not to have known of the candidate's impromptu campaign stop, for the train started up, leaving the candidate clutching at the rails while a comparison of McKinley and King George III went unfinished.[36]

As the special train headed east, the Great Commoner and the Golden Rule mayor had much to discuss. Bryan had been influenced by many of the same men who had set Sam Jones on the road to reform. The Bible, Jefferson, the writings of Lloyd, George, Bellamy, and Tolstoy had helped shape Bryan's views. Bryan had made the trip to Yasnaya Polyana to see Tolstoy that Jones so hoped to make. He found that "notwithstanding his great intellect, his colossal strength lies in his heart more than in his mind." Bryan was more cautious in 1900 than he had been in the 1896 campaign; in 1897 he had written an article to distance himself from the radicals in which he said he was not a socialist. Jones tried to persuade him otherwise. He freely spoke of his own sense of the "redeemed social state," which the Bible described in socialist terms. He urged Bryan to consult Acts, Chapter 4, and Isaiah for descriptions of true communism. This redeemed social state, Jones argued, would come to be on American soil, under an American flag, but it would not be brought about by political revolution, by a "mere victory of 51% who will then force the other 49% to do business according to the Golden Rule."[37]

They spoke together at stops in Ohio and New York. The high point of the trip for both men was a rally at Madison Square Garden. Jones was overwhelmed at the size of the audience. Fifteen thousand people listened to Sam Jones, a self-styled "free, untrammeled soul," passionately argue that imperialism was so important a question that William McKinley must be stopped. The people stamped their feet in approval throughout the evening. Catcalls greeted the sound of Mark Hanna's name. After listening to the nonpartisan working the crowd for the Democratic standard-bearer, the *Chicago Record* reported the view of one "Ruggy" Moore, who thought Jones had an unbeatable system: "The politicians can't get to him at all. They can't even tell if he's on the square. Any time they get him in a corner he springs a bunch of talk about the silence and solitude of your soul."[38]

Sam Jones had an important influence on William Jennings Bryan—more influence than any historian has noted. Bryan's biographer, Paolo Coletta, observed that the "significant development" of the 1900 campaign was Bryan's new conviction that "love was the only truly uplifting force in the world." Coletta does not attribute this development to Golden Rule Jones's influence, for he mentions only in passing that Jones accompanied Bryan (and places Jones on the wrong trip, one to Maryland, not Madison Square Garden). But there is good reason to think that this "new conviction" had come to Bryan as the train steamed east to New York. Bryan held the crowd at the Garden for two hours, and his words make direct reference to Sam Jones, who had just spoken: "We are to be a great nation, but a great nation of friends not a great nation of fighters. I want that we shall be the great peace nation of the world so that when difficulties arise between other nations, instead of organizing great armies to kill each other they will say, 'Let us leave it to the United States; there is a nation that will settle it according to the Golden Rule.'" Jones helped lead Bryan to this new conviction.[39]

Bryan was, Jones found, "a great personality, the greatest, to my mind, that we have had as the candidate for the presidency in many years." The four-day intimacy greatly increased Jones's admiration for and love of Bryan. As they parted, Jones turned to Bryan to say he thought he had an even chance of winning both Ohio and New York but that it made "no difference" because Bryan would surely "campaign for truth always." The candidate seemed nonplussed, if only for a moment. He paused briefly and then said, "certainly, certainly."[40]

Back in Toledo, Jones campaigned for yet another Democrat. He spent three days with Neg Cochran stumping the Ninth Congressional District. Jones was the better campaigner. He had had more practice at it than Cochran, he loved the contact with people, and he believed wholeheartedly in the Democratic anti-imperial stand, which Cochran did not. At a packed meeting in Memorial Hall one wet night, Tom Johnson was working the crowd when Jones arrived. Tremendous cheers greeted his entrance. Johnson looked at his friend, paused, and said: "And this is the man Mark Hanna says can control but one vote." The cheers continued through the mayor's speech. Clearly, Neg Cochran could not keep up with the more experienced and more flamboyant Johnson and Jones. He often took the podium after Jones had warmed the crowd to say: "I wish to endorse what Mayor Jones has said today. He has expressed just my sentiments." Toledo Republicans took to calling him "Me Too Cochran." Perhaps Cochran thought the Jones magic would work for him as it had for the mayor in the spring of 1899, but he did not seem to work much magic for himself on the campaign trail. He clearly was more comfortable hurling political barbs from the pages of the *Bee*. Three years later, he saw that himself. Cochran wrote Jones: "It will take people a long time to forget that I was once a politician. I am trying to live it down; although I am more of a politician than ever, in a different sense."[41]

The national race was thought to be closest in New York, Ohio, Indiana, Illinois, and Nebraska. Jones was confident he could turn out the vote for Bryan. He predicted, "At least 75% of the vote of my personal following will go for Bryan." But despite his predictions, he was genuinely unconcerned about winning: "I think I care nothing at all about winning, in the sense that you are so interested about. I know the truth is winning, is gaining ground, all the time, and I am content to work for the truth, whether it shall win or lose."[42]

Even the week before the election Jones was still arguing with Nelson over his own non-partisan stand. Nelson, like Cochran, thought Sam Jones was really a Democrat. Thinking back on the past two months, Jones contemplated doing it all over again. He would have "simply said what I was for, refusing to say whom I was for," and he would still have been able to make every speech he had delivered. It would have made it "impossible for you, or any of those who find so much comfort in saying that I am a Democrat, to have said such a thing."[43]

The election results did not bring good news to Cochran, Bryan, or Jones. Cochran lost to Congressman James Harding Southard, though he did carry Toledo. In the national election, 7,219,530 votes were cast for McKinley to 6,359,061 for Bryan. It was a disappointing loss because McKinley had received 61 percent of the popular vote four years earlier and earned 65 percent this time. Bryan had some cause to agree with Jones about the evils of the party system. Bryan often told the story of a man who came to hear him out west, and, given Sam Jones's view of parties, it is likely that Jones heard the story from the candidate himself. The man approached Bryan, told him that he had come fifty miles to hear him speak, that he had read every speech he could get his hands on, that he would come one hundred miles to hear him speak "and, by gum, if I wasn't a Republican I'd vote for you."[44]

As 1900 came to a close and the nation prepared for McKinley's second term, Jones had a cogent suggestion for improving municipal life in Toledo. In his December 1900 annual message to the city council, Jones advocated, like Mayor Major before him, a new city charter, which, he argued, would have made a more efficient municipality and enabled citizens better to determine who was responsible for public policy decisions. Jones's changes included expanding his mayoral power, electing a seven-member city council at large, and creating only four departments headed by mayoral appointees. The revised charter was narrowly defeated in November 1901, another potent sign of Jones's failing political muscle: 9,505 for and 10,242 against.[45]

Jones tried to dispel his loneliness by sharing his ideas with the Acme Sucker Rod employees in a formal fashion. He began to send them short letters on social and political questions because the act of letter writing had become an integral part of living the Golden Rule. He wrote of his love for his employees; at the end of the year he published them in a book he called *Letters of Love and Labor.* It was another manifestation of his contract of the heart. He included in the book his letters to Eugene Debs and Clarence Brown on the Bryan controversy. Writing to Debs, he distanced himself from an alliance with everything the Democrats stood for. With reference to the Democrats' attempt to limit Negro voting in the South, he wrote, "I am against imperialism in North Carolina as much as in Luzon." Writing to

Clarence Brown, Jones distanced himself from the Tammany Democrats in New York: "I must be true to my own soul. I must follow the light within, the 'light that lighteth every man that cometh into the world.' And I would not be true to this Higher Self did I not plainly tell you in the face of your doubt of my integrity, that this is what I am doing in the present political campaign. I am following the highest and best impulses that I have; more I have not claimed, less I cannot do; I may be mistaken; I am not false." What hurt most was the criticism that he was false. "I admire your candor," he wrote Brown, "but am profoundly sorry that you have lost faith in me, as you frankly say over your signature that you have 'misgivings' as to my integrity. . . . I want to meet frankness with frankness by saying I do not doubt your integrity. I believe in you though you do not believe in me." He ended his letter to Debs with a revealing bit of doggerel:

> It takes great strength to live where you belong,
> When other people think that you are wrong;
> People you love, and who love you, and whose
> Approval is a pleasure you would choose,
> To bear the pressure and succeed at length
> In living your belief—well, it takes strength.[46]

What Sam Jones did best was live his belief. And by the time of the presidential campaign it had become clear that he stood virtually alone. He did not want an organized structure, but he surely did desire compatriots willing to live their belief in collective enterprises. Jones was frankest when discussing matters with Nelson. While the letters to Debs and Brown were couched in love and respect, and he seemed to turn the other cheek, in writing to Nelson he was angry. He sent Nelson a recent column from the *Blade* that attacked his stand on Bryan and asked Nelson to put it next to Debs's letter to him and "distinguish, if you can, between the abuse that is heaped upon me by one kind of partyism and the other. If anything, the social democratic press has been more villainous in the very personification of infamy." Bryanism had no chance, his socialist friends said, in hopes that Jones would then support a candidate who had even less chance. "Would that be any reason why I should shift and go for Debs? I never believed for one moment that Jones had any chance in the Non-Partisan campaign last fall, except the chance that he embraced and that was to stand for, and proclaim in season and out of season, the highest and holiest conception of truth."[47]

10

I Fail Utterly When It Comes to Depending upon Love

In the next several years Sam Jones focused on dispensing judgments, in favor of others in Toledo's police court and against himself in the court of his own conscience. Although he would still turn out the vote in 1901 and 1903, he would suffer significant defeats at the hands of the Ohio General Assembly and Governor Nash. Jones continued to handle those defeats with calm good grace but not so his own self-diagnosed failures to perfect his love. There is an odd disjunction between the two. Jones calmly accepted the orchestrated attacks against him. External attacks seem only to have convinced him of the validity of his position. But internal criticism was another matter; he suffered from a self-imposed suffering because he was unable to perfect his love. Sam's despair intensified as he continued to fail to meet the extraordinary demands he placed on himself. He wrote Horace Traubel, "I continually seem to feel that I am carrying the world on my shoulders."[1] Sam pushed himself so hard that he almost died in 1902.

In an extraordinary letter to Nelson after his recovery, Jones revealed just how critically his evangelical conscience was judging his failure to achieve perfection. Golden Rule Jones felt himself an utter failure. He failed because self intruded: "Love is the only measure, but love is so elusive, I sometimes think, and we get so mixed, we get so much Sam Jones philosophy mixed up with the Golden Rule. . . . Sometimes, I think my experience is unique. There is where the 'self-centered' idea comes in. I only need to refer to Isaiah to learn that the Master is he who has met and overcome." His antinomian inability to see anything of value in institutions such as the party or the church was turned upon himself; he could make no distinction between his efforts and the worst of mankind. "The best of us," he told Nelson, "are no better than the worst of us. That is my trouble all of the time. I *fail utterly* when it comes to depending upon love entirely. I'll trust love 'to a certain extent,' and yet I know that we must learn to trust it fully, that love will accept no compromise, wants no half-hearted service." Sam thought his illness was his failure to love perfectly; in fact, it was the relentless judgment that dismissed anything short of perfect love as failure that led him to a nervous breakdown. As he put it, "It has been my miserable shifty attitude towards love that cost all the pain that my body has had to endure, but love is teaching me the most important lesson that I have yet met and I believe I am learning it." Because he strove to live the Golden Rule, Sam Jones knew full well what the Puritans knew: "self is against the good of our neighbors." As a politician running for governor it had seemed incomprehensible that Sam Jones continually dismissed his own importance, his charisma, his ability to make the people believe in *him*. As a man defined by evangelical Christianity, though, what seemed politically incomprehensible makes sense. His faith required him to love unconditionally; it is a requirement that allows no room for self. But self intruded, however valiantly he tried to suppress it. The Golden Rule places the self as the touchstone: am I loving others as I wish to be loved? And so Sam Jones found himself compromising daily, giving halfhearted service, giving with a "miserable, shifty" sort of love. And this pain was eating away at him.[2]

Sam Jones's inner turmoil was carefully masked from the public, so the discouraged Republican Party had no reason for hope in the campaign against Jones in 1901. The people had not embraced their Golden Rule mayor's ideas, but they still loved the man. There was no likely candidate who could beat Sam Jones. Reynold Voit, the mayor's clerk, had begun circulating petitions to "nominate" Jones by the people themselves. On March 1, just before the Republicans met to propose a candidate in a more traditional way, Jones wrote a letter "To the People of Toledo" which the newspapers ran: he had received three thousand petitions and would run again as an independent for mayor. The Republicans sought a mayor "who would have more interest in the duties of the office than having his picture in the *Chicago Record* or his poetry in the *New York Journal*."[3]

Convinced of the political clout of a war hero, if not of the need of military strategy, the Republicans found their man in Brigadier General William McMaken, a national guard officer who had commanded the Sixth Ohio Volunteer Infantry during the Spanish-American War. McMaken had made it plain he was not interested in trying to beat Sam Jones, but he was a party man who responded to the call when it came. One Republican delegate had sighed, "I thought General McMaken had enough friends to prevent that nomination."[4]

It was, Jones characteristically thought, "the best and brightest experience in politics" that he had ever had. Each new campaign seemed both the best and brightest. "You have never seen anything like it," he wrote Ernest Crosby; "there has never been anything like it in the politics of America." He was proud that the campaign worked perfectly—without a machine.

He had but one man working for the campaign, finding halls where meetings could be held, advertising those meetings, and doing the paperwork. He had not asked for campaign donations from anyone. Meanwhile, the Republicans, he told Crosby, had a "great force of clerks, stenographers, heelers, runners, etc.," and they were spending thousands of dollars. He wrote to the theosophist J.D. Buck, as he did to many others, that it was a "campaign of faith, more so, if possible, than was the campaign for the governorship. I am trusting wholly and entirely to the good, the God, that is in the people; trusting to their ability to do their own voting without the paternal care of self-constituted committees, and we have no organization whatever."[5]

The peculiarity about this election was that the Democratic convention endorsed Sam Jones. Cochran had reason to hope that if Democrats supported Jones, they would control the city council. The Democrats followed Cochran's lead, though not without opposition within the party. Meanwhile, Jones's willingness to work with the Democrats cost him the support of Toledo's Socialists. For the first time, early in 1901, they nominated a full ticket to municipal offices. They were finished with Sam Jones: "We fail to recognize any distinction between the Republican, Democratic, and any other partisan or non-partisan movement. They are all apologists of the present system, and seek to continue it by unsubstantial palliatives."[6]

According to Cochran, the Democratic machine filled the void left by the candidate's lack of interest in organization. The Democratic machine worked for Jones; it assisted in circulating his petitions and remained in close contact with his managers. Jones may not have known it, suggested Cochran two years later, but "there was such a thing as a Jones machine . . . nevertheless."[7] In this campaign, as in his previous mayoral races, Sam Jones did not seem to be competing against anyone but was using the campaign to advance his own ideas.

The *Blade* cast aspersions on Jones's patriotism by asking why he had not served in the Civil War. "According to the biography of Mayor Jones, he was eighteen years old when the Civil War was at its height. Did he defend his country? Did he fight for the freedom of the slaves? Did he, in his young and vigorous manhood, give his services to the perpetuity of the nation. Not a bit of it. . . . He stood for peace then and now." Jones found the *Blade*'s coverage as "pestiferous, though perhaps not quite as venal as two years ago."[8]

"Two More Years of Sam Jones" ran the *Blade* on April 2, 1901, having had enough practice by now to be philosophical. That Jones won surprised nobody. But the results, if not surprising, do indicate a significant loss of support. Jones received 12,576 votes to 9,433 for William McMaken. Jones had only one opponent in this race, yet he polled 25 percent fewer votes than he had in the three-way race two years earlier. Clearly, Sam Jones had not used the 1899 mandate to put through his ideas for municipal reform, and it seems to have weakened the voters' faith in him.

Since winning reelection came naturally, Sam was able to turn his energies to prison reform at the same time. Prison reform became an opportunity to trust love fully and without compromise. He personally tried to change the criminal justice system, case by case. Jones had been interested in the plight of petty criminals from his first year in office when he had begun sitting in as police judge in the judge's absence. As a direct result of his courtroom experiences, he had become convinced as early as 1900 that "in no department of our municipal life is there more crying need for reform than in our method of dealing with unfortunates who fall into the hands of the police. . . . Our police courts actually perpetrate more crime than they prevent."[9]

Jones thought prison reform was the most significant work of his life. When he could not appear in court, he appointed Brand Whitlock in his place. In this manner he had managed to deal compassionately with many people for three and a half years before he created controversy. Those most frequently brought before him were poor people with long records as tramps, prostitutes, gamblers, drunks, or petty thieves. He seems to have moved from attempts to deal compassionately with these people to an unwillingness to incarcerate anyone. At a time when those who could not afford legal representation simply did without, Sam Jones and Brand Whitlock took on cases they considered worthy: Jones paid the court costs and Whitlock provided his services as a lawyer. Both were appalled by the police practice of picking people up "on suspicion" and keeping them in jail without charging them with a crime. Once the mayor began intervening, these people were brought to court. Jones's action had more far-reaching consequences: once the police saw that such people would receive legal counsel and a jury trial, which, under Whitlock's able skills, usually dismissed the charges, much of the police harassment ceased. At the end of his life, when Sam Jones assessed the good he had done in the world, he doubted that his charity had accomplished much, but his work to keep people out of prison seemed significant: "Almost every day I have an opportunity to help get some fellow out of jail or keep some one from going to jail, and whenever I realize that I have done that, I always feel that I have not lived in vain."[10]

By now Whitlock had become Jones's closest friend in Toledo, despite their differences in temperament. Because they worked so closely together during this period, Whitlock had many opportunities to witness Jones's love in action. His extraordinary magnanimity and trust astounded Whitlock, for Jones felt more trust than Whitlock could even imagine and he was continually surprised by its effect. One night as they were walking in downtown Toledo a tramp approached the mayor and asked him for some change. Jones reached for his wallet, found he only had a $5 bill, and handed the man the money. He asked him to go get change and bring the remainder back. Never expecting that they would see the man or the money again, Whitlock was stunned when he returned and handed Jones $5 in change.[11]

Jones spent the summer of 1901 in a confrontation with Judge Lyman W. Wachenheimer that would ultimately be settled by the Ohio legislature. The Democratic Wachenheimer had won more votes than did Sam Jones in the April election. During the intervening months, the judge had been repeatedly irritated by what he saw as the mayor's interference in his courtroom through his administration of Golden Rule justice. But in July battle lines were drawn.

The case was hardly a desperate one. A farmer visiting Toledo had gone to a brothel, ordered a beer, and never received the change from his two dollar bill, so he called the police. He would have done well to have taken the loss, for the police came only to raid the place. The farmer found himself in jail for visiting a brothel. Mayor Jones was present in court the day of the trial; Judge Wachenheimer presided. As the farmer was about to get down after testifying, Jones got up, went to the witness stand, and asked to see the man's hands. The farmer dutifully showed the mayor a pair of well-worn hands. The mayor then asked if the farmer had a bank account. "Naw," was the reply. At this, Wachenheimer interrupted the mayor's untoward cross-examination to find out why he had asked the question. Jones shrugged his shoulders, turned his hands heavenward, and replied: "Oh, that's obvious. The man is here in court without counsel." Then the mayor turned to leave. The judge sought to stop him, saying, "Wait a minute, Mayor, I have something to say," but Jones kept on walking. Furious, Wachenheimer sent a policeman for the mayor. The patrolman caught up with the mayor downstairs getting his bicycle; he brought him back in custody, a large grin on his face. "I consider your conduct and especially your remarks as a direct insult to this court," said the judge. "You are fined five dollars and costs for contempt." The mayor smiled even more broadly as if to say the judge had just proven his point. Said Jones, "This is nothing to me. All that I have to do is write my name and I am free. I am surprised that I got off as light as I did." Jones "pulled out his check book with a flourish," remembered Whitlock, wrote a check, and left; Wachenheimer dismissed the case against the farmer. The clerk of court, a Lincoln

Club Republican, said, "I never received five dollars that I wanted to take so much as that one." Jones later said his "only object . . . was to demonstrate that so-called police court justice outraged can be and is satisfied with a money consideration." The judge himself was not convinced; he thought Jones was engaged in these antics "to gain notoriety. He hopes that the story will be spread broadcast, and that it will be taken up by the outside papers. In that way, he will advertise himself." In the final event, it did give Sam Jones notoriety—of two very different sorts.[12]

Jones continued his one-man campaign against incarceration. In Judge Wachenheimer's absence Sam Jones held court for a four-day stretch in February, dismissing every case that came before him. As the caseload included a charge against a man who had pleaded guilty to burglary, Jones's actions created something of a stir in Toledo. He defended his reasoning on the principle of love; he dismissed the charges "because I saw no way of helping the persons so charged by punishing them as proscribed by law." He confided to Ernest Crosby, "If the prosecutor should instruct me that the law prescribed something I felt would be an insult to my soul, something that I could do as a judge that I could not do as a man," he would dismiss the charges anyway. "I thought it would be a splendid occasion for declaring myself and saying that I would not do either as a mayor or judge that which I could not do as a man, and therefore, the necessity was upon me to resign both offices, for I could not hold the office of mayor and appoint some other man as judge and ask him to do that which I myself refused to do." Harold W. Fraser, representative from Toledo, was so concerned by the cases the mayor dismissed that he introduced a bill in March to the General Assembly which, if passed, would remove Jones's power to select someone to fill a vacancy on the police bench.[13]

His experience in court led Jones to write a speech, "What Is Crime, and Who Are the Criminals," which he gave in Lima, to the State Board of Charities, in Cleveland, and in Cincinnati from October 1901 to February 1902. In it, Jones took his beliefs about the justice system to their logical—and radical—extreme. Jones came as close to being the Tolstoyan anarchist he was frequently accused of being when he said that "dealing out justice through the administration of punishment inflicted upon one man by another man or set of men is absolutely without a leg to stand on—that is, without foundation in any recognized philosophy of life." God metes out justice, therefore it was "an impious sort of blasphemy for me to make laws which tried to improve on God's." The response in Cleveland was understandable: two police court judges deemed Toledo's Golden Rule mayor "crazy" and "a fool." Most in Cincinnati agreed with that assessment three months later when Jones said: "If I could I would open the penitentiaries. Anything which today separates me from the lowest soul in the penitentiary or tenderloin district is the very opposite of religion."[14]

Just as Mayor Jones's dealings with Judge Wachenheimer were heading toward direct confrontation, the mayor's power was assaulted from another front. In January 1902, a bill was introduced into the General Assembly which would replace Toledo's elected Police Board with a board appointed by the governor. The governor was to select two Democratic and two Republican members, who, once selected, were to abstain from politics. This police ripper bill was designed to remove from power Raitz, an ardently political chief who continued to be somewhat lax in enforcing the laws. The *Bee* objected to it on the grounds of Home Rule: why should the governor interfere with Toledo's self-government? "If the object be to get rid of Mayor Jones it is inexcusable," wrote Cochran.[15]

In March the legislature took up the issue that Sam Jones had repeatedly attacked in his speeches as the "crowning infamy" of the system: the Habitual Criminal Act, which sentenced a person convicted of three felonies to prison for life. Repeal of the bill passed the lower house unanimously, and after passage in the Senate the law was changed. But if the General Assembly endorsed Golden Rule Jones's view of the Habitual Criminal Act, it did not endorse his ability to fill vacancies on the police bench. The Fraser bill passed, giving that power to the clerk of the court. That same month the General Assembly passed the police ripper bill which gave the governor the power to appoint four police commissioners. Both actions undermined Sam Jones's power.[16]

The police judge happened to be absent the day the Fraser Bill passed so Mayor Jones sat as judge one last time. He summarily dismissed every case before him and took the opportunity to observe to the court: "I have done by them just as I would have another judge do by my son if he were a drunkard or a thief, or by my sister or daughter if she were a prostitute, and for thus being true to the highest and holiest impulses of my soul, the power of appointing a police judge is taken away from the mayor and conferred on a subordinate office of the court—the clerk."[17]

One final ruling was entirely characteristic. A man named Walker, arrested for carrying a concealed weapon, appeared before the mayor. Jones took the weapon, held it over his head, and said it was a devilish thing, a thousand times worse than whiskey. Walker nodded his agreement with every word, that is, until Jones sentenced him to smash the gun to bits with a sledgehammer. Walker was told to wait until court adjourned. Then everyone, including the mayor, chief of police, clerks of court, policemen, reporters, and bailiff went to the engineer's room. The mayor placed his arm affectionately around the shoulders of the visibly stunned Walker. Jones placed the gun in a vice; Walker had no recourse but to destroy it.[18]

Jones decided to fight the governor on the police ripper bill. Jones, once an ex officio member of the Police Board, now had no role in the new four-member board; he managed to convince a majority of the members of the old board and the chief of police to continue to function as they always had, thus defying Governor Nash's board. Jones hired Brand Whitlock to argue the case before the state supreme court. The court agreed to consider the case on the issue of special legislation. Before the court rendered its decision in late June, both police boards vied for power in Toledo. Jones won: the court ruled that the bill was special legislation and was unconstitutional. "The supreme court," observed Jones, "is bound to be right once in awhile."[19]

Despite his conflicts with Wachenheimer and the city council, Jones had the sense that he was in the best health he had enjoyed in years. He had begun a regular exercise program during the year and had kept steadily at it. He now limited himself to two meals each day. As a result of his diet and exercises, his weight dropped 30 pounds to 170 pounds and he was free from asthma. He thought he was cured. But that was an illusion.

Jones spent a great deal of time thinking about the requirements for good health in the winter of 1902. His eldest brother, John Hugh Jones, died at his farm in upstate New York. Jones spoke to the gathered family at the funeral of his belief that "what we call death is the beginning of life on a higher plane." John now seemed to symbolize something that was missing in his own life. His brother represented the simple working life which, like Tolstoy's, greatly appealed to his younger brother. He wrote Nelson that John "was guilty of the injustice of overwork to his own body and . . . he died twenty years sooner than he would, had he the enlightenment that would have taught him how to work rationally."[20]

Shortly after John's death, Jones suffered a nervous breakdown. His physical illness forced him finally to pay attention to the mental and spiritual strain he was experiencing. To some extent, certainly, the strain was a by-product of the age. By the 1890s, the medical community in both England and the United States had defined the dramatic increase in nervous disorders as a direct result of the industrialized world. In England, a scientist observed in 1890, "Our age suffers from nervous weakness; it is the malady of the nineteenth century," the "consequence of a way of life altered with the progress of civilization, which strains the mind and neglects the body." In 1895, the New York health commissioner observed that "in no nation at any time have the demands on the nervous forces been as great as in the United States."[21]

In the month preceding his nervous breakdown, Jones wrote longingly of the simple life—a life of hard work such as his brother John had lived. He told Nelson that he was "very much in need, not of rest, but of *work*, real live work; that will be a change that will be a great relief to a brain and mind that has been exceedingly active because of continual confronting with 'problems.'"[22]

His eldest son, Percy, was now one of his principal problems. While Jones was yearning for a far simpler life, Percy desired the best that money could buy. Now Percy too, like Paul, had come to think money an end in itself. For the past year he had run with a wild crowd, but now Percy had fallen in love. Attending a Broadway show, he had been so struck by the ingenue that he had gone backstage after the show to meet her. Blond, beautiful Marion Cullen was a Boston-born Irish Catholic. She was one of seven children of Thomas Cullen, a stockbroker. Percy knew immediately that he wanted to marry her. A disheartened Jones wrote Percy in February that "I cannot see any way in which I can promise you the 'big income' that you seem to think just now is necessary to your happiness."[23]

After discussing the future together, Jones had written his son, "In thinking about the talk that we had about the theatre, I do not want you to get the impression that I condemn it. I do not condemn anything—at least, I do not want to. . . . I should say that for me the worst thing about the life of an actor would be that, to a certain extent, it has the same defect as has the life of a preacher, though it is quite clear that the preacher's is the worse of the two. The evil is in the artificiality that there is in both. Neither the actor nor the preacher can live a natural life. By the conditions of their life, they are denied the right of working with their hands, which I believe to be an absolute necessity to any complete life." Out of the oil fields for more than five years now, Sam also was denying himself the right of working with his hands.

Jones realized that he was no more living this kind of life than was the actress or the preacher. The conflict Jones felt between the life he was living and the life he ought to live brought on the crisis of the spring of 1902. He continued to Percy, "My failure is in the fact that I do not *do* my best. . . . Though I admire simplicity and I see that the true life, true happiness, is only found in a complete life, in a condition that will admit of the work of hand and brain and body—though I see all this, I have not yet been able to go bravely forward and live the life that I so much admire and for which I have inexpressible longings; but I am not without hope."[24] With no sign of similar longings, Percy married Marion Cullen on August 19, 1902.

Jones collapsed at a Los Angeles banquet where he was to speak. He suffered an attack of pleurisy and was so ill he was forced to remain in

California for three weeks before he could make the return trip to Toledo. Jones thought his illness the result, not the cause, of his problem: "I have been in very bad health ever since I left home," he wrote from California; it was, he felt, "the result I believe of a nervous break down."[25] At a seaside cottage the sunshine, sea air, mountains, and ten days with Nelson spent talking and reading Whitman did much to restore his soul. This was perhaps the last defining experience of his life. Because of this collapse, Sam transformed his way of living.

For at least a year before the Los Angeles nervous breakdown, Sam had experimented with fasting in an effort to purge his body of all defilements. He seems to have been engaged in what the Puritans called a "self civil war." He adopted Edward Hooker Dewey's *No Breakfast Plan and the Fasting Cure* and fasted each day until noon; at times he went on extended fasts. The previous spring he even had persuaded John Merrell, once so intent on prosecuting Chief Raitz, of the virtues of fasting. Merrell, who had suffered intestinal trouble for years, underwent a two-week fast at Jones's suggestion. "Faith has made him whole," reported the mayor. When Jones fasted, he first washed out his system before a fast of from three to seven days with "a good thorough syringing." The night before breaking the fast, he drank three quarters of a glass of pure olive oil, then went immediately to bed, sleeping on his right side. The next morning, he got up, took a full bottle of citrate of magnesia, and at noon broke the fast by eating popcorn and zwieback. He continued this extraordinary practice during his illness. By the end of the California fast, he weighed 154 pounds—some 50 pounds lighter than he had been a year and a half earlier, almost 15 pounds lighter than when he left Toledo. He believed he was "going to be better for the experience."[26]

In California, he was suffering, though he did not know it, from both the physical and the psychic conditions that would shorten his life. He was diagnosed as having abscesses on the lungs, caused, he thought, by the "catarrhal difficulty that I have had for twenty-five years." When his abscesses broke, he was "pretty nearly broken." It was a life-threatening illness. Word of the severity of his illness spread through the reform community. Tom Johnson was "greatly shocked." Even the *Chicago Tribune* cautioned Jones to take care of himself: Toledo could not afford to lose him. His recovery was slow. Despite the good weather and the company of Nelson, it was a greatly weakened Sam Jones who returned home. Feeling unfit for the train trip to Toledo, Sam pushed on for he thought he needed to be in Toledo to "get at the real work of getting my mind at rest before my body could get into a normal condition."[27]

Jones had come to believe that "every experience that comes to us has a meaning and purpose." He invested his collapse with meaning: the "nervous and spiritual collapse . . . was just the experience I needed," he thought. It confirmed the truths of his evangelical childhood. He felt his trouble had been "mainly mental or spiritual. I have been 'self-centered'; that is, I have felt that I had to carry the world on my shoulders—in short, I separated myself in this way from God; I forgot that I am one with and a part of God," he wrote the editor of *Perfect Health*. In fact, self had long been seen in direct opposition to God. As Augustine put it, "Two loves have given origin to these two cities, self-love in contempt of God unto the earthly . . . [and] love of God in contempt of one's self to the heavenly." The Puritans placed the conflict between self and God at the center of their theology. They added a host of new compound words to the language to define the damned more precisely: "self-affection, self-confident, self-credit, self-fullness, self-honor, self-intended, self-practice, self-safety, self-sufficiency." Two new terms defined the redeemed: "self-emptiness" and "self-revenging." Raised within a tradition that rigorously sought to destroy the self, Jones was continually attracted to an ideal he could never meet—"self-emptiness." At this point, he was hopeful that his breakdown would set him on the right road. He assured the editor of *Perfect Heath* that his illness had made him aware of the truth; he felt he was approaching "tranquility of mind, learning something about the 'peace that passeth understanding,' and propose to be physically and spiritually whole, because that is my privilege." In that last thought, the idea that *he* could decide, he could propose to be whole, lies the theology of Methodist sanctification. In James' *Varieties of Religious Experience,* in the chapter "The Religion of Healthy-Mindedness," James wrote and Jones highlighted: "To the believer in moralism and works, with his anxious query, 'What shall I do to be saved.' Luther and Wesley replied; 'You are saved now, if you would but believe it'. . . . 'God is well and so are you.' You must awaken to the knowledge of your real being." Jones marked boldly in the margin, "No doubt a truth, but hard to grasp."[28]

His illness and the intensity with which he took up a variety of health fads over the next two years clearly show how self-denial has the treacherous capacity to become self-affirmation. This tension drives one to Christ through self-loathing but then forces one back to the self "by the recognition that his labors are an assertion of what he loathes."[29] Jones's particular form of "self-emptying" or "self-revenge" necessarily forced his attention back upon the self he sought to deny. The fasting body demands that one pay attention to it. The regime, with its attention to peculiar drinks, sleeping positions, and an eye on the clock, called for a particularly vigilant form of self-monitoring.

Jones determined to follow through on the lessons he had been taught on the West Coast. He became, as the lingo of the day had it, a "thorough physical culturist." After recovering from a bout of bronchitis that summer, Jones told the press, "I am going out into the country to take up physical culture and plain work, such as my father took." Physical culture, then, for Sam Jones, represented the simple life. Jones spent some of the summer of 1902 with Paul but most of it alone, in northern Michigan. While there, he slept outdoors. He fell asleep that first night "with the thought in my mind that I was drawing great drafts of life in every breath; that I did not have to take it warmed over, poisoned or mixed with the fumes or gases of an unhealthy nature, but that I could breathe health and life straight from headquarters." Jones rented a house, living, he said, "like Robinson Crusoe." He kept hens and a rooster, gardened, pitched hay with nearby farmers, and on one occasion joined a section gang to work on the railroad line. He was happier than he had been in years. Real work made him feel he was "in a real sense a partner with God." Those two months in the Upper Peninsula, which were a direct result of his illness in Los Angeles, changed the way he lived the rest of his life. In his copy of *Walden,* Jones marked Thoreau's famous passage, "I went to the woods because I wished to live deliberately, to front only the essential facts of life, and see if I could not learn what it had to teach." The quotation continues and Jones underscored twice the remaining thought: "and not, when I came to die, discover that I had not lived. I did not wish to live what was not life, living is so dear; nor did I wish to practise resignation, unless it was quite necessary."[30] It was far easier to "trust love fully" alone on the Upper Peninsula.

Sam Jones's longing for a simpler life of real work connects to his "right to work" platform. Jones had been arguing that honest, useful work was essential to the development of a healthy personality. As mayor, Sam had certainly found *useful* work that expanded his vision. His social reforms were good for the health of the city. But as the breakdown in 1902 clearly suggests, this work was not providing him the opportunity to develop a healthy personality. The pursuit of perfect health sums up the paradox of Jones's final years. Becoming a "thorough physical culturist" was both a victory and a defeat. As with his reform agenda, he made remarkable progress, but, as in politics, progress was not perfection and he drove himself too hard.

Jones's interest in physical culture was as logical an outgrowth of his political ideology as it was of his health problems. The belief that he was part of the problem, part of the "machine" that produced great suffering, did not confine itself to his political philosophy. As the body politic was suffering, so was his own body. In 1903, Jones wrote an article for *Arena* called "A Plea for Simpler Living." Much of his own secular preaching in the remaining years of his life was devoted to this ideal. "We have not yet begun to understand how very little we really require—how easily our actual necessities incident to a happy life may be supplied." To the degree that we get away from artificiality "and from the slavery that requires us to do as other people do," we will become ever freer.[31]

Though many laughed at what they called "Jones fads," Sam Jones was not alone in his interest in physical culture. Magazines that Jones wrote for or that covered his career such as *Outlook*, the *North American Review*, and the *Independent* all featured articles on simple living during this period. Even mainstream magazines such as *McClure's* and the *Ladies Home Journal* devoted pages to the subject. As early as 1894, *McClure's* ran an article titled "Nervousness: The National Disease." The *Ladies Home Journal*, under the editorial leadership of Edward Bok, campaigned that simple living was the key to personal happiness.[32]

Compared to this growing national interest in good health, Sam Jones chose a rather idiosyncratic health plan. Once back in Toledo in the autumn of 1902, he built an "outdoor sleeping apartment," one of the country's first screened porches, on the back of the house. It seems he slept out there for the rest of his life in all but the worst of weather—which suggests much about his physical relations with Helen. His day began at 6 A.M. with a regimen of deep breathing exercises, followed by a regular exercise routine stripped naked in a cold room which he concluded by doing handstand push-ups. Next followed a cold bath. He made the transition from his home workout to political responsibilities by running or riding his bicycle to his office. He had become a vegetarian.[33]

Prisoners in Toledo had good reason to complain about the mayor's health fads. In March 1903, the prisoners went from a standard three-meal-a-day fare to a two-meal plan. Accustomed to a breakfast of bread, bologna, and coffee, the prisoners awoke one morning to dry cereals by Battle Creek such as "U-Need-Me" and "U-Ought-To-Eat-It" laced with corn syrup. "What t'hell's this stuff?" asked one prisoner. "Don't ask me," said the turnkey, "it's your breakfast and you'd better eat it for you'll see no more until four o'clock." "Nothing but Battle Creek food goes," mused the *Bee*. "Imagine trying to sober a man on such dry food."[34]

Jones's health fads had a potentially dangerous effect on public health policy. He had become convinced that his culture's addiction to medicines contributed greatly to corporate bad health. He had suffered from "asthma, rheumatism, lumbago, toothache, neuralgia, and sour stomach" for years, but after he stopped taking medicine he felt cured. Jones argued against mandatory vaccination when an outbreak of smallpox occurred that summer in Toledo's tenements. Dr. W.W. Brand, the health officer, who fought the smallpox all that summer and fall in the tenements, also had to fight the fears of the immigrants most likely to be infected. On one occasion, Brand had to break down the tenement door to inoculate a man who had been exposed to the disease and refused to be vaccinated. By January, when the mayor spoke against compulsory vaccination, Brand gave up the fight.[35]

Prisoners and Dr. Brand were not the only ones to complain of Jones's new ideas. His experience with Nelson in California and with Paul in Michigan persuaded Jones to make changes in his home. In a revealing letter, Jones wrote Nelson: "I feel as I have told my wife, that I am done forever with the to me blasphemy of the aristocratic life of separateness. This does not mean, of course, that I propose to separate from my wife, but I am going to get into a position to let her be free to live her way and give me as much liberty as possible to live mine. The big house, the servants, the refinement of it and all of that is more and increasingly distressing to my soul." Clearly, the grand house and servants were not distressing to Helen's soul; it seems likely that her husband's increasingly peculiar ideas would have been.[36]

If Sam was not in perfect accord with Helen, he had sustaining understanding from his sister Nell. Since the death of Alma in 1875, she had devoted her life first to Jones's children and then to his concerns. Brand Whitlock saw "perfect sympathy" between sister and brother as she made his ideas reality by running the Golden Rule Settlement House. She had, he felt, the "simplicity . . . [that] comes from innate honesty and sincerity of purpose. It was this that drew her so closely to the people. . . . The children, the boys in the shop, the mothers and wives of the boys, all felt this genuine sympathy. . . . To her they came with their troubles and sorrows, and she gave to them the greatest gift she had—herself."[37]

Throughout that autumn the mayor was buoyed by his regained good health. He felt young again and was proud of his athletic skills. He demonstrated his physical prowess to a gathering of grade school students at the Congress Street School playground in Grand Rapids, Michigan. The children seemed stunned to see an old man demonstrating his skill at the Athabascan Indian game of high kick. On another occasion, he challenged a group of firefighters to see who could shinny up the pole: at twice the age of anyone present Jones was the only one to get to the top. He had become so famous for his quirks that the *Cincinnati Post* sent cartoonist E.A. Bushnell to Toledo to capture some typical Jones poses. Cochran thought it a natural combination: politics and acrobatics. "When [politicians] get tired of running for office on their feet they can flop over and run on their hands a while. The Mayor may set the example this spring." The *New York Sun* could not resist comment: "The effete east fails to understand and properly appreciate the robust, vigorous west. . . . What harm is there in the mayor of Toledo standing on his head? We venture to say New York in all its interesting history never had a mayor who could stand on his head."[38]

What is most worth noting is Jones's need to perform. He had begun a rigorous fitness plan because his nervous collapse suggested that self intruded too much. He made his body submit to extraordinary demands. But his pride in his body's compliance pushed him to exhibit his skills and self intruded once again. One day when Paul and some friends were home, the mayor burst in the house, running. He said to the teenagers as he passed them, "Can you do this?" and did a handspring, ending with his legs against the wall. The kids thought they could do anything the "old man" did, but none of them had arms strong enough. "Our arms just wouldn't hold us," remembered one. "We got our feet up into the air—then we simply crumpled. The old boy wasn't above crowing a bit over his better showing."[39]

Clearly, Sam Jones was far ahead of his culture in searching for systemic good health. But just as clearly, there was something unhealthy in the extremity of his approach. At fifty-five, Jones worked frantically to deny death, and he sought atonement through the punishing dietary and physical regime. While at the heart of all Jones did there were true health benefits, the desperate energy dedicated to these fads indicates that the evangelical was striving to purge the body that had failed him into submission. The shame of Pithole had been a defilement that he had sought to purge by the acquisition of wealth. Yet his wealth had become a defilement that he needed to expurgate. That had not sufficed, so he turned to his body. The man who sought to deny self did so by a rigorous physical regimen that would have only made him more conscious of his physical self. Although he had the heady sense that he had regained his youth, in the summer of 1902 Sam Jones might almost be said to have begun to die. His failure to live according to the impossibly high demands he made on himself was killing him. Death would be the ultimate compensatory gesture. The physical culture regimen was an intense attempt to fight back against his failing health, but the battle was being fought on the wrong front. Despite the number of handstands, he was not addressing the real problem—it was a spiritual torment that he could not ease.

As party officials began to prepare for another municipal election in the spring of 1903, Sam Jones thought longingly of giving up his job. By early February Jones considered his political career over: "I am getting ready to 'let go' the mayor's job at the end of my term," he wrote a trusted friend. Jones was sure he could be reelected but felt that "I can do a larger work as a man than I can as a mayor and I think there is no doubt it will enforce the lesson that I have been trying to teach when I voluntarily lay down what is considered such a desirable 'honor.'" If physical work was "an absolute necessity to any complete life," Sam had compelling reason to retire from public life. But it was very difficult for him to retire. To Nelson he said, "The bosses and the newspaper editorial writers are terribly anxious to know what Jones is going to do, and I will say to you frankly that I do not know." On March 2, 1903, he used his annual message to the city council primarily to discuss the potential campaign. He frankly admitted, "I am painfully conscious of my lack of ability and often mourn my want of that essential genius for detail, that makes the competent executive." It is clear that had his good health not returned, Jones would not have run for a fourth term. By mid-March, still in energetic good health, he decided to run again. He had attempted to get someone else nominated by petition but received three thousand petitions for his own renomination. He trusted the people's love fully. He justified his decision, saying he felt he could not retire leaving the people to choose between two machine candidates. In short, he found that he had "reached the point where I had to be a candidate or a coward. I could not voluntarily consent to the latter. . . . I fear neither defeat, death, nor the devil."[40]

The *Bee,* which had endorsed him in 1901, did not endorse Jones in this campaign. Cochran explained that the Democratic nominee, Charles Edson, was a man he believed in. "We have quoted poetry from Walt Whitman for him," wrote Cochran of Mayor Jones, "we have loved our fellow men with him, we have yelled for Bryan with him, we have stood by the Golden Rule with him until the last ring of the bell. . . . And if the Democrats hadn't nominated a clean, honest man . . . for mayor we would probably be tramping the streets now behind the Golden Rule band." If Sam Jones was not a political animal, Negley Cochran was an inveterate one. It had been clear in the two years since Jones had won with Democratic support that Sam Jones would never join the Democratic Party.[41]

If the Democrats put up a man Cochran thought was good, the Republicans had what Sam Jones thought a good man in John W. Dowd. Dowd, a former superintendent of schools and a friend of Sam Jones's, supported many of the mayor's ideas. Earlier that spring, both Dowd and Lem Harris, a friend and Jones supporter, had wanted the Republican nomination. Each man came to see the mayor in private to talk about their own political plans. A visibly nervous Dowd walked into a closet instead of the mayor's office when he went to discuss his political future. Jones told the reporters gathered in his outer office after Dowd had left that he himself was not a candidate, but "if my own brother was a partisan candidate and the people demanded that I should be, I would be." This could hardly have been calming news to Dowd. Once Dowd became the Republican standard-bearer, Jones had to remind himself to "judge not lest . . . ," for he had hoped, he told Clarence Darrow, that in the future Dowd would stand "with the rest of us." Perhaps Jones had tried to persuade Dowd to accept nomination by petition as an independent that day he was so rattled he walked into the closet.[42]

On March 17, the day the Republicans convened, the mayor announced that he would run as a nonpartisan because no one else had agreed to do so. The German-language *Express* was the only newspaper to print the the text of Jones's announcement. Cochran had printed the facts but not Jones's account. The first meeting of the campaign was held outdoors at a busy downtown intersection. The mayor's son Paul played the saxophone, and the black Golden Rule quartet entertained the crowd from the back of a wagon. "Every daily paper in the city is closed tight against us, so far as news is concerned," observed Jones the day of the next meeting. They would not even announce his upcoming public appearances. That night, the meeting began at the same downtown intersection, but it turned into a "progressive" meeting in both senses of the word. After speaking to those gathered downtown, the mayor led the Golden Rule band in a march to the doors of every Toledo newspaper office. At each stop the crowd gathered to listen to the band and Jones announced the time and location of his next scheduled meeting.[43]

A reluctant candidate just the month before, Jones gloried in this contest more, perhaps, than any of his other campaigns. He was up against a Republican who shared many of his views, a Democrat, and a Socialist; the press had no ties to him, the machines were at work against him, and the people were at work for him. It was, he told William Randolph Hearst, "pure Democracy." A self-described "buoyant and jubilant" Jones confided to Tom Johnson, then conducting his own campaign in Cleveland, that it was "really the most inviting prospect that I have ever had." His emotions ran high in all the letters that discuss the campaign. His ebullient good spirits were in part owing to the response of the organized press: "All the forms of 'organized' society are either openly hostile or decidedly indifferent"; afterward he thought it "quite evident . . . that the opposition of the papers helped us out this time." It made him freer than he had been with Negley Cochran's support. Sam Jones was utterly alone, outside any organization, and he gloried in it. That the official world thought him wrong proved him right.[44]

Jones had to cast the election as a test of the independent principle as though it had nothing to do with him personally. He seems to have realized that in this election the results would not suggest such solid support as he had seen previously; on election eve he was optimistic that "the people will win, but I shall stand for the principle [of people over parties] tomorrow morning just the same regardless of what the vote may reveal." The next day Jones won 10,350 votes to Dowd's 7,491 and the Democrat Edson's 4,266. Even though he received the smallest number of votes of any election and won by only a plurality, he felt it was a clear test and a real victory. His second election had been colored, he believed, by the people's anger over the Republican convention, while the third election's results had been affected by the lack of a Democratic candidate. Even two years after the fact, Jones was still stung by the charge "that the democrats helped Jones out."[45]

This experiment in democracy did not provide Jones with a power base in office. That spring Jones's power was tested and shown to be severely limited. Certainly, his idiosyncratic disregard of political organization played a large role in his failure to implement his policies. But perhaps even more important was Toledo's intricate city government that provided little real power to the mayor. In the autumn of 1902, the Ohio General Assembly had passed a new municipal code for the state. The desire to make government more efficient consolidated power in the hands of the city council at the cost of the mayor.[46]

Nothing better reveals the city council's absolute unwillingness to share power with the mayor than the fight over the Police Board. It is hard to conceive of a struggle more likely to make one fail at "depending upon love entirely." The new municipal code permitted the governor to step in and appoint members to these boards when the council did not approve the mayor's appointments. The ensuing arguments were held on strictly party lines. At a May 18 city council meeting the mayor pleaded with the council to support him in the interests of home rule: "I don't care to have the city governed from Columbus, and I do not believe that you do." Proof of his "earnest desire" to cooperate came in an offer to substitute a second slate of four new names. Jones offered to provide the council with one hundred names to choose from; a week later the council voted to postpone consideration of the nominees indefinitely. It was a conflict in which "depending upon love entirely" would have strained the heart of a saint.[47]

Proof of the strain Sam was under can be seen in his dissatisfaction with himself: "I am tired of books, tired of reading, tired of talk, tired of libraries and lectures, tired of respectability. My soul seems to long for nothing but the open air, the simple life and the chance to earn my living by working with my hands rather than working my jaw." His new despair came from the knowledge that his skills—talk and letters—would not enable him to transform the city.[48]

The political fight continued throughout June. The governor had said he would name a board on July 1 if there was no local agreement by then. Jones had made an unsuccessful effort to persuade Nash to support him. Given Jones's disturbing impact on the election that had won Nash the governorship, it is not surprising that he participated in Jones's humiliation. Jones went to Columbus to ask Nash to select four men from the sixteen he had submitted to the council. When he arrived, the governor's waiting room was full. Along with the requisite hangers-on and newspapermen, several important Toledo Republicans were waiting to see the governor, including Waldorf and Brown. Nash emerged from his office to ask Jones to join him first. There was a pause, and Sam Jones declined. Instead, he spoke to the governor in front of those who opposed him and the press. He was brief and to the point, outlining the crisis and asking Nash to select from his nominations. The governor thanked him, then turned to Brown, who asked for a private meeting with the governor. It was granted; Nash renamed his original choices. If Jones "failed utterly" in depending upon love, reasoned political discourse failed him too.[49]

W.D.P. Bliss surely must have been thinking of Toledo's famous mayor when he wrote four years after Jones's death: "Men have tried to carry out the Golden Rule on individual lines, and they have failed. We do not say they have wholly failed. No earnest effort, even tho mistaken, wholly fails. But, generally speaking, they have failed. Large numbers of business men say to-day that the Golden Rule cannot be applied to business. They are right on the present system of business, because the system is wrong. You 'cannot serve God and Mammon.' Pathetic, noble but impractical are the desperate efforts of Christian men and women to do good and be Christ-like in modern business. It is a hopeless task. God's way demands a social basis."[50]

11

The Greatest Victory of My Life

In the last two years of his life the battle Jones was waging within his soul intensified. Brand Whitlock watched as his dear friend experienced "the greatest victory of [his] life"—and he saw the price it exacted from him. Jones tried to respond with love to those who fought him. He tried to deny his anger and meet the expectations of the Golden Rule. It is not surprising that this attempt struck him differently than it did his good friend Whitlock. One day Jones visited a man who had publicly "persecuted" him, hoping for a reconciliation. He was sure that if they simply talked, man to man, they would arrive at a better understanding. Jones brought with him to this interview a written statement of his position. He offered it to the man and asked him to read it so that then they might discuss the question. But the man grabbed it out of his hands and summarily tore it into bits. Jones said nothing, did nothing. He turned on his heel and marched straight to Brand Whitlock's office. At a glance, Whitlock could tell that his friend was "trying to master some unusual emotion." Jones sat down, remaining silent for some time. At last, the concerned Whitlock saw "his face [break] into that beautiful smile of his, more beautiful than I had ever seen it." Jones said, "Well, I've won the greatest victory of my life; I have won at last a victory over myself, over my own nature. I have done what it has always been hardest for me to do." Again, there was silence. Whitlock waited. "You know, it has always seemed to me that the most remarkable thing that was ever said of Jesus was that when he was reviled, he reviled not again. It is the hardest thing in the world to do." Whitlock thought Jones had paid a terribly high price: "He had never, it seemed to me, been quite the same after the day when he had that experience of insult which he did not resent." According to Christianity, a victory that can be expressed that way—with the emphasis on *I*—is a defeat. Sam's failure and his pain came from pride; he needed to be the victor; he could not surrender to God's grace. On some level Sam knew this: it accounts for his pessimism about his own ethical journey. [1]

Within three weeks of his death, he still had not found perfect mastery. Control was such a burden, it seems, because he had decided that he alone was to blame for all the troubles of his life. He wrote a woman imprisoned in Toledo for keeping a house of prostitution: "I am not as 'good' as many people think I am. . . . If you knew my inner life, you would understand as you do not, that it is not one of unalloyed happiness as doubtless you suppose it to be." He had learned, he went on to tell her, that he could find all the troubles of his life in himself "if I just look inside and think it out carefully I always make up my mind that *I alone* am to blame. I have not learned the art of self-mastery, and just in proportion as I do learn to master myself, my troubles diminish." Deceit was central to Jones's portrayal of his experience as a young man at Pithole. In his second life, he seemed to anguish over the discrepancy between his exterior and interior selves: he wanted not to deceive the world about the truth about himself.[2]

Texts so attracted Sam Jones that he worked out his philosophy in the margins of treasured books, carrying on a "conversation" with the author. Jones's copy of William James's *Varieties of Religious Experience* provides a remarkable window to his inner life. When James quotes from Horace Fletcher's *Menticulture* to the effect that one should rid oneself of the "cancer spots of worry and anger," Jones scrawled in the margin, "A most desirable state of mind, to which I will attain." To seal this vow he added: "SMJ July 1903."[3] Within six weeks of his death, Jones read *How to Live Forever: The Science and Practice* and noted in the margin, "I would rather lose $100 than lose my temper."[4]

Jones's marginal notes in *The Varieties of Religious Experience* suggest that he was particularly attracted to James's chapter "The Sick Soul." It is hardly surprising since Jones suffered from exactly this spiritual complaint. Jones underlined James's assessment of Martin Luther: "What single-handed man was ever on the whole as successful as Luther? Yet when he had grown old, he looked back on his life as if it were an absolute failure." Sam Jones's correspondence in the remaining months of his life suggest that, like Luther, he felt himself a failure. Similarly, Jones's pencil was attracted to these words by Tolstoy in James' book: "I felt . . . that something had broken within me on which my life had always rested. . . . This took place at a time when so far as all my outer circumstances went, I ought to have been completely happy. I had a good wife who loved me and whom I loved; good children and a large property which was increasing with no pains taken on my part. I was more respected by my kinsfolk and acquaintance than I had ever been; I was loaded with praise by strangers." These words of the Russian he so admired echoed Jones's own experience.[5]

Sam Jones's life is a story of a doubly divided man—the self-made millionaire turned Progressive idealist and, more significant, the successful man who publicly symbolized the Golden Rule in action yet privately was deeply troubled by the inadequacies of his soul. It is hardly surprising, then, that in James' next chapter, "The Divided Self," the author's assessment of Tolstoy's problem matches Jones's analysis of his situation. Both men laid the blame on an overly cerebral life: Tolstoy's trouble, wrote James (and Jones underscored the words), had been with the "upper, intellectual, artistic classes, the life which he had personally always led, the cerebral life, the life of conventionality, artificiality, and personal ambition." Jones's letters confirm James's insight about Tolstoy. Unlike Sam Jones, however, Tolstoy had given up that artificial life and taken on the simple life of a peasant. In the last twelve months of Jones's life that image of Tolstoy seemed to haunt him. James writes and Jones underscored this sentence: "And though not many of us can imitate Tolstoy, not having enough, perhaps, of the aboriginal human marrow in our bones, most of us may at least feel as if it might be better for us if we could."[6]

Yet he never took up the simple life except during his stay in Michigan in the summer of 1902. The letters throughout the last months of his life reverberate with his struggle. Jones wrote a friend: "Much of the time I am in a good deal of a quandary to know what the turmoil I am in is all about. When I reflect upon what a simple thing life really is, I marvel that it has become so complex in my case. When I think how easily I could earn my living by working with my hands, how much happier and healthier I should probably be if I were really doing it, I find myself wondering why I have not long since taken the Jesus plan and gotten rid of the hindrance of property and gone about it quietly." The Commonwealth Colony in Georgia, though it had been disbanded for four years, would have presented a vision of the life Jones longed to lead. Those people had "taken the Jesus plan" and lived it, creating for five years a place of work and ideas, where everyone was welcome—"tramp, college professor, minister, or one-legged man with nine children"—and property was jointly owned. Writing to Nelson, Sam paraphrased the poetry of Brigham to say, "But I, like one possessed of some disease, / Within the cells of fashion chafe and rail." "Why should I have drifted into it," he wondered. "How did I become enslaved? Certainly none but myself can be blamed or charged with fault. Perhaps some day I can see that it was in order that I, and the humanity of which I am a part, might through me learn a needed lesson."[7]

From midsummer 1903 through the autumn Toledoans focused their civic attention on the Toledo Railway and Light Company, the city council, and the mayor. The details of the traction fight in Toledo are complex. The problem began when rival lines began operating independently in 1889. In 1901, when a new company took over the system, ninety ordinances were in effect and no transfers were permitted between the rival lines. The Railway and Light Company pushed for a twenty-five-year franchise; the mayor argued that the city council should let the franchise expire.[8]

Neg Cochran kept the issue a hot one throughout August in the pages of the *News-Bee.* On August 24, the city council passed a twenty-five-year franchise; on September 8, the mayor vetoed it. In his veto, Jones questioned the council's moral right "to mortgage the future" of the city. On September 21, when the council was to take up the issue of the mayor's veto, a bold headline read "Danger That Council Will Pass Franchise Ordinance Tonight."[9]

Sam Jones was able to rally the people behind him. The people came out in numbers to let their councilmen know how they felt. "Petition in Boots Was Effective," proclaimed the *Bee*'s headline the next day, while the *Blade* did not cover the story. The lobby was so packed no one could enter. Everyone was "talking, yelling and shouting at the top of their voices," making it impossible for the council to enact business. At 8 P.M. a "roar went up" by the elevator: "Make way for the mayor. Mayor Jones wants in." He scrambled over the backs of chairs because the room was packed so tightly. When he jumped to the top of the railing that separated the crowd from the council, he turned and acknowledged their courtesy but would not give them the speech they begged for. Once before the council recessed to caucus, the mayor had to take to the top of a desk to quiet the outraged crowd. Pandemonium broke out. But a "stentorian voice from the rear of the hall cautioned. . . . 'Shut up; Mayor Jones wants to talk." He quieted the crowd; the council returned to business. During the caucus, "the crowd gave vent to its feelings in its own particular way," expressing their opinions about various council members in no uncertain terms. The mayor, atop a desk again, remonstrated: "All things come to him who waits." A voice suggested they should spend their time waiting by throwing the council members out the window.[10]

When Barton Smith, attorney for the Toledo Railway and Light Company, attempted to answer questions later that night, he was met with stony silence. Then he suggested that the company would have to reduce wages, and the crowd "raised a howl of disapproval that nearly swept the attorney off his feet." It was followed by "derisive cries, insults, cat calls," and other interruptions. As the noise increased, Smith grew red and trembled "visibly in a rage." "This, I suppose, is the kind of government we may expect when the Golden Rule is in force." The mayor sprang from his chair: "No, Mr. Smith, this is the kind of government you will have when the rule of gold is in full force." His adversary, with an eye to the crowd, interrupted: "Might I ask the Mayor a question? How much gold did it take to bring them here?" Jones "advanced . . . with his frame quivering and his eyes flashing. It was," said the newspaper, "a meeting of the gladiators and each was in a fighting mood." But "the mayor recovered himself and in a voice that trembled with excitement remarked; 'Mr Smith, your insinuation about the Golden Rule was uncalled for." He had read William James just two months earlier and was living by the vow he made in the margin to rid himself of anger. In the face of universal popular opposition, the council tabled the ordinance. Outside, after the meeting, the crowd, thrilled by its political muscle, wanted to hear from Jones. The triumphant mayor got up in an automobile so the crowd could hear him. When he told those gathered that "the hope of America is in the self-owning man, and the independent voter is the ideal American," they responded with the most "genuine hurrah" he had ever heard. It was a doubly powerful experience for Sam Jones: a victory over himself and a dramatization that the people would act. Jones considered it "the most exciting time in the history of the municipality," for "the day was saved in the truly American style."[11]

That autumn he began again to "wrestl[e] almost nightly with my old enemy the asthma." The asthma may well have been a response to the pressures of the traction fight, but the pressures he placed on himself surely added to his ill health. Not only did he attempt to repress his feelings of anger, he rebelled against the entire world he had created around him. He wrote Ernest Crosby in January: "I have very firmly fixed upon me the conviction that only myself can save myself and no one but myself can ruin myself. In my own case, each day's setting sun finds me more rebellious against even the moderate degree of luxury that I seem to be compelled to live in. It is degradation pure and simple, and I do not differentiate between the drunkenness that goes with luxurious living and the ordinary, kind of whiskey drunkenness and licentiousness. . . . They all alike destroy the body and damn the soul."[12]

The next spring Jones interceded with Police Chief Perry Knapp on behalf of two eleven-year-old boys to keep them out of prison. The boys had been charged with stealing a pair of boots. The *News-Bee* printed a photograph of the shoes worn by the thief. They were "water stained and so badly worn that they are more holes than shoes." The picture spoke dramatically of the boys' needs. The mayor "tried on them the principles of brotherly love and the golden rule," reported the newspaper. In turn, "the boys tried on new shoes, and are the possessors of suitable footwear." Five days later, standing at a Chicago pulpit, in a speech titled "The Debauchees of Luxury," Jones held up those dilapidated shoes in one hand and "an imaginary sofa pillow" in the other and said, "I look with equal pity on the starved children of the poor and those that dwell in the mansions along our avenues whose little souls are being choked by the doctrines they learn from their parents." He went on in a way that could only have shocked his audience: "'Dope fiends' at times have wanted to break away from their habit but the debauchee of luxury knows nothing of that feeling. What but the densest ignorance could cause a person to be happy living in a house wherein all is warmth while human beings outside are freezing?" Some of Jones's passion surely stems from his sense that Paul's soul had been "choked" by the doctrines learned in his own home.[13]

Philanthropic impulses did not correct the social problems nor did they save the rich man's soul, Jones had found. He had wrestled with his own ideas about charity for more than a decade. From the time work began to bring the factory on Segur Avenue back to life in 1894, through his years as a Golden Rule employer and a reform politician, he had been inundated with requests for aid. In 1899, Jones wrote to Josephine Shaw Lowell, founder of the New York Charitable Organizing Society, who believed there were two classes of people, workers and idlers: "The appeals for help that come to me from all over the country are simply overwhelming, and to answer them in the expected way would bankrupt a Carnegie or a Rockefeller in a year."[14]

The daily requests for aid while he was mayor led him to think that his age's great commitment to charity "is after all only a sort of apology for the unrighteous conditions that we are content to live in, an apology for our failure to be Christian. . . . I often think that the most pathetic words that Jesus ever uttered, except perhaps, His last expiring cry on the cross, were . . . 'why call me Lord, Lord, and *do* not the things that I say?' and I feel that I am as deep in the mud as any of the others are in the mire. I really feel often times that if I would actually go and sell what I have and give to the poor and be poor, voluntarily manifesting my willingness to be anything, to be nothing, as He did, as St. Francis did, and as all of the martyrs who gave their life for truth have done." Such sentiments set him apart from the founders of charitable organizations such as Lowell. In Thoreau he found confirmation of his belief. He marked the following passage in *Walden*: "There are a thousand hacking at the branches of evil to one who is striking at the root, and it may be that he who bestows the largest amount of time and money on the needy is doing the most by his mode of life to produce that misery which he strives in vain to relieve. . . . Some show their kindness to the poor by employing them in their kitchens. Would they not be kinder if they employed themselves there? You boast of spending a tenth part of your income in charity; may be you should spend the nine tenths so, and be done with it."[15]

Sam increasingly despaired about the good his own charity had done. "People tell me that I have done good with money, that I would not have been able to do the things I have done, to get the publicity, etc., etc., ad libitum, ad nauseam, had I not been armed with money. I do not know how much 'good' I have done. I think in my best moments that I am unconscious of ever having done any. I believe that money has been an agency that has put me into a position where I can see how hopeless the thought that good can be done with money really is."[16]

Jones's struggle with the implications of radical Christian moralism also set him apart from philanthropists such as Rockefeller and Carnegie. Rockefeller spent millions in charitable efforts, virtually building the University of Chicago, yet his dramatic gifts could not keep up with dividends Standard Oil produced. Rockefeller felt the burden of his wealth deeply because he adhered to the doctrine of stewardship, but Carnegie had reinvented that doctrine. In relation to the other books still in his library, no book outraged Jones as much as *The Gospel of Wealth*. Throughout its pages Jones scrawled in the margin: "This is the highest pitch of absurdity," or "Oh Mercy," or "Oh Horrors." The passage that horrified Jones advises against small charitable gifts to the poor because the money would be "wasted . . . in the indulgence of appetite, some of it in excess, and it may be doubted whether even the part put to best use, that of adding to the comforts of the home, would have yielded results for the race, as a race, at all comparable to those which are flowing and are to flow from the Cooper Institute from generation to generation." "Let the advocate of violent or radical change ponder well this thought," Carnegie concluded his paragraph. Sam Jones did, and it horrified him. In the margin of the book's first paragraph Jones wrote, "It is difficult to conceive how to crowd more fallacy into a paragraph than this contains. It is the result of unimaginative thought."[17]

Continually attracted by the example of Christ and by the contemporary example of Tolstoy, Jones wrestled with his proper response to the suffering in the world. He was convinced that the charity that he had been practicing had come to naught. The people he had "helped" were no better off a month or a year later. On several occasions he watched as someone he had loaned money to in the past crossed the street so as not to have to meet him. After his father's death, Percy found over $2,000 in outstanding IOUs, stuffed in all the pigeonholes and in every drawer of his rolltop desk. The notes bore the words "NO INTEREST" in Jones's handwriting. The *Toledo Times* observed: "There are other thousands of dollars lying about in various nooks in the late mayor's office, in this same form. And the death of the mayor cancelled for good, what in fact were cancelled the minute the cash was turned over to the debtors of the worthless bits of paper. And the mayor knew it. Of late years, he simply refused to have a note made out for this kind of loan. He simply turned over the cash." Some of the names on these notes were "well known in business and official circles. And they are considered very well up and 'honorable men—all honorable men.'" Noting that the mayor was not "methodical" in these matters, the newspaper reported, "It has been asserted that during the last year of his life charities, and friendship for men with bad business propositions cost him $22,000."[18]

Money vexed him because everyone—the poor, the rich, and the reformers—saw it as all-important. He wrote to Nelson that "the part of the world I seem to be surrounded and hemmed in with is apparently daft" on the need for endowments. "One and all seem to be a unit in the belief that money is a prerequisite and necessity to the carrying forward of any good work. And I do not believe it. . . . I know that every good worker, on the other hand, from Buddha to Nelson and from Jesus to Jones, not only did not have money, but through all their teachings have plainly pointed out that it was a curse and hindrance rather than a help. . . . I am certain sure that I will not let it damn me or be the cause of the loss of my soul."[19]

But if personal charity was a source of distress, Jones was comforted by the new leadership in the White House. Jones had the opportunity to meet with President Roosevelt in the White House in mid-October 1903. Not much is known about their conversation, but Jones felt that he had been made welcome "in truly American style." The conversation dealt with questions Jones was truly interested in, and there seems to have been a lively interchange. Jones would not live long enough to endorse and vote for a Republican for president, but there was much in Roosevelt's energy and ideals that would have been attractive to Toledo's Golden Rule mayor.

A bad bout of bronchitis dogged Jones through much of the month of October. He did not feel well during his trip to Washington. He avoided all medicine and tried to regain his strength by taking multiple cold baths daily and enduring week-long fasts while continuing his hectic schedule. Ten days after his visit with Roosevelt he was depressed by his inability to heal himself. He wrote Macfadden for help: "I dreadfully hate to turn to the drug doctors, and I greatly dread to have the stories in the newspapers about my ill health. Can you suggest anything?" The newspaper accounts invariably initiated responses such as the one from Tom Johnson: "I was terribly grieved to see by the papers this morning that you were taken ill last evening and do hope that it isn't anything serious. . . . Above all, take care of yourself." In response, he usually understated his illness—unless he wrote to a fellow sufferer, or a convert to physical culture, or to his dear friend Nelson.

This time he hesitated even to tell Nelson of his ill health because it seemed a personal failure. His body did not fully respond to the new demands. His health had not become perfect. As with his inability to love unconditionally, he saw partial success as total failure. The bronchitis and asthma coming, as it did, "at a time when I felt like boasting of my splendid vigor and strength" disheartened him. He had thought he had found the answer. Because he was practicing physical culture, he "did not know what to make of it." He considered his work over the past two years of building up his impaired health as truly "heroic": "I really feel that I have sound reason for being disheartened. A year ago I believed that I had overcome the asthma entirely, yet I did not lapse back into old habits; have grown gradually onto a higher plane of living in every respect, and still I must suffer these relapses and be made the subject of newspaper comment that distresses me beyond expression." There seems to be a desperate edge in the words, "I suppose it is an experience that will make me better when I am through with it, because I am going to be in perfect health. I am on the road to that condition. Mark what I say."[20] In seven months, he would be dead.

While battling his own ill health, Sam Jones took heart in Tom Johnson's political success. He was, as Jones saw it "making a great campaign" in Cleveland. Jones thought Johnson "the freest man, that is at all prominent in partisan politics in America. . . . Of course, he has a machine, that is the unpleasant part of it." Jones was never critical of Tom Johnson the man, but historians have since noted that along with Johnson's municipal successes, Johnson "and his associates had created an effective political apparatus that dominated Cleveland politics for fifteen years."[21] Thus Johnson's reliance on a political party created precisely the thing Jones most feared: another machine.

Johnson himself was hardly sanguine about his ability to accomplish much. He found himself, he wrote Jones, fighting a city council that was "running wild. . . . Corrupt combinations are, I think being formed and I have less influence over them than any time since my first election. . . . They seem to be trying to hamper the administration in every way possible. The trouble has bothered you a great deal, I know, and I am trying to adopt your philosophy and believe that things will come out all right."[22]

Jones experienced a good deal of pleasure in the last year of his life, though one gets only a fleeting sense of it from the correspondence. In the autumn of 1903 he had encouraged Tom Johnson to attend the first annual municipal picnic at a park along the river. He promised to give Johnson a "handicap" for the fat man's race. That same season he orchestrated a

Welsh festival. The boy who loved "wrastling" in Collinsville was still very present in the man. He wrote business associates that he was "ready for a 'go' a la Marquis of Queensbury or London Prize ring with you," though he feared they would be too busy "to take time for fun; but let me just suggest that it pays to do that. It pays to take time to live."[23]

In early January 1904, Lincoln Steffens, at work on his series "The Shame of the Cities" for *McClure's* magazine, came to Toledo. With a laugh, Jones jokingly invited him to "look around all you want to and do what you please. If you find anything wrong, give it to them. Only make an exception of the mayor's office. If there is anything crooked there, do your best to gloss it over." Steffens did not find the mayor crooked, certainly; but he did find him strange. After dining with Whitlock, Steffens accompanied the lawyer to the Jones home for a visit. Steffens was nonplussed. For two hours he listened to the Golden Rule mayor read aloud from the New Testament and the poetry of Walt Whitman. Afterward, on the walk outside in the chill January night air, Steffens said, "Why, that man's program will take a thousand years!"[24]

Steffens eventually changed his mind about Sam Jones. Whitlock thought Jones had perplexed him in those first days, "though he knows now that Jones was wholly . . . right." Although it is doubtful that Steffens ever thought Jones wholly right, he seems to have influenced Steffens's thought in much the same way he influenced Bryan's. Louis Filler suggests that Steffens's advocacy of the Golden Rule as a practical principle, some six years after Sam Jones's death, can be linked to Jones. "That he should have hit upon the Golden Rule as a working principle may seem incredible," wrote Filler, "but it should be remembered that he had seen it work for 'Golden Rule' Jones." After meeting Jones, Steffens described himself picking up the New Testament, "without reverence, with feet up on a desk and a pipe in the mouth, as news."[25]

Jones had read Steffens's essays as they came out in *McClure's* and was pleased when Steffens sent him a copy of the book *Shame of the Cities* "in permanent form." He greatly appreciated the work Steffens was doing. "The bosses," wrote Steffens, "have split us up into parties. To him parties are nothing but means to his corrupt ends. . . . It is idiotic. This devotion to a machine that is used to take our sovereignty from us." Elsewhere, when Steffens discusses muckraking, one notes an emotion and a purpose similar to Jones's: "I did not gather with indifference all the facts and arrange them patiently for permanent preservation and laboratory analysis. I did not want to pressure, I wanted to destroy the facts."[26]

If Sam Jones felt any personal anger toward Mark Hanna he suppressed it publicly when he learned of his death. Hanna, a man long revered or feared as just the sort of boss Steffens describes, came down with typhoid fever on February 1, 1904. By the fifteenth, he was dead. Mayor Jones, asked to comment on Hanna, said characteristically that Hanna's strength of character was founded on his "devotion and fidelity to his own convictions of truth." Sam Jones the pacifist could be perceptive, honest, and hide the intended criticism from those who chose not to think about what he said when he observed that Hanna, a great organizer and fighter, "had he been engaged in real war would have been as great a general on the field of blood as he was in the field of party politics."[27]

While Jones wrestled to overcome his feelings of anger, many of his adversaries continued to vent their feelings. One of the last occasions when Jones incited the ire of many of Toledo's most respectable citizens came in March 1904. Jones and Whitlock had persuaded Toledo representative John C. Jones to introduce a bill in the General Assembly that would abolish capital punishment. The mayor went to Columbus to testify in behalf of the bill: what he had to say shocked most of the people who heard him or read the published reports. The night before he testified, a mob had stormed the Springfield, Ohio, jail, took a black man charged with killing a police officer, and hung him on a telephone pole. When the authorities brought him down, his body was riddled with bullets. Sam Jones, greatly shocked by the news, saw an analogy to the criminal justice system. He told the legislative committee: "If there must be killing of men, I believe the Springfield plan is better than the lugubrious killing by law."[28] As he told Nelson: "Of the two, I believe the methods of the mob are the least reprehensible. There is, at least some excuse for that; men are heated angry and insane, but the state! What language can adequately express the depth of depravity of the premeditation and cruelty involved in the judicial or legal murder?"[29]

The Ohio General Assembly passed a series of laws that affected municipal governance, one of which further eroded the little power Toledo's mayor had. Walter Brown had helped draft the Chapman bill, which amended sections of the municipal code of 1902. A clause that had given the mayor the general right of appointment was dropped in the Chapman bill. The effect was to limit Jones's ability to make appointments only to the board of public safety and to fill any other offices that became vacant when someone resigned or died. The *Blade* printed the *Columbus Journal*'s assessment: "Walter Brown is gradually undermining the strength of Golden Rule Jones."[30]

With his power to appoint greatly restricted, Jones became increasingly unwilling to enforce the laws. In the final months of his life Sam Jones sounded very much the anarchist: "Really and frankly, my brother, I am indifferent to man-made laws," he wrote to his socialist friend Walter Young. "Laws always follow, never lead the population."[31]

Jones, of course, did not see himself as an anarchist. He saw himself connected to the Christian martyrs. "It was devotion to His conviction of truth that led Jesus to willingly suffer death on a cross in obedience to sentence of the 'law.' The same is true of the martyrs in all ages who suffered torture, imprisonment, beheading, burning, hanging, and every sort of ignominy that could be heaped upon them, and always in the name of 'law and order,' and often times in the name of 'religion,' as in the case of the pious council that burned Jeanne D'Arc, and John Calvin who burned Michael Servitus. In one of his lectures on Anti-Slavery Wendell Phillips said: 'The highest crime may be the written law of the land.'"[32]

That spring Sam had one last opportunity to see Nelson. They spent the day together on the World's Fair grounds. Helen was attending a convention of women's clubs in St. Louis to read a paper. Writing Nelson in advance for hotel suggestions, Jones had said, "What can you tell me about a reasonable place to stop at? Of course, you know I shall not be as free with my wife along or I would not be asking questions, but even with her, I do not want to go to the Platers or any other five dollar a day hotel." Perhaps the tone of this letter makes as clear as any other document the strain between husband and wife. The final line reads, "I write about the hotel because my wife wanted me to, so you will please reply promptly." He helped to close the business in Beaumont, Texas, and investigated a New Orleans plant where his company's engines would be produced before returning to Toledo in mid-June. Almost as soon as he returned from the trip, Jones became critically ill.[33]

In a section of *The New Right* headed "Service for Service the Only Just Recompense," Jones wrote that he would not do one thing to help a young man get rich, but "I gladly give my life to the work of helping all men to realize the kingdom of God, which consists of brotherhood" (*NR*, 467-68). Dying at the age of fifty-seven, he did exactly that.

How does one sum up such a life? Sam Jones clearly was significantly ahead of his time—and life is better for us in America because of his work. Think of how much our world today was brought to life by reform pioneers like Sam Jones: an eight-hour workday, company benefits, paid vacations, public kindergartens, city parks, and recreation facilities. Our world would be greatly impoverished by the absence of such things. Thinking about it from this perspective, it is possible to appreciate the impact Jones had on Toledo and the important role he played in the transformation of civic culture in America. It is also possible to imagine an even better

America at the turn of the twenty-first century: one that had done more to inculcate his values.

Christian socialism is not even a minority movement in America today, but one need not look at Jones's life from that perspective—in fact, one need not look at him from within the Christian faith—to appreciate Jones's convictions and commitment. All of the world's major religions are built on love. Sam Jones is a unique figure in American history: a politician who turned the guiding principle of love into municipal policy. Speaking from within his religious tradition, Jones eloquently affirmed values central to the most positive aspects of American culture today: a deep appreciation for workers; the conviction that work creates self-respect; a recognition that we are connected to others, regardless of background or ethnicity; an abiding faith in all the people, without which democracy is a sham; an understanding of the systemic nature of health.

It was not as easy for Sam Jones to implement reforms in the city as it had been at his factory. Nevertheless, while he worked without the support of the Republican machine at first and later against the relentless animosity of the city council, Golden Rule Jones improved life in Toledo. In 1897, the *Blade* had prayed for one man out of 135,000 who "would conduct the affairs of the city as they should be conducted—for the benefit of all."[34] That was Jones's guiding principle, and he remained faithful to it throughout his seven-year mayoralty. All his programs sought to defend the public interest against private interest, to enrich the value of the commonwealth, to govern so that all of Toledo might benefit. His greatest disappointment was losing the opportunity to continue and expand municipal ownership of utilities. Jones believed that the people together had a common right to the natural resources of the earth.

Toledo was better in 1904 because Sam Jones had served all the people. Life had improved thanks to a few overarching structural improvements and to the smaller changes, the ones people notice. Jones had some successes in defending the principle of home rule—protecting the rights of the city against the state. Instituting civil service reform and hiring municipal employees on an eight-hour day made for a more professional and humane city government. All this was important work but less tangible to residents than the social reforms. People could see and benefit from the new public kindergartens, the increased public park acreage, the zoo, free swimming facilities in summer and municipal sleigh rides in winter, playgrounds, free concerts, a free golf course. He sought to reform the environment because of his passionate conviction that "each person could reach a kind of perfection, just as plants reach perfect beauty" living under the proper conditions. Municipal government was the means for fostering proper conditions.[35]

Sam thought his effort to reform the criminal justice system was the most significant work of his life. Together with Whitlock, he decreased police harassment of the most vulnerable citizens; they took personal responsibility for ensuring that the poor received a fair trial. His work later led to changes in the Ohio penal code.

No one saw more clearly than Sam did how far removed he was from the ideal of running the city on the principle of the Golden Rule: "To say that I have put the Golden Rule into practice in the conduct of the private business with which I am connected is to overstate the truth. To say that I have put it into practice in the city government of Toledo is a greater exaggeration," he wrote in 1898.[36] Certainly, his sudden death at fifty-seven left much of his work unfinished. But it is also true, that, given his temperament, it was unlikely that additional terms would have greatly expanded his accomplishments. Once again, he saw that most clearly. Writing a letter in May 1904, Jones described his vision of his strengths and inadequacies and in so doing he assessed his political strengths and weakness. "I know I lack those qualities of so-called leadership that are essential in a 'political boss,'" he wrote. "I do not use the word boss in an obnoxious sense, but you know he is a kind of dictator, and I can neither boss nor be bossed. I know there are millions of men who think they must be bossed, but I cannot boss them." The role he played as mayor, he went on to say, using a phrase that had no Orwellian connotation then, was that of "big brother in a loving family." Had he the management qualities of a leader, the people of Toledo would have reaped other benefits: lower prices for gas and electricity and cheaper municipal transportation. In fact, Toledo benefited in these areas when the furor over transit created a new Independent Party, which elected three councilmen in 1904 and Brand Whitlock as mayor in 1905.[37]

Certainly Sam Jones bore responsibility for failures to implement his vision, though significantly less responsibility than he so willingly accepted. But Toledo shared responsibility that the "city on a hill" that Jones built did not shine more brightly. To take just one example with contemporary resonance, Jones planned "at the city's expense, a place where the working mother might leave her child to be cared for. They told him it was paternalism." A little pamphlet circulated in Toledo at some point in Jones's tenure which reminded its readers that a great city must be a cooperative effort: "The charge is that a man admittedly able to serve the public, and admittedly anxious to do it, has not yet succeeded in making Toledo as fine a city as it should be. But why should it be left to one man to make a city fine? To criticize Jones because he has not washed and dressed the city and fed it with a spoon is to misunderstand a little the meaning of American democracy." "Is not the building of a city a communal enterprise?" asked Charles Ferguson in the pamphlet. "Only a great people can build a great city. The most that one can do—mayor or scavenger—is to manage his own job in so great a way that the sight of it will make other men great."[38]

The paradox at the center of Jones's reform career was that it was both a defeat and a victory. Clearly, there were tangible defeats: losing the gubernatorial race, failing to translate his 1899 landslide into pressure to enact his public policy reforms, failure to maintain and expand municipal ownership in Toledo. But taken out of the purely political sphere, there were victories as well. Sam truly was genuinely unconcerned about political victories: "I think I care nothing at all about winning, in the sense that you are so interested about. I know the truth is winning, is gaining ground, all the time, and I am content to work for the truth, whether it shall win or lose."[39]

One must read the mayoral years as a paradox, juxtapose the political plot against the reform agenda, and see how complete a transformation of our culture Jones was working for. If we put his goal in sight—to enact the Kingdom of God here on earth—then it is possible to understand that he saw victory where the seasoned political eye would see only defeat. We should see victories as well.

What is most important about Sam Jones's life is his life. Even the *Blade* saw that early on: "His earnest words . . . backed by the eloquence of his private life, have made a powerful impression on the people of Toledo." Neither a list of accomplishments nor a catalog of his reforms enacted provide the measure of the man. His greatness lay in his courageous willingness to confront and reexamine everything he believed, his energetic search for answers to the problem of poverty that still plagues our culture, and his valiant spiritual journey. As the *Detroit Journal* said at his death, "The moral which his spectacular career teaches . . . lie[s] in the spectacle which his life presented of a generous, open-hearted, charitable man, tremendously energetic in the pursuit of his convictions." Close examination of his inner life makes that "spectacle" all the more impressive. His pessimism about his own ethical journey reveals a profound integrity.[40]

The Welsh look to Owain Glyndwr's brief years of achievement as the essence of what it means to be Welsh. Sam Jones's ideals and his hopes for the city of Toledo and for the United States of America have their roots in Glyndwr. Both men built their respective places as human entities, places for fellowship. In his attempt to transform the Golden Rule into public policy, Sam Jones, like Glyndwr centuries before him, sought "a reconciliation of time, in which the the affairs of the remotest past might overlap the present and engage the future."[41]

Victory and defeat, validation and inadequacy were his in his last days. He recognized that his love had been reciprocated. "Toledo has poured out her love upon me in a way that at times quite overwhelms me with gratitude." Notice his feelings of inadequacy as he thinks about compensating them: "And I feel deeply my inefficiency, my inability to render service that will in any way recompense for this wealth of affection." He briefly discussed future work in improving love and comradeship in the world and then concluded, "Having said this, it would really add nothing to it for me to say that to work to this end, Toledo has my heart and my life." Toledo would have the opportunity within eight weeks to pour out its love for Sam Jones in an overwhelming way.[42]

By the end of his life he had moved far from the grief he felt in the mid-1870s after the deaths of his daughter, Midgie, and his wife, Alma. Three months before he died he wrote an old friend: "Old Walt. Whitman said 'No array of terms can say how much I am at peace about death and about God.' That is just the way I feel, but I feel very sure that there is no such thing as an end to my life. Death is merely an incident in life, not the end of it."[43]

Toledoans last saw their mayor in public on June 23. Jones and city council members made a tour of Toledo organized by the public service board. Jones had ridden in an open car, dined with the group at the Toledo Yacht Club, and continued on the tour. At lunch, used to the criticism that he would not enforce the laws, he joked that the motorcade had broken the speed limit. But the tour was cut short: the mayor was suddenly taken ill and driven home.[44]

Helen called in Dr. John Pyle the next morning. He diagnosed Jones's illness as pleuro-pneumonia. His weakened lungs, now lined with abscesses, had finally given in. The doctors, his family, and the mayor himself were not concerned about his recovery for the first week; but on July 1 one of the abscesses broke. The doctors thought he could not survive. There was some discussion of an operation as a last resort, but his doctors feared the shock of surgery would be more of a drain to his body than absorbing the fluid. The city rallied to support the mayor: all the churches offered special prayers, people called or wrote suggesting trusted remedies. And it seemed, for a time, to work. On July 4 the people were told their mayor had recovered. His secretary, Helen Wheeler, writing for the mayor on July 5, said, "We have had some very anxious days, but yesterday morning there was a decided change for the better, which continues this morning, so that all are hopeful of his recovery. Political opponents have seemed as solicitous as friends, and for once we can say that his beloved Toledo has been truly non-partisan." On July 7 Nelson sent a telegram: "Hurrah for you.

Come . . . join [us] as soon as possible." Toledoans were startled the next Monday by the banner headline of the July 11 *News-Bee*: "Mayor Jones Is Once More in the Shadow of Death." The *Blade,* since it had castigated Jones for more than five years, felt the need to be properly reverential now: "Mayor Jones is Dying; All Hope has been Abandoned and he is Sinking; But a Flutter of Life Remains," read its headline.[45]

But if the city was stunned that Monday, the eleventh, the family had been in shocked mourning all weekend. Although he had seemed to be steadily improving all the previous week, on Saturday, the ninth, he had such a high fever he lost consciousness. On Sunday, Jones himself seemed to give up hope for the first time. Daniel was called; fearing the end, he made it from his home on the river to Monroe Street in eleven minutes. Doctors administered an injection of saline solution that afternoon and then again Monday morning. The high fever continued; Jones was delirious.

He lay on his bed, reported one of his doctors, "with his mouth wide open. His tongue appeared parched and his eyes were covered with a film." The family gathered at his bedside: Helen, with her sister Mrs. S.R. Maclaren to support her; Percy with Marion at his side; Paul; Daniel and his wife; Nell; and Bertha and Roy Jones, his late brother John's two eldest children. On Wednesday the gathered family was joined by relatives of his first wife, Alma, John Ley from Bradford, Pennsylvania, and Mrs. Matteson of Montpelier, Indiana. But there was nothing for them to do: on Monday afternoon, July 11, he had slipped into a coma; he never regained consciousness. His brother Dan came downstairs shortly after 5 P.M. on Tuesday, July 12, to tell those waiting in the parlor that Sam was dead. The *New York Times,* in reporting his death, noted that the asthma that he had suffered from for years "was the primary cause of his fatal illness."[46]

The *Blade* was inclined to sentimentalize the end. On Tuesday anxious Republicans read that their mayor "with a tenacity that is little short of miraculous, [was] hanging to the little thread of life remaining in his body." A man who had lived such a controversial life did not die without some critics, of course. While most were saying he died as he lived, others observed that he died *because of* the way he lived. The *News-Bee* special issue "Account of the Mayor's Death," price one cent, contained an implicit criticism of his way of life. Of course, the *News-Bee* could afford to be straightforward now as the newspaper staff had little reason to regret their past treatment of the Golden Rule mayor. The mayor was so "pulled down in flesh and strength by what seemed to many people his peculiar ideas of living, and eating and fasting and exercise, there was little left for the disease . . . to feed upon." This implicit criticism was nothing compared to the actions of the Toledo Railway and Light Company, which urged investors to buy its stock now in the last days of Jones's life because "in the event of Mayor Jones's death the stock should go considerably higher." The *News-Bee* saw it as "a splendid tribute to the well-known character of mayor Jones. It shows that everybody expected him to protect the interests of the people." Washington Gladden likewise called the rise in stock prices a "ghastly tribute to his integrity."[47]

Word of his death quickly traveled far beyond Toledo. Helen soon received condolence telegrams from, among others, Washington Gladden, William Jennings Bryan, N.O. Nelson, Tom Johnson, Eugene Debs, and Lincoln Steffens. Newspapers from Brooklyn to Montreal to San Francisco reported his passing. Five newspapers in Chicago reported his death, including the *Chicago Farm, Field, and Fireside,* which wrote "'Golden Rule' Jones was, perhaps, the best beloved man living. He was of the Abraham Lincoln type in the honesty and purpose of his motives and his sympathy with the masses of people." One San Francisco newspaper saw fit to observe that "he took a strangely distorted view of things. . . . He said 'As long as the capital crime of capital punishment exists there will be murder. . . . Borrowers of money are life's real derelicts.'" The *Boston Universalist* dismissed his critics: "That sounds very much like things that were said of Christ and other personal masters."[48]

On Thursday the mayor's body was quickly prepared for burial and on Friday was placed at Memorial Hall to lie in state. Viewing began at 5:30 A.M. and continued to midnight to "accommodate the laboring man."[49]

Sam Jones seemed to have kindled a recompensatory spirit in all of Toledo. The city council, which had been even less reconciled to the mayor than the *Blade* had been, showed its respect by sending flowers to Memorial Hall in the shape of the mayor's chair; the fire department sent flowers in the shape of a miniature net; the waterworks had flowers sculpted into a model water tower. But it was not these formal testimonials that impressed seasoned reporters, it was the people. Toledo had never witnessed such an outpouring of love as was demonstrated that Friday and Saturday. The people came, more than fifty-five thousand of them, passing by his bier from dawn till midnight on the first day and continuing to pack the hall all the next morning. "Keep close to me Minnie," whispered a mother who held a toddler by the hand. "I want you to [be able to] say that you have seen the mayor." "I wouldn't go to the funeral of my own sister," another woman was heard to say. "But this is Sam Jones and my conscience wouldn't let me rest if I hadn't shown him what little honor I can."[50]

It was hardly a simple affair. Sam Jones would have disavowed the display if he could—the copper-lined cedar casket cost $300, the use of twenty-two carriages cost $110. But he would have been cheered by the presence of the Golden Rule band, which escorted his hearse from Memorial Hall to the cemetery as it had escorted him during his political campaigns. Five thousand people observed the grave-side ceremony at which his friend the Rev. Albert Marion Hyde of the Congregational church presided. Several of Toledo's unions, including the Typographical Union, attended the funeral en masse. Wrote the *Bee*: "The numbers were there, but it was the feeling of the numbers that kept them quiet that was so marvelous for a crowd of that size: not quite of awe but of respect."[51]

Percy and Marion, Paul, little Mason, then only six, Jones's secretary, Helen Wheeler, his clerk Reynold Voit, N.O. Nelson, Brand Whitlock, and Tom Johnson with fifteen Cleveland officials all waited solemnly in the steaming afternoon heat. Helen was not present. Various officials occupied the 150 waiting chairs. Johnson turned to Cowell, the labor journalist who first suggested Jones as an ideal mayor, and whispered, pointing to the officials: "They're all here: they want to make sure he's dead." His real mourners, aside from his family, were the people. J. Ellery Eaton wrote afterward, "I stood for nearly two hours, half hidden in the branches of an evergreen tree and only a few feet from the waiting grave. Outside the ropes were a throng of people, 'just people you know,' waiting patiently."[52]

Whitlock, who gave the eulogy, pointed out to Newton Baker a hefty saloon keeper, "his face tense with grief," staring straight ahead in stunned bereavement. In recent years, he had stopped serving liquor at midnight and never permitted a man to drink more than was good for him "because Sam had asked him not to." In his way, said Whitlock, he "was trying to follow the 'golden rule.'"[53]

In the end, the people recognized the reciprocal nature of his contract of the heart. They were there to make amends for any failure on their part to meet love with love. "It was different yesterday. That was no ordinary funeral," rhapsodized Cochran at the *News-Bee*:

> And the funeral was FREE. It wasn't an invitational affair. Every human being in Toledo who wasn't locked up in jail or otherwise unable to get out and walk, felt that he had a right to fall in line and follow the hearse.
>
> The thousands who stood for two long hours on the Jones lawn, in the street and on the lawns of neighbors—all of these felt that they were a part of the funeral, they were in it—not mere onlookers. It was their funeral.
>
> If there was any inequality at all it was because those who loved Mayor Jones stood in the broiling sun while some who had hated him sat in the seats of the mighty, and were the chief mourners.
>
> Undoubtedly that was noticed by some. But they didn't understand as Jones might understand could he but have directed his own funeral. . . .

Yes, it was a remarkable funeral, a marvelous harmony of thought, a glorious demonstration of love, a hopeful promise of peace in this community this Toledo of ours.

Cochran ended with an allusion to Christ: "In his great love for humanity Mayor Jones would have gladly died to bring about this getting together of all the people under such wholesome references and with such a promise for the future." Sam had written his dear friend Nelson in 1899, "I can stand for truth; I can tell truth; I can live for it; I am just as willing to die for it, if that shall be in the programme."[54]

The *Chicago Chronicle*'s views serve as a reminder of the chorus that always thought Jones dangerous: "There are various grades of anarchism, the emotional, the philosophical, the sentimental, the benevolent, the violent. Mr. Jones was one of the benevolent type. Personally he 'would not hurt a fly,' in the common phrase, but all types of anarchism are revolutionary and dangerous to civilized society, and the Jones type is even more dangerous than the more truculent type, because the personal inoffensiveness of such representatives as Mr Jones tends to mislead and disarm society." At his death, this vision was decidedly the minority view.[55]

His secretary, Helen Wheeler, went in to the office the morning after he died—she had one letter to answer. On July 8, as Sam Jones was near death, Samuel Gompers, president of the American Federation of Labor, had written to Jones to solicit an article for the September issue of the *American Federationist*. "I am confident," he wrote, "that anything which you may write will be interesting and educational." On July 13, Helen Wheeler answered: "Mr. Jones was very ill when your letter came, and I delayed answering, hoping that he might improve sufficiently to promise to write the desired article, but as you must have learned from the morning papers, Mr. Jones's work here is finished, and Toledo today mourns her most beloved citizen."[56]

There is an ancient Jewish tradition dating back to the days of Isaiah, a poet and a prophet Sam Jones loved, that tells of the Lamed-Vov, or the Just Men. Tradition has it that the world "reposes upon thirty-six Just Men, the Lamed-Vov, indistinguishable from simple mortals"; they are "the hearts of the world multiplied, and into them, as into one receptacle, pour all our griefs." It is a useful notion, that there are special individuals who seem to carry within them "the hearts of the world multiplied." Sam Jones had such a heart. It was not perfect—far from it. But it prompted Jones to become a just man who tried to create a more just world. Those who argue that he did not succeed in implementing his ideas, that he made obvious political blunders, miss the point. Perhaps people cannot be reformed, but surely the world becomes a better place, if only temporarily, when people such as Sam Jones with childlike naïveté believe that they can be.

Sam Jones had changed. He had lived two very different lives. At times he looked back in despair at the waste of the first life. But more frequently he embraced his own change, seeing in it a hope for the future. In 1900, he read Florence Converse's *Burden of Christopher*. After suffering bankruptcy, having relied on humane business practices that benefited his employees, Philip says to his wife in that novel, "I would do it all over again tomorrow. I would do everything—that I have done—just as I have done it." Jones read those words and wrote in the margin: "So would I. I cannot change the past and I am doing the best I know in the present." Twice in the pages of Converse's novel Jones noted in the margin, "There is no sin but the sin of *trifling with your own soul*."[57]

On July 24 five thousand people gathered in tribute to Sam Jones in Cleveland. Welsh singers sang the native anthems. Cleveland mayor Tom Johnson spoke to those gathered in Rockefeller Park: "With a smile for a friend and a kind word for an opponent, he won his way in Toledo, in Ohio and in the nation. As my tribute to Mayor Jones I desire to say that Toledo is better; Ohio is better; the nation is better and the whole world is better for his having lived."[58]

Notes

Introduction: If You Knew My Inner Life

1. *New Orleans Sunday States,* May 4, 1902; *Denver Post,* Obituary, July 18, 1904, in the Memorial Scrapbook, complied upon his death, Jones Papers. Peter J. Frederick argues in *Knights of the Golden Rule: The Intellectual as Christian Social Reformer in the 1890s* (Lexington: University Press of Kentucky, 1976), 22, that these reformers turned to Jones in this way; Jones to Loretto French, May 28, 1904. Jones Papers. Both the letters written by Jones and those written to him cited in this book can be found at the Toledo–Lucas County Public Library and, on microfilm, through the Ohio Historical Society in Columbus.

2. Memorial Scrapbook; *Toledo News-Bee,* special issue, July 13, 1904; *Toledo Blade,* October 8, 1904.

3. Clippings in the Memorial Scrapbook.

4. Reprinted in the *Toledo Bee,* July 8, 1902.

5. Paul Boyer, *Urban Masses and Moral Order in America, 1820-1920* (Cambridge, Mass.: Harvard University Press, 1978), 168-69. Boyer sees the effort to impose moral order as the dominant stimulus to reform from 1820 to 1920 (viii); Jones to Henry Demarest Lloyd, April 16, 1897.

6. Jones to Washington Gladden, April 1897.

7. Brand Whitlock, *Forty Years of It* (New York: D. Appleton, 1925), 269-70.

8. The Roosevelt and Riis comments come from Boyer, *Urban Masses,* 176; Ruth Rosen, *The Lost Sisterhood: Prostitution in America, 1900-1918* (Baltimore: Johns Hopkins University Press, 1982), 16.

9. See Susan Curtis, *A Consuming Faith: The Social Gospel and Modern American Culture* (Baltimore: Johns Hopkins University Press, 1991). She and Boyer both persuasively demonstrate that middle-class reformers sought to use institutional means to increase the state's ability to repress the most visible forms of vice.

10. Jones to Rev. M. Crafts, October 28, 1897; Jones to N.O. Nelson, July 13, 1898.

11. Josiah Strong, *Our Country* (New York: Baker and Taylor, 1891), 55. Copy in Jones Papers.

12. Melvin G. Holli, *Reform in Detroit: Hazen S. Pingree and Urban Politics* (New York: Oxford University Press, 1969), 163, 169.

13. Ernest S. Griffith, *A History of American City Government: The Conspicuous Failure, 1870-1900* (New York: Praeger, 1974), 144, 252. Griffith's surprise suggests much about the tone historians have taken toward Jones. All too frequently historians have considered him outside the context of applied Christianity so strong at the century's end and condescendingly dismissed him. An example is Robert Crunden: "Rather than fight for jobs or a bill that he and his supporters wanted . . . Jones

would orate for it, disdaining any backstairs conniving. Such an Olympian attitude made for much purity and *no progress* and caused some of Jones's supporters to declare, probably unjustly, that all Jones cared about was the publicity" (*A Hero in Spite of Himself: Brand Whitlock in Art, Politics and War* [New York: Knopf, 1969], 94; emphasis added). Even one of the few researchers to consult the primary sources misunderstands the application of the Social Gospel. Robert Smith asserts that Jones was "a throw back to an earlier age," when reform was more "utopian than pragmatic." Completely missing Jones's repeated assertion that we are to create the Kingdom of God here, today, he argues that Jones and Nelson O. Nelson "looked to a distant simple day when the kingdom of God would be ushered in on earth" ("Beyond Progressivism: The Careers of Samuel 'Golden Rule' Jones and Nelson O. Nelson," *Midwest Review: Journal of History and Culture of the Missouri Valley* 10 (Spring 1988): 43-54.

14. George W. Knepper, *Ohio and Its People* (Kent: Kent State University Press, 1989), 328, calls Jones "the extraordinary mayor of Toledo," "the pacesetter in municipal government." Wendell Johnson asserts (*Toledo's Non-Partisan Movement* [Toledo: H. J. Chihenden Co, 1922], 10), that "probably in no other American city has the non-partisan idea been more thoroughly tested" than in Toledo. As Morgan Barclay and Charles N. Glabb point out in *Toledo: Gateway to the Great Lakes* (Tulsa: Continental Heritage, 1982), 85, Jones did not initiate a culture of independence at the century's end; Toledo's independent thinking can be traced back to the earliest Quaker settlers and to German immigrants fleeing the failed revolution of 1848.

15. As Christopher Lasch notes in *The New Radicalism in America, 1889-1963: The Intellectual as Social Type* (New York: Knopf, 1965), 253, Walter Lippmann, John Dewey, Brand Whitlock, Frederic C. Howe, and Lincoln Steffens criticized Progressivism as another form of Puritanism. I want to stress (see Lasch, 32-33) that it is not my intention to "question the validity of radical action by exploring its psychic origins," nor do I mean to suggest that "it was wrong or abnormal for a member of the urban middle class in 1900 to feel guilt about living in comfort when millions of immigrant families battled tuberculosis and the sweat-shop in filthy and overcrowded tenements." But as we shall see, Sam Jones's response was all-consuming.

16. Freud himself was notoriously hostile to religious feeling, especially in *The Future of an Illusion* (1927; rpt. Garden City, N.Y.: Doubleday, 1964). He believed religious thinking had a narcotic effect and that religious feeling was rooted in the obsessional neurosis of the Oedipal complex. Psychoanalysis has generally cast religion in terms of neurotic fantasy, sublimation, and psychopathology. But there have been important revisionist psychoanalysts—beginning with Erik Erikson—and it is this revisionist tradition on which I rely. The work of Donald Nathanson, the psychoanalyst most responsible for awakening the psychoanalytic community to the role shame plays in identity formation, has played a central role in the process of my coming to understand Jones's complicated emotional response to money. In addition, both the Jesuit psychoanalyst William Meissner's *Life and Faith: Psychological Perspectives on Religious Experience* (Washington, D.C.: Georgetown University Press, 1987) and Ana-Maria Rizzuto's work, phenomenological in its assumptions, *The Birth of the Living God: A Psychoanalytic Study* (Chicago: University of Chicago Press, 1979) have also provided useful ways to help make sense of the mind's search for meaning in the spiritual dimension.

17. Jones to Henry Demarest Lloyd, April 16, 1897; Frances Fitzgerald, *Cities on a Hill: A Journey Through Contemporary American Cultures* (New York: Simon and Schuster, 1981), 23.

18. Daniel Walker Howe persuasively demonstrates the connection between the two in "Religion and Politics in the Antebellum North," in *Religion and American Politics: From the Colonial Period to the 1980s*, ed. Mark A. Noll (New York: Oxford University Press, 1990), 121; Nathan Hatch, *The Democratization of American Christianity* (New Haven: Yale University Press, 1989), 3-13.

19. Richard Baxter's *Christian Directory* quoted in Sacvan Bercovitch, *The Puritan Origins of the American Self* (New Haven: Yale University Press, 1975), 19.

20. Jones to W. H. Kinnier, November 11, 1897.

1. Stirred with Ambition

1. Samuel Jones, *The New Right: A Plea for Fair Play Through a More Just Social Order* (New York: Eastern Book Concern, 1899), 39. Subsequent quotations from this work, which includes his "Autobiography," a memoir chapter of seventy pages, will be made parenthetically in the text abbreviated as *NR*. The title refers not to one end of the political spectrum, but rather to Jones's conviction that the right to work was all-important.

2. Jones to S.M. Jones of Springfield, Massachusetts, August 31, 1898. His close friend Brand Whitlock, the novelist who became mayor of Toledo the year after Jones's death, concurred: "It was his Welsh blood, this Celtic strain in him, that accounted for . . . his wit, his humor, his instinctive appreciation of art, his contempt for artificial distinctions, his love of liberty, his passionate democracy" (Whitlock, *Forty Years of It*, 129).

3. *Caernarvonshire Historical Society Transactions* 15 (1954): 55; translated by Aled Davies, a member of the extended Jones family.

4. Jan Morris, *The Matter of Wales: Epic Views of a Small Country* (Oxford: Oxford University Press, 1984), 158.

5. Gwyn Williams, *When Was Wales? A History of the Welsh* (1985; rpt. London: Penguin, 1988), 229; emphasis added. Just as Jones began advocating a cooperative municipal agenda in Toledo in the 1890s, a strong socialist movement was gaining power in Wales. One of its early heroes, Thomas Edward Ellis, who combined Welsh poetry and Methodism with a strong semisocialist populism, emphasized the collectivist emphasis of Cymraeg (Welsh).

6. Ruth Janette Ruck, *Place of Stones* (London: Faber and Faber, 1961), 172. Ruck moved to Ty Mawr just after World War II.

7. 1 Sam. 2:26, *The New Revised Standard Version.*

8. Ruck, *Place of Stones*, 7.

9. Williams, *When Was Wales?*, 154-55.

10. Morris, *Matter of Wales*, 110.

11. Williams, *When Was Wales?*, 155; R.R. Williams, *Flames from the Altar: Howell Harris and His Contemporaries* (Caernarvon, Wales: Calvinistic Methodist Book Agency, 1962), 93. This church is not simply an offshoot of Wesleyan Methodism. Both John Wesley and George Whitefield played their parts, but neither

man was the true leader of this denomination. *Flames from the Altar* and Rev. William Williams, *Welsh Calvinistic Methodism: A Historical Sketch of the Presbyterian Church of Wales* (London: Presbyterian Church of England, 1884), 27-44, provide detailed background on the formation of this church.

12. Williams, *Welsh Calvinist Methodism,* 155-63.

13. Jones to Rhys T. Williams, February 27, 1902.

14. Jones to John R. Edwards, February 15, 1904; Williams, *When Was Wales?,* 176-80. Up to the 1860s Wales lost people to emigration at a rate of 28-47 per 10,000 per decade. By the 1880s that figure fell to 11 per 10,000; by the 1890s Wales became a country of new immigration. During the decade before World War I, Wales, with an immigration rate of 45 per 10,000, ranked second to the United States as a center of world immigration. The demographics can largely be explained by the attraction of the industrial south.

15. Hugh Jones's "Declaration of Intention to become a U.S. Citizen," filed on February 23, 1858, in Lewis County, New York, swears that he was born "on or about the 24th day of September in the year of our Lord one thousand eight hundred and eight as he is informed and believes" (Jones Papers). Dudley Baines, *Migration in a Mature Economy: Emigration and Internal Migration in England and Wales, 1861-1900* (Cambridge: Cambridge University Press, 1985), 58-62. Imre Ferenczi and Walter F. Wilcox, *International Migration* (New York: National Bureau of Economics and Social Research, 1929-31), 2:114, report that between 1840 and 1930, 65 to 75 percent of immigrants who arrived in the United States were between fifteen and forty years old. Thus Hugh Jones was in a minority. In the first half of the nineteenth century males emigrating from England and Wales typically ranged in age from seventeen to twenty-five.

16. Philip J. Greven, *The Protestant Temperament: Patterns of Child-Rearing, Religious Experience, and the Self in Early America* (New York: Knopf, 1977). Greven focuses his attention on how what he terms Evangelical, Moderate, and Genteel temperaments are shaped by childhood religious experience. Although his focus is on early American culture, Greven notes that these three temperaments persist through many generations. See also Warren Kinston, "The Shame of Narcissism," in *The Many Faces of Shame,* ed. Donald L. Nathanson (New York: Guilford Press, 1987), 200, 225-28.

17. Donald L. Nathanson, "Shaming Systems in Couples, Families, and Institutions," in *The Many Faces of Shame,* ed. Nathanson, 249.

18. Alan Conway, ed., *The Welsh in America: Letters from the Immigrants* (Minneapolis: University of Minnesota Press, 1961), 15.

19. Ibid., 28-29. Cruffydd Rhisiart sailed from Liverpool on board the *John Bright* six years after the Jones family emigrated; in the absence of more detailed information about the Joneses' own journey, his account provides some sense of the transatlantic experience for the Welsh at mid-century.

20. Ibid., 9; Edwin C. Guillet, *The Great Migration: The Atlantic Crossing by Sailing Ship, 1770-1860* (1937; rpt. Toronto: University of Toronto Press, 1963), 75-76, 84.

21. Williams, *When Was Wales?,* 161. In Collinsville, the Joneses joined an established community of Welsh present since 1796. The 1790s had been a turbulent

decade in rural Wales as the enclosure movement threatened rural life. A famine in 1795-96 pushed prices up; troops were called out to quell civil disobedience in Bala, the center of Calvinist Methodism, and in the pubs there, toasts were drunk to the French Revolution.

22. Rev. Lewis Williams, "Lewis County, New York," *Cambrian* 25 (September 1905): 372-76; statistics on the Welsh Calvinists are from Byron G. Bower, *History of Lewis County, New York, 1880-1965* (Lowville: Willard Press, 1970), 536.

23. Whitney R. Cross, *The Burned-Over District: The Social and Intellectual History of Enthusiastic Religion in Western New York, 1800-1850* (Ithaca: Cornell University Press, 1950), 3-4, 13. The Great Revival in western New York began in the winter of 1799-1800, preceding the revival in Beddgelert by almost twenty years. Evangelism dominated the area until 1850: it reached its height in 1825.

24. Nathan O. Hatch, "The Democratization of Christianity and the Character of American Politics," in *Religion and American Politics: From the Colonial Period to the 1980s*, ed. Mark A. Noll (New York: Oxford University Press, 1990), 93. Hatch deals with the period 1780-1830, but a similar phenomenon existed at mid-century; see William Martin, *A Prophet with Honor: The Billy Graham Story* (New York: William Morrow, 1991), 43. Richard Carwardine, "Methodist Ministers and the Second Party System," in *Rethinking Methodist History: A Bicentennial Historical Consultation*, ed. Russell E. Richey and Kenneth E. Rowe (Nashville: Abingdon, 1985), 140, demonstrates that Methodists were more likely than other denominations to separate politics from religion. The same cannot be said for their Welsh Calvinistic brethren.

25. Jones shared with other evangelicals the characteristic internalization of religious life, the turn away from external authority, a lay orientation, and an emphasis on the transformation of character. America had been founded by such people and by the nineteenth century anti-institutionalism had become the nation's dominant cultural attitude. As a reformer, like the abolitionists who came before him, Sam Jones's antinomian vision blinded his ability to see any good in institutions. His political effectiveness was consequently limited. See Claude Welch, *Protestant Thought in the Nineteenth Century*, 2 vols. (New Haven: Yale University Press, 1972, 1985), 1:27-28. In *Slavery: A Problem in American Institutional and Intellectual Life* (Chicago: University of Chicago Press, 1976), 255, Stanley Elkins accounts for characteristic American anti-institutionalism thus: "The anti-institutionalism . . . so impressive in the cultural attitudes of this period was in fact perennially inherent in American experience virtually from the first. [Seventeenth-century immigrants] had in their way been challenging institutions in the name of liberty for years before their voyage, which was itself a plenary repudiation of institutional continuities." There may be something else at work here: Frank Sulloway's *Born to Rebel: Birth Order, Family Dynamics, and Creative Lives* (New York: Pantheon Books, 1996) convincingly argues that scholars have missed the essential issue in understanding social change. Birth order [not social class, gender, or ethnicity] is the most accurate predictor of social radicalism. Sulloway analyzes vast data to show that later-borns, like Sam Jones, are more predisposed to adopt radical or anti-institutional ideas.

26. James Hastings, *The Encyclopaedia of Religion and Ethics* (New York: Scribners, 1908-1926), "Wales," 10:218a.

27. Jean B. Quandt, *From the Small Town to the Great Community: The Social*

Thought of Progressive Intellectuals (New Brunswick, N.J.: Rutgers University Press, 1970), 40.

28. Martin, *Prophet with Honor,* 33.

29. Williams, *Flames from the Altar,* 97: "When one considers the spiritual forces released by the Calvinistic Methodist Revival, its effect seems epochmaking. It gave birth to a democracy. . . . Politics has had a religious implication, its strength measured by its adherence to principles and ideas." Williams notes that these ideas "anticipated much of what British socialism has stressed in recent years" (93). Claude Welch notes there were quietist evangelicals but that "the dominant pietist evangelical stream insisted that the inner religion of the heart be expressed in an outward and visible quality and shape of existence: Christianity consists rather in practice than in knowledge . . . and specifically the practice of love" (*Protestant Thought,* 1:29).

30. The actions and feelings of Jones's reform life, as well as the known facts about Calvinistic Methodism, combined with Sam's early life, suggest that he fits Philip Greven's evangelical paradigm. The paradigm also confirms suggestions hidden in Jones's autobiography. See Greven, *Protestant Temperament,* 12-13.

31. Welch, *Protestant Thought,* 1:27; Greven, *Protestant Temperament,* 35-36, 93.

32. Harvey S. Ford, "The Life and Times of 'Golden Rule' Jones," 2 vols. (Ph.D diss., University of Michigan, 1953), 1:31. Ford does not discuss Jones's relations with his mother. He simply quotes from an unpublished manuscript dated 1938 by Robert J. Plate entitled "A Message from the President of the YMCA." The manuscript was then in Plate's possession; it is not in the Toledo archive. Sam Jones was the Lima Y's second president.

33. The developmental model that makes most sense of the role of shame in Sam Jones's life sees shame as the guardian of a person's separate self (Kinston, "Shame of Narcissism," 200, 225-28). The evangelical child has two options: to defy the parents' wills or to acquiesce. Any child who feels the parents are rejecting his or her unique self feels pain and anger. Those children who successfully tolerate and manage the negative feelings continue to develop their unique identity. They experience little shame. The child who complies with parental projection, however, destroys his or her own experience. In the short term, the child experiences parental approval. But it is a spurious sense of self-worth, for the child fuses with the parents' definition of the self and feels shame. Shame is a self-protecting mechanism: it reminds the self of the self before it can be totally absorbed by the other. Thus shame carries with it the sense of disappearing into nothingness.

34. George Herron's article "The Philosophy of the Lord's Prayer" helped prompt Sam's conversion to Christian socialism in the 1890s (Greven, *Protestant Temperament,* 37; Rizzuto, *Birth of the Living God,* 15). A marginal comment in his copy of Washington Gladden's *Ruling Ideas of the Present Age* (Boston: Houghton Mifflin, 1895), 20, presents a clue to his view of his father. Gladden argues, "You must tell men that God is their Father, but you must be very careful not to let them get the idea that they are his children." He then goes on to discuss the disobedience and ingratitude of children to earthly fathers' impulses to "save" them. Sam scrawled in the margin: "An exact statement of the ridiculous and wicked conception of the Fatherhood of God that I learned from the popular teaching and kept me confused and [illegible word] in my so-called Christian life for 20 years" (Jones Papers).

35. Greven documents the parental strategy that could build such a conscience by analyzing the journals of evangelicals who were as inclined to record the experience as they were to deny their children. Greven finds that children left on their own, without a sense of being loved, were "utterly devastated and destroyed. . . . For the rest of their lives they would never be entirely freed from the pangs of guilt. . . . planted within them during their earliest years" (*Protestant Tempermen*t, 55).

36. Martin, *Prophet with Honor,* 39; Jones to William Cocolough, February 22, 1902.

37. Robert M. Crunden, *Ministers of Reform: The Progressives' Achievement in American Civilization, 1889-1920* (Urbana: University of Illinois Press, 1984), 3-12. Crunden does not do as much to explain why evangelicals should become Progressives as does Greven. See also Nick Salvatore, *Eugene Debs: Citizen and Socialist* (Urbana: University of Illinois Press, 1981), 10.

38. Cross, *Burned-Over District,* 93.

39. Greven, *Protestant Temperament,* 54. Small wonder, then, that Jones needed feelings of oneness and unity later in life. One of the most powerful desires of the evangelical temperament, notes Greven, is the desire for oneness with Christ (85).

40. Hoyt Landon Warner argues in *Progressivism in Ohio, 1987-1917* (Columbus: Ohio State University Press, 1964), 30, that Jones's lack of formal training led him to rely "upon intuition more than logic in attacking problems"; Clarence Darrow, *Farmington* (Chicago: A.C. McClurg, 1904), 58-60.

41. Lewis County had erected a poorhouse in 1846 at a cost of $2,461 in support of thirty-one men and twenty-nine women. By 1855, the county spent $5,012 in support of forty-nine men and forty-five women. Statistics on the poor are from Franklin Hough, *A History of Lewis County in the State of New York from the Beginning of Its Settlement to the Present Time* (Albany: Munsell and Rowland, 1860), 18.

42. Nathanson observes that shame requires the presence of another person: "In order for shame to occur, there must be a relationship between the self and the other in which the self cares about the other's evaluation" ("Shaming Systems," 250, 108). As Kinston's model has it, shame protects the self from the other's projection.

43. His feelings of resentment are recast in *The New Right,* 41, into an exhortation to parents and teachers to discover what work children are best suited for: parents and teachers should do "their utmost to put them into a position where they can have free play for their natural talents." But feelings of abandonment and angry resentment are surely there.

44. Thomas C. O'Donnell, *Snubbing Posts: An Informal History of the Black River Canal* (Boonville, N.Y.: Black River Books, 1949), 44.

45. Crunden, *Ministers of Reform,* 5. For many of the reformers of Sam Jones's generation, Lincoln's death defined the present. Jane Addams, for example, remembered seeing her father in tears for the first time in her life.

2. The Only Problem

1. *Titusville Morning Herald,* September 27, 1865.

2. Carl Resek, ed., *The Progressives* (New York: Bobbs-Merrill, 1967), xxxiii. Autobiographies written by people close to Jones include Whitlock's *Forty Years of It,* Johnson's *My Story,* Gladden's *Recollections,* and Steffens's *Autobiography.*

3. Amasa M. Eaton, "A Visit to the Oil Regions of Pennsylvania," *Western Pennsylvania Historical Magazine* 18 (1935): 189; Paul H. Giddens, *Pennsylvania Petroleum: Contemporary Accounts, 1859-1872* (Philadelphia: Lippincott, 1975), 268. The Industrial Revolution gave oil real monetary value. Edwin Drake had first successfully drilled for oil in Titusville, Pennsylvania, in 1859. He adapted the techniques for drilling salt to drill a six-inch pipe into the rock strata with a pressure of nine hundred pounds. But the Civil War halted the development of the new industry.

4. Morris, *Matter of Wales,* 115-16.

5. Helen Block Lewis, "Shame and the Narcissistic Personality," ed. Donald L. Nathanson (New York: Guilford Press, 1987), 109, in *The Many Faces of Shame,* noted that it is often difficult to recognize shame because "shame and guilt are often fused and therefore confused. Shame and guilt may both be evoked simultaneously by a moral transgression."

6. *Titusville Morning Herald,* October 23, 1865.

7. Charles Leonard [Crocus, pseud.], *The History of Pithole* (Pithole City: Morton, Longwell, 1867), 31.

8. Paul H. Giddens, *The Birth of the Oil Industry* (New York: Macmillan, 1938), 138.

9. *Pithole Daily Record,* December 30, 1865. This newspaper, a rich resource, unfortunately is incomplete. The first newspaper (Monday, September 25) still exists at the Drake Well Museum, in Titusville, but nothing remains of the newspapers from Tuesday, September 26, through Friday, November 24, 1865.

10. The *Nation* reprinted in *Titusville Morning Herald,* October 13, 1865; *Titusville Morning Herald,* June 14, 1865.

11. *Pithole Daily Record,* April 2, 1866.

12. William C. Darrah, *Pithole, the Vanished City: A Story of the Petroleum Industry* (Gettysburg, Pa.: Published by the author, 1972), 35; *Titusville Morning Herald,* October 26, September 21, 1865; Giddens, *Pennsylvania Petroleum,* 288.

13. Darrah, *Pithole,* 38; *Pithole Daily Record,* December 11, 1865.

14. *Titusville Morning Herald,* October 11, 1865; Darrah, *Pithole,* 223-31; Giddens, *Pennsylvania Petroleum,* 344.

15. Jones to L.O. Vaight, February 15, 1899.

16. Eric Hoffer, *True Believers: Thoughts on the Nature of Mass Movements* (New York: Harper & Row, 1951), 26.

17. Jones to S.H. Comings, August 11, 1898.

18. Elkins, *Slavery,* 168, 261. "The entire logic of reform," he writes, "placed enormous burdens on the individual and the individual conscience and grossly magnified the personal role of everything" (158).

19. William James, *The Varieties of Religious Experience: A Study in Human Nature* (New York: Longman's, Green, 1902), 213. Copy in Jones Papers.

20. Only a handful of the thousands of extant letters written from 1897 to 1904 look back to this period. These glimpses of life in the oil regions come from Jones to John Mahan, March 15, 1904, and Jones to D.M. Riordan, July 25, 1899.

21. Kenneth Harris, *The Wildcatter: A Portrait of Robert O. Anderson* (New York: Weidenfeld and Nicolson, 1987), 27. In about 1871, when he was twenty-four, Sam again invested in a wildcat well, but this one became a "producer." "I became a

profit taker or employer myself and the payer instead of the taker of wages. In modern parlance, this is called 'business'" (Jones to H.E. Kile, editor of *Good Times*, January 29, 1902).

22. The cause of Moses's death is unknown. See Jones to Professor J.H. Dillard, January 28, 1904.

23. Jones to Paul Jones, February 25, 1903.

24. Assessment of the young Sam Jones by his friends from the *Detroit Free Press*, reprinted in *Toledo Saturday Night*, April 22, 1899. Its masthead reads: "An Independent Paper Devoted to the Reforms Advocated by Mayor S.M. Jones."

25. Samuel P. Bates, *Our County and Its People: A Historical and Memorial Record of Crawford County, Pennsylvania* (Bradford, Pa.: W. A. Ferguson, 1899), 571; *Crawford County* Deed Book, Meadville, Pa., I-1, 463; *Deed Book* N-1, 577; *Deed Book*, W-1, 136.

26. Remarks made by Sam Jones at the marriage service of Minnie C. Baller and George Shelty, February 29, 1904.

27. Obituary notice, *Bradford Era*, December 28, 1885.

28. E. Willard Miller, "Population and Functional Changes of Villages in Western Pennsylvania," *Western Pennsylvania Historical Magazine* 43 (1960): 67; Joseph A. Caldwell, *Illustrated Historical Combination Atlas of Clarion County Pennsylvania*, N.p.: Atlas Publishing Company, 1877. *Clarion County Pennsylvania* (1877), 158, 227. At its height the population numbered four hundred; by 1880, it had fallen to one hundred; by then many, including Sam Jones, had moved on, following the oil strikes further west. The 1878 Turkey City *Directory* lists S.M. Jones as "Oil Producer."

29. Barbara Leslie Epstein, *The Politics of Domesticity: Women, Evangelism, and Temperance in Nineteenth Century America* (Middletown, Conn.: Wesleyan University Press, 1981), 2, roots the late nineteenth-century source for the emergent female consciousness in the changing economic relations between husbands and wives. Market forces that rewarded efficiency as well as the beginning of industrialization removed business from the home (where women had participated). Thus women were more completely separated into the domestic, as opposed to the economic, sphere of life.

30. Walt Whitman, *Notes and Fragments* (N.p., n.d), in the Jones Papers. Margaret Williams Jones is buried in the Turin, New York, cemetery.

31. H.L. Cartwright, *History of Duke Center Together with a Complete Business Directory of the Borough* (Duke Center, Pa.: Wellington and Carr, 1880), 22-24.

32. Robert G. McClosley, *American Conservatism in the Age of Enterprise: A Study of William Graham Sumner, Stephen J. Field, and Andrew Carnegie* (Cambridge, Mass.: Harvard University Press, 1951), 3; Beecher quoted in Henry May, *Protestant Churches and Industrial America* (New York: Harper, 1967), 69. The eleven million new immigrants arriving between 1870 and 1900 strained urban structures. Many of the middle class saw the attempt to meet those new structural needs as a threat to their economic freedom. Thus the arguments from Protestant pulpits such as Beecher's appealed to their economic self-interest.

33. Sidney E. Mead, in "American Protestantism Since the Civil War," *Journal of Religion* 36 (1956): 1-15, analyzes the denominational periodicals and finds that church leaders no longer felt estranged from society; rather, they began "to bless and

defend it in a jargon strangely confounded out of the language of traditional Christian theology, common-sense philosophy, and *laissez-faire* economics." As Nathan Hatch observes, the essentially democratic spirit of American Protestantism "had the ironic effect of accelerating the breakup of traditional society" in that it helped promote the culture of competition and free enterprise ("Democratization of Christianity," 109).

34. Ronald C. White Jr. and C. Howard Hopkins, *The Social Gospel: Religion and Reform in Changing America* (Philadelphia: Temple University Press, 1976), 147. Its brief life suggests much about the lack of interest in applying the principles of Christianity to the questions of late nineteenth-century industrial reform. Twenty years later, such publishing ventures were far more numerous and more successful.

35. Page Smith, *The Rise of Industrial America,* vol. 6 in A People's History (1984; rpt. New York: Penguin, 1990), 187.

36. There is no record of the cause of Alma's death.

37. Crunden, *Ministers of Reform,* 42, 24, 16. Crunden finds that in their youth Progressives experienced the "mechanism of conversion" even if they lost their theology.

38. Jones to J.S. Willard, December 24, 1898; Jones to Paul Jones, May 14, 1900. There is no record of Hugh Jones's death; he does not lie beside Margaret in the Turin cemetery; the census records show that he was alive in 1880.

39. Marathon Oil Company, *Five Eventful Decades: A History of the Ohio Oil Company, 1887-1837* (Findlay, Ohio: N.p., 1937), 8. Joining Sam from the Bradford fields in forming the company were H.M. Ernst (who became the company's president), J. R. Leonard, (vice-president), E.M. Cobb (secretary), I.E. Dean, and W.H. Mandeville.

40. Smith, *Rise of Industrial America,* 131; Marathon Oil Company, *Five Eventful Decades,* 8, 9. The *Toledo Bee* for February 9, 1902, reported that Sam Jones had sold out at $100 a share.

41. The name Ohio Oil Company remained. Marathon Oil Company's official history, *Five Eventful Decades,* does not name Standard Oil at any point, nor does it mention that the original founders sold out.

42. Ford, "Life and Times of 'Golden Rule' Jones," 1:30. Ford located people in Lima in the late 1940s who still remembered Jones.

43. Ibid., 31; Jones to N.O. Nelson, May 13, 1904.

44. Boyer, *Urban Masses,* 116-17. Boyer's insights into the nature of the YMCA as a strategy to impose social control is entirely persuasive. But once again, even in his pre-reform life, Sam Jones seems not to fit the pattern. See Ford, "Life and Times of 'Golden Rule' Jones," 1:31.

45. Jones to J.W. Van Dyke, May 10, 1899.

46. *Toledo News-Bee,* September 26, 1930; Ford, "Life and Times of 'Golden Rule' Jones," 1:32-33.

47. *Toledo Blade,* August 24, 1892.

3. The First Radical Move

1. James, *Varieties of Religious Experience,* 206.

2. Jones to William Barringer, November 14, 1899. The assessment that Jones

was an anarchist is that of Jack Tager, Brand Whitlock's biographer, in *The Intellectual as Urban Reformer* (Cleveland: Case Western Reserve University Press, 1968), 52. Silvan S. Tomkins, in "The Psychology of Commitment: The Constructive Role of Violence and Suffering for the Individual and for His Society," in *The Anti-Slavery Vanguard: New Essays on the Abolitionists*, ed. Martin Duberman (Princeton: Princeton University Press, 1965), 281-82, analyzes the motivations of the abolitionists Garrison, Phillips, Weld, and Birney and notes that these men's commitment to reform could not have been predicted. So it is with Jones. He shared with these abolitionists a deeply Christian background, an extroverted personality, physical courage, and an increasing identification with the oppressed.

3. Ford, "Life and Times of Golden Rule Jones," 1:36-37, Charles N. Glabb and James C. Marshall, *Toledo Profile: A Sesquicentennial History* (Toledo: Toledo–Lucas County Public Library, 1987), 63. During Jones's tenure, Toledo's most significant immigrant growth shifted from the German and Irish to Polish and Hungarian communities.

4. Charles Hoffmann, "The Depression of the Nineties," *Journal of Economic History* 16 (1956): 139. Manufacturing unemployment never dipped below 9 percent from 1893 to 1898. Although there were brief recovery periods in 1895 and again in 1899, even at those points the national economy was functioning at 5 to 10 percent below capacity. In 1894 and 1897, the worst low points, the economy was functioning at 25 percent below capacity.

5. Samuel Rezneck, "Unemployment, Unrest, and Relief in the United States During the Depression of 1893-97," *Journal of Political Economy* 61 (1953): 325-29.

6. Samuel M. Jones, unpublished talk, "The Acme Sucker Rod Company: The Economic and Social Conditions Which Influenced Its Business Philosophy," January 1899, Jones Papers. One Who Knew Him, "Samuel Milton Jones: The Golden-Rule Mayor," *Arena* 35 (1906): 128.

7. William T. Stead, *If Christ Came to Chicago!* (Chicago: Press of the Eight Hour Herald, 1894), 23.

8. Curtis, *Consuming Faith,* 29.

9. Charles Hoffmann, "Depression of the Nineties," *Journal of Economic History* 16 (1956), 156. The figures for the decline in real earnings related unemployment, estimates of money earnings, and the cost-of-living indexes to one another. Over the course of the depression, the decline ameliorated somewhat. Real earnings declined 18 percent from 1892 to 1894; they averaged 15 percent from 1892 to 1898.

10. Washington Gladden, *Tools and the Man: Property and Industry Under the Christian Law* (New York: Houghton Mifflin, 1894), 210-13, copy in Jones Papers.

11. William G. McLoughlin, "Jones vs. Jones," *American Heritage* 12 (April 1961): 59.

12. Hoffer, *True Believers,* 14-15.

13. Boyer, *Urban Masses,* 164; Henry Adams, *The Education of Henry Adams* (New York: Modern Library, 1931), 337; Rezneck, "Unemployment," 331- 32.

14. Rezneck, "Unemployment," 334-36. Altgeld is one of the few reformers, who, like Sam Jones, was not born into the middle class. Unlike Jones, he never condemned the economic system. Altgeld spoke at Golden Rule Park and stayed with Sam and Helen.

15. Even before the panic, Pingree had been losing the support of Detroit's business elite and his friends in the social register because his ideas were thought to be radical (Holli, *Reform in Detroit,* 62). The antiethnic views of the period were made clear when Michigan voters overwhelmingly supported, a constitutional amendment in 1893 to disfranchise aliens by 117,088 to 31,537, (ibid., 52).

16. James, *Varieties of Religious Experience,* 213.

17. Ibid., 206; Peter Frederick locates William Dean Howell's conversion to reform in these terms (*Knights of the Golden Rule,* 20).

18. Charlotte (Perkins) Stetson Gilman, *Women and Economics: A Study of the Economic Relation Between Men and Women as a Factor in Social Evolution* (Boston: Small, Maynard, 1898), 80, copy in Jones Papers. She stayed with the Joneses and spoke to a crowd of four hundred in Golden Rule Hall in January 1899 (Jones to Herbert Casson, January 10, 1899).

19. Gordon Allport, *The Individual and His Religion: A Psychological Interpretation* (New York: Macmillan, 1950); Jones to W.H. Kinnier, November 11, 1897.

20. Jones to Johnathan J. Carter, June 15, 1897. I rely on Jones's description of his ailment in 1897, the year the letters begin, to describe his first illness.

21. Henry Hyde Salter, *On Asthma: Its Pathology and Treatment* (Philadelphia: Blanchard and Lea, 1864), 33-34; John C. Thorowgood. *Notes on Asthma: Its Nature, Forms, and Treatment* (Philadelphia, Lindse and Blakiston, 1873), 35; Jones to Jonathan Carter, October 21, 1903.

22. Jones to Bernarr Macfadden, December 22, 1903.

23. George Albert Coe, *The Psychology of Religion* (Chicago: University of Chicago Press, 1916), 171-72; Samuel M. Jones, "The Way to Purify Politics," *Independent* 54 (February 27, 1902): 512-13. Developmental psychologists see religious conversion as a step toward an awareness of the relationship between individual rights and the social contract. See Lawrence Kohlberg, "Religion, Morality, and Ego Development," in *Toward Moral and Religious Maturity: International Conference on Moral and Religious Development,* ed. Christine Brusselmans (Morristown, N.J: Silver Burdett, 1980), and Erik Erikson, *Insight and Responsibility: Lectures on the Ethical Implications of Psychoanalytic Insight* (New York: Norton, 1964), for the developmental psychologist's view of how religious integration leads to greater social consciousness.

24. Charles Sheldon, *In His Steps* (1896; rpt. New York: Grosset and Dunlap, 1961), 8-9.

25. Caro Lloyd, *Henry Demarest Lloyd, 1847-1903: A Biography,* 2 vols. (New York: Putnam's, 1912), 2:308, 316; *In Memoriam: Henry Demarest Lloyd* (Chicago: N.p., November 29, 1903), n.p.

26. Jones to Henry Demarest Lloyd, March 25, 1897.

27. *In Memoriam.*

28. Jones to Herbert Casson, June 20, 1899; Jones to editor, the *Coming Nation,* February 8, 1900; Frederick, *Knights of the Golden Rule,* 67, quotes Lloyd from *Men the Workers,* 16. In a letter of February 27, 1900, to Charles H. Kerr, while ordering a copy of Frederick Engels's *Socialism: Utopian and Scientific,* Sam wrote, "I am sure I do not know why the class conscious socialists need to be troubled about my attitude."

29. Jones to Nelson O. Nelson, July 13, 1898; George Herron, *Between Caesar and Jesus* (1898; rpt. Westport, Conn.: Hyperion Press, 1975), 241-43.

30. Frederick, *Knights of the Golden Rule,* 161-83; Jones to William Stead, May 11, 1897. Jones was such a successful student of Herron that he was asked by the president of Iowa College to give the commencement address in 1899. The next year he was asked to teach in Herron's summer institute at Gull Lake, Michigan, though mayoral commitments made that impossible (Jones to A.C. Wisner, January 30, 1900).

31. Frederick, *Knights of the Golden Rule,* 162, 174-75; Jones to Nelson O. Nelson, June 20, 1899; Herron to Jones, May 10, 1901. In a letter in which Herron described keeping "silent and see[ing] the supreme sacrifice of one's life converted into a thing of evil," he told Jones, "I thank you and bless you for your words of loving faith; they shall abide with me forever. You are one of the few to whom I have wanted to talk of this whole matter; and one of the few upon whose faith I counted."

32. George D. Herron, *The Christian State: A Political Vision of Christ* (New York: Crowell, 1895), 31, 26, copy in Jones Papers.

33. George D. Herron, *The New Redemption* (New York: Crowell, 1893), 99-100, copy in Jones Papers. Herron's vitality depended on his failure, argues Frederick, *Knights of the Golden Rule,* 178-79.

34. Frank Luther Mott, *A History of American Magazines, 1885-1905,* 4 vols. (Cambridge, Mass.: Harvard University Press, 1957), 4:174, 405.

35. Jones to Henry Demarest Lloyd, December 26, 1896.

36. Gladden, *Ruling Ideas of the Present Age,* 20, copy in Jones Papers; *The Bible* (Oxford: Oxford University Press, 1891), Luke 6:27-28, in Jones Papers.

37. Ernest Crosby to L.N. Tolstoy, March 19, New Style, 1898; Jones to Crosby, March 15, 1898; Crosby to L.N. Tolstoy, April 8, 1898, Tolstoy Museum, Moscow. The books remaining in Samuel Jones's personal library include Tolstoy's *The Suppressed Book of the Peasant Bondareff: Labor, the Divine Command* (1890) and the following later works: *The Beginning of the End, Essays, Letters, Miscellanies, The Gospel in Brief, and What Is Art?* In all likelihood, Tolstoy's *My Religion, My Life* would also have been important to Jones. Many of Jones's books were given to friends after his death. Thus the absence of books in the Jones archives is not significant.

38. Jones to L.N. Tolstoy, September 8, 1898.

39. Tolstoy letter and the description of Jones's office are in Memorial Scrapbook.

40. John Ruskin, *Unto This Last: Four Essays on the First Principles of Political Economy* (New York: Merrill and Baker, n.d.), 25, 39, copy in Jones Papers; Jones's Oxford *Bible.*

41. Ruskin, *Unto This Last,* 40.

42. Gladden, *Ruling Ideas of the Present Age,* 116, copy in Jones Papers; *Los Angeles Herald,* March 9, 1902, clipping in Memorial Scrapbook.

43. Lewis A. Coser, *Men of Ideas: A Sociologist's View* (New York: Macmillan, 1965), viii.

44. Frederick, *Knights of the Golden Rule,* 170. Readers interested in the scope of the Social Gospel should consult Charles Hopkins, *The Rise of the Social Gospel in American Protestantism, 1865-1915* (New Haven: Yale University Press, 1967).

45. Welch, *Protestant Thought,* 2:257.

46. W.D.P. Bliss, *The New Encyclopedia of Social Reform* (New York: Funk and Wagnalls, 1908), 204; Samuel Jones, "Municipal Expansion," *Arena* 21 (1899): 767.

47. Flower quoted in Boyer, *Urban Masses,* 168.

48. Frederick, *Knights of the Golden Rule,* 22; Gladden, *Tools and the Man,* 144-45, copy in Jones Papers.

4. Produce Great Persons

1. Jones to George Howard Gibson, Commonwealth, Ga., January 6, 1899.

2. Boyer, *Urban Masses,* 237-38; Randolph C. Downes, *Industrial Beginnings,* Lucas County Historical Series, 4 vols. (Toledo: Historical Society of Northwest Ohio, 1954), 4:75; James H. Rodabaugh, "Samuel M. Jones: Evangel of Equality," *Historical Society of Northeastern Ohio Quarterly Bulletin* 15 (1953): 24.

3. Jane Addams, *Thirty Years at Hull House* (New York: Macmillan, 1938), 93.

4. Samuel M. Jones, "The Religious Condition of the Working Men in America at the Close of the Nineteenth Century," in *Theology at the Dawn of the Twentieth Century: Essays on the Present Status of Christianity and Its Doctrines,* ed. John Vyrnwy Morgan (Boston: Small, Maynard, 1901), 40.

5. Jones to Joseph Griffith, April 28, 1899.

6. Washington Gladden Sermon, Eulogy for Sam Jones, July 17, 1904.

7. The house is presently the site of Toledo's Art Museum; the only link to Sam Jones's time is the oak trees that shelter the museum. Jones to Miss J.A. Stewart, December 29, 1898; "Homes with a History," *Toledo News-Bee,* October 30, 1930.

8. Chester MacArthur Destler, *Henry Demarest Lloyd and the Empire of Reform* (Philadelphia: University of Pennsylvania Press, 1963), 212, 216-17. "Homes with a History," *Toledo News-Bee,* October 30, 1930.

9. Epstein, *Politics of Domesticity,* 2.

10. Jones to Mrs. David E. Matteson, January 11, 1899.

11. I do not mean to suggest that Helen's Golden Rule husband did not influence her, but surely her concern for the people at large seems to have been kept comfortably within the bounds of traditional philanthropy. In 1921, Helen helped create a shelter for homeless women, Beach House, named in honor of her mother. It continues to provide shelter for homeless families to this day. See "Reasons Why I Like Toledo," an unidentified news article by "Mrs. S.M. Jones" in the Toledo "Biography" collection at the Toledo–Lucas County Public Library; *Toledo Blade,* October 5, 1908; Jones to Nell Jones, January 6, 1899.

12. Arthur Henry, "Millionaire Socialists," *Ainselee's Magazine* 4 (August 1899): 30.

13. Boyer, *Urban Masses,* 237-38. The first movement toward creating municipal parks had begun in New York in the 1850s, but by 1894 parks still had not become a feature of working-class communities. Since the 1850s, when Frederick Law Olmsted designed Central Park (with Calvert Vaux) and oversaw its construction, there had been those who argued that parks were vital improvements needed to combat the deleterious effects of urban life.

14. Downes, *Industrial Beginnings,* 4:235.

15. Frank T. Carlton, "The Golden-Rule Factory: The Late Mayor Jones's Contribution Toward the Solution of Industrial Problems," *Arena* 32 (1904): 409.

16. "Address at the Anniversary of Golden Rule Park," September–October 1897, Jones Papers; Whitlock, *Forty Years of It*, 117.

17. Boyer, *Urban Masses*, 239. In creating the park and in improving working conditions at his factory, Sam Jones comes close to what Boyer calls a "positive environmentalist" rather than a "coercive crusader." Both types of reformers shared the same implicit moral assumptions, but environmental reformers sought to destroy vice by creating a city where humane conditions made it less likely to flourish, while the crusaders used the tactics of denunciation and repression. Jones did seek to build a positive environment, but he does not fit the profile.

18. Downes, *Industrial Beginnings*, 4:235-37. Riverside Park was enlarged (at a cost of $2,000); the city acquired Collins Park (in accordance with the will of William A. Collins); Walbridge Park at sixty-one acres included the old reform school; Ottawa Park at 280 acres ($125,000); and Central Grove Park that adjoined Woodlawn cemetery.

19. Boyer, *Urban Masses*, 242; Ford, "Life and Times of Golden Rule Jones," 1:62; Jane Addams to Jones, May 20, 1898. Although municipal parks had been around for forty years, the first public playground was not created until the summer of 1886, shortly after the Haymarket riots.

20. Boyer, *Urban Masses*, 245.

21. Downes, *Industrial Beginnings*, 4:238-39; Jones, "Opening of the Children's Playground," July 26, 1899, manuscript in Jones Papers.

22. Downes, *Industrial Beginnings*, 4:239.

23. Addams, *Thirty Years at Hull House*, 188; Ford, "Life and Times of Golden Rule Jones," 1:57.

24. Jones, *The Eight Hour Day in the Oil Fields* (Toledo, 1897). Twenty thousand copies of this pamphlet were printed in 1897.

25. Jones, Christmas Message to Working-Men of the Acme Sucker Rod Company, 1897.

26. Jones to Ernest Hammond October 20, 1897; Jones to Jim Harrison, September 28, 1898; Jones to Walter Burrows, November 15, 1898.

27. Ford, "Life and Times of Golden Rule Jones," 1:66-67.

28. Ibid., 69.

29. Ibid., 58-59.

30. Samuel Jones was interested in both social and structural reform. As Arthur Link and Richard L. McCormick see it, "The distinction between urban 'structural reform' and 'social reform' was often less sharp than Holli has made it. In many cities structural and social reforms went hand in hand" (*Progressivism* [Arlington Heights, Ill.: Harlan Davidson, 1983], 30). Many of Jones's programs were social reforms that would make Toledo a better place to live—lower trolley fares, better schools, better sewers, hospitals, playgrounds, concerts. But he was also interested in correcting defects in the structure of government: giving the mayor real power; electing councilmen at large, rather than from wards; reducing state interference in city affairs; making appointments according to civil service rules.

31. Herron, *The New Redemption*, 61, copy in Jones Papers.

5. Not the Mayor of Any Faction

1. *Toledo Bee,* March 21, 1897.

2. Boyer, *Urban Masses,* 124, 141.

3. Clark Waggoner, *History of the City of Toledo and Lucas County, Ohio* (New York: Munsell, 1888), 640; *Toledo Blade,* November 13, 1899.

4. Downes, *Industrial Beginnings,* 4:153-56; Ford, "Life and Times of Golden Rule Jones," 1:86-87. In 1896, Major had a bill introduced into the General Assembly in Columbus that would restructure Toledo's government: a one-house legislature of fifteen would replace the two-house legislature of forty-five; all elected and appointed boards and commissions would be replaced with a board of administration of five members appointed by the mayor to serve as his cabinet. The Foraker machine supported Major's bill, but both parties and the Socialists united in attacking the plan and the bill was withdrawn. Had either political party been able to pass such a reform, Sam Jones's experience would have been quite different and perhaps Toledo's history remarkably changed. Eugene Debs argued that this bill would make Toledo's mayor an "autocrat" (*Toledo Bee,* January 21, 1896).

5. Warner, *Progessivism in Ohio,* 12-13; Rodabaugh, "Samuel M. Jones," 24-25.

6. Holli, *Reform in Detroit,* 3, 7.

7. Ibid., 17, 30, 74.

8. Ibid., 61-62, 74.

9. *Toledo Bee,* February 10, 1898. Toledo's partisan press, the virulently anti-Hanna *Bee* and the lukewarm Republican *Blade,* help explain how the view of Hanna's power has lingered. Lewis L. Gould, *The Presidency of William McKinley* (Lawrence: Regents Press of Kansas, 1980), 8, believes that McKinley was a much stronger leader than he was being given credit for. "The notion lingers that Hanna made McKinley president when, in fact, the politician used the businessman to reach the White House. . . . [Hanna's] position with McKinley was always that of a subordinate."

10. Herbert Croly, *Marcus Alonzo Hanna: His Life and His Works* (Hamden, Conn.: Archon Books, 1965), 137-38. Hanna had been Joseph Foraker's close friend and political promoter for at least a year before Foraker became governor of Ohio in 1885. Foraker, aspiring to be the party's presidential standard-bearer in 1887, considered Hanna's support of John Sherman treachery.

11. Everett Walters, *Joseph Benson Foraker: An Uncompromising Republican* (Columbus: Ohio Historical Press, 1948), 273; Croly, *Hanna,* 112; Harvey Scribner, *Memoirs of Lucas County and the City of Toledo from the Earliest Historic Times down to the Present,* 2 vols. (Madison: Western Historical Association, 1910): 2:35; *Toledo Blade,* February 22, 1897; Rodabaugh, "Samuel M. Jones," 26.

12. *Toledo Blade,* February 18, 22, 1897; Ford, "Life and Times of Golden Rule Jones," 1:99-100.

13. Ford, "Life and Times of Golden Rule Jones," 1:90-91; Interview with William Cowell.

14. *Toledo Blade,* February 16, 2, 1897.

15. *Toledo Blade,* February 25, 1897.

16. Downes, *Industrial Beginnings,* 4:153: "Ripper" was a term first used by the

Republican *Blade* in reference to a bill sponsored by the Democrats for popular election of members to the Board of Public Affairs. Since the board in 1890 was made up of Republicans, the newspaper thought that it was meant to rip Republicans out of office. The term entered the local vocabulary and was used loosely to signal anyone who wanted to alter the political establishment.

17. *Toledo Bee,* February 26, 1897.

18. *Toledo Bee,* February 26, 1897; Ford, "Life and Times of Golden Rule Jones," 1:107.

19. *Toledo Bee,* February 26, 1897, March 7, 1898.

20. *Toledo Bee,* February 26, 1897.

21. *Toledo Blade,* February 26, 1897.

22. Whitlock, *Forty Years of It,* 126-27. This description of Jones's campaigning style comes from Brand Whitlock's account of the last election. But as Jones seems to have relished this sort of contact with the people—"all the people"—from the beginning, it seems sufficiently representative to include it here.

23. Herbert Casson, "Draining a Political Swamp," *Arena* 21 (1899): 770.

24. *Toledo Blade,* April 2, 1897; Whitlock, "Golden Rule Jones," *World's Work* 8 (September 1904): 5308.

25. *Toledo Blade,* November 20, 1897.

26. *Toledo Bee,* December 23, 1987; advertisement in the *Toledo Bee,* January 7, 1898.

27. Jones to Ellen Smith, November 3, 1897; Jones to E.W. Tolerton, July 7, 1898.

28. Jones to Henry Demarest Lloyd, July 12, 1898.

29. Rodabaugh, "Samuel M. Jones," 24.

30. "National and Municipal Politics, an Address Before the 14th Ward Jackson League Club," 1-15, manuscript in Jones Papers.

31. Jones to Henry Demarest Lloyd, March 22, 1897; *Toledo Blade,* March 29, 1897, April 3, 1897. The catalog of complaints against Jones comes from Whitlock, "Golden Rule Jones," 5308-9.

32. *Toledo Blade,* March 31, 1897. He had turned to Macaulay's definition of good government at the Good Government Club. "Macaulay's definition, that . . . 'it is to compel us to get a living by industry rather than robbery,' implies the logical conclusion that men would have an opportunity to get a living by work."

33. *Toledo Blade,* April 3, 1987.

34. Ford, "Life and Times of Golden Rule Jones," 1:133.

35. *Toledo Blade,* April 6, 1897.

36. Ford, "Life and Times of Golden Rule Jones," 1:135-36; *Toledo Blade,* April 8, 1897; *Toledo Bee,* April 6, 1897.

37. Lloyd's article discussed in *Toledo Blade,* May 3, 1897; Jones to Henry Demarest Lloyd, May 28, 1897.

38. B.O. Flower, "The Significance of Mayor Jones's Election," *Coming Age* 1 (June 1899), 653-55; Henry Demarest Lloyd, *London Review of Reviews* (May 1897); Clipping enclosed in letter, Hartley to Jones, August 28, 1897.

39. Thomas Beer, *Hanna* (New York: Knopf, 1929), 308.

6. The Time to Think

1. Robert Bremner, "Samuel M. Jones: The Man Without a Party," *American Journal of Economics and Sociology* 8 (1948-49): 154, 152.

2. Ibid., 159.

3. *Annual Statement of the Finances of Toledo, together with the Mayor's Message and Reports of the Various Departments,* 1898. Jones Papers.

4. The Police Board approved the change to civil service rules with a three-to-two vote (*Toledo Blade* September 2, 1897). Democrat Charles Stager recommended the use of walking sticks with Jones's enthusiastic endorsement (*Toledo Bee,* October 7, 1897). In November, Jones instituted an eight-hour day for policemen (*Toledo Blade,* November 4, 1897).

5. *Toledo Blade,* April 15, 22, 1897; *Toledo Bee,* April 22, 1897.

6. Obituary in the *Toledo Blade,* August 19, 1902.

7. Ibid.

8. *Toledo Blade,* June 3, 1897.

9. *Toledo Bee,* June 3, 5, 1897.

10. *Toledo Bee,* May 6, 1897.

11. *Toledo Bee,* December 16, 1897.

12. Obituary in the *Toledo Blade,* August 14, 1903.

13. Jones to D.M. Fisk, June 2, 1897; Jones to N. O. Nelson, August 26, 1898. Mark Edward Lender and James Kirby Martin, in *Drinking in America: A History* (New York: Free Press, 1982), demonstrate that temperance in the second half of the nineteenth century was not a response to an increase in drinking but an anti-immigration issue. Per capita alcohol consumption actually dropped significantly in the nineteenth century.

14. Details of his experience are from Jones to Jonathan Carter, June 15, 1897; Salter, *On Asthma,* 34. The *Toledo Bee* reported on April 7, 1897, that Jones missed the monthly Humane Society meeting the day after the election because he was ill.

15. Jones to J.H. Kellogg, February 1, 1898; Edward Hooker Dewey, *The No-Breakfast Plan and the Fasting Cure* (N.p.: Published by the author, 1900), 57, copy in Jones Papers; Harry Gaze, *How to Live Forever: The Science and Practice* (Chicago: Stockman, 1904), 33, copy in Jones Papers.

16. Greven, *Protestant Temperament,* 109-13.

17. Thorowgood, *Notes on Asthma,* 35.

18. Jones to "Billy" J.W. White, July 2, 1897; Jones to Mrs. V.W. Curtiss, July 2, 1897; Jones to C.B. Fillerbrowne, July 16, 1898.

19. *Toledo Bee,* April 18, 1897, 1.

20. *Toledo Blade,* June 14, 1897. Jones had written Lloyd on May 28, 1897, estimating the unemployed figure at somewhere between five and ten thousand people. "Idle men throng the market places and congregate on the street corners," he told Lloyd.

21. Jones to H.V. Caton, August 23, 1897; James, *Varieties of Religious Experience,* 185-86.

22. *Toledo Bee,* June 16, 1897.

23. Ernest Crosby, *Golden-Rule Jones* (Chicago: Public Publishing Co., 1906), 60; Whitlock, *Forty Years of It,* 269.

24. Frederick, *Knights of the Golden Rule,* 225.

25. Ernest Crosby, "Golden-Rule Jones, the Late Mayor of Toledo," *Craftsman* 7 (February–March 1905): 682-83.

26. Justin Kaplan, *Walt Whitman: A Life* (New York: Simon and Schuster, 1980), 21.

27. Ibid., 34; Inscription in *Complete Poems and Prose of Walt Whitman* (Philadelphia: Ferguson, 1881), copy in Jones Papers; Horace Traubel to Jones, June 7, 1901; July 28, 1902.

28. "Specimen Days," *Notes and Fragments: Left by Walt Whitman and Now Edited by Dr. Richard Maurice Bucke, One of His Literary Executors* (N.p., 1899), 69, 58.

29. *Toledo Blade,* October 16, 1897.

30. *Toledo Blade,* August 2, 1897, 6, July 30, 1897.

31. *Toledo Bee,* September 12, 1897, 8; *Toledo Blade,* September 11, 1897.

32. *Toledo Blade,* August 11, 1897.

33. *Toledo Bee,* September 13, 1897. Jones pointed with pride (and historians have since congratulated him on it) that arrest statistics were down during his years as mayor. One can understand, especially with a mayor dismissing every police case he adjudicated, that this did not persuade middle-class Toledoans that the crime problem was being addressed.

34. Jones to F.H. Boke, February 2, 1898. Jones said Herron had been more useful than anyone else in making him understand economic issues (Jones to N.O. Nelson, April 28, 1898; Jones to George Herron, March 10, 1898).

35. Jones to Dr. W.H. Kinnier, November 11, 1897.

36. Hatch, *Democratization of American Christianity,* 13, 41-42. One example is Abner Jones (no relation), ordained "A Free Man" by the Freewill Baptists in 1801. He had said he would become ordained on the condition of complete independence: "I will never be subject to one of your rules; but if you will give me the right hand as a brother, and let me remain a *free man,* just as I am, I should be glad."

37. Roy Harvey Pearce, *The Continuity of American Poetry* (Middletown, Conn.: Wesleyan University Press, 1987), 5, 40-41.

38. Jones to Rev. D.M. Fisk, December 23, 1897; Jones to Frank Parsons, December 23, 1897; Salvatore, *Eugene Debs,* 192.

39. *Toledo Blade,* December 23, 1897.

40. The only record of Debs's speech comes from the glimpses provided by the Toledo press. It is not mentioned in *The Writings and Speeches of Eugene Debs,* nor does it exist at Cunningham Memorial Library, Indiana State University, which houses the Debs Papers.

41. D.M. Fisk to Jones, January 6, 1898; Jones to Fisk, January 8, 1898.

42. Jones to Jane Addams, December 29, 1897; *Toledo Bee,* December 24, 1897; Jones to Negley Cochran, December 29, 1897.

43. Ford, "Life and Times of Golden Rule Jones," 1: 39-40.

44. Ibid., 38.

45. *Toledo Bee,* February 7, 1898.

46. *Toledo Bee,* February 6, 7, 1898.

47. *Toledo Bee,* February 7, 8, 1898.

48. *Toledo Blade,* March 22, 1899; Whitman, "Specimen Days," 69.

49. Samuel M. Jones, "Municipal Expansion," *Arena* 21 (1899), 766-67.

7. Democracy Has Never Yet Been Tried

1. Whitlock, *Forty Years of It,* 137-38.

2. *Toledo Bee,* February 18, 19, 20, 1899.

3. Jones's marginal note in Josiah Strong, *The Twentieth Century City* (New York: Baker and Taylor, 1898), 60-61, 79, 89, copy in Jones Papers.

4. John Dewey, "Ralph Waldo Emerson," in *Characters and Events: Popular Essays in Social and Political Philosophy,* ed. Joseph Ratner, 2 vols. (New York: Henry Holt, 1929), 1:75-76.

5. Samuel M. Jones, "Patience and Education the Demands of the Hour," *Arena* 25 (1901): 544-46.

6. *Toledo Blade,* October 14, 1897.

7. Jones to James L. Cowles, January 13, 1898; Jones to F.H. Baker, February 2, 1898.

8. *Toledo Bee,* October 17, 1897; Jones to P.C. Boyle, October 21, 1897.

9. *Toledo Blade,* October 18, 22, 1897.

10. *Toledo Bee,* October 27, 21, 1897.

11. *Toledo Bee,* October 27, 1897. While Jones was on a visit to Hull House just after the election, a Chicago newspaper discussed Jones and Hanna in glowing terms: Chicagoans had read that Mayor Jones "went to the Republican committee and frankly notified it he could not support the candidates friendly to the Senator." Cochran could not bear this representation. Jones "didn't have the moral courage to openly oppose Hanna's election" (*Toledo Bee,* November 8, 1897).

12. Eltweed Pomeroy, "Samuel Jones: An Appreciation," *American Fabian* 4 (July 1898): 1.

13. Jones to Governor Asa Bushnell, January 4, 1898, printed in the *Toledo Bee,* January 6, 1898.

14. *Toledo Blade,* January 12, 1898.

15. *Toledo Bee,* January 12, 1898.

16. Frederic C. Howe, *The Confessions of a Reformer* (1925; rpt. New York: Scribner's, 1975), 147; *Toledo Bee,* January 14, 13, 1898.

17. *Toledo Bee,* January 14, 1898.

18. *Toledo Bee,* February 1, 1898.

19. Jones to Frank Rhines, September 8, 1898.

20. Jones to Thomas Nelson Page, Secretary, National Arbitration Conference, December 28, 1903; Kim McQuaid, "Businessman as Social Innovator: N.O. Nelson, Promoter of Garden Cities and Consumer Cooperatives," *American Journal of Economics and Sociology* 34 (1975): 418.

21. Jones to Frank Maxwell, July 2, 1898; Jones to C.B. Fillebrowne, July 14, 1898.

22. *Toledo Blade,* September 5, 1898; Barbara Tuchman, *The Proud Tower: A Portrait of the World Before the War, 1890-1914* (New York: Macmillan, 1962), 230.

23. *Toledo Blade,* January 24, 1899; S.W. Ewing to Jones, June 3, 1899.

24. *Toledo Blade,* January 24, 1899.

25. Jones to Sara Worsfold, February 2, 1898.

26. *Toledo Blade,* February 7, January 17, 1899; Jones to M.A. Neff, January 6, 1899.

27. Downes, *Industrial Beginnings,* 4:158-59, 166, 142. The modified Baber Law,

in use since 1895, gave voters in each ward the chance to vote for delegates to the nominating convention. Major was the nominee under the first modified Republican Baber primary. The effect was no more democratic than the machine-controlled convention: the city board of elections later proved that some seven pro-Major delegates had not received majorities in their wards. The *Blade* was so outraged by the abuse of the system it supported Democrat Parks Hone for mayor.

28. *Toledo Blade,* February 25, 1899, February 27, 1899. Cochran and Dowling, who had fought in the past, met for the first time at the Boody House Hotel for their reconciliation. Sam thought it "one of the best practical illustrations of the Golden Rule" since he had begun preaching it (*Toledo Blade,* March 1, 1899).

29. *Toledo Bee,* February 22, 1899.

30. *Toledo Blade,* March 2, 1899. Governor Pingree wrote Jones on December 27, 1898: "You are one of the few acquaintances of mine who can use my name for most anything you like."

31. *Toledo Bee,* March 2, 1899.

32. Jones to Billy White, March 3, 1899.

33. *Toledo Blade,* March 4, 1899. The "Cooney" Sherman story is from Walter Brown to Jones, March 8, 1899.

34. *Toledo Blade,* March 4, 1899.

35. Ibid.

36. Ibid. Tager, *Intellectual as Urban Reformer,* 61, calls Brown Jones's "implacable foe" who "manipulated the Republican convention so that Jones was deprived of the nomination."

37. Jones to Governor Pingree, March 6, 1899.

38. Walter Brown to Jones, March 8, 1899; Negley Cochran featured the letter on the front page of the *Toledo Bee* the day it was written.

39. "Opening of the Campaign of Education," March 1899.

40. Jim Ashley to Jones, March 11, 1899, reprinted in the *Toledo Bee,* March 11, 1899.

41. Jones to Edwin Wheelock, March 9, 1899; Jones to John Brisbane Walker, March 13, 1899.

42. *Toledo Bee,* March 15, 14, 1899.

43. McLoughlin, "Jones vs. Jones," 87; *Toledo Bee,* March, 23, 1899.

44. Jones to Mr. and Mrs. Ernest Hammond, March 14, 1899; Jones to William Riley Boyd, March 31, 1899; Holli, *Reform in Detroit,* 170.

45. *Toledo Blade,* March 3, 1899; Jones to Dr. J.P. Haynes, March 18, 1899; Jones to Rufus W. Weeks, April 1, 1899.

46. Helen Jones's comments in clipping in Memorial Scrapbook from the *Toledo Times,* July 6, 1937, Jones Papers.

47. Quoted in the *Toledo Blade,* March 13, 1899.

48. *Toledo Non-Partisan and Saturday Night,* September 16, 1899; *Toledo Blade,* March 27, 1899.

49. *Toledo Bee,* March 31, 1899.

50. The *Toledo Bee,* April 4, 1899, carried the news on pages 1 and 2; the *Toledo Blade,* on the same day, buried its humiliation a bit deeper, carrying the story on page 4.

51. Jones to Josiah Strong, April 8, 1899; *Toledo Bee,* April 5, 1899.

52. Ernest Crosby to L.N. Tolstoy, April 6, October 17, 1899, in the Tolstoy Museum, Moscow.

8. That I May Rid Myself of Guilt

1. Ralph Waldo Emerson, "The Conservative," in *The Collected Works of Ralph Waldo Emerson,* ed. Joseph Slater, 3 vols. (Cambridge, Mass.: Belknap Press of Harvard University Press, 1971-), 1:189; Jones to Rev. George Candee, August 15, 1899; Jones to Ernest Hammond, July 15, 1898. The idea of complicity has been of special interest to scholars in recent years. Hatch notes that the strident individualism of lay preachers created a democratic religious culture that helped create the competitive market-driven culture (*Democratization of American Christianity,* 14). Recent critics of Emerson find that he falls victim to the fundamental irony of modernity: the culture co-opts those who strive to change it. See David Marr, *American Worlds Since Emerson* (Amherst: University of Massachusetts Press, 1988), 67, and Carolyn Porter, *Seeing and Being: The Plight of the Participant Observer in Emerson, James, Adams, and Faulkner* (Middletown, Conn.: Wesleyan University Press, 1981), 106.

2. Samuel Jones, *A Christmas Message from Samuel M. Jones to the Working-Men of the Acme Sucker Rod Co.* (1902), 2-3

3. Harry N. Robins to Jones, May 5, 1899; S.H. Ewing to Jones, June 3, 1899; W.F. Lamson to Jones, August 26, 1899.

4. Jones to R.H.H. Wheeler, July 22, 1899; *Cleveland Leader* item as reported in the *Toledo Bee,* July 19, 1899.

5. *Toledo Bee,* June 22, April 24, 1899.

6. Beer, *Hanna,* 308; *Toledo Bee,* June 8, 1899. Waldorf denied that Hanna had made these remarks (*Toledo Bee,* June 12, 1899).

7. *Toledo Blade,* May 22, 1899.

8. Speech quoted in full, *Toledo Saturday Night,* June 3, 1899.

9. Jones to Rev. George Candee, August 15, 1899.

10. Jones to Lloyd, July 12, 1898; Jones to Nelson O. Nelson, July 6, 1898.

11. *Henry Demarest Lloyd,* 2:265-66.

12. Ibid. Lloyd ended with an apology: "I know that you can forgive me for entering into so private a matter as this, for I know you will understand the spirit in which I write."

13. Jones to S.H. Comings, August 11, 1898; Jones to John P. Gavitt, May 3, 1899; Jones to Josephine Shaw Lowell, July 21, 1899; Jones to Bert Myers, July 21, 1899; Jones to *Christian Endeavorer,* September 8, 1897.

14. Jones to Mrs. Teresa R. Clen Dening, November 3, 1898; Jones to James L. Cowles, July 19, 1897.

15. T. J. Dawson to Jones, June 16, 1899.

16. The phrase is Horace Traubel's in Traubel to Jones, July 28, 1902.

17. Jones to T.J. Dawson, June 19, 1899.

18. Jones to Eugene Debs, June 22, 1899.

19. But Sam was not to hear from Debs, who was out of town. A month later he wrote again; this time he was upset by a letter Debs sent to the *Toiler,* which seemed, to him, "to question the genuineness of my socialism." Debs had said that Jones

would have accepted the Republican gubernatorial nomination if it had been given him, which Jones denied: "The only thing I hoped to accomplish by keeping silent was that enough of the independent Jones element might get into the convention to break up the slate of the G.O.P. and give the necessary impetus for an independent campaign" (Jones to Eugene Debs, July 20, 1898).

20. Eugene Debs to Jones, July 24, 1899. He regretted that speaking obligations made it impossible to come to Toledo. Debs had spoken positively of Sam Jones from hundreds of platforms.

21. *Non-Partisan Candidate for Governor,* brochure; Jones to Walter Young, July 19, 1899.

22. James Bryce, *The American Commonwealth,* 2 vols. (New York: Macmillan, 1888), 2:642; N.O. Nelson to Jones, May 11, 1899.

23. Jones to N.O. Nelson, July 29, 1899.

24. "To the People of Ohio I," July 29, 1899, in Jones Papers. Reactions to the Jones candidacy reprinted in the *Toledo Bee,* August 2, 1899, 4; *Post* assessment reprinted in the *Toledo Bee,* July 19, 1899, 4.

25. Jones to N.O. Nelson, July 31, 1899. The law required that he gather 1 percent of the number of voters from the last comparable election; see *Toledo Bee,* August 3, 1899; Jones, "To The People of Ohio II," August 26, 1899. There is a chance for confusion. Jones wrote two letters "To the People of Ohio." I have designated the one written July 29 inviting petitions as "To the People of Ohio I" and the one accepting their nomination by petition on August 26 as "To the People of Ohio II."

26. *Toledo Non-Partisan and Saturday Night,* September 30, 1899.

27. Ibid., Jones to Charlie Davidson, December 13, 1899.

28. Jones to H.V. Caton, August 23, 1897; Jones to *Christian Endeaveror,* September 8, 1897.

29. Commencement Address, Iowa College, Grinnell Iowa, June 1899, Jones Papers.

30. Joseph F. Wall, "A Second Look at Andrew Carnegie," in *Introspection in Biography,* ed. Samuel H. Baron and Carl Pletsch (Raleigh, N.C: Analytic Press, 1985), 215.

31. Jones to Herbert Casson, July 4, June 20, 1899; see Jones to Keller and Potts, July 19, 1899, regarding Casson's contribution to other chapters mentioned; Jones to Henry Demarest Lloyd, July 29, 1899; Jones to N.O. Nelson, July 14, 1899.

32. Jones to Keller and Potts, July 12, 1899; Jones to N.O. Nelson, June 3, 1899.

33. *Toledo Bee,* July 31, 1899.

34. *Annual Report of the Secretary of State to the Governor of Ohio, 1899* (Columbus, 1899), 148-50, for the Democratic platform, 156-57 for the nonpartisan platform.

35. *Toledo Bee,* September 4, 1899; *Toledo Non-Partisan and Saturday Night,* September 9, 1899.

36. Jones to N.O. Nelson, July 12, 1899, reprinted in *Toledo Non-Partisan and Saturday Night,* October 7, 1899; both the *Toledo Bee,* October 4, 1899, and *Toledo Blade,* September 19, 1899, carried the controversy.

37. *Toledo Bee,* October 1, 5, 1899; *Toledo Non-Partisan and Saturday Night,* September 30, 1899.

38. *Philadelphia North-American* reprinted in *Toledo Non-Partisan and Saturday Night,* September 23, 1899; Akron statistics, *Toledo Bee,* October 22, 1899; Springfield statistics, *Toledo Bee,* October 26, 1899; Cleveland statistics, *Toledo Bee,* November 5, 1899.

39. *Toledo Bee,* September 23, 1899, October 13, 1899.

40. *Toledo Bee,* September 23, 1899, October 18, 1899.

41. *Toledo Bee,* October 7, 13, 1899.

42. Beer, *Hanna,* 308.

43. *Toledo Bee,* November 8, 1899; Jones to Edwin D. Wheelock, November 21, 1899. Jones would not agree with my formulation as he did not wage a third-party campaign but a no-party campaign.

44. Jones to N.O. Nelson, November 13, 1899; *Toledo Bee,* November 9, 1899; Jones to Rev. W. M. Kain, November 11, 1899.

45. The *New York Sun* thought it natural that Cuyahoga County, "the capital of anarchism in this country, voted for him. The human and gentle souls that blew up cars and passengers with dynamite, the Cleveland rioters and boycotters, responded to the call of the man who proposed to break up the existing order of things and found a sort of despotic labor trust government" (reprinted in the *Toledo Non-Partisan and Saturday Night,* November 18, 1899).

46. *Washington Post* projections reprinted in the *Toledo Bee,* October 21, 1899; Salvatore, *Eugene Debs,* 186.

47. Jones to Herbert Welsh, November 11, 1899; Jones to George Herron, November 16, 1899.

48. Jones to Willard Barringer, November 14, 1899.

49. Frederick, *Knights of the Golden Rule,* 3, 95.

50. Jones to Eltweed Pomeroy, November 11, 1899; Jones to John McLean, November 10, 1899; Jones to N.O. Nelson, November 13, 1899.

9. I'm a Man Without a Party

1. *Toledo Bee,* May 4, 1900; Jones to Paul Jones, May 4, 1900.

2. *Toledo Bee,* December 12, 1899; Jones to Hazen Pingree, December 13, 1899; Jones to William S. Crandall, Editor, *City Government,* February 27, 1900. Consolidated Edison had been charging the city $90 per streetlight. In response to Jones's proposed public facility, the company, facing the expiration of its franchise at the end of the year, offered to reduce its charge to $80 per light for a ten-year contract. Thus even the threat of a municipal plant had a salutary effect on pricing. Under Jones's plan, in ten years the city would have owned the lighting facility.

3. *Toledo Blade,* December 19, 1899. The history of the Toledo municipal gas crisis predated Jones by a decade. Henry Demarest Lloyd had discussed the pipeline controversy in *Wealth Against Commonwealth* (New York: Harper and Brothers, 1894). The city-owned pipelines had proved a financial disaster because the gas wells in Findlay were not, as was originally thought, unlimited in supply.

4. *Toledo Blade,* December 27, 1899.

5. *Toledo Blade,* January 16, 1900.

6. Jones to Clarence Darrow, April 12, 1900.

7. Jones to Henry Demarest Lloyd, January 2, 1900.

8. Jones to Mark Strange, November 5, 1902; Jones to Tom L. Johnson, September 1, 1903.

9. Jones to Henry Demarest Lloyd, January 2, 1900; *Toledo Bee*, October 11, 1901.

10. Whitlock, *Forty Years of It*, 117-18.

11. Tager, *Intellectual as Urban Reformer*, 66-69. Whitlock's assessment of Jones comes from words spoken July 12, 1905, at the grave site on the first anniversary of Jones's death. The last years of Whitlock's life, spent as a recluse in Cannes, France, unconcerned with the disastrous effects of the Great Depression on Americans, demonstrate that the concern for convention finally dominated. His biographer says, "Whitlock shut himself off from all contact with the outside world and turned more and more toward that fastidious, illusory world of aristocratic make-believe which he had erected for himself. . . . To fend off the offensive attacks of a 'vulgar' society, Brand Whitlock had retired into the comforting domain of social and religious elitism" (ibid., 176-77).

12. Jones to N.O. Nelson, July 19, 1900; Jones to Lem Harris, July 31, 1900.

13. *Toledo Bee*, August 29, 24, 1900.

14. *Toledo Bee*, September 4, 1900; Arthur Brisbane to Jones, December 17, 1898; *New York Journal*, December 13, 1898; Clipping of article running under a half-inch bold headline "Wall St. Scored by Mayor Jones," Mark Twain Scrapbook 5, Jones Papers.

15. Jones to A.W. Files, July 23, 1900; Jones to Clarence Darrow, June 28, 1900.

16. Jones to N.O. Nelson, April 16, 1900, July 29, 1898.

17. Jones to Ernest Hammond, April 9, 1900.

18. Ibid.

19. Jones to Ernest Hammond, March 30, 1901; Jones to William E. Cady, April 1, 1901, emphasis added.

20. Jones to N.O. Nelson, April 16, 1900; Jones to Ernest Hammond, April 16, 1900.

21. Jones to Ernest Hammond, May 3, 1900.

22. Jones to Mrs. V. Curtiss, May 3, 1900.

23. Jones to Percy Jones, June 18, 1900.

24. Jones to Paul Jones, May 24, 1900; Jones to Ernest Hammond, July 3, 1900; Jones to Ellen Parker Grant, April 4, 1902.

25. *Toledo Blade*, September 13, 1900. His friend Eltweed Pomeroy called him a "philosophical anarchist . . . not a socialist." As Pomeroy saw it, Jones did not "believe the way Debs does at all but more the way that W.J. Bryan thinks. You are attracted to Debs by his strong humanitarian spirit and if you vote for him, that will be the reason and not because you believe the remedies he believes in" (Eltweed Pomeroy to Samuel Jones, April 3, 1900).

26. Jones to B.O. Flower, May 12, 1900.

27. Jones to J.F. Levelle, September 24, 1900.

28. *Toledo Blade*, March 29, 1900, 1; Jones to James K. Jones, September 24, 1900; Keith Melder, *Bryan the Campaigner*, Contributions from the Museum of History and Technology, Paper 46, Bulletin 241 (Washington, D.C.: Smithsonian Institution, 1965), 72.

29. Melder, "Bryan," 78; Paolo E. Coletta, *William Jennings Bryan: Political Evangelist, 1860-1908* (Lincoln: University of Nebraska Press, 1964), 194.

30. *Toledo Blade,* September 14, 1900; William Jennings Bryan to Jones, n.d. (September 1900?).

31. William Schulz to Jones, September 20, 1900; Nicholas Klein to Jones, September 15, 1900.

32. Jones to J.F. McShane, September 17, 1900; Jones to C.L. Titus, September 20, 1900; Jones to Gen. Frank S. Monnett, September 26, 1900.

33. *Toledo Blade,* September 20, 21, 1900.

34. Eugene Debs to Jones, October 8, 1900; *Toledo Blade,* November 2, 1900.

35. *Toledo Bee,* September 20, 1900; William Jennings Bryan to Jones, n.d. (September 1900?).

36. *Toledo Bee,* October 12, 1900.

37. Paul W. Glad, *The Trumpet Soundeth: William Jennings Bryan and His Democracy, 1896-1912* (Lincoln: University of Nebraska Press, 1960), 30; Jones to Charles H. Kerr, October 19, 1900.

38. *Toledo Bee,* October 17, 18, 19, 1900.

39. Coletta, *William Jennings Bryan,* 289; Bryan's speech as reported in Jones to N.O. Nelson, 19 October 1900.

40. Jones to N.O. Nelson, October 19, 1900.

41. *Toledo Bee,* October 23, 1900; Negley Cochran to Jones, September 18, 1903.

42. Jones to *New York Journal,* reprinted in the *Toledo Bee,* November 2, 1900; Jones to Charles F. Howard, October 29, 1900.

43. Jones to N.O. Nelson, November 5, 1900.

44. Coletta, *William Jennings Bryan,* 277; Paolo E. Coletta, "The Bryan Campaign of 1896," in *William Jennings Bryan: A Profile,* ed. Paul W. Glad (New York: Hill and Wang, 1968), 29.

45. *Annual Statement of the Finances of Toledo, Together with the Mayor's Message and Reports of the Various Departments, 1900,* 13-38, Jones Papers; Ford, "Life and Times of Golden Rule Jones," 2:550-58.

46. Jones to Clarence Brown, October 31, 1900; Jones to Eugene Debs, reprinted in Jones, *Letters of Love and Labor,* 1:92-99. There is room for confusion: Jones oversaw the publication of the two volumes of *Letters of Love and Labor;* Brand Whitlock oversaw publication of a third collection, with the words in the title inverted, after Jones's death: *Letters of Labor and Love* (Indianapolis: Bobbs-Merrill, 1905).

47. Jones to N.O. Nelson, October 12, 1900.

10. I Fail Utterly

1. Jones to Horace Traubel, April 3, 1902.

2. Jones to N.O. Nelson, April 9, 1902; Bercovitch, *Puritan Origins,* 18.

3. *Toledo Blade,* March 1, 2, 1901.

4. *Toledo Bee,* March 2, 1901.

5. Jones to Ernest Crosby, March 25, 1901; Jones to Dr. J.D. Buck, March 25, 1901.

6. *Toledo Bee,* March 16, 7, 1901; *Toledo Blade,* January 9, 1901.

7. *Toledo Bee*, November 22, 1902.

8. *Toledo Blade*, March 14, 1901; Jones to W.J. Ghent, March 28, 1901.

9. See chapter 6 for the beginning of this practice; *Annual Message, 1900*, 29-30.

10. Whitlock, *Forty Years of It*, 119-20; Jones to Frank Maxwell, April 13, 1904.

11. Whitlock, *Forty Years of It*, 143-45: "By the operation of the same law that brought the vagrant back to Jones's side with all the money, I with my distrust might have been treated far differently."

12. *Toledo Bee*, July 17, 1901; *Toledo Blade*, July 17, 1901; Whitlock, *Forty Years of It*, 120.

13. *Toledo Bee*, February 14, March 16, 1902; Jones to Ernest Crosby, February 26, 1902.

14. Jones, "What Is Crime and Who Are the Criminals?" in Jones Papers; *Toledo Bee*, November 22, 1901, February 10, 1902. After President McKinley's assassination, Jones had received an anonymous letter on September 7, 1901: "I suppose you are very glad that Presidente [*sic*] McKinley is shot for you did not want to see him in office you will do all you can to help the murder [*sic*] get off for that is your way of doing." But Jones saw Czolgosz's crime as symptomatic of the entire culture.

15. *Toledo Bee*, March 11, 1902.

16. The Fraser bill seems to have been a personal attack on Jones and not motivated by anti-reform sentiment, for the same legislators who voted for this bill also passed the Habitual Criminal Act (Ford, "Life and Times of Golden Rule Jones," 2:591).

17. *Toledo Bee* April 30, 1902.

18. Ibid.

19. *Toledo Blade*, June 26, 1902; *Toledo Bee*, July 2, 1902.

20. Jones to Frank Maxwell, February 7, 1902; Jones to N.O. Nelson, February 8, 1902.

21. Peter Gay, *The Tender Passion*, Vol. 2 of *The Bourgeois Experience: Victoria to Freud* (New York: Oxford University Press, 1986), 337; David E. Shi, *The Simple Life: Plain Living and High Thinking in American Culture* (New York: Oxford University Press, 1985), 176.

22. Jones to N.O. Nelson, January 28, 1902.

23. Jones to Percy Jones, February 12, 1902.

24. Jones ended the letter by saying, "Now, my dear boy, if you want to let your histrionic friend know the kind of a crank your father is, you have my consent to forward this letter, and to take for yourself and for her and all others my most beneficent blessing" (Jones to Percy Jones, January 28, 1902).

25. Jones to C.P. Rogers, March 19, 1902.

26. The metaphor of a "self civil war" comes from George Goodwin's poem, quoted in Bercovitch, *Puritan Origins*, 19:

> I sing my self; my Civil Warrs Within;
> The Victories I howrely lose and win;
> The dayly Duel, the continuall Strife,
> The Warr that ends not, till I end my life.

Jones to J.P. Gavit, March 28, 1901; Jones to Frank Maxwell, April 4, 1902.

27. Jones to Tim Spellacy, April 2, 1902; Chicago article reprinted in the *Toledo*

Bee, July 8, 1902; Tom Johnson to Jones, May 3, 1902. Johnson's letter, sent when Jones was back in Toledo, continues, "The good news soon came which relieved our minds of anxiety. . . . May God bless you in your good work and give you strength and health to continue the struggle, is the prayer of Your devoted friend, Tom L. Johnson."

28. Jones to James T. Van Rensselaer, April 1, 1902; Jones to D. Bell, April 4, 1902; Jones to Charles J. Hakel, of *Perfect Health*, April 4, 1902; Bercovitch, *Puritan Origins*, 17; James, *Varieties of Religious Experience*, 108.

29. Bercovitch, *Puritan Origins*, 19-20.

30. Jones, "Thorough Physical Culturist," *Physical Culture* 10 (September 1903): 263-64; Henry David Thoreau, *Walden*, Vol. 2 of *The Writings of Henry David Thoreau* (New York: Houghton Mifflin 1899), 148, copy in Jones Papers.

31. Samuel M. Jones, "A Plea for Simpler Living," *Arena* 25 (April 1903): 346-47.

32. Shi, *Simple Life*, 176-79. Shi points out that the revival "assumed the status of both a cult and a fad" at the turn of the century.

33. Jones, "Thorough Physical Culturist," 264.

34. *Toledo Bee*, March 5, 1903.

35. *Toledo Bee*, July 16, 1902. In Toledo 143 people contracted the disease; 11 died of it. In a related health issue Jones vetoed an ordinance passed by the city council in October 1903 which set health standards for barbershops to protect customers. There is hardly a more telling—and, in this case, distressing—proof that Jones does not fit the pattern of Boyer's "coercive reformers." Jones argued that it was "class legislation" that would only close the poor shops and represented an "unwarranted interference with the individual liberty of the citizens." The union president argued that regulations were as important for this industry as for slaughterhouses and garbage disposal; see *Toledo News-Bee*, October 27, 28, 1903.

36. Jones to Nelson O. Nelson, September 13, 1902.

37. Whitlock's words spoken at her funeral service, *Toledo Times*, July 11, 1905. Nell died almost one year to the day after her brother.

38. *Toledo Bee*, March 6, 1903; *Sun* comment reprinted in *Toledo Bee*, March 29, 1903.

39. Personal interview conducted by Ford, in "Life and Times of Golden Rule Jones," 2:653-54.

40. Jones to Frank Maxwell, February 5, 1903; *Annual Message of Mayor Samuel M. Jones to the Common Council of Toledo, Ohio, 1902*, 20-21; Jones to N.O. Nelson, March 18, 1903.

41. *Toledo Bee*, April 3, 1903. Rodabaugh, in "Samuel M. Jones," 39, implies that Cochran deserted Jones because the editor had sold the newspaper to the Scripps-McRae chain. At that point, the *Toledo Bee* became the *Toledo News-Bee*. But as the sale did not occur until summer, that explanation cannot account for Negley Cochran's change of heart.

42. *Toledo Bee*, February 12, 1903; Jones to Clarence Darrow, March 19, 1903.

43. Jones to Horace Traubel, March 21, 1903; *Toledo Bee*, March 18, 22, 1903.

44. Jones to William Randolph Hearst, March 20, 1903; Jones to Tom L. Johnson, March 21, 1903; Jones to W.D. Sherwood, March 26, 1903; Jones to Charles Ferguson, April 7, 1903.

45. Jones to Homer C. Fritts, April 6, 1903; Jones to Professor Oscar Triggs, March 30, 1903.

46. *Toledo Bee,* October 22, 1902. Toledo restructured its fifteen wards into thirteen and switched from a two-chamber council of forty-five to a single council of sixteen. The independent board system was made more cumbersome, however. Three new boards—of health, public service, and public safety—were added to the existing fourteen to oversee city governance.

47. *Toledo Bee,* May 12, 19, June 2, 1903; *Toledo Blade,* May 12, 1903.

48. Jones to W.F. Copeland, June 3, 1903.

49. *Toledo News-Bee,* July 3, 1903. One of Nash's original nominees had moved away from Toledo so one of the names was not on his original list. Nor was it on Jones's (*Toledo News-Bee,* July 1, 1903).

50. Bliss, *New Encyclopedia of Social Reform,* 204.

11. The Greatest Victory

1. Whitlock, *Forty Years of It,* 204.

2. Jones to Loretto French, May 28, 1904.

3. James, *Varieties of Religious Experience,* 181.

4. Gaze, *How to Live Forever,* 33, copy in Jones Papers.

5. James, *Varieties of Religious Experience,* 137, 153-54.

6. Ibid., 184-86.

7. Jones to W.L. Young, January 6, 1904; Jones to N.O. Nelson January 20, 1904. A harsh winter and typhoid brought an end to the Commonwealth Colony (Charles Hopkins, *Rise of the Social Gospel, 1865-1915* [New Haven: Yale University Press, 1967], 196).

8. Charles Sumner Van Tassel, *Story of the Maumee Valley, Toledo and the Sandusky Region,* 4 vols. (Chicago: S.J. Clarke, 1929), 2:1489-90.

9. *Toledo News-Bee,* September 9, 21, 1903; The Denman ordinance, which seemed to promise universal transfers, was deemed by the *Bee* "to be dangerously incomplete and misleading." The paper argued that the more precise language of the Columbus provision would protect the people of Toledo. Downes, *Industrial Beginnings,* 105-24 covers in detail the conflict up through 1900. Sam Jones had been arguing for universal transfers and lower ticket prices since the month before his first election. Jones had written a letter to the editor (*Toledo Bee,* January 7, 1897) arguing for eight tickets for twenty-five cents, universal transfers, and municipal ownership, based on information gathered during his recent trip to Glasgow.

10. *Toledo News-Bee,* September 22, 1903.

11. Ibid., Jones to Clinton Rogers Woodruff, September 24, 1903.

12. Jones to Frank Maxwell, September 22, 1903; Jones to Ernest Crosby, January 27, 1904.

13. *Toledo News-Bee,* March 19, 24, 1904.

14. Robert Bremner, *American Philanthropy* (Chicago: University of Chicago Press, 1960), 101; Jones to Josephine Shaw Lowell, July 21, 1899.

15. Thoreau, *Walden,* 120-21.

16. Jones to Rev. W.S.H. Heerman, March 15, 1904.

17. Bremner, *American Philanthropy,* 106-11. An English critic had been "astounded by the brashness of Carnegie's scheme" and had dubbed it the "Gospel of Wealth." Carnegie embraced the implicit criticism wholeheartedly, using it as his title. Andrew Carnegie, *The Gospel of Wealth* (New York: Century, 1900), 13, 2, copy in Jones Papers. Jones seems to have followed the careers of both Carnegie and Rockefeller with interest; newspaper clippings about both men are to be found in his Mark Twain Scrapbook 6, Jones Papers.

18. Clipping in the Memorial Scrapbook.

19. Jones to Nelson O. Nelson, August 4, 1903.

20. Jones to Bernarr Macfadden, October 21, 1903; Tom L. Johnson to Jones, October 28, 1903; Jones to Nelson O. Nelson, October 23, 1903.

21. Jones to Nelson O. Nelson, October 17, 1903; Knepper, *Ohio and Its People,* 330.

22. Tom L. Johnson to Jones, May 18, 1904.

23. Jones to Tom Johnson, October 29, 1903; Jones to William Ap Madoc, September 1, 1903; Jones to J.S. Cullinan, March 22, 1904.

24. *Toledo News-Bee,* January 7, 1904; Whitlock, *Forty-Years of It,* 164-65. Steffens's research led him to believe there was corruption in the police department (Lincoln Steffens to Jones, January 22, 1904). He wrote a letter to Jones within a month of his visit which began "My Dear Good Friend." In it Steffens wrote, "There are things going on in the Police Department which you do not know about. Neither does your Chief, I trust. But there are a great many things going on in Toledo, which have not yet come to the surface."

25. Whitlock, *Forty Years of It,* 166; Louis Filler, *Crusaders for American Liberalism* (1939; rpt. New York: Harcourt, 1950), 302, 350.

26. Jones to Lincoln Steffens, April 13, 1904; Lincoln Steffens, *The Shame of the Cities* (1904; rpt. New York: Peter Smith, 1948), 8, 18.

27. *Toledo News-Bee,* February 16, 1904.

28. Both the *Toledo Blade* and *Toledo News-Bee* carried the Springfield events, March 8, 1904; the *Toledo Blade* printed the mayor's remarks.

29. *Toledo Blade,* March 9, 1904; Jones to Nelson O. Nelson, March 10, 1904.

30. Ford, "Life and Times of Golden Rule Jones," 2:723-24.

31. Jones to Walter Young, March 15, 1904.

32. Jones to Judge R.D. Parker, May 12, 1904.

33. Jones to Nelson O. Nelson, May 25, June 23, 1904; Jones to Frank Maxwell, June 15, 1904.

34. *Toledo Blade,* January 21, 1897.

35. *Toledo Bee,* February 22, 1899.

36. Jones to Sara Worsfold, February 2, 1898.

37. Jones to Frank Hillenkamp, May 16, 1904. Barclay and Glabb, *Toledo,* 92, note that Whitlock recognized the need for organization and during his eight years in office, Independents gained control of the city council, making strides in municipal ownership. It was "not the municipal ownership Jones, Whitlock, and the Independents had advocated, but it was a limited victory and an important one."

38. Unidentified newspaper article in Scrapbook 42, in Jones Papers; Charles Ferguson, *The Toledo of Jones,* pamphlet (N.p, n.d.).

39. Jones to *New York Journal*, reprinted in the *Toledo Bee*, November 2, 1900; Jones to Charles F. Howard, October 29, 1900.

40. *Toledo Blade*, April 3, 1987; Clippings in the Memorial Scrapbook.

41. Morris, *Matter of Wales*, 5.

42. Jones to Frank Hillenkamp, May 16, 1904.

43. Jones to John Mahon, April 11, 1904.

44. *Toledo Blade*, June 23, 1904.

45. *Toledo Blade*, July 2, 1904; Helen Wheeler to Clinton Rogers Woodruff, July 5, 1904; Nelson O. Nelson to Jones, July 7, 1904; *Toledo News-Bee*, July 11, 1904; *Toledo Blade*, July 11, 1904.

46. *Toledo Blade*, July 11, 13, 1904; *New York Times*, July 13, 1904. The certificate of death lists "Bronchial Pulmonary Abscess" as the chief cause of death, meningitis septicemia as the contributing cause (Burial Permit 2270), Jones Papers.

47. *Toledo Blade*, July 12, 1904; *Toledo News-Bee*, special issue, July 13, 1904; Gladden, "Sermon," in Jones Papers.

48. The newspaper obituaries are found in the Samuel Milton Jones Memorial Scrapbook, complied at his death by his secretary, Helen Wheeler, who was paid $70 for her services. The scrapbook is in the Jones Papers.

49. *Toledo Blade*, July 14, 1904.

50. *Toledo Blade*, July 14, 1904.

51. Probate Court Appraisal #4147, October 6, 1904, Samuel Milton Jones Death and Estate, shows a total expenditure of $469: $300 for casket, $12 for embalming, $8 for use of hearse at funeral, $110 for use of twenty-two carriages, $20 for personal services, $10 for use of 150 chairs, $3 for gloves for pallbearers, $6 for use of hearse from residence to hall, $35 for gravestone, $4 for burial, $5 for removing earth and decorating the grave, $3 for extra labor (*Toledo Blade*, July 15, 1904).

52. Nell was reported having "suffered a slight nervous relapse" shortly after his death. See *Toledo News-Bee*, special issue, 16; Ford interview with Cowell, in Ford, "Life and Times of Golden Rule Jones," 2:732; letter from J. Ellery Eaton in Memorial Scrapbook.

53. Crunden, *A Hero in Spite of Himself*, 104-5.

54. *Toledo News-Bee*, July 16, 1904; Jones to N.O. Nelson, November 13, 1899.

55. Memorial Scrapbook.

56. Samuel Gompers to Jones, July 8, 1904; Helen Wheeler to Samuel Gompers, July 13, 1904.

57. Andre Schwartz-Bart, *The Last of the Just* (New York: Atheneum, 1960), 5; Florence Converse, *The Burden of Christopher* (New York: Houghton Mifflin, 1900), 143, 82, 170.

58. *Toledo News-Bee*, July 25, 1904.

Selected Bibliography

Books and Articles

Abel, Aaron. *The Urban Impact on American Protestantism, 1865-1900*. Cambridge, Mass.: Harvard University Press, 1943.

Adams, Henry.*The Education of Henry Adams*. New York: Modern Library, 1931.

Addams, Jane. *Thirty Years at Hull House*. New York: Macmillan, 1938.

Allport, Gordon. *The Individual and His Religion: A Psychological Interpretation.* New York: Macmillan, 1950.

Baines, Dudley. *Migration in a Mature Economy: Emigration and Internal Migration in England and Wales, 1861-1900*. Cambridge: Cambridge University Press, 1985.

Barclay, Morgan, and Charles N. Glabb. *Toledo: Gateway to the Great Lakes*. Tulsa: Continental Heritage, 1982.

Bates, Samuel P. *Our County and Its People: A Historical and Memorial Record of Crawford County, Pennsylvania*. Bradford, Pa.: W.A. Ferguson, 1899.

Beer, Thomas. *Hanna*. New York: Knopf, 1929.

Bercovitch, Sacvan. *The Puritan Origins of the American Self*. New Haven: Yale University Press, 1975.

Bliss, W.D.P. *The New Encyclopedia of Social Reform.* New York: Funk and Wagnalls, 1908.

Bower, Byron G. *History of Lewis County, New York, 1880-1965*. Lowville, N.Y.: The Willard Press, 1970.

Boyer, Paul. *Urban Masses and Moral Order in America, 1820-1920*. Cambridge, Mass.: Harvard University Press, 1978.

Bremner, Robert. *American Philanthropy*. Chicago: University of Chicago Press, 1960.

———. "Samuel M. Jones: The Man Without a Party." *American Journal of Economics and Sociology* 8 (1948-49): 151-61.

Bryce, James. *The American Commonwealth.* 2 vols. New York: Macmillan, 1888.

Caernarvonshire Historical Society Transactions 15 (1954).

Caldwell, Joseph A. *Illustrated Historical Combination Atlas of Clarion County Pennsylvania.* N.p.: Atlas Publishing Company, 1877.

Carlton, Frank T. "The Golden-Rule Factory: The Late Mayor Jones' Contribution Toward the Solution of Industrial Problems." *Arena* 32 (1904): 408-10.

Carnegie, Andrew. *The Gospel of Wealth*. New York: Century, 1900.

Cartwright, H.L. *History of Duke Center Together with a Complete Business Directory of the Borough*. Duke Center, Pa.: Wellington and Carr, 1880.

Carwardine, Richard. "Methodist Ministers and the Second Party System." In *Rethinking Methodist History: A Bicentennial Historical Consultation*, edited by Russell E. Richey and Kenneth E. Rowe. Nashville: Abingdon, 1985.

Casson, Herbert. "Draining a Political Swamp." *Arena* 21 (1899): 768-72.

Clark, Frank M. "The Theatre of Pithole, Pennsylvania, Oil Boom Town." *Western Pennsylvania Historical Magazine* 56 (1973): 39-57.

Coe, George Albert. *The Psychology of Religion*. Chicago: University of Chicago Press, 1916.

Court, Elaine. "Toledo's Golden Rule Mayor." *Toledo Magazine*, August 28, 1983, 6-8.

Coletta, Paolo E. "The Bryan Campaign of 1896." In *William Jennings Bryan: A Profile*, edited by Paul W. Glad. New York: Hill and Wang, 1968.

———. *William Jennings Bryan: Political Evangelist, 1860-1908.* Lincoln: University of Nebraska Press, 1964.

Converse, Florence. *The Burden of Christopher*. New York: Houghton Mifflin, 1900.

Conway, Alan, ed. *The Welsh in America: Letters from the Immigrants*. Minneapolis: University of Minnesota Press, 1961.

Coser, Lewis A. *Men of Ideas: A Sociologist's View*. New York: Macmillan, 1965.

Crawford County Deed Books I, N, and W. Meadville Library.

Croly, Herbert. *Marcus Alonzo Hanna: His Life and His Works*. Hamden, Conn.: Archon Books, 1965.

Crosby, Ernest. *Golden Rule Jones*. Chicago: Public Publishing Co., 1906.

———. "'Golden-Rule' Jones, the Late Mayor of Toledo." *Craftsman* 7 (February–March 1905): 530-47, 679-88.

Cross, Whitney R. *The Burned-Over District: The Social and Intellectual History of Enthusiastic Religion in Western New York, 1800-1850.* Ithaca: Cornell University Press, 1950.

Crunden, Robert M. *A Hero in Spite of Himself: Brand Whitlock in Art, Politics and War.* New York: Knopf, 1969.

———. *Ministers of Reform: The Progressives' Achievement in American Civilization, 1889-1920.* Urbana: University of Illinois Press, 1984.

Curtis, Susan. *A Consuming Faith: The Social Gospel and Modern American Culture.* Baltimore: Johns Hopkins University Press, 1991.

Darrah, William C. *Pithole, the Vanished City: A Story of the Petroleum Industry*. Gettysburg, Pa.: Published by the author, 1972.

Darrow, Clarence. *Farmington.* Chicago: A.C. McClurg, 1904.

———. *The Story of My Life*. New York: Charles Scribner's Sons, 1934.

Destler, Chester MacArthur. *Henry Demarest Lloyd and the Empire of Reform.* Philadelphia: University of Pennsylvania Press, 1963.

Dewey, Edward Hooker. *The No-Breakfast Plan and the Fasting Cure*. Published by the author, 1900.

Dewey, John. "Ralph Waldo Emerson." In *Characters and Events: Popular Essays in Social and Political Philosophy,* edited by Joseph Ratner. 2 vols. New York: Henry Holt, 1929.

Downes, Randolph C. *Industrial Beginnings.* Lucas County Historical Series, 4 vols. Toledo: Historical Society of Northwest Ohio, 1954.

———. "Jones and Whitlock and the Promotion of Urban Democracy." *Northwest Ohio Quarterly* 28 (Winter 1955-56): 26-37.

Eaton, Amasa M. "A Visit to the Oil Regions of Pennsylvania." *Western Pennsylvania Historical Magazine* 18 (1935): 189-208.

Elkins, Stanley. *Slavery: A Problem in American Institutional and Intellectual Life.* Chicago: University of Chicago Press, 1976.

Emerson, Ralph Waldo. "The Conservative." In *The Collected Works of Ralph Waldo Emerson,* edited by Joseph Slater. 3 vols. Cambridge, Mass.: Belknap Press of Harvard University Press, 1971-.

Epstein, Barbara Leslie. *The Politics of Domesticity: Women, Evangelism, and Temperance in Nineteenth Century America.* Middletown, Conn.: Wesleyan University Press, 1981.

Erikson, Erik. *Insight and Responsibility: Lectures on the Ethical Implications of Psychoanalytic Insight.* New York: Norton, 1964.

Ferenczi, Imre, and Walter Francis Wilcox. *International Migration.* 2 vol. New York: National Bureau of Economics and Social Research, 1929-31.

Ferguson, Charles. *The Toledo of Jones.*

Filler, Louis. *Crusaders for American Liberalism.* 1939. Reprint. New York: Harcourt, 1950.

Fitzgerald, Frances. *Cities on a Hill: A Journey Through Contemporary American Cultures.* New York: Simon and Schuster, 1981.

Flower, Benjamin O. "The Late Mayor Jones: His Life and Ideals." *Arena* 32 (1904): 323-24.

———. "The Significance of His Victory." *Arena* 29 (1903): 653-55.

———. "The Significance of Mayor Jones' Election." *Coming Age* 1 (June 1899): 1-2.

Ford, Harvey S. "The Life and Times of Golden Rule Jones." 2 vols. Ph. D. diss., University of Michigan, 1953.

Frederick, Peter J. *Knights of the Golden Rule: The Intellectual as Christian Social Reformer in the 1890s.* Lexington: University Press of Kentucky, 1976.

Freud, Sigmund. *The Future of an Illusion.* 1927. Reprint. Garden City, N.Y.: Doubleday, 1964.

Gaustad, Edwin Scott. *Historical Atlas of Religion in America.* New York: Harper & Row, 1962.

Gay, Peter. *The Tender Passion.* Vol. 2 of *The Bourgeois Experience: Victoria to Freud.* New York: Oxford University Press, 1986.

Gaze, Harry. *How to Live Forever: The Science and Practice.* Chicago: Stockman, 1904.

Giddens, Paul H. *The Birth of the Oil Industry.* New York: Macmillan, 1938.

———. *Pennsylvania Petroleum: Contemporary Accounts, 1859-1872.* Philadelphia: Lippincott, 1975.

Gilman, Charlotte (Perkins) Stetson. *Women and Economics: A Study of the Economic Relation Between Men and Women as a Factor in Social Evolution.* Boston: Small, Maynard, 1898.

Ginger, Ray. *Altgeld's America: The Lincoln Ideal vs. Changing Realities.* New York: Funk and Wagnalls, 1958.

Glabb, Charles N., and James C. Marshall. *Toledo Profile: A Sesquicentennial History.* Toledo: Toledo–Lucas County Public Library, 1987.

Glad, Paul W. *The Trumpet Soundeth: William Jennings Bryan and His Democracy, 1896-1912.* Lincoln: University of Nebraska Press, 1960.

Gladden, Washington. "Mayor Jones of Toledo." *Outlook* 62 (May 6, 1899): 17-21.

———. *The Ruling Ideas of the Present Age.* Boston: Houghton Mifflin, 1895.

———. *Tools and the Man: Property and Industry Under the Christian Law.* New York: Houghton Mifflin, 1894.

Gould, Lewis L. *The Presidency of William McKinley*. Lawrence: Regents Press of Kansas, 1980.

Greven, Philip J. *The Protestant Temperament: Patterns of Child-Rearing, Religious Experience, and the Self in Early America*. New York: Knopf, 1977.

Griffith, Ernest S. *A History of American City Government: The Conspicuous Failure, 1870-1900*. New York: Praeger, 1974.

Guillet, Edwin C. *The Great Migration: The Atlantic Crossing by Sailing Ship, 1770-1860*. 1937. Reprint. Toronto: University of Toronto Press, 1963.

Harris, Kenneth. *The Wildcatter: A Portrait of Robert O. Anderson*. New York: Weidenfeld and Nicolson, 1987.

Harrison, John. *The Blade of Toledo: The First Fifty Years*. Toledo: Toledo Blade Co., 1985.

Hastings, James. *The Encyclopaedia of Religion and Ethics*. New York: Scribners, 1908-1926.

Hatch, Nathan O. *The Democratization of American Christianity*. New Haven: Yale University Press, 1989.

———. "The Democratization of Christianity and the Character of American Politics." In *Religion and American Politics: From the Colonial Period to the 1980s*, edited by Mark A. Noll. New York: Oxford University Press, 1990.

Henry, Arthur. "Millionaire Socialists." *Ainselee's Magazine* 4 (August 1899): 22-32.

Herron, George. *Between Caesar and Jesus*. 1898. Reprint. Westport, Conn.: Hyperion Press, 1975.

———. *The Christian State: A Political Vision of Christ*. New York: Crowell, 1895.

———. *The New Redemption*. New York: Crowell, 1893.

Hoffer, Eric. *True Believers: Thoughts on the Nature of Mass Movements*. New York: Harper & Row, 1951.

Hoffmann, Charles. "The Depression of the Nineties." *Journal of Economic History* 16 (1956): 137-64.

Hofstadter, Richard. *The Age of Reform*. New York: Knopf, 1955.

Holli, Melvin G. *Reform in Detroit: Hazen S. Pingree and Urban Politics*. New York: Oxford University Press, 1969.

Hope, Derrill. "The Golden Rule in Toledo." *Social Gospel* 39 (May 1901): 7-11.

Hopkins, Charles. *The Rise of the Social Gospel in American Protestantism, 1865-1915*. New Haven: Yale University Press, 1967.

Hough, Franklin. *A History of Lewis County in the State of New York from the Beginning of ItsSettlement to the Present Time*. Albany: Munsell and Rowland, 1860.

Howe, Daniel Walker. "Religion and Politics in the Antebellum North." In *Religion and American Politics: From the Colonial Period to the 1980s*, edited by Mark A. Noll. New York: Oxford University Press, 1990.

Howe, Frederic C. *The Confessions of a Reformer*. 1925. Reprint. New York: Scribner's, 1975.

Howe, Irving. *Socialism and America*. New York: Harcourt Brace Jovanovich, 1985.

In Memoriam: Henry Demarest Lloyd. Chicago: N.p., November 29, 1903.

James, William. *The Varieties of Religious Experience: A Study in Human Nature*. New York: Longman's, Green, 1902.

Johnson, Tom. *My Story*. New York: B. W. Huebsch, 1911.

Johnson, Wendell. *Toledo's Non-Partisan Movement*. Toledo: H.J. Chihenden Co., 1922.

Jones, Marnie. "Before Pollsters and Sound Bites: The 1897 Election of 'Golden Rule' Jones." *Toledo Magazine,* December 18, 1992, 6-13.

———. "Writing Great-Grandfather's Biography." *American Scholar* 57 (Autumn 1987): 519-34.

Kaplan, Justin. *Walt Whitman: A Life.* New York: Simon and Schuster, 1980.

Kinston, Warren. "The Shame of Narcissism." In *The Many Faces of Shame,* edited by Donald L. Nathanson. New York: Guilford Press, 1987.

Knepper, George W. *Ohio and Its People.* Kent: Kent State University Press, 1989.

Kohlberg, Lawrence. "Religion, Morality, and Ego Development." In *Toward Moral and Religious Maturity: International Conference on Moral and Religious Development,* edited by Christine Brusselmans. Morristown, N.J.: Silver Burdett, 1980.

Lasch, Christopher. *The New Radicalism in America, 1889-1963: The Intellectual as Social Type.* New York: Knopf, 1965.

Lender, Mark Edward, and James Kirby Martin. *Drinking in America: A History.* New York: Free Press, 1982.

Leonard, Charles [Crocus, pseud.]. *The History of Pithole.* Pithole City: Morton, Longwell, 1867.

Lewis, Helen Block. "Shame and the Narcissistic Personality." In *The Many Faces of Shame,* edited by Donald L. Nathanson. New York: Guilford Press, 1987.

Link, Arthur, and Richard L. McCormick. *Progressivism.* Arlington Heights, Ill.: Harlan Davidson, 1983.

Lloyd, Caro. *Henry Demarest Lloyd, 1847-1903: A Biography.* 2 vols. New York: Putnam's, 1912.

Lloyd, Henry Demarest. *Wealth Against Commonwealth.* New York: Harper and Brothers, 1894.

———. "The Man Without a Party" *Outlook* 74 (2 May 1903): 73.

Marathon Oil Company, *Five Eventful Decades: A History of the Ohio Oil Company, 1887-1937.* Findlay, Ohio: N.p., 1937.

Marr, David. *American Worlds Since Emerson.* Amherst: University of Massachusetts Press, 1988.

Martin, William. *A Prophet with Honor: The Billy Graham Story.* New York: William Morrow, 1991.

May, Henry. *Protestant Churches and Industrial America.* New York: Harper, 1967.

McClosley, Robert G. *American Conservatism in the Age of Enterprise: A Study of William Graham Sumner, Stephen J. Field, and Andrew Carnegie.* Cambridge, Mass.: Harvard University Press, 1951.

Macfadden, Bernarr, and Felix Oswald. *Fasting, Hydropathy, Exercise: Nature's Wonderful Remedies for the Cure of All Chronic and Acute Diseases.* London: Published by the authors, 1903.

McLoughlin, William G. "Jones vs. Jones." *American Heritage* 12 (April 1961): 56-59, 84-89.

McQuaid, Kim. "Businessman as Social Innovator: N.O. Nelson, Promoter of Garden Cities and Consumer Cooperatives." *American Journal of Economics and Sociology* 34 (1975): 401-18.

Mead, Sidney E. "American Protestantism Since the Civil War." *Journal of Religion* 36 (1956): 1-15.

Meissner, William. *Life and Faith: Psychological Perspectives on Religious Experience.* Washington, D.C.: Georgetown University Press, 1987.

Melder, Keith. *Bryan the Campaigner.* Contributions from the Museum of History and Technology, Paper 46 Bulletin 241. Washington, D.C.: Smithsonian Institution, 1965.

Miller, E. Willard. "Population and Functional Changes of Villages in Western Pennsylvania." *Western Pennsylvania Historical Magazine* 43 (1960): 59-74.

Morris, Jan. *The Matter of Wales: Epic Views of a Small Country.* Oxford: Oxford University Press, 1984.

Mott, Frank Luther. *A History of American Magazines, 1885-1905.* 4 vols. Cambridge, Mass.: Harvard University Press, 1957.

Nathanson, Donald L. "Shaming Systems in Couples, Families, and Institutions." In *The Many Faces of Shame,* edited by Donald L. Nathanson. New York: Guilford Press, 1987.

O'Donnell, Thomas C. *Snubbing Posts: An Informal History of the Black River Canal.* Boonville, N.Y.: Black River Books, 1949.

One Who Knew Him. "Samuel Milton Jones: The Golden-Rule Mayor." *Arena* 35 (1906): 126-32.

Pearce, Roy Harvey. *The Continuity of American Poetry.* Middletown, Conn.: Wesleyan University Press, 1987.

Philip, Jordan D. *Ohio Comes of Age, 1973-1900.* Vol. 5 of *The History of the State of Ohio.* Columbus: State Archaeological and Historical Society, 1943.

Pomeroy, Eltweed. "Samuel Jones: An Appreciation." *American Fabian* 4 (July 1898): 1-3, 9.

Porter, Carolyn. *Seeing and Being: The Plight of the Participant Observer in Emerson, James, Adams, and Faulkner.* Middletown, Conn.: Wesleyan University Press, 1981.

Quandt, Jean B. *From the Small Town to the Great Community: The Social Thought of Progressive Intellectuals.* New Brunswick, N.J.: Rutgers University Press, 1970.

Resek, Carl, ed. *The Progressives.* New York: Bobbs-Merrill, 1967.

Rezneck, Samuel. "Unemployment, Unrest, and Relief in the United States During the Depression of 1893-97." *Journal of Political Economy* 61 (1953): 325-29.

Rizzuto, Ana-Maria. *The Birth of the Living God: A Psychoanalytic Study.* Chicago: University of Chicago Press, 1979.

Rodabaugh, James H. "Samuel M. Jones: Evangel of Equality." *Historical Society of Northeastern Ohio Quarterly Bulletin* 15 (1953): 17-46.

Rosen, Ruth. *The Lost Sisterhood: Prostitution in America, 1900-1918.* Baltimore: Johns Hopkins University Press, 1982.

Ruck, Ruth Janette. *Place of Stones.* London: Faber and Faber, 1961.

Ruskin, John. *Unto This Last: Four Essays on the First Principles of Political Economy.* New York: Merrill and Baker, n.d.

Salter, Henry Hyde. *On Asthma: Its Pathology and Treatment.* Philadelphia: Blanchard and Lea, 1864.

Salvatore, Nick. *Eugene Debs: Citizen and Socialist.* Urbana: University of Illinois Press, 1981.

Saulsbury, Elwood. "Samuel M. Jones, Golden Rule Mayor of Toledo." *Frank Leslie's Popular Monthly* 53 (April 1902): 642-47.

Schwartz-Bart, Andre. *The Last of the Just*. New York: Atheneum, 1960.

Scribner, Harvey. *Memoirs of Lucas County and the City of Toledo from the Earliest Historic Times down to the Present*. 2 vols. Madison: Western Historical Association, 1910.

Sheldon, Charles. *In His Steps*. 1896. Reprint. New York: Grosset and Dunlap, 1961.

Shi, David E. *The Simple Life: Plain Living and High Thinking in American Culture*. New York: Oxford University Press, 1985.

Smith, Page. *The Rise of Industrial America*. Vol. 6 of A People's History. 1984. Reprint. New York: Penguin, 1990.

Smith, Robert M. "Beyond Progressivism: The Careers of Samuel 'Golden Rule' Jones and Nelson O. Nelson." *Midwest Review: Journal of History and Culture of the Missouri Valley* 10 (Spring 1988): 43-54.

Stave, Bruce M., ed. *Urban Bosses, Machines and Progressive Reformers*. Lexington, Mass.: Heath, 1972.

Stead, William T. *If Christ Came to Chicago!* Chicago: Press of the Eight Hour Herald, 1894.

Steffens, Lincoln. *The Shame of the Cities*. 1904. Reprint. New York: Peter Smith, 1948.

Strong, Josiah. *Our Country*. New York: Baker and Taylor, 1891.

———. *The Twentieth Century City*. New York: Baker and Taylor, 1898.

Sulloway, Frank. *Born to Rebel: Birth Order, Family Dynamics, and Creative Lives*. New York: Pantheon, 1996.

Tager, Jack. *The Intellectual as Urban Reformer*. Cleveland: Case Western Reserve University Press, 1968.

Thoreau, Henry David. *Walden*. Vol. 2 of *The Writings of Henry David Thoreau*. New York: Houghton Mifflin, 1899.

Thorowgood, John C. *Notes on Asthma: Its Nature, Forms, and Treatment*. Philadelphia: Lindse and Blakiston, 1873.

Tomkins, Silvan S. "The Psychology of Commitment: The Constructive Role of Violence and Suffering for the Individual and for His Society." In *The Anti-Slavery Vanguard: New Essays on the Abolitionists*, edited by Martin Duberman. Princeton: Princeton University Press, 1965.

Tuchman, Barbara. *The Proud Tower: A Portrait of the World Before the War, 1890-1914*. New York: Macmillan, 1962.

Van Tassel, Charles Sumner. *Story of the Maumee Valley, Toledo and the Sandusky Region*. 4 vols. Chicago: S.J. Clarke, 1929.

Waggoner, Clark. *History of the City of Toledo and Lucas County, Ohio*. New York: Munsell, 1888.

Wall, Joseph F. "A Second Look at Andrew Carnegie." In *Introspection in Biography*, edited by Samuel H. Baron and Carl Pletsch. Raleigh, N.C.: Analytic Press, 1985.

Walters, Everett. *Joseph Benson Foraker: An Uncompromising Republican*. Columbus: Ohio Historical Press, 1948.

Walzer, Michael. *The Revolution of the Saints: A Study in the Origins of Radical Politics*. Cambridge, Mass.: Harvard University Press, 1965.

Warner, Hoyt Landon. *Progressivism in Ohio, 1887-1917*. Columbus: Ohio State University Press, 1964.

Welch, Claude. *Protestant Thought in the Nineteenth Century*. 2 vols. New Haven: Yale University Press, 1972, 1985.

White, Ronald C. Jr., and C. Howard Hopkins. *The Social Gospel: Religion and Reform in Changing America*. Philadelphia: Temple University Press, 1976.
Whitlock, Brand. "Campaigning with Sam Jones." *Commons* 9 (1904): 355-56.
———. *Forty Years of It.* New York: D. Appleton, 1925.
———. "Golden Rule Jones." *World's Work* 8 (September 1904): 5308-9.
———. *The Letters and Journal of Brand Whitlock,* edited by Allan Nevins. New York: D. Appleton, 1936.
Whitman, Walt. *Complete Poems and Prose of Walt Whitman.* Philadelphia: Ferguson, 1881.
———. In "Specimen Days." *Notes and Fragments: Left by Walt Whitman and Now Edited by Dr. Richard Maurice Bucke, One of His Literary Executors.* N.p., 1899.
Williams, Gwyn. *When Was Wales? A History of the Welsh.* 1985. Reprint. London: Penguin, 1988.
Williams, Rev. Lewis. "Lewis County, New York." *Cambrian* 25 (September 1905): 372-76.
Williams, R.R. *Flames from the Altar: Howell Harris and His Contemporaries.* Caernarvon, Wales: Calvinistic Methodist Book Agency, 1962.
Williams, Rev. William. *Welsh Calvinistic Methodism: A Historical Sketch of the Presbyterian Church of Wales.* London: Presbyterian Church of England, 1884.

Newspapers

Bradford Era, 1885.
Pithole Daily Record, 1865-66.
Titusville Morning Herald, 1865.
Toledo Bee, 1895-1903.
Toledo Blade, 1895-1930.
Toledo News-Bee, 1903-30.
Toledo Saturday Night: A Paper Devoted to the Reforms Advocated by Mayor S.M. Jones, 1899.

Government Documents

Annual Messages of Mayor Samuel M. Jones to the Common Council of Toledo, Ohio 1898-1904.
Annual Report of the Secretary of State to the Governor of Ohio, 1899. Columbus.

Publications by Samuel M. Jones

"American Workingmen and Religion." *Outlook* 65 (July 14, 1900): 640-42.
Annual Christmas Messages to the Workers of the Acme Sucker Rod Company, 1897-03.
"The Eight Hour Day in the Oil Fields." Toledo, 1897.
"Government by the Golden Rule." *Munsey's Magazine* 28 (January 1903): 506-9.
Letters of Labor and Love. Indianapolis: Bobbs-Merrill, 1905.
Letters of Love and Labor. 2 vols. Toledo: Franklin Printing, 1900-1901.
"Municipal Expansion." *Arena* 21 (1899): 766-67.

"The New Patriotism." *Municipal Affairs* 3 (September 1899): 455-61.

The New Right: A Plea for Fair Play Through a More Just Social Order. New York: Eastern Book Concern, 1899.

"The Non-Partisan in Politics." *Independent* 55 (August 20, 1903): 1963.

"Patience and Education the Demands of the Hour." *Arena* 25 (1901): 544-46.

"A Plea for Simpler Living." *Arena* 29 (April 1903): 345-61.

"The Religious Condition of the Working Men in America at the Close of the Nineteenth Century." In *Theology at the Dawn of the Twentieth Century: Essays on the Present Status of Christianity and Its Doctrines,* edited by John Vyrnwy Morgan. Boston: Small, Maynard, 1901.

"The Rights and Obligations of the Municipality." *Coming Age* 1 (April 1899): 544-46.

"Thorough Physical Culturist." *Physical Culture* 10 (September 1903): 263-64.

"The Way to Purify Politics." *Independent* 54 (February 27, 1902): 512-13.

"What Should the City Own." *American Monthly Review of Reviews* 18 (1898): 462-63.

Women and City Government. N.p.: N.d.

Index

abolitionists, 10, 26, 27, 51, 243 n 25, 249, n 2
Acme Oil Company, 101-2
Acme Sucker Rod Company, 91, 108, 113-14, 117, 127, 148, 187; reforms of, 69-70, 77, 96-7, 118-19, 127, 197
Adams, Henry, 60, 72
Addams, Jane, 77, 81, 97; as autobiographer, 39; correspondence between Jones and, 99, 135; depression of, 60; as evangelical, 87; on Lincoln's death, 36, 245 n 45; reformers and, 11, 27, 87, 99-100, 130, 165; on urban isolation, 92-93
alcohol, 4-5, 25, 123-24, 136-38, 152-53, 191, 256 n 13
Altgeld, John Peter, 72, 249 n 14
American Civic Association, 99
American Federationist, 237
American Federation of Labor, 163, 237
American Protective Association, 124
American Revolution, 133
anarchists, 87, 108, 136, 262 n 44. *See also* Jones: Politics, as anarchist
Anderson, S.G., 63, 127, 132
Andersonville Prison, 107
Anglican Church, 21
anti-imperialism, 175, 196. *See also* Jones: Politics, anti-imperialism
anti-institutionalism, 51, 243 n 25. *See also* Jones: Politics, anti-institutionalism
Anti-saloon League, outraged by Jones, 136-37
Arbuckle-Ryan Company, 182-83
Arena, 81, 211
Ashley, Jim, 110-13, 154; correspondence between Jones and, 151; role in Jones's nomination, 141, 149-50
Association of American Playgrounds, 99
Atlanta Penitentiary, 168
Augustine, Saint, 209

Baber law, 162, 258 n 27
Baines, Dudley, 242 n 15
Barclay, Morgan, 240 n 14, 268 n 37
Bartlett, J.A., 122-24
Baxter, Richard, 14
Beach House, 252 n 11
Beddgelert, Wales, 19-25, 93-94, 243 n 23
Beecher, Henry Ward, 58, 247 n 32
Bellamy, Edward, 194
Bercovitch, Sacvan, 13, 241 n 19
Bible, as educational tool for Welsh, 21, 58. *See also* New Testament
Black River Valley, 26, 35
Bliss, W.D.P., 87-88, 99; sees Golden rule in business, a "hopeless task," 217; sees need for unity among reformers, 179
blue laws, 136-38, 153
Bok, Edward, 211
Boyer, Paul, 3-4, 239 n 5, 248 n 44, 252 nn. 17, 19, 266 n 35
Brand, W.W., 212
Bremmer, Robert, 267 n 17
Brown, Clarence, 162, 217; on the Golden Rule, 193; correspondence between Jones and, 197-98
Brown, T.P., 149-50
Brown, Walter, 108, 146, 149, 151, 154, 166, 217, 228, 259 n 36. *See also* machine

Bryan, William Jennings, 7, 11, 103, 112, 130, 140, 151, 214, 235; "Cross of Gold" speech of, 191; and evangelism, 32; interested in Jones's support, 181-82, 185, 186-87; Jones and, 190-198; Jones influences, 195-97
Bryce, James, 170
Buck, J.D., 97; correspondence between Jones and, 201
Buddha, 225
Burden of Christopher, 238
burned-over district, 26, 33, 243 n 23
Burns, Robert, 183
Bushnell, Asa; praises Jones, 162; repudiates Hanna, 142-43; repudiates Jones, 175

Calvinist impulses, 14, 27, 173. *See also* Jones: religious life, Calvinist training; Welsh Calvinist Methodism
Candee, George: correspondence between Jones and, 163
Carnegie, 3; autobiography of, 173, 267 n 17; Jones horrified by, 224; philanthropy of, 71, 165
Casson, Herbert, 174, 261 n 30
Children's Playground Association, 99
cholera, 25
Christ. *See* Jesus
Christian Endeavorer, 165
Christian socialism, 1-2, 27, 29, 78, 230; intellectual basis for 79, 88; principle behind, 87. *See also* Jones: religious life, Christian socialism
Circuit Court of Appeals, 183
civil war, 36; Pingree and, 107; prompts complacent view of labor hardships, 52-53; Raitz and, 121; veterans of, 44-45, 109, 136
Clemens, Samuel. *See* Twain, Mark
Cochran, Negley, 112, 139, 141, 142, 147, 155, 185, 212-13; background of, 135; Congressional campaign of, 193, 195-97; obtains Democratic support for Jones, 186, 193, 201; separates from Jones, 214-16
Coleman, John C., 182-83
Coleridge, Samuel Taylor, 104
Coletta, Paolo, 195-96
Collinsville, New York, 32, 34-35, 93; Welsh connection to, 23, 25-30, 242 n 21
Comings, S.H., correspondence between Jones and, 51, 165
commonwealth, 121, 138, 230
Commonwealth, 51, 165
Commonwealth, Georgia, 86, 92, 220, 267 n 7
community, 10; at Acme Sucker Rod, 114; Bryan's faith in, 190-91; fostered in small towns, 27
Convers, Florence, 238
Cooper Institute, 224
Court of Common Pleas, 183
Cowell, William, 110, 112, 170
Cowles, James L., 166
Coxey's Commonweal Army, 72
Craig, John, as Jones's opponent, 110-113
critics of Jones, 7, 132; clergy as, 152-53, 164; family as, 165, 182, 187; President McKinley as, 177; Republican party members as, 141-43; upper-middle-class Toledoans as, 4-5, 12, 118-19, 132, 153
Croly, Herbert, 254 n 10
Crosby, Ernest, 83, 145; correspondence between Jones and, 200-201, 204; corresponds with Tolstoy about Jones, 82, 155; introduces Jones to Whitman's poetry, 128-29
Crosbyside conference, 128-30, 166
Cross, Whitney R., 243 n 23
Crunden, Robert, 239 n 13, 248 n 37
Cuba, 108-9, 144-45
Culture Extension League, 99
Curtiss family, 55, 189, 234
Curtis, Susan, 239 n 9

Darrow, Clarence, 77; on capitalism in school cirriculum, 33; correspondence between Jones and, 183-84,

187, 215; as George Herron's divorce lawyer, 80; on Negley Cochran as a writer, 135
Dawn, 88
Dowd, John W., 214-16
Debs, Eugene, 11, 72, 97, 103, 130, 131, 143, 165, 166, 178, 235, 254 n 4, 260 n 18; correspondence between Jones and, 168-69, 197-98; gives Jones realistic advice, 161, 168-69, 175, 179; important Toledo speech, 133-35; Jones separates himself from 190, 192
Declaration of Independence, 68, 139
de Lome, Enrique Depuy, 108
democracy, 139, 140-41, 192, 215, 231-32; Christianity yoked to, 13, 26-28, 257 n 36. *See also* Jones: politics, democracy in action
Democratic party: conventions of 1899 of, 147, 175; courts Jones, 181-82, 185-87; forbids press coverage of Jones, 175-77; Jackson League Club of, 116; Jones, Bryan and 190-198; supports Jones, 186, 193, 201; willing to offer Jones as Congressional candidate, 193, 195-97
Denman ordinance, 267 n 9
Dewey, John, 27, 87, 240 n 15
devil, as political analogy, 14, 119, 152, 194
Dickens, Charles: influences Ruskin, 83; shapes Jones's view of the world, 34, 40, 54, 104
Dowles, Randolph C., 254 n 4
Dowling, P.H., as Jones's opponent, 147, 155

economy: attitudes toward, 50, 52-53; Christianity and, 58, 83-84, 247 n 32, 247-48 n 33; Debs' view of, 134; depression of 1873 and, 68; depression of 1890s and, 14, 66, 71-72, 99, 107-8, 249 nn 4, 9; socialist perspective on, 69-70, 81; Toledo prosperity and, 66
Edwards, Johnathan, 32
eight-hour day. *See* Jones: reform, eight-hour day
electricity, 99-100, 262 n 2; municipal utilities and, 182-84, 188
Eliot, George, 104
Elkins, Stanley, 243 n 25, 246 n 18
Ellis, Seth, 177
Ellis, Thomas Edward, 241 n 5
Ely, Richard, 66
Emancipation Proclamation, 136, 145
Emerson, Ralph Waldo, 51, 132-33, 140, 164; on complicity, 159-60, 260 n 1
Engels, 250 n 28
Epstein, Barbara Leslie, 247 n 29
Erikson, Erik, 240 n 16
evangelical culture, 13, 19-22, 26, 243 n 23; agenda for change in, 27-28; child rearing in, 24-25, 29-32, 38, 73, 244 n 33; temperament of individuals in an, 24, 32, 39, 87, 245 nn. 35, 39. *See also* shame; Jones: religious life: evangelical temperament

fabians, 95, 142
Fellows, William, 111
feminist reforms, 26, 140
Ferenczi, Imre, 242 n 15
Filler, Louis, 227
Finney, Charles, 26
Fisk, D.M., 135
Fletcher, Horace, 220
Flower, Benjamin O., 81, 87; assesses importance of Jones's election, 119; correspondence between Jones and, 191; Jones writes article for, 140-41
Flower, Roswell P., 72
Foraker, Joseph B., 109, 162-63, 176-77, 254 n 10
Ford, Harvey S., 244 n 31
Francis of Assisi, Saint, 223
Fraser Bill, 204-5, 265 n 16
Frederick, Peter, 1, 239 n 14
Freud, Sigmund, 9, 51, 240 n 16

Gay, Peter, 265 n 21
George, Henry, 194
Giddings, Franklin, 87
gilded age, 93

Gilman, Charlotte Perkins [Stetson], explains Jones's sensibility, 73, 250 n 18
Glabb, Charles N., 240 n 14, 249 n 3, 268 n 37
Gladden, Washington, 79, 84, 86, 87, 94, 119, 244 n 31; correspondence between Jones and, 70, 67-68, 88, 166; depression of, 60
Glyndwr, Owain, 232
God: Jones family covenant with, 21; will of, 24, 33, 81, 217. *See also* Jones: religious life, God
Golden Rule, 28, 65, 68-69, 73, 77, 82, 86, 88, 92, 139-40, 143, 155, 195, 221. *See also* Golden Rule under Jones: character and formative events; Jones: reform; Jones: religious life; and Jones: politics
Gompers, Samuel, 6; correspondence between Jones and, 237
Gould, Lewis L., 254 n 9
grand central palace, 145
Grant, Ulysses S., 135
Greenback Party. *See* Nationalist Party
Greven, Philip, 9, 24, 242 n 16, 244 n 30, 245 nn 35, 39
Griffin, Charles: campaigns for Jones, 154; defends Jones against Republican attack, 142
Griffith, Ernest, 239 n 13
Guatemala, 144
guilt, and American reform, 51, 240 n 15, 246 n 18. *See also* shame; Jones: character and formative events, shame

Habitual Criminal Act, 205, 265 n 16
Hammell, George, 177
Hammond, Ernest, 165; correspondence between and, 187
Hanna, Marcus (Mark), 11, 110, 139, 145, 152, 176, 195, 254 nn. 10, 258 n 11; control of Toledo, 108-9; death of, 227-28; election to U.S. Senate, 140-44; enmity toward Jones, 119, 131, 134, 162, 177, 196; Jones victory in Hanna ward, 178
Harris, Lem P.: correspondence between Jones and, 185; Jones campaign manager, 154, 155; mayoral hopeful, 110-12
Hatch, Nathan, 241 n 18, 248 n 33, 260 n 1
Hearst, William Randolph, 8 174; correspondence between Jones and, 215; interested in Jones's political career, 186, 193-94
Hegel, Georg, 79
Henderson, David, 177
Herron, George, 1, 88; contrast to Jones, 80-81; correspondence between Jones and, 179; influences Jones, 11, 65, 77, 79-81, 84-87, 104, 244 n 33; outrages Toledo clergy, 132-33
Holli, Melvin, 239 n 12, 250 n 15, 253 n 30
home rule, 87, 144, 205, 216
Hone, Parks ("Punk): and blue laws controversy, 137; as Jones's opponent, 114, 117, 118; Republicans support as Democratic nominee in 1895, 108
Hopkins, Charles, 248 n 34, 251 n 44
How, Daniel Walker, 241 n 18
Howe, Frederick: 27, 87, 240 n 15; on Hanna, intent on "breaking" men, 143
How the Other Half Lives, 99
Hull House, 60, 83, 258 n 11; as model for Golden Rule House, 100

If Christ Came to Chicago, 67
Independent Party, 185; Brand Whitlock elected mayor from, 231; elects 3 to city council in 1904, 231
industrial revolution: makes oil a valuable commodity, 246 n 3; political machines and social gospel, responses to, 106; price American culture pays for 52, 206; technological break-throughs from, 107
In His Steps, 76
immigrants, 5-6, 106, 124, 247 n 32
Independent, 211

Iowa College: Jones's commencement speech at, 172; Jones supports Herron's retention fight against, 80
Isaiah, the "redeemed social state" in, 195, 199

James, William, 67; on the conversion process, 9, 52, 65, 73-76, 103, 120, 127; on "The Sick Soul," 219; on Tolstoy's depression, 220-222
Japan, 144
Jefferson, Thomas, 139-40, 194
Jermain, Sylvanus P., 98, 99
Jesus, 10, 102, 139-40, 165, 180, 225, 245 n 39; economic teachings of, 86, 96, 104, 127, 134, 225; failure to follow, 76-77, 81-82, 131, 153, 209, 223; radical expectations of, 12, 29, 220; selfless sacrifice, 29, 164, 237. *See also* Jones: Religious Life, Jesus
Johnson, Tom: 11, 12, 77, 196, 208, 235-36; correspondence between Jones and, 184, 215, 225-27, 265-66 n 27; eulogy for Jones, 238
Johnson, Wendell, 240 n 14
Jones, Alice (sister), 20, 30, 95
Jones, Alma (first wife): death of, 59-61, 63, 212, 233; Jones's deep love for, 55; importance to reform agenda, 55-56, 73; marriage partnership to, 56-57, 95, 247 n 29
Jones, Bertha (neice), 234
Jones, Daniel (brother), 21, 31, 32, 102, 126, 234
Jones, Ellen (Nell, sister), 20, 30, 61, 62, 96, 100, 103, 212, 234, 269 n 52
Jones, Eva Bell ("Midgie," daughter), 59, 233, 234
Jones, Helen (second wife), 63, 93, 94, 117, 127, 153, 155, 234-36, 249 n 14; structure of marriage, 95. *See also* Jones: character and formative events, marriage, strains in marriage
Jones, Hugh (father), 20, 30, 84, 95, 163; American Dream of, 19; emigration of 23-26; naturalization of, 242 n 15; religious revival upon 21-23; sufferings of, 94, 95, 163
Jones, John C., 228
Jones, John Hugh (brother), 20, 30, 31, 36, 206, 234
Jones, Margaret (mother), 20, 95, 163; death of, 57; religious values of, 22-23, 78; sufferings of, 94
Jones, Marion (daughter-in-law), 207, 234, 236, 265 n 24
Jones, Mary (sister), 20, 30
Jones, Mason (son), 132, 236
Jones, Moses (brother), 21, 32; death of, 54, 247 n 22
Jones, Paul (son), 59, 61, 62, 63, 93, 94, 210, 212, 213, 234, 236; caught up in the "frivolous life," 187-190, 223
Jones, Percy (son), 57, 59, 61, 62, 63, 236; correspondence between Jones and, 207, 265 n 24; material concerns and, 18, 207; finds IOU, 224
Jones, Roy (nephew), 234
Jones, Sam (grandfather), 20
Jones, Samuel Milton
character and formative events
abandoned by parents, 34-35, 43
abstemious, 5, 74
ambition(s): 37, 40, 159, 163; conflict with religious temperament, 163, 167-68, 170, 220
anger: asthma, a result of, 125, 222; at leaving home, 34, 245 n 43; during Raitz case 125-26; suppressed, 218-219, 221-222, 228, 245 n 45
appearance, 4-5, 185, 218
athletic skills, 54-55, 212-13, 226-27
autobiography: gubernatorial race and, 159; handling of Pithole in, 38-42, 50, 51; handling of poverty in, 23, 34-35; intentions of, 43, 173-74; strategies in, 23, 36, 60, 70, 172-74
birth of, 20; birth of children, 57, 59
birth order and radicalism, 243 n 25

Jones, Samuel Milton: character and formative events *(cont'd)*
charisma, 92, 105, 174
charitable and generous, 2, 13, 71, 82, 165, 223-25
civil war: 36; failure to serve a campaign issue, 201
class consciousness, 78, 169, 250 n 28
courage: to create a new identity, 115; to restore his health, 226. *See also* Jones: religious life: valient spiritual journey
"crank," 63, 162, 164
dangerous, 162, 177, 237
Debs's speech in Toledo, profound impact upon Jones, 134
death: charity revealed at, 224-25; funeral, 235-37, 268 n 46 n 51; press reaction to, 3, 234-35
defender of the weak, 54-55, 74, 127-28, 202-6, 222-23
defining texts: Gospels, 10, 82, 84, 87, 96, 102; *Caesar and Jesus,* 70; *Christian State,* 80; *Duties of Man,* 79; *Faith and the Future,* 85; *Fors Clavigera,* 84; rails against *Gospel of Wealth,* 173; *New Redemption,* 81, 104; *Philosophy of History,* 79; "Philosophy of the Lord's Prayer," 224 n 34; *Social Morality,* 79; *Unto This Last,* 79, 83-85; *Varieties of Religious Experience,* 9, 73, 209; *Walden,* 223-24; *Wealth Against Commonwealth,* 77; disagrees with Gladden, *Tools and the Man,* 70, 84; *Ruling Ideas of the Present Age,* 81, 84, 244 n 34; *Twentieth Century City,* 140. *See also* James, William
depression and despair, 40, 59-61, 165, 172, 199, 216-19, 224-25
determined and forceful personality, 40-41, 46-49, 128, 139, 150, 171, 176
divided self, 1, 8, 14, 171-72, 75, 220
dreamer and visionary, 154, 175, 183-84, 230 n 13
education of: 32-33; love of learning, 62
elicits a powerful response from people: 117, 145, 148, 159, 160-61, 167-77, 192, 200, 221, 233, 235; needs to shun adulation, 174
emigration of, 14, 23-26
empathy, 11, 65, 67-71, 74, 85, 92
energy, 2, 161, 176, 200-201, 212-13
failure: to accept God's grace, 218-19; to find peace, 160; when Paul succumbs to "frivolous" life, 187-190; to depend on love, 199; to live up to his impossibly high demands, 51, 126, 164, 199, 213, 226
faith in the American Dream, 14, 19, 49
first self, 14, 19, 27, 30-31, 58, 74, 172
Golden Rule: as business maxim, 1, 2, 19, 73, 91; as habit of life, 1, 2, 8, 14, 185, 220; impacts the self, 10, 31, 124-26, 139, 174; inability to meet standard of, 9, 13, 71, 125-26, 145; psychological need for, 24; textual power of, 10, 165. *See also* Golden Rule; Golden Rule under Jones: reform; Jones: religious life; and Jones: politics
guilt. *See* Jones: character and formative events, shame
health, concerns over: asthma, 2, 75, 124-6, 189-90, 222, 225-26, 234; mental and emotional breakdown, 60, 199, 206-13; pleuro-pneumonia, 208, 233; relative health of emotional response, 79-80, 128
health, cures for chronic illness: exercise and fasting, 125, 225; *How to Live Forever,* 125, 220; *The No-Breakfast Plan and the Fasting Cure,* 125, 208; physical culture,

75, 210-13, 226; standing on head, 2, 212-13; vegetarianism and, 2, 211
isolation: 30, 34, 40, 54, 57, 60, 78-79, 190, 198; desire for unity with Jesus, 245 n 39
losses, 24, 30, 35, 59-60
love for Alma, 55
marriage: with Alma, 55-57; with Helen, 63; strains in, 95-96, 187, 211-212, 229, 252n 11
meets Whitlock, 185
mother: relations with, 29, 63; need for forgiveness from, 57. *See also* Jones, Margaret
music: love of, 57, 147; used in campaigns, 101, 215
non-judgmental toward others, 80, 251 n 31
oil: first wildcat well, 53-54, 246-47 n 21; strikes Tunget Well, Ohio, 61
optimism and confidence of, 7, 31, 40, 54, 76, 81, 88, 91, 159, 173, 179, 200-210, 215-16
patent: of sucker rod, 63-64; troubled by, 96
Pithole: failure at, 52; haunts imagination, 117, 172; defining experience of life, 49, 51; moral parable of, 38, 172; traumas of, 40-48
poverty: connects Jones to the unemployed, 67-70; shamed by, 23-24, 33, 42, 70; at Pithole, 38, 40-50
return to Collinsville, 93
return to Wales, 20, 93-4
second self, 14, 19, 24, 32, 39, 65, 71, 74, 77, 139, 172
self-consciousness: 9-10, 12, 50, 91, 165-67; lack of, 38-39, 113, 173
selflessness, 2, 12, 77, 91, 102-3, 113
sense of humor, 13, 227, 241 n 2
sexual nature, 31, 39, 130, 133, 211
shame as shaper of identity, 29-31, 34, 39, 57, 103, 159-60, 163, 172, 244 n 31. *See also* shame
simple life, 56, 83, 206-7, 210-11, 220
sympathy of Nell, 61, 212
transatlantic voyage, 25
travel: through Ohio, 143, 176; to California, 98, 143; to Glasgow, Scotland, 93, 267 n 9; to Los Angeles, 93, 207; to Mexico, 93; to Pithole, 93, 189; to St. Louis, 43-44; to Texas, 143; to Venice, 93
Ty Mawr, 20, 24, 35, 93
unconventional behavior, 2, 62, 102, 128, 132-33, 151, 208, 211
upper-middle-class values: 137; rejects, 28, 93, 152-53, 220, 222-23
victory: against criminal justice system, 202, 205, 230; in commitment to good health, 210-11; in freedom, 185; from gubernatorial loss, 179; in lasting influences, 8, 229-232; as a "just man," 237-38
wealth: discomfort with, 91, 96, 127, 131, 164, 222-23; divesting fortune, 2, 10, 13, 23-24, 165, 188, 213, 223-24; patents sucker rod, 63-64; pursuit of, 38, 52-64; shamed by, 11, 24, 33, 39, 71, 74, 165
Welsh values, 19-24, 26-28, 78, 241 n 2. *See also* Welsh
Whitman's importance, 128-30, 131-33, 208, 233
work history: farming, 30, 34; sawmill, 35; Black River canal 35-36; St. Louis and Pithole Petroleum Company, 47-48; oil fields, 52-53; first large well in Lima, 60-63; Ohio Oil Company 61; buy-out by Standard oil, 62; President of Geyser Oil, 62-63; first all metal sucker rod, 63-64, move to Toledo, 63; founding Acme Sucker Rod Company, 67-70
writing, importance of, 9-11, 166-69, 173-74

Jones, Samuel Milton *(cont'd)*
reform
ability to implement change, 1, 7, 69, 86, 128, 173
alcohol, attitude toward, 4-6, 12, 102, 123-4, 136-37, 152-53
brotherhood, 4, 85, 114, 139, 145, 172
complicity with the "system," 50, 159-60, 163, 166-67, 260 n 1
community inspired by the Bible, 88, 91
conversion to, 65-66, 73-74, 250 n 23
co-operative insurance plan as, 96, 101-3
economic principle: 3, 10; business as synonym for war, 70; defined by the nightmare of Pithole, 50; unemployment destroys the soul, 49-50; profit is wrong, 69, 73. *See also* economy
eight-hour day as: 2, 49, 91, 119, 229, 230; for city servants, 100; McLean platform supporting, 175; for oil workers, 101-2
emotional price paid for, 71, 75-76
environmental, 91, 96
equality, essential to, 68-69, 77-78, 85
failure, paradox of, 1, 210, 231-232
fair wages as, 69, 75, 77, 101
Golden Rule: band, 214, 215; as business maxim, 1, 2, 19, 73, 82, 91, 227; hall, 100, 147, 250 n 18; in factory, 63, 68-69, justice and, 121-24, 127-28, 202-3; park, 91, 95-101, 103, 249 n 14, 252 n 13; as public policy, 232; settlement house, 96, 100, 101, 212. *See also* Golden Rule; Golden Rule under Jones: character and formative events; Jones: religious life; and Jones: politics
identifies with working class: 78; need for "useful" work, 206, 210
impact on Steffens, 227
increasing radicalism of ideas, 69, 73, 79-82, 116, 166-67, 175
industrial workers as abject slaves, 68-69
just relations with employees: 74, 84, 85, 91, 110, 118-19, 120; more important than making money, 69-70, 101-3
labor: creates humane environment for, 69-70, 93, 96, 100-103, 110, 230; pride in support from labor, 112
middle class values, unwilling to impose upon immigrants, 3-7, 124, 239 n 5, 248 n 44, 252 nn 17, 19, 266 n 35
municipal ownership: 6-7, 154, 119, 220-22, 234-35, 267 n 7; failure to implement in city government, 184
paid vacations, 2, 69, 101
parks and playgrounds, 12, 98, 121, 138, 229, 230
paternalism, 84, 231
police department, 121, 256 n 4
progressive, 1, 3-4, 6, 8, 11, 27, 220
profit sharing as, 2, 69
prostitution, attitude toward, 5
public kindergartens, 96 121, 229, 230
social, 103, 230. *See also* social and structural reform
sensibility of, 73-74
structural, 12, 197, 230. *See also* social and structural reform
union wages, 175
vice, definition of, 2, 4, 93; closure of pool rooms, 126-27; satirization in support of, 137-38
wealth, connection to, 100, 102. *See also* Jones; character and formative events
works of: *Letters of Love and Labor,* 84, 166, 197; *New Right,* 38, 39, 78, 83, 172-74
work and self-respect: 67, 87;

essential to municipal health, 120
YMCA, 62
religious life
Abraham and Isaac, symbols in, 187-89
applies Christian principles to municipal problems, 8, 12, 13, 63, 76, 77-79, 86, 88, 104, 127-28, 202-3, 206, 228, 231, 230 n 13; "Holy" Toledo, 12-13, 103
atonement, need for, 10, 39, 71, 74, 213
baptism, refuses ritual for third son, 132
broken-hearted, 1, 199
Calvinist training: 27, 29; cynical view of, 62; limitations on political effectiveness, 13-14, 173-74
changing values, 28, 77, 79
Christian socialism: 27, 73, 78, 81 87-88, 192; Jones's definition of, 169-70. *See also* Christian socialism
church hypocrisy, 12, 82, 146, 223-24; belief in Christianity, not the church, 132
compensatory impulses in, 10, 71, 74-75, 164, 166, 213, 233
conventional Christian, 30, 41, 62-63, 77, 172, 244 n 34
evangelical temperament: 3, 28, 168-69; agenda for change, 27; conscience in, 161, 164, 185, 245 n 35; hostility to self in, 24, 28-32, 180, 199-200. *See also* evangelical culture
God: and criminal justice, 204; led by, to a career in social justice, 65; immanent in all people, 201; linked to Hugh Jones, 30, 32; Paul and the will of, 189; view of, 32-33, 40, 65, 102, 104, 132-33, 192-93, 209, 233, 244 n 34. *See also* God
Golden Rule: as habit of life, 1, 2, 8, 14, 128, 185; textual power of, 10, 165. *See also* Golden Rule; Golden Rule under Jones: character and formative events; Jones: reform; and Jones: politics
grace, 30-31, 218
interest in the occult, 53
Jesus: 218; radical expectations of, 175, 224; as practical model, 82, 153; "What would Jesus do?" 12-13, 75
love: supreme confidence in, 1, 19, 31, 51, 128; failure to depend fully on, 199
Methodist impulse to perfect the self, 19, 31, 199, 209, 219. *See also* Methodist sanctification
poverty: Calvinism and, 42; as God's plan, 33, 65; Methodism and, 43
raised in Welsh Calvinist Methodist Church, 21-22. *See also* Welsh Calvinist Methodist Church
religion as life, 23, 28, 244 n 29
religious crisis, 59, 73
sacrifice, attracted to, 80-81, 164, 229, 237
self-denial, in, 14, 24, 29-31, 173-74, 180
sensitivity to the sacred, 85-86
social gospel: 11, 12, 86-87; more radical than, 70. *See also* social gospel valiant spiritual journey, 11, 12, 65, 75-86, 91, 128, 218, 232-33
politics
articulates new vision for America, 7, 12, 14, 121, 130, 230
as anarchist, 66, 87, 167, 237, 228-29, 204-5, 237, 249 n 2. *See also* anarchy
anti-imperialism: 144; criticizes McKinley, 191. *See also* anti-imperialism
anti-institutionalism, 27

Jones, Samuel Milton: politics *(cont'd)*
antinomianism, 132-33, 140, 199, 228-29, 243 n 25
burden of responsibility, 75, 160-61
campaign skills: 105, 113-14, 116-17, 175-76; municipal campaigns of education, 184, 215
closure of gambling outfits, 126
combined with theology, 129, 175, 232
considers leaving mayoral office, 213-14, 220
contract of the heart, 11, 121, 160, 166-67
criminal justice reform: 2, 127-28, 231; as police judge, 199, 202-206; legislation against capital punishment, 228; "What is Crime, and Who are the Criminals?" 204-5
democracy in action, 119, 121, 129, 139, 145, 231. *See also* democracy
elected treasurer of Duke Center (Pa.) Borough Council, 58
election campaigns: aborted 1900 congressional, 185-86, 190, 193: 1899 non-partisan gubernatorial, 2, 38, 39, 159, 161-63, 170-72, 200; hesitations about, 167-68; platform of, 175; results of, 177-80, 198; 1897 mayoral, 4, 105, 110-18: 1899 re-election as Independent, 139, 147-52, 159, 171, 153-55: 1901 mayoral, 200-201; democrats support Jones, 201; loss of electoral support, 201-2; 1903 mayoral, 213-16; press boycott, 215: presidential, 193-96
failure: 8, 9, 219, 232; as administrator, 214, 231; with Governor Nash, 199, 216-17; of gubernatorial election, 179; in losing the city-owned gas plant, 182-84; removed from police court, 199, 205; translation of political success to public policy reform, 172, 232; maintainance of popular support, 7, 216
faith in all people, 31-32, 74, 85, 129, 203, 230, 265 n 11
Golden Rule: influence on Bryan about, 195-96; as political platform, 10, 114-16, 118, 120, 190-91, 223. *See also* Golden Rule; Golden Rule under Jones: character and formative events; Jones: reform; Jones: religious life
good government, 4, 120, 121, 140, 230, 255 n 32
Hanna, conflicts with, 119, 141-43, 178. *See also* Hanna
immigrants: ability to reach 7, 113; refusal to support mandatory vaccines of, 212. *See also* immigrants; middle-class values
independent politician *See* non-partisan
Jesus, 218; as campaign figure, 194. *See also* Jesus and Jones: religiouslife, Jesus
machines, commitment to avoid, 114-15, 163, 171-72, 176-80, 198, 200-201, 215-16. *See also* machines
non-partisan career: 7, 139; gubernatorial race 175-80; works for abolition of parties, 163, 175-80
pacifism, 144-45, 201, 228
passivity, 10, 170-71
power over electorate, 221-22
Republican party, affiliation with: 2, 36; convention fight with, 146-51; lukewarm support of, 116-18, 230; Jones read out of, 141-43; race and support, 153, horrified by lynching in Ohio, 228; supports voting rights in the South, 197
revolution, tentative acceptance of, 119
self-denial and gubernatorial race,

161, 173-74
socialism of: 79-82, 116, 147, 169-70; as "gas and water" socialist, 138
Toledo Press, shifting attitudes toward Jones: *Bee,* negative coverage, 136, 139, 141; *Bee,* positive coverage; 135, 142, 143, 175-77, 181, 186, 205; *News-Bee,* 234-37; *Blade* negative coverage; 135, 143, 146, 154, 201, 228; *Blade* positive coverage; 10, 110, 113, 117, 118, 232, 234-37
unions: active support of, 130-31; campaigns on union wages, 175
Jones, Samuel M., II (grandson) viii-ix
Jones, Samuel P., 152-53

Kellogg, John: breakfast foods in prison, 211; speaks in Toledo, 97; economic conference of, 130
Kemp, 176
Kerlin Company, 183
Kimes, Ed, 122
Kind, Richard, 136
kindergartens. *See* Jones: reform, public kindergartens
King, Harry E., 119, 149
King, Frank L., 110
Kinston, Warren, 242 n 16, 244 n 31, 245 n 42
Klotz, Solon T., 8
Knepper, George W., 240 n 14
Knapp, Perry, 222

labor: conditions destroy the dignity of, 52-53, 74; supports Jones, 110, 163, 178; violence and, 58, 262 n 44. See Jones: reform, labor
Ladies Home Journal, 211
Lamed-Vov, Jones as "just man," 237-38
Lamson, John D.R., 150
Lasch, Christopher, 240 n 15
League of Ohio Municipalities, 144
Lee, Joseph, 98
Lender, Mark Edward, 256 n 13
Ley, John, 234
Lincoln, Abraham, 105, 118, 136, 180; progressive ideal, 36; as political "marker" 139-40, 145, 150, 155, 235
Lloyd, Henry Demarest, 1, 11, 65, 101, 119, 135, 194, 262 n 3; correspondence between Jones, and, 116, 164-65, 174, 184, 260 n 11; influence on Jones, 77-79, 81, 82, 88, 93
Locke, David Ross, 135-36
Locke, Robmson: attacks Major, 108; background of, 135-36; criticizes Jones supporters, 154. *See* Jones: politics, toledo press, shifting attitudes, toledo, *Blade*
Longfellow, Henry Wadsworth, 183
Low, Seth, 4, 153
Lowell, Josephine Shaw, 223
Luther, Martin, 209; spiritual complaint of, 219
Lynch, Edward J., 8
L.R. Lyon, 25-37, 67
Lyon, Lymon R., 35
Macfadden, Bernarr, 75, 225
McClosley, Robert G., 247n 32
McClure's, 211; *Shame of the Cities,* 227
McLean, John R. Jones's opponent, 169, 175, 177; correspondence between Jones and, 179-80
McKinley, William, 2, 7, 11, 103, 108, 151, 186, 254 n 9; assassination of, symptomatic of the culture, 265 n 14; Jones critical of, 191; on Jones, 162, 177; Bryan on, 194; re-election of, 197
McMaken, William, Brigadier General, Jones's opponent, 200-201; response to chaos of industrial conditions, 106; Brown machine, 108, 138; Foraker machine, 110, 155, 162-63, 254 n 4; Hanna machine, 108-10; Johnson machine, 226; Jones and, 1, 106-7; Major machine, 107, 109. *See also* Jones: politics, machines
Maine, 108
Major, Guy, 105-8, 113, 254 n 4, 258-59 n 27. *See also* machines; municipal corruption

Malthus, Thomas, 100
Marr, David, 260 n 1
Marshall, James C., 249 n 3
Martin, James Kirby, 256 n 13
Marx, Karl, 78, 79
Maumee River, 92, 93
Maurice, Frederick Denison, 79, 104
Mazzini Giuseppe, 164; influence on Jones, 65, 77, 85, 87
Meissner, William, 240 n 16
Melvin, James, 109-12
Memorial Hall, 133-34, 147-48, 235-36
Men the Workers, 79
Merrell, John B. 111, 208; and Ben Raitz 121-24, 136
Methodist sanctification, 19, 31, 209; and poverty, 43
middle class morality: repression of imigrants with 5-6; oppression of sexuality, 6. *See also* Boyer and Jones: reform, middle-class values
Mills, Benjamin Fay, 128, 29
Miner, Samuel, as role model, 41, 47, 70, 76
Monroe street home, 94-95, 252 n 7
Moses, as political metaphor: by the *Blade*, 105; by Debs, 193; to describe Bryan, 191; to describe Jones, 167
municipal corruption, 4, 8, 107-8
municipal ownership of utilities: 2, 6, 87, 121, 138, 175, 262 n 3, 268 n 37; city council thwarts mayor over, 182-84

Nash, George, Jones's opponent, 162; wins gubernatorial election, 177; limits Jones's power, 199, 206
Nathanson, Donald, 240 n 16, 242 n 17, 245 n 40
Nationalist Party, 146-47
Nelson, Nelson 0., 79, 124, 143, 161, 179, 212, 235-36; correspondence between Jones and, 164-65, 174, 175, 180, 187-88, 196-97, 199-200, 220, 225, 228, 229, 233-34; pacifism of, 144; support during Jones's illnesses, 207-8
nervous disorders, 206
New Deal, 106
New York Charitable Organizing Society, 223
New Testament, 65, 82, 84, 87, 96, 102, 166, 194-95, 227
Nicaragua, 144
Nicholas II, Czar of Russia, 145
nihilists, 108
North American Review, 211

Oberlin, 26
Ohio: constitution of, 155; General Assembly, 106, 143, 199, 203-5, 216, 228; gubernatorial race of 1899, 175-78; Hanna and, 141; Ninth Congressional race, 193, 196-97; Ohio Oil Company, 62; penal code, 213; Republican party and, 109; Sixth Ohio Volunteer Infantry, 200; Supreme Court, 138, 206
Oliver Twist, 40
Olmsted, Frederick Law, 92, 98, 252 n 13
Ottawa park golf course, 99, 138
Outlook, 211

Protestant Church: capitalism and, 247-48 n 32; fails immigrants, 106
philanthropy, 71, 223-24, 165
Philippines, 144, 191
Phillips, Wendell, 10
Phelen, James, 4
phenomenological perspective, 8, 39, 240 n 16
pietism, 27, 31
Pingree, Hazen: campaigns for Jones, 147; compared to Jones, 142; correspondence between Jones and, 150, 259 n 30; as mayor, 4, 6, 11, 72; political career of, 106-8, 161, 119, 165, 166, 250 n 15; on vice, 153
Pithole, Pennsylvania, 38, 44, 55, 57, 70, 71, 76, 93, 102, 126, 219; 44-48; gateway to hell, 43; ghost town, 49; *Nation*, 45; *New York Herald*, 45; *New*

York Observer, 46; *New York Tribune, 49; Pithole Daily Record,* 45; *Titusville Morning Herald,* 38, 46. *See also* Jones: character and formative events, Pithole
Pomeroy, Eltweed, 142; correspondence between Jones and, 179
Populist party, 171
Porter, Carolyn, 260 n 1
post-structuralist view of self, 9-10
poverty, 43, 245 n 40
Press, attitude toward Jones: *Boston Universalist,* 235; *Chicago Chronicle,* 237; *Chicago Farm, Field, and Fireside,* 235; *Chicago Record,* 195, 200; *Chicago Tribune,* 3, 208; *Cincinnati Enquirer,* 168, 170; *Cincinnati Post,* 212-13; *Cincinnati Times-Star,* 170; *Cleveland Leader,* 161; *Cleveland Plain-Dealer,* 3; *Columbus Journal,* 228; *Detroit Journal,* 3, 232; *London Review of Reviews,* 119; *Los Angeles Herald,* 85; *Milwaukee News,* 3; *New Orleans Sunday States, 1; New York Journal,* 168, 186, 200; *New York Sun,* 213; *New York Times,* 154, 234; *Philadelphia North-American,* 176; *Tiffin Tribune,* 170; *Toledo Express,* 215; *Washington Post,* 170, 178
prison reform, 223
progressive reformers, 39, 87, 98, 103; burden of guilt upon, 51; evangelism and, 32; depression and, 60; interested in increasing institutional moral control, 5-7, 124, 248 n 44; Lincoln on, 36, 245 n 45. *See* Jones: reform, progressive
prohibition, 5, 136-38, 171; Prohibitionist party, 177
prostitution, 4-6, 14, 219
psychoanalytic perspective, 9, 11, 240 n 16
Pullman; layoffs at, 66; strike of, 72
puritan roots of American culture, 10, 13-14, 200, 240 n 15; self-civil war, 208-9, 265 n 26
Pyle, John, 233

Quincy, Josiah, 4

Raitz, Ben, 136, 148, 206; causes Jones's first controversy, 121-24
Rauschenbusch, Walter, 1, 8, 87, 166
Republican party: animosity toward Jones, 230; courts Jones in gubernatorial race, 161-62; effectiveness limited by Jones, 1, 108, 119, 152, 200; Lincoln Club, 205; and Pingree, 106; role in saving the Union, 109
Resek, Carl, 245 n 2
Richardson, Judd, 118, 121-24, 136
Riis, Jacob, 5, 99
ripper bill, 254-55 n 16
Rizzuto, Ana-Maria, 240 n 16
Robbins, Harry N., 160
Rockefeller, John D., 3, 61, 165, 267-68 n 17; buys Jones out, 71; philanthropy of 223-24
Romeis, Jacob, 146
Roosevelt, Theodore, 99; criticizes Bryan, 192; as evangelical, 32; meets Jones in the White House, 225; on vice 5
Royce, Josiah, 87
Ruskin, 11, 65, 71, 77, 79; influence on Jones, 100-101, 104, 166; just relation with employees, 83-85, 88
Russell, Charles, Jones's opponent, 147, 149-50, 154-55
Russia, 144
Ryan, Henry ("Sport"), 183

saloons, 4, 119, 124, 136-38
Salter, Henry Hyde, 75, 250 n 21
Schieren, Charles, 4
Schreiber, Cornell, 8
Scudder, Vida, 1
Seldon, Charles, 76
Sermon on the Mount, 13, 14
shame, 11; defined, 24, 245 n 42, 246 n 5; evangelicals and, 30-31, 58, 125, 163; by-product of Methodism, 31-32; and money, 43. *See also* Jones: character and formative events, shame

Sherman, John, 108, 254 n 10
Shi, David, 265 n 21
sin, 14, 29, 51
Sinclair, Upton, 81
single tax, 95
smallpox, 212, 266 n 35
Smith, Adam, 61
Smith, Barton, 221-22
Smith, Page, 248 n 35
Smith, Robert, 240 n 13
Snowdon, Mount, 19, 21, 23
social and structural reforms, 12, 103, 197, 230, 253 n 30. *See also* Jones: reform, social; Jones: reform structural
social gospel, 11, 12, 67, 76, 79, 95, 99, 106, 165, 251 n 44; defined, 86-87; *Equity*, 58; *Social Gospel*, 51; to inspire faith in the economic teachings of Jesus, 86
Social Unity, 179
socialists, 108, 145, 254 n 4
Socialist Labor Party: Debs urges Jones to join, 168-70; Jones debates supporting Debs, 190; election results for, 177
Society of Christian Socialists, 88
Southard, James Harding, 197
Spain, 145
Spanish American War, 144-45, 200
Stager, Charles, 122-24, 256 n 4
Standard Oil, 77, 109, 224; antitrust laws and, 61; and Senator Foraker, 109
State Board of Charities, 204
Stead, William T., 67, 72, 88
Steffens, Lincoln, 8, 165, 235, 240 n 15; finds corruption in Toledo, 268 n 24; Jones's influence upon, 227
Strobel, Charles, 137
Strong, Josiah, 6, 80, 140
Strong, William, 4
Sulloway, Frank, 243 n 25
Swayne, Noah, H., 112

Tager, Jack, 249 n 2
tariff, 135
temperance, 5, 124, 136-38
Tennyson, Albert, (Lord), 183
Thoreau, 210; on the simple life, 223-24
Thorowgood, John C., 250 n 21
Toledo, 4; Chapman bill, 228; city charters, 8, 197, 216; city council, 138-39, 182, 216, 226, 230, 235; community in, 91-100, 121; crime statistics in, 257 n 33; demographics of 92, 116, 249 n 3; economic prosperity and, 66; as governed by Guy Major, 105-8; as governed by Jones, 86, 120-21, 138, 149, 230; governmental structure of, 106, 216, 254 n 4, 266-67 n 46; Hanna's effect on, 108-10; "Holy," 12-13; international attention from Jones's election, 119; Jones's estimate of unemployment in, 256 n 20; Jones's impact upon, 229-33; McKinley concerned about, 162; municipal gas crisis and, 262 n 3; police board, 216-17, 256 n 4; police department, 121-24, 268 n 24; public parks, 96-100; responds to Jones as police judge, 204, 206; responds to Jones's death, 234-37; support for Jones in gubernatorial race, 178; support of third party candidates, 146-47; tax burden of, 105, 107; prosperity and depression in, 66; unemployment in, 127; tests blue laws, 136-38; Toledo Railway and Light Company, 220, 234-35; Toledo Yacht Club, 233; transit fight 119, 220-22, 267 n 9; Welsh festival in, 226-27; zoo, 99, 138, 230
Tolstoy, 101, 172; Bryan on, 194-95; model for Jones, 204, 224; receives news of Jones, 82-83, 155; spiritual complaint of, 65, 77, 127, 219-20; works influence Jones, 11, 88, 104, 166
Traubel, Horace, 129
Tucker, William, 141-42, 143
Twain, Mark, 36, 78

typhoid, 267 n 7
Tsanoff, Stovyan Vasil, 99
unions, 102; National Association of Letter Carriers, 145, 190; Newsboys and Bootblacks Union, 155; Toledo Ministers Union, 155; Union Reform Party, 163, 170, 177, 179, 186
unemployment, 118, 120, 127
University of Chicago, 224
U.S. Constitution; 140; Eighteenth Amendment to, 190
U.S. House of Representatives, 109, 144, 177, 185
U.S. Senate, 109, 141, 143, 144, 177

Valentine building: 4, 170, 177; Jones's office in, 5
vice, economics of, 6, 12, 31, 39. *See* Jones: reform, vice
Voit, Reynold, 148

Wachenheimer, Lyman W., 203-5
Waldorf, George P., 109, 142, 150, 217
Wales, connected to Lewis County, N.Y., 25-26; democratic ideal of, 19; tension with English, 20
Waggoner, Clark, 254 n 3
Warner, Hoyt Landon, 245 n 40
Warner, Mason, 110
Walters, Everett, 254 n 11
Wayside, 94
Weld, Theodore,10, 27
Welch, Claude, 243 n 25, 244 n 29
Welsh, 232; anti-institutionalism in, 27; emigration of, 23-26, 242 n 14, 242 n 15; language (Cymraeg), 19-20, 26, 241 n 5; powerful preaching of, 26, 27; Welsh anthems, at memorial service, 238
Welsh Calvinistic Methodism, 241-42 n 11; activist, 243 n 24, 243 n 25, 244 n 29; Christianization of Wales, 21; emphasizes brotherhood, 26-28, 241 n 5; fidelity to Sabbath, 41; revival of 1818, 21-23; shame and, 31-32; supportive of French Revolution, 243 n 21
Wesley, Charles, 52
Wesley, John, 29, 30, 209, 241-42 n 11
Wesley, Susanna, 29
Western Oil Men's Association, 91
Wheeler, Helen, 233, 237
White, Ronald C., 248 n 34
White, William Allen, 87
Whitefield, George, 29, 241-42 n 11
Whitlock, Brand, 5, 11, 124, 138, 139, 149, 212, 240 n 15, 241 n 2; growing friendship with, 184-85; insight into Jones, 203, 265 n 11, 218; reform of criminal justice system, 202-3, 206, 228
Whitman, Walt, 13, 57, 85, 91, 138, 145, 183; becomes Jones's favorite poet, 128-30; antinomianism of 131-33
Williams, Gwyn, 241 n 5
Williams, R.R., 241 n 11
Williams, William, 242 n 11
Woman and Economics, 73-74
World War I, 144, 242 n 14
World's Work, 81

YMCA, 62, 124
Young, Walter, correspondence between Jones and, 228-29

www.ingramcontent.com/pod-product-compliance
Lightning Source LLC
Chambersburg PA
CBHW020405100426
42812CB00001B/203

* 9 7 8 0 8 1 3 1 2 0 6 2 1 *